INTERNATIONAL COMMUNISM
IN THE ERA OF LENIN

HELMUT GRUBER is Professor of History at the Polytechnic Institute of Brooklyn. A graduate of City College, New York, he received the M.A. and Ph.D. degrees at Columbia University. His articles on international communism and German intellectual history have appeared in American, English, Dutch and Italian journals. He is author of the forthcoming *International Communism in the Service of Stalin* and *International Communism in the Shadow of Fascism* both to be published in Anchor Books.

International Communism in the Era of Lenin

A DOCUMENTARY HISTORY

Helmut Gruber

ANCHOR BOOKS
DOUBLEDAY & COMPANY, INC.
GARDEN CITY, NEW YORK

1972

INTERNATIONAL COMMUNISM IN THE ERA OF LENIN: A
Documentary History was originally published as a paperback by
Fawcett Publications, Inc., in 1967, and in hardcover by Cornell
University Press, in 1967. The Anchor Books edition is published by
arrangement with the author.

Anchor Books edition: 1972

TO CAROL

ACKNOWLEDGMENTS

The editor has made every effort to determine and credit the holders of copyright of the selections in this book. Any errors or omissions may be rectified in future printings. The editor wishes to thank the following for permission to reprint the material included in this volume:

PART ONE

I, Document 1, *What Is to Be Done?*, by V. I. Lenin. Copyright, 1929, by International Publishers Co., Inc. Reprinted by permission of the publishers.

II, Documents 1 and 3, from *Collected Works*, by V. I. Lenin, copyright, 1930, International Publishers Co., Inc. Reprinted by permission of the publishers.

II, Documents 4 and 5, reprinted from *The Bolsheviks and the World War* by Olga Hess Gankin and H. H. Fisher with the permission of the publishers, Stanford University Press. Copyright 1940 by the Board of Trustees of the Leland Stanford Junior University.

III, Document 2 (and PART THREE, III, Document 1), from *The Communist International 1919–1923: Documents,* Volume I, edited by Jane Degras, published by the Oxford University Press under the auspices of the Royal Institute of International Affairs. Reprinted by permission of Oxford University Press. Copyright, 1956.

PART TWO

I, Documents 2 and 3, from *The Spartacist Uprising of 1919 and the German Socialist Movement* by Eric Waldman, 1958, pp. 169–170; 175–176. Reprinted by permission of Marquette University Press.

IV, Documents 1 and 5, from *Die Arbeiterräte in Deutschösterreich* by Julius Braunthal. Copyright, 1919. Reprinted by permission of Wiener Volksbuchhandlung.

IV, Documents 3 and 4, from *Aus Österreichs Revolution* by Julius Deutsch. Reprinted by permission of Wiener Volksbuchhandlung.

V, Document 1, *"Left-wing" Communism, an Infantile Disorder,* by V. I. Lenin. Copyright, 1940, by International Publishers, Inc. Reprinted by permission of the publishers.

PART THREE

III, Document 2, by permission of *Rivista storica del socialismo.*

PREFACE

The general reader interested in international communism will find few readily accessible works which treat this subject from an historical viewpoint. It is the aim of this documentary history, in which a concise narrative framework serves as the underpinning and continuity for documents and a small number of interpretive essays, to help remedy this situation. In departing from the standard form of an anthology or collection of documents I have attempted to give the general reader that amount of narrative guidance without which the raw materials of history are all too often incomprehensible. The reader should be alerted to the fact that I have added explanatory footnotes to the documents. These footnotes are designated by lower-case alphabetical headings rather than numerals. In making a selection from the numerous doctrinal statements, manifestoes, analyses, tactical decisions, and polemics of the communist movement I have been guided by a desire to highlight the important events in Lenin's era rather than merely to trace institutional developments.

Although the orientation and content of the book are my responsibility alone, I am indebted to many who assisted me in removing at least some of the flaws by challenging my assumptions and questioning my judgments. I owe a special measure of gratitude to Professors Eugene D. Genovese and John M. Cammett of Rutgers University, Professor István Deák and Miss Manuela Dobos-Schleicher of Columbia University, and Professor Louis Menashe of the Polytechnic Institute of Brooklyn, whose careful and telling criticism forced me to view the subject from perspectives other than my own. I have been assisted by the members of the Universities' Seminar on International Communism at the Polytechnic Institute of Brooklyn, whose searching discussion of my Introduction helped me to reduce its bravura. I also want to express my appreciation for the patience with which my own students, acting as a trial audience, received various portions and versions of this book. Much of the collection and selection of documents would have been impossible without the generous help and counsel of Mr. Otto Bauer, librarian of the Library for Political Studies in New York, who allowed this excellent archive to become my scholarly home for several years. My profound thanks are also due to the Polytechnic Institute of Brooklyn which, by awarding me a research grant in the summer of 1964, made it possible for me to steep myself in the literature necessary for my work. The tremendous burden of translation was lightened considerably by the expert assistance of Miss Manuela Dobos-Schleicher, Mrs. Waltraud Ireland, Mrs. Charlotte Smokler, and Professor John M. Cammett. I am also grateful to Mrs. Jean Lester and Mrs. Nita Woods, who cheerfully transformed many handwritten versions into typed drafts.

Above and beyond these acknowledgments I want to pay special tribute to my wife, Carol S. Gruber, who put aside her own scholarly labors to subject the manuscript to relentless criticism and shared with me the frustration and genuine pleasure which were at the heart of this venture.

H. G.

New York City
November, 1966

PREFACE TO THE ANCHOR EDITION

In this edition the body of the 1967 original remains intact. The only significant change is the deletion of the "Interpretations" which, friendly critics convinced me, added little to the substance of the book.

Of course I have been tempted on the occasion of this new printing to add or substitute just a few documents, to append just one more explanatory footnote, and most of all to greatly expand my analytic text. To do so even in a minor way could easily have led me to fashion an entirely new book. Such an undertaking would have violated my original intention of making *International Communism in the Era of Lenin* the first part of a trilogy of both independent and intrinsically connected volumes tracing the history of international communism from left-wing social democracy before the First World War to the dissolution of the Communist International in 1943.

Now that this plan is nearly realized, my decision to leave this book essentially in its original form seems justified. *International Communism in the Service of Stalin* should appear in the spring of 1973 and *International Communism in the Shadow of Fascism* one year later. Both will be published by Anchor Books; both should be more fully realized documentary histories by providing an equal division of space between analysis and sources. The final part of this project will be a historical overview of the Communist International that will combine analysis with an attempt to evaluate present research and to assess the nature and extent of scholarship that will be necessary before a systematic and exhaustive history of the subject can be written.

It is impossible to thank individually all those who have helped me with suggestions and criticisms, least of all my own students who have been tolerant and patient. I hope that the successful completion of the entire project will serve as a token of appreciation. I do want to single out two friends,

Professor Harvey Goldberg of the University of Wisconsin and Professor Georges Haupt of the École Pratique des Hautes Études, Paris, whose kind counsel helped me to see new perspectives of the subject and most of all encouraged me to get on with the work.

HELMUT GRUBER

New York City
December 1971

CONTENTS

INTRODUCTION   1

PART ONE   FORMATIVE YEARS: DEFINITION
           AND ORGANIZATION OF LEFT-WING SOCIAL
           DEMOCRACY   9

I. PARTY STRUCTURE AND FUNCTION   14
   1. V. I. Lenin, *What Is to Be Done?: Burning
      Questions of Our Movement*   15
   2. Rosa Luxemburg, *Leninism or Marxism?*   29

II. ZIMMERWALD AND KIENTHAL CONFERENCES   44
   1. "The Tasks of Revolutionary Social Democracy
      in the European War"   50
   2. "Manifesto of the International Socialist Confer-
      ence at Zimmerwald"   53
   3. "Draft Manifesto Introduced by the Left-Wing
      Delegates at the International Socialist Confer-
      ence at Zimmerwald"   58
   4. "Theses Submitted to the International Socialist
      Committee by the German 'Internationale'
      Group"   61
   5. "To the Peoples Who Suffer Ruin and Death:
      Manifesto of the Kienthal Conference"   65
   6. "The Attitude of the Proletariat toward the
      Question of Peace: Resolution of the Kienthal
      Conference"   69

III. CREATION OF THE THIRD INTERNATIONAL   73
   1. "German Reservations about the Founding of
      the Comintern"   79
   2. "Manifesto of the Communist International to
      the Proletariat of the Entire World"   82

FURTHER READING   93

PART TWO 1919—WORLD REVOLUTION ON
THE   HORIZON: BERLIN,   BUDAPEST,
MUNICH, VIENNA   97

I. SPARTACUS IN BERLIN   100
    1. *The German Spartacists: Their Aims and
        Objects*   104
    2. "Joint Declaration by the Independent Socialist
        Party and the Communist Party"   114
    3. "Proclamation by the Revolutionary Committee
        Representing the Revolutionary Shop Stewards,
        the Central Committee of the Berlin USPD, and
        the Central Committee of the KPD"   116

II. BÉLA KUN'S 133 DAYS   117
    1. "The Constitution of the Hungarian Socialist
        Federated Soviet Republic"   123
    2. Béla Szántó, "The Real Reason for the Collapse
        of the Federal Hungarian Soviet Republic"   132
    3. Karl Radek, "The Lessons of the Hungarian
        Revolution"   137
    4. Paul Levi, "The Lessons of the Hungarian Rev-
        olution"   143

III. THE BAVARIAN SOVIET REPUBLIC   153
    1. The Revolutionary Central Council of Bavaria,
        "Proclamation of the Soviet Republic"   157
    2. "Declaration of the Communist Party Regard-
        ing the 'Pseudo'-Soviet Republic"   159
    3. Paul Frölich, "The Munich Experience"   162
    4. Paul Levi, "The Munich Experience: An Op-
        posing View"   168

IV. VIENNA: WINDOW TO THE WEST?   175
    1. "Declaration by the Executive Committee of
        Workers'   Councils   to   the   Proletariat   of
        Hungary"   181
    2. "Declaration of the Communist Workers' Coun-
        cilors"   182
    3. "Austrian Communist Broadside of June 14,
        1919"   183
    4. "Directive of the Action Committee of Austrian
        Communists"   184

Contents   xiii

5. "Declaration of the Viennese Workers' Councilors"   185
6. Karl Radek, "The Lessons of an Attempted
   Putsch: The Crisis in the German-Austrian
   Communist Party"   186
7. Ernst Bettelheim, "The 'Bettelheimerei': A
   Contribution to the History of the Austrian CP
   and at the Same Time an Answer to Radek's
   Criticism of the Events of June 15th"   194

V. VOICES OF ORTHODOXY—CRITICS AND
   JEREMIAHS   203
1. V. I. Lenin, "'Left-Wing' Communism, an Infantile Disorder"   205
2. Hermann Gorter, Open Letter to Comrade
   Lenin: An Answer to Lenin's Pamphlet "'Left-
   Wing' Communism, an Infantile Disorder"   216

FURTHER READING   227

PART THREE ORIGIN OF BOLSHEVIK HE-
GEMONY: ITALIAN SPLIT AND GERMAN
OFFENSIVE   231

I. THE TWENTY-ONE CONDITIONS AND COMMUNIST
   DISCIPLINE: THE ITALIAN EXAMPLE   234
1. Conditions of Admission into the Communist
   International   241
2. G. M. Serrati, "The Second Congress of the
   Third International"   247
3. "Declaration of the Representative of the Communist International"   250
4. "Order of the Day of the Unitary Communists"   254
5. "Order of the Day of the Concentration
   Faction"   256
6. Paul Levi, The Beginning of the Crisis in the
   Communist Party and International   258
7. Karl Radek, "The Italian Question"   263

II. THE GERMAN MARCH ACTION   267
1. Paul Levi, Our Course against Putschism   274
2. Karl Radek, "The Levi Case"   296
3. Waldemar, "Behind the Scenes of the March
   Action"   301
4. Clara Zetkin, Reminiscences of Lenin   305

5. "Preparation for the Struggle" and "Lessons of
the March Action"   309

III. VOICES OF ORTHODOXY—CRITICS AND
JEREMIAHS   314
1. "Directives on the United Front of the Workers
and on the Attitudes to Workers Belonging to
the Second, Two-and-a-Half, and Amsterdam
Internationals, and to Those Who Support
Anarcho-Syndicalist Organizations"   318
2. Amadeo Bordiga, "Manifesto"   327

FURTHER READING   336

PART FOUR 1923—END OF WORLD REVO-
LUTION: BULGARIAN JUNE AND GERMAN
OCTOBER   339

I. BULGARIANS SPURN THE UNITED FRONT   343
1. "The Situation in Bulgaria and the Communist
Party"   348
2. "Manifesto of the Enlarged Executive of the
Communist International on the Events in Bul-
garia"   355
3. "The Communist Party of Bulgaria and the Re-
cent Coup D'Etat"   359
4. Mátyás Rákosi, "The Latest Attitude of the CP
of Bulgaria"   361

II. A SECOND RED OCTOBER?   365
1. Ruth Fischer, "On the Situation in Germany
and on the Tactics of the Party"   377
2. A. Thalheimer and H. Brandler, "Theses on the
October Defeat and on the Present Situation"   381
3. "Speech of Comrade Zinoviev on the Situation
in the KPD"   383

FURTHER READING   403

SELECTED GENERAL BIBLIOGRAPHY   405

CHRONOLOGY   410

INDEX   417

INTRODUCTION

It is more metaphorically apt than historically accurate to characterize the infancy and early adolescence of the communist movement as "the era of Lenin." Between the turn of the century and the Russian October Revolution Lenin was essentially a national, not an international, figure. He was prominent among Russian socialist émigrés, and his work was a vital text in their fierce and uninterrupted debates. But few of the Western socialist leaders, not to speak of the socialist rank and file, really knew the man or his work. Some of Lenin's ideas received currency during the war in the Zimmerwald movement's left-wing manifestoes, which were part of the underground literature circulated in many countries, but these collective proclamations were only opaque statements of Lenin's ideas. They did not really advertise his unique position on party organization, revolution, imperialism, and internationalism in the strongholds of Western social democracy. It was not until Lenin led the Bolsheviks in capturing state power that he became socialism's man of the hour, speaking with an authority vested in accomplishment to an international socialist audience. It was then that the corpus of his theoretical and programmatic writings began to be translated, read, and respected. As his reputation grew at the end of the war and in the postwar years, it extended backward in time and retroactively cast him as a prime mover in the development of international communism of which he had been only one of many organizers.

The course of describing the genesis and early years of the Third International under the rubric "era of Lenin" has been adopted here as a convention and in an honorific sense in full realization that it may well still be misleading. Historians have frequently made the communist movement appear to be Lenin's creation in order to divide and quarantine socialism from communism and their respective movements from each other. Hermetically sealed from its past, the Communist International has then been viewed as a debased and uniquely radical version of its predecessor.[1] Seen from this perspective the communist movement and its International represented a sharp break with the past. It can also be argued with equal conviction based on ample evidence that the Third International in its early years was a historical continuation of the Second.

The Comintern in Lenin's era still had important roots in the Second International. Many of those who commanded the fledgling communist parties after the war and gave a measure of prestige to the movement had cut their socialist wisdom teeth in party and trade union work during the heyday of the old international. These old hands (among them the Germans Rosa Luxemburg, Clara Zetkin, and Paul Levi, the Poles Leo Jogiches and Juljan Marchlewski, the Dutch Hermann Gorter and Anton Pannekok, the Italian G. M. Serrati, the British Sylvia Pankhurst and Jack Tanner, the Bulgarian Dmitri Blagoev and the French Marcel Cachin and L. O. Frossard), who had fought both for and against social democracy from its left wing, brought a spirit compounded of tradition and innovation to the Comintern which helped to set its tone. They considered the International an organization of peers, each entitled to speak for his own position and not only for that of his party. Among them there was a widespread belief in the power of ideas and "correct" theories to attain acceptance in the working class because of their intrinsic Marxist merits and not only because they were backed by organizations. In the operation of their parties and activity in the Comintern they championed an openness of disagreement and public airing of disputes, and preferred plenary sessions to small committees and commissions as the arena for thrashing out theoretical and tactical differences. By com-

[1] A sampling of the literature in which this view is either explicit or implicit might include: Bertram D. Wolfe, *Marxism: One Hundred Years in the Life of a Doctrine* (New York, 1956), pp. 252–312; Alfred G. Meyer, *Communism* (New York, 1960), pp. 89–91; Adam B. Ulam, *The Unfinished Revolution: An Essay on the Sources of Influence of Marxism and Communism* (New York, 1964), p. 168 ff; James Joll, *The Second International* (New York, 1966), pp. 191–95; Theodore H. Von Laue, *Why Lenin, Why Stalin: A Reappraisal of the Russian Revolution* (Philadelphia and New York, 1964), p. 169 ff; and Günther Nollau, *International Communism and World Revolution* (New York, 1961), pp. 20–59.

mon tradition they were part of a minority opposition in a capitalist society and therefore more effective as critics and gadflies than as people's tribunes.

The influence of those who had broken with social democracy, but in many ways remained its spiritual descendants, on the nature and direction of the Comintern was more than balanced by that exercised by the Bolsheviks and those whom they influenced and trained. The latter group (represented by the Russians Lenin, Trotsky, Zinoviev, and Bukharin, the Pole Karl Radek, the Finn Otto Kuusinen, the Bulgarians Vasil Kolarov and Khristo Kabakchiev, the Hungarians Béla Kun and Mátyás Rákosi, the Austrian Karl Tomann, the Swiss Fritz Platten, and the German Willi Münzenberg) brought a new radicalism to the movement and at first challenged and later struggled against their partners who did not share their particular revolutionary élan. They were tough-minded and unimpressed with precedents save those which they created, and therefore were blinded by the success of the October Revolution, which they adopted as the guide to future actions. Sharing the loyalties of a small and disparaged sect, they valued group discipline more than individual theoretical insight, and favored centralization and oligarchical control of national parties and the Comintern. They were conscious of being innovators without debt to socialism of the immediate past, and although they gave obeisance to Marx and Engels, they disregarded or discounted their epigones. Perhaps most pronounced was their desire to cleanse the Comintern of all vestiges of the Second International, in the belief that contamination by that which they regarded as outmoded and corrupt would undermine their purpose and will in establishing a revolutionary world order.

The struggle of these two forces in the Comintern runs as a counterpoint to its activities in the first few years of its existence. Thus the history of the movement at that time is a combination of organizational and revolutionary activity in various European countries and trouble spots superimposed on the struggle within the Comintern itself, which was largely subterranean until the Bolshevik tendency in skillful Russian hands emerged victorious. International communism during Lenin's lifetime can, therefore, best be understood as a dialectical development in which historical socialist forces and traditions, at least as much as individual actors, hold the center of the stage.

The artificial separation of the communist movement from the socialist mainstream is not the only obstacle to an understanding of its inner history and relation to the events of this century. It is equally distorting to subordinate the continuity between the era of Lenin and that of Stalin to differences between these two periods of international communism. Lenin's era did have a distinct flavor, imparted by the revolutionary spirit of segments of the European working class and by communist and left-wing socialist leaders who, inspired by Bolshevik success, displayed a millenarian fervor even in the face of situations where the conditions for revolution were far from favorable. The most unique feature of the Leninist International was its central political aim of bringing about a communist world revolution, although under the impact of continuous reverses this had ceased to be regarded as an attainable goal before Lenin's death. By contrast the communist movement in Stalin's era was undynamic and subservient to the Russian state machine. Most striking was Stalin's direct use of the Comintern as an instrument of Russian foreign policy and indirect use as a lever in his struggle to gain and keep power in the Soviet Union, which ultimately transformed the Comintern into an anti-revolutionary organization. Consequently, Stalin has been charged with perverting Lenin's purpose by placing the movement in the service of socialism in one country.

But the existence of these differences must not obscure the lines of continuity between the eras of Lenin and Stalin. During Lenin's time the main course which the movement was to follow in later years had been charted, and its subordination to the needs of the Russian party and state had been firmly established. The structure of the Comintern was centralized and russified before Stalin came to power, and its directing organs attained a hegemony over the individual communist parties that extended to their internal affairs. Some historians have implied that Lenin was not responsible for the centralized structure which emerged by pointing out that he objected to making the Russian party the prototype for the Comintern's organization.[2] Considering Lenin's pres-

[2] E. H. Carr points out that Lenin, speaking at the Fourth World Congress, attacked the resolution on organization adopted by the

tige and the power of intervention in organizational matters at his command, his offhand objection in 1922 was extremely weak. It seems as if he had not yet assimilated the improbability of world revolution in the foreseeable future or seriously considered the extreme alternative of building socialism in only one country. With the future course of the Comintern so uncertain, it seems likely that he found it difficult to take a firm stand on its structural development and allowed russification to begin. Furthermore, policies laid down on the united front, the peasantry, and the national and colonial question while Lenin was the putative head of the movement remained its broad guidelines long thereafter, although modifications were made to adjust them to the anti-revolutionary context of the Stalin era.

In documenting the formative years of international communism it is important to dispel the myth of a golden age under Lenin, whose experimental and optimistic hallmarks were destroyed by Stalin, who transformed the Comintern into a mere tail to the Russian comet after 1924.[3] Continuity is as much a part of historical process as change, and from that vantage point the communist movement in the era of Lenin bequeathed as much to its Stalinist followers as it inherited from its social democratic predecessors.

Many of those who have polemicized against the Comintern in Stalin's era have fastened upon the twistings and turnings of its theory and practice without realizing that they originated in Lenin's time. If one examines some milestones

---

Third World Congress the year before as too exclusively Russian. This detailed resolution, which carefully defined the functions and obligations of the Comintern and its members and stressed the need for centralization, promoted a Soviet-style dual subordination of party executives to their own national congresses and to the ECCI. See *The Bolshevik Revolution 1917–1923* ("A History of Soviet Russia;" New York, 1961), Vol. III, pp. 392–93, 445. Lenin's objection to russification was feeble and came late; earlier he had been instrumental in furthering the tendency against which he warned.

[3] The notion of a Leninist golden age followed by Stalinist degeneration is prevalent among Trotskyists who attempt to link their mentor with Lenin and his time, when, they believe, communism was still "pure." See, for instance, Alfred Rosmer, *Moscou sous Lénine: les origines du communisme* (Paris, 1953) and C. L. R. James, *World Revolution 1917–1936: The Rise and Fall of the Communist International* (New York, 1937).

of the Communist International's revolutionary activity during its first four years (particularly the Bulgarian September uprising in 1923 and the abortive German October of 1923) from a Marxist perspective, its policies appear to have been remarkably undialectical. In these and other instances actions were undertaken by communist parties under circumstances where the possibility for revolution appeared extremely slim because the pregnant moment had passed.[4] In their support for these actions or in their subsequent justification the Comintern Executive appeared to express the belief that moments in history auspicious for revolution could be recaptured if they had been allowed to pass. Comintern pronouncements generally made it appear as though missed revolutionary opportunities resulted from the wrong strategy and tactics of practitioners, and that the proper moment could be recreated if the Comintern helped the party in question to apply the correct prescription. This outlook signified a naïve substitution of communist will for historical process and did violence to Marxist dialectical materialism.

Moreover, it calls into question whether "orthodox" Marxism was really the guiding philosophy of the Third International any more than it had been of the Second. The last remnants of reformism were almost completely extirpated by a series of cataclysmic party splits in Lenin's lifetime, but the communist movement continued to be plagued by anarcho-syndicalism (particularly in the Italian, French, and Spanish parties). This anti-Marxist aberration was finally excised when Stalin brought bolshevization and russification to completion. But the categorical Marxism-Leninism, already elevated to dogma in Lenin's lifetime and used so adroitly thereafter by Stalin to cloak his policies, no longer conformed to some of the leading ideas of the master. As the documentary history of Lenin's era illustrates, dialectical materialism was abandoned for a rough-and-ready pragmatism at

[4] Both in 1923 and now it could be argued that possibilities for revolution existed in Bulgaria and Germany. But neither the parties in question nor the Comintern Executive acted or made plans to ready the forces necessary for revolution while the possibility existed. Only afterward, when the propitious time had lapsed and the probability of defeat far outweighed that of success, were revolutions attempted in apparent disregard for the changed realities.

first used sparingly, and later exclusively, in adapting the whole movement to the needs and furtherance of socialism in one country.

Throughout its existence, the Comintern suffered from a chronic disease whose symptoms were already pronounced during Lenin's time and became acute thereafter. Far more serious than the "infantile disorder" against which Lenin polemicized, it stemmed from the Comintern's tendency to view reverses in the movement as a result of errors. In practice these errors and failures generally were attributed to individuals who were then reprimanded or disciplined. This disease was certainly manifest in the charges of irresponsibility against Ernst Bettelheim after the failure of communist uprisings in Vienna, in Lenin's condemnation of Hungarian and German "romantics" for espousing the offensive strategy which led to the disastrous March Action in Germany, in the Comintern Executive's blame of Lukanov and Kabakchiev for the inaction of the Bulgarian party in June 1923, and in the postmortem conviction of Heinrich Brandler for the German October defeat of 1923. The belief that error or perhaps even betrayal could explain revolutionary setbacks implied that things would have gone right if only individuals had behaved as they should have. Thus, according to the Comintern, individuals were found to err, but the general line or dogma of the moment remained unassailable. It changed only in the hands of those in command, in the Executive or its inner bureau, but not visibly, or admittedly through pressure from below. At the heart of the malady was an implicit conception of history as manipulated by individuals, which was as essentially undialectical as the Comintern's notion of historical time.

It is only natural that the Comintern should have altered its theoretical and tactical course after serious reversals in 1919, 1921, and 1923. It is most unnatural that the reason for and purpose of these turnings should have been hidden from communist parties and their members behind the smokescreen of accusations of error and treason. The quest always to be correct—never responsible for what transpired in the movement although often the instigator or director of particular actions—turned the Comintern Executive into an omnipotent authority to which many who refused to be guided by "faith alone" refused ultimately to bow. The defectors from the movement and the cause included not only the expendable salon Bolsheviks and summer soldiers for whom "God had failed," but also some of the greatest talents and freest spirits.

PART ONE

FORMATIVE YEARS:
DEFINITION AND ORGANIZATION OF
LEFT-WING SOCIAL DEMOCRACY

The Third or Communist International which came into being after the end of the First World War was the dialectical descendant of the Second International; its taproot reached to the very foundations of socialism. The shortcomings of the Second International, manifested in its structural weaknesses, theoretical and tactical ambiguities, and inability to promote international socialist solidarity in the face of war, prompted the small left wing in various socialist parties (the nascent communists) to create a more militant international organization of its own. Although it would be impossible to review here the complex intellectual and organizational history of socialism, some consideration of it is indispensable in tracing the genesis of the communist movement.

In 1889, thirteen years after the collapse of the First International, which had been rent by the struggle between Marx and Bakunin, socialists of various countries decided to call an international congress in Paris. This effort to establish a new international of labor was the culmination of the steady growth of trade union organizations and socialist parties. In the more advanced capitalist countries socialist parties strove for organizational unity and increasingly relied on political action. The two wings which strove for domination over the socialist movement were the revolutionary socialists, who were predominantly Marxists, and the moderate reformists, who believed in class collaboration. These two forces met separately in Paris and formal unity between them could not be achieved until the Brussels congress in 1891.

Like its predecessor, the Second International was a loose organization of autonomous units without common theory or

tactics and central authority. The apparent strength of the
socialist forces which comprised the Second International—
the party organizations, newspapers, trade union organizations, parliamentary representatives, cooperative societies,
and welfare agencies—was offset by fundamental incompati-
bilities. The basic weakness of the International stemmed
from disagreement between reformists who believed that a
gradual evolution toward socialism based on day-to-day economic, social, and parliamentary advances was possible, and
revolutionaries who believed that political activities leading
to class consciousness were only the prelude to proletarian
revolution.

On a philosophic plane this dispute was waged between
reformists and orthodox Marxists in Germany, Austria, and
Russia, countries in which Marxism had become the official
doctrine of social democracy. Germany was the major arena
for this controversy, not only because of its leading position
in Europe, but also because its large and well-developed
socialist party dominated the International. Eduard Bernstein,
the principal theoretician of revisionism, taking issue with
some of the basic tenets of Marxism, argued that the collapse
of the capitalist system was not imminent; that there was
evidence of increasing order, security, prosperity, and more
equitable distribution of wealth; that the middle class was
not diminishing; and that ownership of property was becoming more widespread. Bernstein regarded the democratic
state as an instrument to be mastered and used for the realization of socialism and not as a tool of class repression to be
overthrown. His tactics were reformist, and the establishment
of socialism would consist, therefore, essentially in the extension of the area of freedom already existing under liberal
democracy.

To the orthodox, Bernstein's argument was a virtual abandonment of Marxism. Karl Kautsky, the spokesman for orthodoxy, rejected Bernstein's notion of capitalist resilience and
viability and reasserted Marx's postulates concerning the inevitability of capitalist decay. Socialism, he asserted, could
only come about by revolution, but the proletariat could use
the tools of the democratic state to gain political experience
and consolidate its powers. The weight of Kautsky's argument rested on the belief in the inevitability of socialism
which, reminiscent of crass economic determinist formulas,

diminished the need for revolutionary struggle. The German Socialist party (SPD) formally rejected Bernstein's formulation and the majority of its membership followed the orthodox leadership of Kautsky and August Bebel. A left wing of the SPD under the leadership of Rosa Luxemburg, Franz Mehring, Karl Liebknecht, and Clara Zetkin, was dissatisfied with Kautsky's rather tame rebuttal of revisionism. The left was not content with the cautious tactics of the party majority (the centrists) and demanded revolutionary action, such as the general strike, in place of tepid reform.

The divisions in the German party were reflected in the factional alignment within the International. There, the revolutionary left group included the Bolshevik supporters of Lenin and the "narrow" (left-wing) Bulgarian socialists; the reformist right comprised the French Possibilists, the Fabian Socialists, and the followers of Jaures; the center of orthodox Marxists numbered among its supporters the French Guesdists, the Menshevik supporters of Plekhanov, the Hyndman group in Britain, the followers of Victor Adler in Austria-Hungary and of Hillquit in the United States.[1] The center was the largest group in the International and theoretically based its policies on an unreconstructed Marxist framework. In reality, along with a majority of the International, it continued to give lip service to Marxist formulations while engaging in reformist practices. The growth of trade unions and the success of socialist parties in gaining a mass base, together with their increasing respectability, had dampened their revolutionary fires. Socialist organizations became bureaucratic institutions with funds and treasuries safely invested in national economies, with numerous officials, agents, lawyers,

[1] The Possibilists, as the followers of Paul Brousse were derisively called by the Marxists, were more concerned with present possibilities for social change than with striving for the final goal. They were part of the gradualist movement within socialism of which the Fabian Society in England and later the revisionists in Germany were also a part. Jules Guesde, who had the personal confidence of Marx and Engels, was the exponent of a narrow and orthodox Marxism in France. In a singleminded manner reminiscent of Kautsky, Guesde projected the socialist society of the future as the dialectical unfolding of an inevitable confrontation between capital and labor which in its final phase of struggle would blend democratic and violent means.

managers, and parliamentary representatives, and with a considerable stake in the societies in which they had become well integrated.[2] It is understandable that, save for a small militant minority, the spirit of moderation prevailed at various international congresses.

Two developments had a profound effect upon the discussions of the Second International: the Russian Revolution of 1905, which suggested that violent upheavals were still possible and might even be expected in eastern and central Europe; and dangerous imperialist clashes from the Moroccan crisis of 1905 to the Balkan crisis of 1912, which threatened a general European war. The problem of war and militarism became the leitmotiv of many international congresses, creating a conflict of loyalties for most socialists between their national identification and their international aspirations. Denunciations of war were universal, but concrete proposals for dealing with war varied considerably and generally followed the pattern of factional divisions within the International.

From the point of view of the right, national loyalty took precedence over class identity and international socialist unity. This attachment to their country was a natural consequence of their belief that the capitalist state was in gradual transition toward socialism and that the interests of the proletariat and the states were becoming identical. The position of the centrists was more complicated and contradictory. They believed that war was inevitable under capitalism but at the same time assumed that under pressure of the working class the warlike tendencies of capitalism could be directed into peaceful channels. To the left the notion that war is inherent in capitalism was a logical Marxist conclusion, and it called

[2] The German Social Democratic party is an excellent example of the growth and bureaucratization of socialist parties which led to increased accommodation to the state and eventual identification with it. The Mannheim agreement of 1906 ratified the equal status of party and trade unions and marked the surrender of the former to the latter. It cleared the way for the rise of party bosses who knew how to "get along with" union leaders. By 1914 the party had become a vast institution that was staffed by more than 4,000 paid functionaries and 11,000 salaried employees, had twenty million marks invested in business, and published over 4,000 periodicals.

for the conversion of international war into class war to end capitalism. The clearest exposition of these views took place at the Congress of Stuttgart in 1907, where the International attempted to establish a position on the question. The official resolution of the congress blended the positions of the contending factions and relied on a compromise formula open to the widest and most divergent interpretations. Following the postulate that war was inherent in capitalist society and could only disappear with its demise came an exhortation to all socialists to pressure parliaments into reducing armaments and standing armies. In case an outbreak of war threatened, the working class and their parliamentary representatives were directed to use whatever means appeared most effective to forestall catastrophe. Specific commitment to insurrection or to a general strike was carefully avoided although not excluded. Surprisingly the resolution ended on a revolutionary note which Luxemburg, Lenin and Martov had injected: in the event of war it was the duty of the working classes to intercede for its speedy end and utilize the economic and political crisis created by the war to rouse the masses and thereby hasten the abolition of capitalist rule.

The weakness of the International lay not only in the ambiguity and timidity of its position on vital issues. Even had its stand been firmer, it lacked the necessary machinery to make its decisions binding on its members. To be sure, an International Socialist Bureau (ISB) had been created in 1900, but its responsibility and powers had been cast in the most nebulous terms.

The assassination of Archduke Ferdinand on June 28, 1914 had at first been regarded by the socialist leaders as another passing crisis, but as Austria's belligerence increased and war began to threaten in earnest, they called mass meetings and directed their press to attack militarism and secret diplomacy. Frenzied and uncoordinated protests did little to stem the tide of nationalist euphoria released by the mobilization of nation after nation. The working classes and their leaders were swept along by the tide as patriotism vanquished internationalism. The International collapsed and only the ISB, a weak administrative body without direction, remained to command the breached international fortress.

I: Party Structure and Function

In tracing the transformation of left-wing socialism into communism it is important to realize that the unity of the radical socialists in the Second International did not extend to theoretical and tactical questions. There were important differences on the left not only between segments of national groups in applying Marxism to their historical conditions (leading in the case of the Russian Social Democratic Labor party [RSDLP] to a split between Bolsheviks and Mensheviks in 1903) but also in the international arena between the leading spokesmen of the left on strategy in preparing for proletarian revolutions. In the selections that follow, the organization of social democracy was the main theme, but broader issues involving the direction, pace, and historical context of revolutionary socialism were the real subjects of the controversy between V. I. Lenin and Rosa Luxemburg. This somewhat specialized dispute, with its overtone question of revolution from above or below, was taken up again repeatedly in the early years of the Communist International.

Lenin's *What Is to Be Done?: Burning Questions of Our Movement* of 1902 has become a classic of revolutionary polemics. Its initial reception was far from spectacular, for Lenin led only one of many energizing forces working and pamphleteering for Russian social democracy, and in international socialist circles he was decidedly a newcomer. Lenin voiced a profound skepticism about the ability of the Russian working class spontaneously to acquire social democratic consciousness. Spontaneity, he declared, could lead to trade unionism and had led to Economism, the Russian counterpart of reformism; it would never lead to true socialist consciousness. Only a highly centralized party directed by professional revolutionists was the correct road to social democracy in the backward environment of Czarist Russia.

Lenin argued for recognition of particular Russian conditions which imposed a development on Russian social democracy different from that in western Europe. His demand for strict centralism was intended to be more than a theoretical scheme for Russian consumption. Implied in his proposal for placing all power in the hands of professional revolutionists was a fierce critique of the leaders of European social democracy who, infected with the "disease of reformism," had failed to build strong revolutionary parties. Implicit in his conception of Russian social democracy was a blueprint for socialist movements everywhere.

Luxemburg took strong issue with Lenin's polemic in two articles of 1904 titled "Organizational Questions of the Russian Social Democracy," which appeared simultaneously in *Iskra* and in *Die neue Zeit*. Luxemburg was a critic to be reckoned with, for she was a leading figure in the German Social Democratic party and, unlike Lenin, was well known and respected in international socialist circles. She saw dangers to the advance of social democracy, not only in the abandonment of socialist goals for bourgeois social reform, but also in the loss of mass character and deterioration into a mere sect. The greatest danger to the young Russian labor movement, she lectured Lenin, was a centralized bureaucratic straitjacket and the mechanical substitution of an absolute central committee for the yet unrealized rule of the majority of politically conscious workers in the party.

Luxemburg warned against loose talk of "opportunism" and against pat formulas. By innuendo she called Lenin and his followers opportunists, for she considered opportunism a by-product of the development of the labor movement. During the formative stages of development, as in Russia, it was represented by the quest for despotic centralism; under parliamentary regimes and strong labor parties, as in western Europe, it expressed itself in the drive for decentralization. In either case the working class had to overcome opportunism by making mistakes and learning from the dialectic of history.

DOCUMENT 1: V. I. Lenin, *What Is to Be Done?: Burning Questions of Our Movement*

(New York: International Publishers, 1929). By permission. Lenin's polemic on the relations of party to class was first published in March, 1902.

. . . In the previous chapter we pointed out how universally absorbed the educated youth of Russia were in the theories of Marxism in the middle of the nineties. The strikes that followed the famous St. Petersburg industrial war of 1896 also assumed a similar wholesale character. The fact that these strikes spread over the whole of Russia showed how deep the reviving popular movement was, and if we must speak of the "spontaneous element" then, of course, we must admit that this strike movement certainly bore a spontaneous character. But there is a difference between spontaneity and spontaneity. Strikes occurred in Russia in the seventies, and in the sixties (and also in the first half of the nineteenth century), and these strikes were accompanied by the "spontaneous" destruction of machinery, etc. Compared with these "revolts" the strikes of the nineties might even be described as "conscious," to such an extent do they mark the progress which the labor movement had made since that period. This shows that the "spontaneous element," in essence, represents nothing more nor less than consciousness in an *embryonic form*. Even the primitive rebellions expressed the awakening of consciousness to a certain extent: the workers abandoned their age-long faith in the permanence of the system which oppressed them. They began . . . I shall not say to understand, but to sense the necessity for collective resistance, and emphatically abandoned their slavish submission to their superiors. But all this was more in the nature of outbursts of desperation and vengeance than *struggle*. The strikes of the nineties revealed far greater flashes of consciousness: definite demands were put forward, the time to strike was carefully chosen, known cases and examples in other places were discussed, etc. While the revolts were simply uprisings of the oppressed, the systematic strikes represented the class struggle in embryo, but only in embryo. Taken by themselves, these strikes were simply trade union struggles, but not yet social democratic struggles. They testified to the awakening antagonisms between workers and employers, but the workers were not and could not be conscious of the irreconcilable antagonism of their interests to the whole of the modern political and social system, i.e., it was not yet social democratic consciousness. In this sense, the strikes of the nineties, in spite of the enormous progress they represented as compared with the "revolts," represented a purely spontaneous movement.

We said that *there could not yet be* social democratic

consciousness among the workers. This consciousness could only be brought to them from without. The history of all countries shows that the working class, exclusively by its own effort, is able to develop only trade union consciousness, i.e., it may itself realize the necessity for combining in unions to fight against the employers and to strive to compel the government to pass necessary labor legislation, etc.

The theory of socialism, however, grew out of the philosophic, historical and economic theories that were elaborated by the educated representatives of the propertied classes, the intellectuals. The founders of modern scientific socialism, Marx and Engels, themselves belonged to the bourgeois intelligentsia. Similarly, in Russia, the theoretical doctrine of social democracy arose quite independently of the spontaneous growth of the labor movement; it arose as a natural and inevitable outcome of the development of ideas among the revolutionary socialist intelligentsia. At the time of which we are speaking, i.e., the middle of the nineties, this doctrine not only represented the completely formulated program of the Emancipation of Labor group[1] but had already won the adhesion of the majority of the revolutionary youth in Russia.

. . . There is a lot of talk about spontaneity, but the *spontaneous* development of the labor movement leads to its becoming subordinated to bourgeois ideology; it means developing *according to the program* of the *Credo,* for the spontaneous labor movement is pure and simple trade unionism—*Nur-Gewerkschaftlerei*—and trade unionism means the ideological subordination of the workers to the bourgeoisie. Hence, our task, the task of social democracy, is to *combat spontaneity,* to *divert* the labor movement with its spontaneous trade-unionist striving, from under the wing of the bourgeoisie, and to bring it under the wing of revolutionary social democracy. . . .

But why, the reader will ask, does the spontaneous movement, the movement along the line of least resistance, lead to the domination of bourgeois ideology? For the simple rea-

[1] The Emancipation of Labor group was formed in Switzerland in 1883 by G. V. Plekhanov, P. B. Axelrod, Vera Zasulich, and other intellectuals. Although the group was initially under the influence of Narodnik ideas, it became Marxist under Plekhanov's leadership, and in 1890 began the publication of *Sotsial Demokrat* for the dissemination of Marxist ideas.

son that bourgeois ideology is far older in origin than social democratic ideology; because it is more fully developed and because it possesses *immeasurably* more opportunities for becoming widespread. . . .

And so, we have become convinced that the fundamental error committed by the "new tendency" in Russian social democracy lies in its subservience to spontaneity, and its failure to understand that the spontaneity of the masses demands a mass of consciousness from us social democrats. The more spontaneously the masses rise, the more widespread the movement becomes, so much the more rapidly grows the demand for greater consciousness in the theoretical, political, and organizational work of social democracy.

The spontaneous rise of the masses in Russia proceeded (and continues) with such rapidity that the young untrained social democrats proved unfitted for the gigantic tasks that confronted them. This lack of training is our common misfortune, the misfortune of *all* Russian social democrats. The rise of the masses proceeded and spread uninterruptedly and continuously; it not only continued in the places it commenced in, but it spread to new localities and to new strata of the population (influenced by the labor movement, the ferment among the students and the intellectuals generally, and even among the peasantry revived). Revolutionaries, however, *lagged behind* this rise of the masses in both their "theories" and in their practical activity; they failed to establish an uninterrupted organization having continuity with the past, and capable of *leading* the whole movement. . . .

Recently, the overwhelming majority of Russian social democrats were almost wholly engaged in this work of exposing factory conditions. It is sufficient to refer to the columns of *Rabochaya Mysl*[2] to judge to what an extent they were engaged in it. So much so indeed, that they lost sight of the fact that this, *taken by itself,* was not substantially social democratic work, but merely trade union work. As a matter of fact, these exposures merely dealt with the relations between

---

[2] *Rabochaya Mysl* or "Workers' Thought" was a newspaper of the right wing of the RSDLP which supported Economism. The Economists insisted that the workers' economic struggles for the improvement of their immediate working and living conditions should be the primary task of the labor movement and that the struggle against czarism should be left to the liberal bourgeoisie.

the workers *in a given trade*, with their immediate employers, and all that it achieved was that the vendors of labor power learned to sell their "commodity" on better terms, and to fight the purchasers of labor power over a purely commercial deal. These exposures might have served (if properly utilized by revolutionaries) as a beginning and a constituent part of social democratic activity, but they might also (and with subservience to spontaneity inevitably had to) have led to a "pure and simple" trade union struggle and to a non-social democratic labor movement. Social democrats lead the struggle of the working class not only for better terms for the sale of labor power, but also for the abolition of the social system which compels the propertyless class to sell itself to the rich. Social democracy represents the working class, not in its relation to a given group of employers, but in its relation to all classes in modern society, to the state as an organized political force. Hence, it not only follows that social democrats must not confine themselves entirely to the economic struggle, they must not even allow the organization of economic exposures to become the predominant part of their activities. We must actively take up the political education of the working class, and the development of its political consciousness. . . .

Let us return, however, to the elucidation of our thesis. We said that a social democrat, if he really believes it is necessary to develop the political consciousness of the proletariat, must "go among all classes of the people." This gives rise to the questions: How is this to be done? Have we enough forces to do this? Is there a base for such work among all the other classes? Will this not mean a retreat, or lead to a retreat from the class point-of-view? We shall deal with these questions.

We must "go among all classes of the people" as theoreticians, as propagandists, as agitators, and as organizers. No one doubts that the theoretical work of social democrats should be directed towards studying all the features of the social and political position of the various classes. But extremely little is done in this direction compared with the work that is done in studying the features of factory life. In the committees and circles, you will meet men who are immersed, say, in the study of some special branch of the metal industry, but you will hardly ever find members of organizations (obliged, as often happens, for some reason or other to give up practical work) especially engaged in the collection of material concerning some pressing question of social and political life which could serve as a means for conducting social democratic work among other strata of the population. In speaking of the lack of training of the majority of present-day leaders of the labor movement, we cannot refrain from mentioning the point about training in this connection also, for it is also bound up with the "economic" conception of "close organic contact with the proletarian struggle." The principal thing, of course, is *propaganda and agitation* among all strata of the people. The western European social democrats find their work in this field facilitated by the calling of public meetings, to which *all* are free to go, and by the parliament, in which they speak to the representatives of *all* classes. We have neither a parliament, nor the freedom to call meetings; nevertheless we are able to arrange meetings of workers who desire to listen to a *social democrat.* We must find ways and means of calling meetings of representatives of all and every other class of the population that desire to listen to a *democrat;* for he who forgets that "the communists support every revolutionary movement," that we are obliged for that reason to emphasize *general democratic tasks before the whole people,* without for a moment concealing our socialistic convictions, is not a social democrat. He who forgets his obligation to *be in advance of everybody* in bringing up, sharpening and solving *every* general democratic question, is not a social democrat. . . .

. . . It goes without saying that we cannot guide the struggle of the students, liberals, etc., for their "immediate interests," but this is not the point we were arguing about, most worthy Economists! The point we were discussing is the possible and necessary participation of various social strata in the overthrow of the autocracy; not only are we able, but it is our duty to guide *these* "activities, of the various opposition strata" if we desire to be a "vanguard." Not only will the students and our liberals, etc., take care of the struggle that will bring them up against our political régime; the police and the officials of the autocratic government will see to this more than anyone. But, if "we" desire to be advanced democrats, we must make it our business to *stimulate* in the minds of those who are dissatisfied only with university or only with Zemstvo, etc., conditions, the idea that the whole political system is worthless. We must take upon ourselves the task of organizing a universal political struggle under the leadership of *our party* in such a manner as to obtain the support of all opposition strata for the struggle and for our party. We must train our social democratic practical workers to become political leaders, able to guide all the manifestations of this universal struggle, able at the right time to "dictate a positive program of action" for the discontented students, for the discontented Zemstvo, for the discontented religious sects, for the offended elementary schoolteachers, etc., etc. . . .

The political struggle carried on by the social democrats is far more extensive and complex than the economic struggle the workers carry on against the employers and the government. Similarly (and indeed for that reason), the organization of revolutionary social democrats must inevitably *differ* from the organizations of the workers designed for the latter struggle. The workers' organizations must in the first place be trade organizations; secondly, they must be as wide as possible; and thirdly, they must be as public as conditions will allow (here, of course, I have only autocratic Russia in mind). On the other hand, the organizations of revolutionists must be comprised first and foremost of people whose profession is that of revolutionists (that is why I speak of organizations of *revolutionists*, meaning revolutionary social democrats). As this is the common feature of the members of such an organization *all distinctions as between workers and intellectuals,* and certainly distinctions of trade and profession, must be dropped. Such an organization must of necessity be not too extensive and as secret as possible. Let us examine this threefold distinction.

In countries where political liberty exists the distinction between a labor union and a political organization is clear, as is the distinction between trade unions and social democracy. The relation of the latter to the former will naturally vary in each country according to historical, legal, and other conditions—it may be more or less close or more or less complex (in our opinion it should be as close and simple as possible); but trade union organizations are certainly not in the least identical with the social democratic party organizations in those countries. In Russia, however, the yoke of autocracy appears at first glance to obliterate all distinctions between a social democratic organization and trade unions, because *all* trade unions and *all* circles are prohibited, and because the principal manifestation and weapon of the workers' economic struggle—the strike—is regarded as a crime (and sometimes even as a political crime!). Conditions in our country, therefore, strongly "impel" the workers who are conducting the economic struggle to concern themselves with political questions. They also "impel" the social democrats to confuse trade unionism with social democracy. . . . Indeed, picture to yourselves the people who are immersed ninety-nine per cent in "the economic struggle against the employers and the government." Some of them never, *during the whole course of their activity* (four to six months), thought of the necessity for a more complex organization of revolutionists; others, perhaps, come across the fairly widely distributed revisionist literature, from which they convince themselves of the profound importance of "the drab daily struggle." Still others will be carried away, perhaps, by the seductive idea of showing the world a new example of "close and organic contact with the proletarian struggle"—contact between the trade union and social democratic movements. Such people would perhaps argue that the later a country enters into the arena of capitalism, the more the socialists in that country may take part in and support the trade-union movement, and the less reason is there for non-social democratic trade unions. So far, the argument is absolutely correct; unfortunately, however, some go beyond that and hint at the complete fusion of social democracy with trade unionism. . . .

The workers' organizations for carrying on the economic struggle should be trade union organizations; every social democratic worker should, as far as possible, support and actively work inside these organizations. That is true. But it would be far from being to our interest to demand that only social democrats be eligible for membership in the trade unions. The only effect of this, if it were attempted, would be to restrict our influence over the masses. Let every worker who understands the necessity for organization, in order to carry on the struggle against the employers and the government, join the trade unions. The very objects of the trade unions would be unattainable unless they united all who have attained at least this elementary level of understanding and unless they were extremely wide organizations. The wider these organizations are, the wider our influence over them will be. They will then be influenced not only by the "spontaneous" development of the economic struggle, but also by the direct and conscious action of the socialists on their comrades in the unions. But a wide organization cannot be a strictly secret organization (since the latter demands far greater training than is required for the economic struggle). How is the contradiction between the necessity for a large membership and the necessity for strictly secret methods to be reconciled? How are we to make the trade unions as public as possible? Generally speaking, there are perhaps only two ways to this end: Either the trade unions become legalized (which in some countries precedes the legalization of the socialist and political unions), or the organization is kept a secret one, but so "free" and "loose" that the need for secret methods becomes almost negligible as far as the mass of the members are concerned. . . .

A small, compact core, consisting of reliable, experienced, and hardened workers, with responsible agents in the principal districts and connected by all the rules of strict secrecy with the organizations of revolutionists, can, with the wide support of the masses and without an elaborate set of rules, perform *all* the functions of a trade union organization, and perform them, moreover, in the manner social democrats desire. Only in this way can we secure the *consolidation* and development of a *social democratic* trade union movement, in spite of the gendarmes.

It may be objected that an organization which is so loose that it is not even formulated, and which even has no enrolled and registered members, cannot be called an organization at all. That may very well be. I am not out for names. But this "organization without members" can do everything that is required, and will, from the very outset, guarantee the closest contact between our future trade unionists and socialism. Only an incorrigible utopian would want a *wide* organization of workers, with elections, reports, universal suffrage, etc., under autocracy.

The moral to be drawn from this is a simple one. If we begin with the solid foundation of a strong organization of revolutionists, we can guarantee the stability of the movement as a whole, and carry out the aims of both social democracy and of trade unionism. If, however, we begin with a wide workers' organization, supposed to be most "accessible" to the masses, when as a matter of fact it will be most accessible to the gendarmes, and will make the revolutionists most accessible to the police, we shall neither achieve the aims of social democracy nor of trade unionism; . . .

I assert that it is far more difficult to catch ten wise men than it is to catch a hundred fools. And this premise I shall defend no matter how much you instigate the crowd against me for my "anti-democratic" views, etc. As I have already said, by "wise men," in connection with organization, I mean *professional revolutionists,* irrespective of whether they are students or working men. I assert: 1. That no movement can be durable without a stable organization of leaders to maintain continuity; 2. that the more widely the masses are drawn into the struggle and form the basis of the movement, the more necessary is it to have such an organization and the more stable must it be (for it is much easier then for demagogues to sidetrack the more backward sections of the masses); 3. that the organization must consist chiefly of persons engaged in revolution as a profession; 4. that in a country with a despotic government, the more we *restrict* the membership of this organization to persons who are engaged in revolution as a profession and who have been professionally trained in the art of combating the political police, the more difficult will it be to catch the organization; and 5. the *wider* will be the circle of men and women of the working class or of other classes of society able to join the movement and perform active work in it. . . .

The question as to whether it is easier to catch "a dozen wise men" or "a hundred fools," in the last analysis, amounts to the question we have considered above, namely, whether it is possible to have a mass *organization* when the maintenance of strict secrecy is essential. We can never give a mass organization that degree of secrecy which is essential for the persistent and continuous struggle against the government. But to concentrate all secret functions in the hands of as small a number of professional revolutionists as possible, does not mean that the latter will "do the thinking for all" and that the crowd will not take an active part in the movement. On the contrary, the crowd will advance from its ranks increasing numbers of professional revolutionists, for it will know that it is not enough for a few students and workingmen waging economic war to gather together and form a "committee," but that professional revolutionists must be trained for years; the crowd will "think" not of primitive ways but of training professional revolutionists. The centralization of the secret functions of the *organization* does not mean the concentration of all the functions of the *movement*. The active participation of the greatest masses in the dissemination of illegal literature will not diminish because a dozen professional revolutionists concentrate in their hands the secret part of the work; on the contrary, it will *increase tenfold*. Only in this way will the reading of illegal literature, the contribution to illegal literature, and to some extent even the distribution of illegal literature *almost cease to be secret work,* for the police will soon come to realize the folly and futility of setting the whole judicial and administrative machine into motion to intercept every copy of a publication that is being broadcast in thousands. This applies not only to the press, but to every function of the movement, even to demonstrations. The active and widespread participation of the masses will not suffer; on the contrary, it will benefit by the fact that a "dozen" experienced revolutionists, no less professionally trained than the police, will concentrate all the secret side of the work in their hands— prepare leaflets, work out approximate plans and appoint bodies of leaders for each town district, for each factory district, and for each educational institution (I know that exception will be taken to my "undemocratic" views, but I shall reply to this altogether unintelligent objection later on). The centralization of the more secret functions in an organization of revolutionists will not diminish, but rather increase the extent and the quality of the activity of a large number of other organizations intended for wide membership and which, therefore, can be as loose and as public as possible, for example, trade unions, workers' circles for self-education, and the reading of illegal literature, and socialist, and also democratic, circles for *all other sections of the population,* etc., etc. We must have *as large a number as possible* of such organizations having the widest possible variety of functions, but it is absurd and dangerous to *confuse these with organizations of revolutionists,* to erase the line of demarcation between them, to dim still more the already incredibly hazy appreciation by the masses that to "serve" the mass movement we must have people who will devote themselves exclusively to social democratic activities, and that such people must *train* themselves patiently and steadfastly to be professional revolutionists. . . .

Against us it is argued: Such a powerful and strictly secret organization, which concentrates in its hands all the threads of secret activities, an organization which of necessity must be a centralized organization, may too easily throw itself into a premature attack, may thoughtlessly intensify the movement before political discontent, the ferment and anger of the working class, etc., are sufficiently ripe for it. To this we reply: Speaking abstractly, it cannot be denied, of course, that a militant organization *may* thoughtlessly commence a battle, which *may* end in defeat, which might have been avoided under other circumstances. But we cannot confine ourselves to abstract reasoning on such a question, because every battle bears within itself the abstract possibility of defeat, and there is no other way of *reducing this possibility to a minimum* than by organized preparation for battle. If, however, we base our argument on the concrete conditions prevailing in Russia at the present time, we must come to the positive conclusion that a strong revolutionary organization is absolutely necessary precisely for the purpose of giving firmness to the movement, and of *safeguarding* it against the possibility of its making premature attacks. It is precisely at the present time, when no such organization exists yet, and when the revolutionary movement is rapidly and spontaneously growing, that we *already observe* two opposite extremes (which, as is to be expected "meet") i.e., absolutely unsound Economism and the preaching of moderation, and equally unsound "excitative terror," which strives artificially to "call forth symptoms of its end in a movement that is developing and becoming strong, but which is as yet nearer to its beginning than to its end."
. . . Only a centralized, militant organization that consistently carries out a social democratic policy, that satisfies, so to speak, all revolutionary instincts and strivings, can safeguard the movement against making thoughtless attacks and prepare it for attacks that hold out the promise of success.

It is further argued against us that the views on organization here expounded contradict the "principles of democracy." . . .

Everyone will probably agree that "broad principles of democracy" presupposes the two following conditions: first, full publicity and second, election to all functions. It would be absurd to speak about democracy without publicity, that is, a publicity that extends beyond the circle of the membership of the organization. We call the German Socialist party a democratic organization because all it does is done publicly; even its party congresses are held in public. But no one would call an organization that is hidden from every one but its members by a veil of secrecy, a democratic organization. What is the use of advancing *"broad* principles of democracy" when the fundamental condition for this principle *cannot be fulfilled* by a secret organization. "Broad principles" turns out to be a resonant, but hollow phrase. More than that, this phrase proves that the urgent tasks in regard to organization are totally misunderstood. Everyone knows how great is the lack of secrecy among the "broad" masses of revolutionists. . . . And yet people who boast about their "sensitiveness to life" come forward in a situation like this and *urge* that strict secrecy and a strict (and therefore more restricted) selection of members is unnecessary, and that what is necessary are—*"broad* principles of democracy"! This is what we call being absolutely wide of the mark.

Nor is the situation with regard to the second attribute of democracy, namely, the principle of election, any better. In politically free countries, this condition is taken for granted. "Membership of the party is open to those who accept the principles of the party program, and render all the support they can to the party"—says paragraph 1 of the rules of the German Social Democratic party. And as the political arena is as open to the public view as is the stage in a theater, this acceptance or non-acceptance, support or opposition is announced to all in the press and at public meetings. Everyone knows that a certain political worker commenced in a certain way, passed through a certain evolution, behaved in difficult periods in a certain way; everyone knows all his qualities, and consequently, knowing all the facts of the case, *every party member can decide for himself whether or not to elect this person for a certain party office.* The general control (in the literal sense of the term) that the party exercises over every act this person commits on the political field brings into being an automatically operating mechanism which brings about what in biology is called "survival of the fittest." "Natural selection," full publicity, the principle of election and general control provide the guarantee that, in the last analysis, every political worker will be "in his proper place," will do the work for which he is best fitted, will feel the effects of his mistakes on himself, and prove before all the world his ability to recognize mistakes and to avoid them.

Try to put this picture in the frame of our autocracy! Is it possible in Russia for all those "who accept the principles of the party program and render it all the support they can," to control every action of the revolutionist working in secret? Is it possible for all the revolutionists to elect one of their number to any particular office when, in the very interests of the work, he *must conceal his identity* from nine out of ten of these "all"? . . . "Broad democracy" in party organization, amidst the gloom of autocracy and the domination of the gendarmes, is nothing more than a *useless and harmful toy*. It is a useless toy, because as a matter of fact, no revolutionary organization has ever practiced *broad* democracy, nor could it, however much it desired to do so. It is a harmful toy, because any attempt to practice the "broad principles of democracy" will simply facilitate the work of the police in making big raids, it will perpetuate the prevailing primitiveness, divert the thoughts of the practical workers from the serious and imperative task of training themselves to become professional revolutionists to that of drawing up detailed "paper" rules for election systems. Only abroad, where very often people who have no opportunity of doing real live work gather together, can the "game of democracy" be played here and there, especially in small groups. . . .

The only serious organizational principle the active workers of our movement can accept is: Strict secrecy, strict selection of members, and the training of professional revolutionists. If we possessed these qualities, "democracy" and something even more would be guaranteed to us, namely: Complete, comradely, mutual confidence among revolutionists. And this something more is absolutely essential for us because, in Russia, it is useless to think that democratic control can serve as a substitute for it. It would be a great mistake to believe that because it is impossible to establish real "democratic" control, the members of the revolutionary organization will remain altogether uncontrolled. They have not the time to think about the toy forms of democracy (democracy within a close and compact body enjoying the complete mutual confidence of the comrades), but they have a lively sense of their *responsibility*, because they know from experience that an organization of real revolutionists will stop at nothing to rid itself of an undesirable member. Moreover, there is a very well-developed public opinion in Russian (and international) revolutionary circles which has a long history behind it, and which sternly and ruthlessly punishes every departure from the duties of comradeship (and does not "democracy," real and not toy democracy, represent a part of the conception of comradeship?). Take all this into consideration and you will realize that all the talk and resolutions that come from abroad about "antidemocratic tendencies" has a nasty odor of the playing at generals that goes on there. . . .

DOCUMENT 2: Rosa Luxemburg, *Leninism or Marxism?*

This answer to Lenin first appeared as two articles published simultaneously in *Iskra,* the theoretical organ of the RSDLP, and in the German social democratic *Neue Zeit* in 1904 under the title "Organizational Questions of the Russian Social Democracy." The condensed version below is taken from the translation by Integer titled *Revolutionary Socialist Organization* (New York, 1934). The title used is taken from another version published by the Anti-Parliamentary Communist Federation in Glasgow, 1935.

An unprecedented task in the history of the socialist movement has fallen to the lot of the Russian social democracy. It is the task of deciding on what is the best socialist tactical policy in a country where absolute monarchy is still dominant. It is a mistake to draw a rigid parallel between the present Russian situation and that which existed in Germany during the years 1878–90, when Bismarck's antisocialist laws were in force. The two have one thing in common—police rule. Otherwise, they are in no way comparable.

The obstacles offered to the socialist movement by the absence of democratic liberties are of relatively secondary importance. Even in Russia, the people's movement has succeeded in overcoming the barriers set up by the state. The people have found themselves a "constitution" (though a rather precarious one) in street disorders. Persevering in this course, the Russian people will in time attain complete victory over the autocracy.

The principal difficulty faced by socialist activity in Russia results from the fact that in that country the domination of the bourgeoisie is veiled by absolutist force. This gives socialist propaganda an abstract character, while immediate political agitation takes on a democratic-revolutionary guise.

Bismarck's antisocialist laws put our movement out of constitutional bounds in a highly developed bourgeois society, where class antagonisms had already reached their full bloom in parliamentary contests. (Here, by the way, lay the absurdity of Bismarck's scheme.) The situation is quite different in Russia. The problem there is how to create a social democratic movement at a time when the state is not yet in the hands of the bourgeoisie.

This circumstance has an influence on agitation, on the manner of transplanting socialist doctrine to Russian soil. It also bears in a peculiar and direct way on the question of *party organization.*

Under ordinary conditions—that is, where the political domination of the bourgeoisie has preceded the socialist movement—the bourgeoisie itself instills in the working class the rudiments of political solidarity. At this stage, declares the *Communist Manifesto,* the unification of the workers is not yet the result of the activity of the bourgeoisie, "which, in order to attain its own political ends, is compelled to set the proletariat in motion. . . ."

In Russia, however, the social democracy must make up by its own efforts an entire historic period. It must lead the Russian proletarians from their present "atomized" condition, which prolongs the autocratic regime, to a class organization that would help them to become aware of their historic objectives and prepare them to struggle to achieve those objectives. . . .

How to effect a transition from the type of organization characteristic of the preparatory stage of the socialist movement—usually featured by disconnected local groups and clubs, with propaganda as a principal activity—to the unity of a large, national body, suitable for concerted political action over the entire vast territory ruled by the Russian state? That is the specific problem which the Russian social democracy has mulled over for some time.

Autonomy and isolation are the most pronounced characteristics of the old organizational type. It is, therefore, understandable why the slogan of the persons who want to see an inclusive national organization should be "Centralism!" . . .

One Step Forward, Two Steps Backward, written by Lenin, an outstanding member of the *Iskra* group,[3] is a methodical exposition of the ideas of the ultra-centralism tendency in the Russian movement. The viewpoint presented with incomparable vigor and logic in this book is that of pitiless centralism. Laid down as principles are: 1. The necessity of selecting, and constituting as a separate corps, all the active revolutionists, as distinguished from the unorganized, though revolutionary, mass surrounding this elite.

Lenin's thesis is that the party central committee should have the privilege of naming all the local committees of the party. It should have the right to appoint the effective organs of all local bodies from Geneva to Liége, from Tomsk to Irkutsk.[4] It should also have the right to impose on all of them its own ready-made rules of party conduct. It should have the right to rule without appeal on such questions as the dissolution and reconstitution of local organizations. This way, the central committee could determine, to suit itself, the composition of the highest party organs as well as of the party congress. The central committee would be the only thinking element in the party. All other groupings would be its executive limbs. . . .

Generally speaking it is undeniable that a strong tendency toward centralization is inherent in the social democratic movement. This tendency springs from the economic makeup of capitalism, which is essentially a centralizing factor. The social democratic movement carries on its activity inside the

[3] Many Russian socialists lived as exiles in western Europe and as deportees in Siberia and Central Asia and carried on their revolutionary activities at a distance.

[4] Outgrowth of the publication of the periodical *Iskra* ("The Spark," 1900–1905), which became the central organ of the RSDLP. The group, which was devoted to orthodox Marxism, fought Economism and ultimately emerged as the dominant force at the second congress of the RSDLP in 1903. It was in connection with the publication of *Iskra* that Lenin went abroad and became acquainted with the international socialist movement and its European leaders.

large bourgeois city. Its mission is to represent, within the boundaries of the national state, the class interests of the proletariat, and to oppose those common interests to all local and group interests.

Therefore, the social democracy is, as a rule, hostile to any manifestations of localism or federalism. It strives to unite all workers and all worker organizations in a single party, no matter what national, religious, or occupational differences may exist among them. The social democracy abandons this principle and gives way to federalism only under exceptional conditions, as in the case of the Austro-Hungarian Empire.

It is clear that the Russian social democracy should not organize itself as a federative conglomerate of many national groups. It must rather become a single party for the entire empire. However, that is not really the question considered here. What we are considering is the degree of centralization necessary inside the unified, single Russian party in view of the peculiar conditions under which it has to function.

Looking at the matter from the angle of the formal tasks of the social democracy in its capacity as a party of class struggle, it appears at first that the power and energy of the party are directly dependent on the possibility of centralizing the party. However, these formal tasks apply to all active parties. In the case of the social democracy, they are less important than is the influence of historic conditions.

The social democratic movement is the first in the history of class societies which reckons, in all its phases and through its entire course, on the organization and the direct, independent action of the masses.

Because of this, the social democracy creates an organizational type that is entirely different from those common to earlier revolutionary movements, such as those of the Jacobins and the adherents of Blanqui.

Lenin seems to slight this fact when he presents in his book (page 140) the opinion that the revolutionary social democrat is nothing else than a "Jacobin indissolubly joined to the organization of the proletariat, which has become conscious of its class interests."

For Lenin, the difference between the social democracy and Blanquism is reduced to the observation that in place of a handful of conspirators we have a class-conscious proletariat. He forgets that this difference implies a complete revision of our ideas on organization and, therefore, an entirely different conception of centralism and the relations existing between the party and the struggle itself.

Blanquism did not count on the direct action of the working class. It, therefore, did not need to organize the people for the revolution. The people were expected to play their part only at the moment of revolution. Preparation for the revolution concerned only the little group of revolutionists armed for the coup. Indeed, to assure the success of the revolutionary conspiracy, it was considered wiser to keep the mass at some distance from the conspirators. Such a relationship could be conceived by the Blanquists only because there was no close contact between the conspiratorial activity of their organization and the daily struggle of the popular masses.

The tactics and concrete tasks of the Blanquist revolutionists had little connection with the elementary class struggle. They were freely improvised. They could, therefore, be decided on in advance and took the form of a ready-made plan. In consequence of this, ordinary members of the organization became simple executive organs, carrying out the orders of a will fixed beforehand, and outside of their particular sphere of activity. They became the instruments of a central committee. Here we have the second peculiarity of conspiratorial centralism—the absolute and blind submission of the party sections to the will of the center, and the extension of this authority to all parts of the organization.

However, social democratic activity is carried on under radically different conditions. It arises historically out of the elementary class struggle. It spreads and develops in accordance with the following dialectical contradiction. The proletarian army is recruited and becomes aware of its objectives in the course of the struggle itself. The activity of the party organization, the growth of the proletarians' awareness of the objectives of the struggle and the struggle itself, are not different things separated chronologically and mechanically. They are only different aspects of the same process. Except for the general principles of the struggle, there do not exist for the social democracy detailed sets of tactics which a central committee can teach the party membership in the same way as troops are instructed in their training camps. Furthermore, the range of influence of the socialist party is constantly fluctuating with the ups and downs of the struggle in the course of which the organization is created and grows.

For this reason social democratic centralism cannot be based on the mechanical subordination and blind obedience of the party membership to the leading party center. For this reason, the social democratic movement cannot allow the erection of an air-tight partition between the class-conscious nucleus of the proletariat already in the party and its immediate popular environment, the nonparty sections of the proletariat.

Now the two principles on which Lenin's centralism rests are precisely these: 1. The blind subordination, in the smallest detail, of all party organs, to the party center, which alone thinks, guides, and decides for all. 2. The rigorous separation of the organized nucleus of revolutionaries from its social-revolutionary surroundings. . . .

In accordance with this view, Lenin defines his "revolutionary social democrat" as a "Jacobin joined to the organization of the proletariat, which has become conscious of its class interests."

The fact is that the social democracy is not *joined* to the organization of the proletariat. It is itself the proletariat. And because of this, social democratic centralism is essentially different from Blanquist centralism. It can only be the concentrated will of the individuals and groups representative of the most class-conscious, militant, advanced sections of the working class. It is, so to speak, the "self-centralism" of the advanced sectors of the proletariat. It is the rule of the majority within its own party.

The indispensable conditions for the realization of social democratic centralism are: 1. The existence of a large contingent of workers educated in the political struggle. 2. The possibility for the workers to develop their own political activity through direct influence on public life, in a party press, and public congresses, etc.

These conditions are not yet fully formed in Russia. The first—a proletarian vanguard, conscious of its class interests and capable of self-direction in political activity—is only now emerging in Russia. All efforts of socialist agitation and organization should aim to hasten the formation of such a vanguard. The second condition can be had only under a regime of political liberty.

With these conclusions, Lenin disagrees violently. He is

convinced that all the conditions necessary for the formation of a powerful and centralized party already exist in Russia. He declares that "it is no longer the proletarians but certain intellectuals in our party who need to be educated in the matters of organization and discipline" (page 145). He glorifies the educative influence of the factory, which, he says, accustoms the proletariat to "discipline and organization" (page 147).

Saying all this, Lenin seems to demonstrate again that his conception of socialist organization is quite mechanistic. The discipline Lenin has in mind is being implanted in the working class not only by the factory but also by the military and the existing state bureaucracy—by the entire mechanism of the centralized bourgeois state.

We misuse words and we practice self-deception when we apply the same term—discipline—to such dissimilar notions as: 1, the absence of thought and will in a body with a thousand automatically moving hands and legs, and 2, the spontaneous coordination of the conscious, political acts of a body of men. What is there in common between the regulated docility of an oppressed class and the self-discipline and organization of a class struggling for its emancipation?

The self-discipline of the social democracy is not merely the replacement of the authority of the bourgeois rulers with the authority of a socialist central committee. The working class will acquire the sense of the new discipline, the freely-assumed self-discipline of the social democracy, not as a result of the discipline imposed on it by the capitalist state, but by extirpating, to the last root, its old habits of obedience and servility.

Centralism in the socialist sense is not an absolute thing applicable to any phase whatsoever of the labor movement. It is a *tendency*, which becomes real in proportion to the development and political training acquired by the working masses in the course of their struggle.

No doubt, the absence of the conditions necessary for the complete realization of this kind of centralization in the Russian movement presents a formidable obstacle.

It is a mistake to believe that it is possible to substitute "provisionally" the absolute power of a central committee (acting somehow by "tacit delegation") for the yet unrealized rule of the majority of conscious workers in the party, and in this way replace the open control of the working masses over the party organs with the reverse control by the central committee over the revolutionary proletariat.

The history of the Russian labor movement suggests the doubtful value of such centralism. An all-powerful center, invested, as Lenin would have it, with the unlimited right to control and intervene, would be an absurdity if its authority applied only to technical questions, such as the administration of funds, the distribution of tasks among propagandists and agitators, the transportation and circulation of printed matter. The political purpose of an organ having such great powers is understandable only if those powers apply to the elaboration of a uniform plan of action, if the central organ assumes the initiative of a vast revolutionary act.

But what has been the experience of the Russian socialist movement up to now? The most important and most fruitful changes in its tactical policy during the last ten years have not been the inventions of several leaders and even less so of any central organizational organs. They have always been the spontaneous product of the movement in ferment. . . .

Our cause made great gains in these events. However, the initiative and conscious leadership of the social democratic organizations played an insignificant role in this development. It is true that these organizations were not specifically prepared for such happenings. However, the unimportant part played by the revolutionists cannot be explained by this fact. Neither can it be attributed to the absence of an all-powerful central party apparatus similar to what is asked for by Lenin. The existence of such a guiding center would have probably increased the disorder of the local committees by emphasizing the difference between the eager attack of the mass and the prudent position of the social democracy. The same phenomenon—the insignificant part played by the initiative of central party organs in the elaboration of actual tactical policy—can be observed today in Germany and other countries. In general, the tactical policy of the social democracy is not something that may be "invented." It is the product of a series of great creative acts of the often spontaneous class struggle seeking its way forward.

The unconscious comes before the conscious. The logic of the historic process comes before the subjective logic of the human beings who participate in the historic process. The tendency is for the directing organs of the socialist party to play a conservative role. Experience shows that every time the labor movement wins new terrain those organs work it to the utmost. They transform it at the same time into a kind of bastion, which holds up advance on a wider scale. . . .

Such inertia is due, in a large degree, to the fact that it is very inconvenient to define, within the vacuum of abstract hypotheses, the lines and forms of still nonexistent political situations. Evidently, the important thing for the social democracy is not the preparation of a set of directives all ready for future policy. It is important: 1, to encourage a correct historic appreciation of the forms of struggle corresponding to the given situations, and 2, to maintain an understanding of the relativity of the current phase and the inevitable increase of revolutionary tension as the final goal of the class struggle is approached.

Granting, as Lenin wants, such absolute powers of a negative character to the top organ of the party, we strengthen, to a dangerous extent, the conservatism inherent in such an organ. If the tactics of the socialist party are not to be the creation of a central committee but of the whole party, or, still better, of the whole labor movement, then it is clear that the party sections and federations need the liberty of action which alone will permit them to develop their revolutionary initiative and to utilize all the resources of a situation. The ultra-centralism asked by Lenin is full of the sterile spirit of the overseer. It is not a positive and creative spirit. *Lenin's concern is not so much to make the activity of the party more fruitful as to control the party—to narrow the movement rather than to develop it, to bind rather than to unify it.*

In the present situation, such an experiment would be doubly dangerous to the Russian social democracy. It stands on the eve of decisive battles against czarism. It is about to enter, or has already entered, on a period of intensified creative activity, during which it will broaden (as is usual in a revolutionary period) its sphere of influence and will advance spontaneously by leaps and bounds. To attempt to bind the initiative of the party at this moment, to surround it with a network of barbed wire, is to render it incapable of accomplishing the tremendous tasks of the hour. . . .

"It is important," says Lenin (page 52), "to forge a more or less effective weapon against opportunism." He believes that opportunism springs specifically from the characteristic leaning of intellectuals to decentralization and disorganization, from their aversion for strict discipline and "bureaucracy," which is, however, necessary for the functioning of the party.

Lenin says that intellectuals remain individualists and tend to anarchism even after they have joined the socialist movement. According to him, it is only among intellectuals that we can notice a repugnance for the absolute authority of a central committee. The authentic proletarian, Lenin suggests, finds by reason of his class instinct a kind of voluptuous pleasure in abandoning himself to the clutch of firm leadership and pitiless discipline. "To oppose bureaucracy to democracy," writes Lenin, "is to contrast the organizational principle of revolutionary social democracy to the methods of opportunist organization" (page 151).

He declares that a similar conflict between centralizing and autonomist tendencies is taking place in all countries where reformism and revolutionary socialism meet face to face. He points in particular to the recent controversy in the German social democracy on the question of the degree of freedom of action to be allowed by the party to socialist representatives in legislative assemblies.

Let us examine the parallels drawn by Lenin.

First, it is important to point out that the glorification of the supposed genius of proletarians in the matter of socialist organization and a general distrust of intellectuals as such are not necessarily signs of "revolutionary Marxist" mentality. It is very easy to demonstrate that such arguments are themselves an expression of opportunism.

Antagonism between purely proletarian elements and the nonproletarian intellectuals in the labor movement is raised as an ideological issue by the following trends: the semianarchism of the French syndicalists, whose watchword is "Beware of the politician!"; English trade unionism, full of mistrust of the "socialist visionaries"; and, if our information is correct, the "pure Economism", represented a short while ago within the Russian social democracy by *Rabochaya Mysl* ("Labor Thought"), which was printed secretly in St. Petersburg.

In most socialist parties of western Europe there is undoubtedly a connection between opportunism and the "intellectuals," as well as between opportunism and decentralizing tendencies within the labor movement.

But nothing is more contrary to the historic-dialectic method of Marxist thought than to separate social phenomena from their historic soil and to present these phenomena as abstract formulas having an absolute, general application.

Reasoning abstractly, we may say that the "intellectual," a social element which has emerged out of the bourgeoisie and is therefore alien to the proletariat, enters the socialist movement not because of his natural class inclinations but in spite of them. For this reason, he is more liable to opportunist aberrations than the proletarian. The latter, we say, can be expected to find a definite revolutionary point of support in his class interests as long as he does not leave his original environment, the laboring mass.

But the concrete form assumed by this inclination of the intellectual toward opportunism and, above all, the manner in which this tendency expresses itself in organizational questions depends every time on his given social milieu.

Bourgeois parliamentarianism is the definite social base of the phenomena observed by Lenin in the German, French, and Italian socialist movements. This parliamentarianism is the breeding place of all opportunist tendencies now existing in the Western social democracy.

The kind of parliamentarianism we now have in France, Italy, and Germany provides the soil for such illusions of current opportunism as overvaluation of social reforms, class and party collaboration, the hope of pacific development toward socialism, etc. It does so by placing intellectuals, acting in the capacity of parliamentarians, above the proletariat and by separating intellectuals from proletarians inside the socialist party itself. . . .

The situation is quite different in Czarist Russia. Opportunism in the Russian labor movement is much more declassed and by far less bourgeois than in western Europe. Added to the immaturity of the Russian proletarian movement, this circumstance is an influence for wide theoretic wandering, which ranges from the complete negation of the political aspect of the labor movement to the unqualified belief in the effectiveness of isolated terrorist acts, or even total political indifference sought in the swamps of liberalism and Kantian idealism.

However, the intellectual within the Russian social democratic movement can only with difficulty be attracted to any act of disorganization. It is contrary to the general outlook of the Russian intellectual's milieu. There is no bourgeois parliament in Russia to favor this tendency.

The Western intellectual who professes at this moment the "cult of ego" and colors even his socialist yearnings with an aristocratic morale, is not the representative of the bourgeois intelligentsia "in general." He represents only a certain phase of social development. He is the product of bourgeois decadence.

On the other hand, the utopian or opportunist dreams of the Russian intellectual who has joined the socialist movement tend to nourish themselves on theoretical formulae in which the "ego" is not exalted but humiliated, in which the morality of renunciation, expiation, is the dominant principle.

The *Narodniki* ("populists") of 1875 called on the Russian intelligentsia to lose themselves in the peasant mass. The ultracivilized followers of Tolstoi speak today of escape to the life of the "simple folk." Similarly, the partisans of "pure Economism" in the Russian social democracy want us to bow down before the "calloused hand" of labor.

If instead of mechanically applying to Russia formulae elaborated in western Europe, we approach the problem of organization from the angle of conditions specific to Russia, we arrive at conclusions that are diametrically opposed to Lenin's.

To attribute to opportunism an invariable preference for a definite form of organization, that is, decentralization, is to miss the essence of opportunism.

On the question of organization, or any other question, opportunism knows only one principle: the absence of principle. Opportunism chooses its means of action with the aim of suiting the given circumstances at hand, provided these means appear to lead toward the end in view.

If, like Lenin, we define opportunism as the tendency that paralyzes the independent revolutionary movement of the working class and transforms it into an instrument of ambitious bourgeois intellectuals, we must also recognize that in the initial stage of a labor movement this end is more easily attained as a result of rigorous centralization rather than by decentralization. It is by extreme centralization that a young, uneducated proletarian movement can be most completely handed over to the intellectual leaders staffing a central committee. . . .

In general, it is rigorous, despotic centralism that is preferred by opportunist intellectuals at a time when the revolutionary elements among the workers still lack cohesion and the movement is groping its way, as is the case now in Russia. In a later phase, under a parliamentary regime and in connection with a strong labor party, the opportunist tendencies of the intellectuals express themselves in an inclination toward "decentralization."

If we assume the viewpoint claimed as his own by Lenin and we fear the influence of intellectuals in the proletarian movement, we can conceive of no greater danger to the Russian party than Lenin's plan of organization. *Nothing will more surely enslave a young labor movement to an intellectual elite hungry for power than this bureaucratic straitjacket, which will immobilize the movement and turn it into an automaton manipulated by a central committee.* On the other hand, there is no more effective guarantee against opportunist intrigue and personal ambition than the independent revolutionary action of the proletariat, as a result of which the workers acquire a sense of political responsibility and self-reliance. . . .

The international movement of the proletariat toward its complete emancipation is a process peculiar in the following respect. For the first time in the history of civilization, the people are expressing their will consciously and in opposition to all ruling classes. But this will can only be satisfied beyond the limits of the existing system.

Now the mass can only acquire and strengthen this will in the course of the day-to-day struggle against the existing social order—that is, with the limits of capitalist society.

On the one hand, we have the mass; on the other, its historic goal, located outside of existing society. On one hand, we have the day-to-day struggle; on the other, the social revolution. Such are the terms of the dialectical contradiction through which the socialist movement makes its way.

It follows that this movement can best advance by tacking betwixt and between the two dangers by which it is constantly being threatened. One is the loss of its mass character; the other, the abandonment of its goal. One is the danger of sink-ing back to the condition of a sect; the other, the danger of becoming a movement of bourgeois social reform.

That is why it is illusory, and contrary to historic experience, to hope to fix, once for always, the direction of the revolutionary socialist struggle with the aid of formal means, which are expected to secure the labor movement against all possibilities of opportunist digression.

Marxist theory offers us a reliable instrument enabling us to recognize and combat typical manifestations of opportunism. But the socialist movement is a mass movement. Its perils are not the product of the insidious machinations of individuals and groups. They arise out of unavoidable social conditions. We cannot secure ourselves in advance against all possibilities of opportunist deviation. Such dangers can be overcome only by the movement itself—certainly with the aid of Marxist theory, but only after the dangers in question have taken tangible form in practice.

Looked at from this angle, opportunism appears to be a product and an inevitable phase of the historic development of the labor movement.

The Russian social democracy arose a short while ago. The political conditions under which the proletarian movement is developing in Russia are quite abnormal. In that country, opportunism is to a large extent a by-product of the groping and experimentation of socialist activity seeking to advance over a terrain that resembles no other in Europe.

In view of this, we find most astonishing the claim that it is possible to avoid any possibility of opportunism in the Russian movement by writing down certain words, instead of others, in the party constitution. *Such an attempt to exorcise opportunism by means of a scrap of paper may turn out to be extremely harmful—not to opportunism but to the socialist movement.*

Stop the natural pulsation of a living organism, and you weaken it, and you diminish its resistance and its combative spirit—in this instance, not only against opportunism but also (and that is certainly of great importance) against the existing social order. The proposed means turn against the end they are supposed to serve.

In Lenin's overanxious desire to establish the guardianship of an omniscient and omnipotent central committee in order to protect so promising and vigorous a labor movement against any misstep, we recognize the symptoms of the same subjectivism that has already played more than one trick on socialist thinking in Russia. . . .

The working class demands the right to make its mistakes and learn in the dialectic of history.

Let us speak plainly. Historically, the errors committed by a truly revolutionary movement are infinitely more fruitful than the infallibility of the cleverest central committee.

II: Zimmerwald and Kienthal Conferences

With the declaration of war in August 1914 the Second International collapsed as an organ of international socialism. Socialist forces in the various national sections were divided into three broad camps: the right or patriotic socialists (generally in the majority), the center or pacifist socialists, and the left or revolutionary socialists. In all but two belligerent countries (Serbia and Russia) socialist representatives voted for war appropriations and agreed to abide by civil peace at home. The worst fears of the left wing within the International became reality as party after party followed the lead of the German Social Democrats in rallying to the national colors on grounds of self-defense.[1] In the neutral countries the socialist parties placed the major responsibility for the war on such general causes as competitive capitalism and imperialism and demanded that their own governments remain above the battle.

Many but not all socialist parties and leaders were content opportunistically to march in step with the times to the beat of national self-defense and civil peace. A small, disunited, and at first disregarded minority attempted to hold together and repair the bonds of international socialist solidarity and to take issue with the war in the spirit of socialism unencumbered by the patriotic mania that had infected the movement. For this purpose a series of conferences were convened. One of the most significant of these was the meeting of Italian and Swiss socialists at Lugano on September 27, 1914, which be-

[1] This capitulation to patriotism and forsaking of internationalism was not unanimous. Hugo Haase and Karl Liebknecht led a minority of fourteen of the German Social Democratic party *Reichstag* deputies in opposing the war credits in caucus. Hopelessly outnumbered, the minority upheld party discipline and abided by the majority decision to approve the credits. Similarly Friedrich Adler led a minority of the Social Democratic party of Austria in opposing the accommodating policy of the majority.

came the organizing nucleus for the subsequent Zimmerwald Conference. Two conferences at Berne, of the Socialist Women's International in March 1915 and of the Socialist Youth International in April 1915, were distinguished by representation drawn from both belligerent sides as well as from neutrals.[2] All of these tentative steps toward socialist internationalism were far from militant; the resolutions which issued from them featured condemnations of war and imperialism and appeals for international socialist cooperation.

Lenin and a small group of Bolsheviks were virtually alone in viewing the war as an opportunity for revolution.[3] In "The Tasks of Revolutionary Social Democracy in the European War," they accused the majority of leaders of the Second International of having betrayed socialism; called for revolutionary propaganda in the armies of all nations; proposed that the imperialist war be turned into a civil war; and spoke about the tasks of a "future" International (Document 1). The Bolshevik leaders in exile presented these theses to various socialist gatherings in 1914 and 1915, but found none willing to adopt them. On the other end of the political spectrum of the international movement was the International Socialist Bureau (ISB), which was hamstrung by the nationalist intransigence of its French and Belgian right-wing members. Its Executive Committee, temporarily transferred to the Hague, appeared immobilized and refused to call a full meeting of the Bureau lest it lead to an open split in the International.

In spite of the unfavorable reception which the Lugano and similar proposals for solidarity had achieved, the Italian So-

[2] Other attempts to revive internationalism which proved abortive (mainly because they were not sufficiently international in composition) were: a meeting called by the American Socialist party for September 19–20, 1914 either at Washington, the Hague, or Copenhagen; a conference of socialists from belligerent and neutral countries at Copenhagen on January 17–18, 1915; a meeting of socialist parties of the Entente countries in London on February 14, 1915; and a conference of socialist parties of the Central Powers in Vienna on April 12–13, 1915.

[3] Lenin was supported by the followers of Liebknecht in Germany, the left wing of the Italian socialist movement, the Polish Social Democrats, the Bulgarian Social Democrats (narrow), the Tribune group in Holland, the followers of Höglund in Sweden, and other splinter groups.

cialist party increased its efforts to restore international socialist relations. Since the ISB had refused the Italians' demand
to convene a general meeting, they acted on their own and
called an international conference of all parties and workers'
organizations ready to act against the war on the basis of the
proletarian class struggle and willing to come out against domestic peace. With the aid of the Swiss socialists they held
a preliminary conference at Berne on July 11, 1915 to formulate plans for the Zimmerwald Conference on September 5–8,
1915. During the preliminaries it was decided to invite all
those who were willing to work for peace. The Bolsheviks thus
failed to make Zimmerwald an exclusive gathering of the left,
and the centrists or pacifist socialists became the majority of
the Conference. Both the ISB and the right-wing socialists
fought bitterly until the last minute to prevent the meeting.

The gathering in the village of Zimmerwald outside Berne
in September was far from imposing, for the illustrious stars
of international socialism, Victor Adler, Eduard Bernstein,
Jules Guesde, Karl Kautsky, Jean Longuet, J. Ramsay Mac-
Donald, G. V. Plekhanov, Pierre Renaudel, and Emile Vandervelde, were conspicuously absent. The thirty-eight delegates from eleven countries who attended the Conference fell
into three rather well-defined groups. The right wing, of some
nineteen or twenty delegates constituting a majority, favored
a general appeal for peace and opposed an open split with
the socialist patriots of the International. This group included
the French delegation, most of the German, some Italians and
Poles, and the Russian Mensheviks. In opposition was a left
group of eight led by Lenin, which favored a break with
the social patriots, a condemnation of civil peace, and the active pursuit of revolutionary class struggle. A moderate center
of five or six included Robert Grimm, Leon Trotsky, Angelica
Balabanoff, and Henrietta Roland-Holst.

One of the main accomplishments at Zimmerwald was the
issuing of a manifesto to the European proletariat. Three
draft manifestoes were submitted to the Conference: by the
right wing of the German delegation; by the Zimmerwald left;
and by the *Nashe Slovo* representative.[4] They were referred

[4] *Nashe Slovo* (*Our Word*) was a newspaper published in Paris
between January 1915 and October 1916 by Russian Social Democrats—Internationalists from both Bolshevik and Menshevik ranks.
Notable contributors included Trotsky, Martov, Kollontai, and

to a commission which hammered out the final version (Document 2). The *Zimmerwald Manifesto* began with an exhortation to the working class to struggle for socialism which, in the existing international context, was synonymous with a fight for peace. It championed a peace without annexations or indemnities that recognized the right of self-determination of peoples, and ended on a high emotional note. Because of pressure by the German delegates it did not include suggestions for concrete parliamentary methods which might be used in activating the class struggle. The draft of the Zimmerwald left (Document 3) went much further than the official manifesto. It demanded that the socialist deputies of the various countries, abiding by the terms of civil peace fulfill their mandate to the workers by refusing to vote for war credits and by withdrawing from positions in the governments. It directed the workers to fight for peace in the streets with the overthrow of capitalist governments in mind and called for a new dynamic International to coordinate this struggle.

An International Socialist Committee (ISC) was elected by the Congress to act as a temporary secretariat in Berne. The ISC was to serve as a clearinghouse for international socialists and as an intermediary between the various protesting socialist minorities; it was not considered a replacement for the International Socialist Bureau. The Conference ended with the general feeling that the first necessary step toward restoring international socialist relations had been taken. To all appearances moderation had triumphed and the left had been held in check; but appearances proved to be deceiving. Although the proposals of the left had been rejected by the Congress, the left had gained a forum for its views. The creation of the ISC, despite protestations to the contrary, did constitute an alternative to the inactive ISB. The fact that leftists and centrists had been able to coexist and create even a temporary international organization did not augur well for continued cooperation between centrists and rightists. Even at this point the left had succeeded in driving a small wedge into the static balance of the international movement.

Although the Zimmerwald Conference was largely ignored

Lunacharsky; the tone was anti-war and anti-imperialist. The periodical had previously been called *Golos* (*The Voice*) and *Nash Golos* (*Our Voice*) and subsequently, when it came under the control of the Bolsheviks, was called *Nachalo* (*A Beginning*).

by the press, its impact on the masses and socialist minority
and opposition groups was considerable. This growing influence was in part due to the legal and illegal propaganda
of the ISC and Zimmerwaldist leaders in various countries.
The manifesto of the Zimmerwald majority and of the left
together with other subversive literature were distributed
openly and circulated underground. Popular opposition to the
war arose as the fighting continued and food shortages, the
rising cost of living, and the mounting number of casualties
made more people receptive to the pacifist and revolutionary
propaganda of the Zimmerwaldians. Under the pressure of
events, of popular discontent, and of the left, the centrist socialists moved more decisively into the pacifist camp and
thereby came closer to the Zimmerwaldians. The majority socialists tenaciously held to their patriotic position and worked
hard to neutralize dissent in the various parties and to curb
the growth of an organized opposition, particularly by keeping the ISB, still the official organ of the international movement, inactive.

Early in 1916 the ISC, desiring a clearer definition of its
responsibilities, made preparations to convene a second Zimmerwald Conference. It met at Berne from February 5th–8th
and drew up a circular letter asking affiliated groups to send
delegates to a conference to be held in April, ostensibly, to
foil the authorities, in Holland, but actually in Kienthal, Switzerland. At Berne the German *Internationale* group led by
Rosa Luxemburg, Karl Liebknecht, and Walter Mehring (already called the Spartacists and later to become the German
Communist party), offered their program as a working document for the ISC and for the congress at Kienthal.[5] The theses
of the *Internationale* group were more radical generally and
on the formation of a new International more pointed and
explicit than the Zimmerwald left had been in its manifesto
five months earlier (Document 4). They blamed the failure
of the Second International on the treason of official leaders
of the socialist parties against the working class; called for
a new International as a center of gravity for the proletariat;

[5] At the Zimmerwald Conference the *Internationale* group had
been pacifist; after it, they moved much further to the left and
became associated with the Zimmerwald left under Lenin, Zinoviev,
and Radek.

and demanded that the resolutions of this International be binding on the national sections.

Forty-four delegates from nine countries attended the Second Zimmerwald or Kienthal Conference from April 24th–30th.[6] Of these, twelve belonged to the Zimmerwald left and seven others identified and voted with it. Thus, although the pacifists still were the majority, the left had made great strides numerically and, as we shall see, ideologically. The official Kienthal Manifesto and Resolution were weaker than the *Internationale* theses on the vital questions of proletarian and socialist activity and on war and peace. (Documents 5 & 6). But they also came much closer to a revolutionary position than the cautiously phrased documents of the Zimmerwald Conference. A final Resolution on the ISB was also a compromise between the majority and the left, although the latter had cause to regard it as a minor victory. The resolution flatly condemned the Executive of the ISB for being chauvinistic and imperialistic; instructed the Zimmerwald Movement, in the event of a full meeting of the ISB, to expose the opportunism and treachery of the social patriots; and empowered the ISC to meet in the event of a general ISB meeting to plan the necessary strategy. The Zimmerwald left was satisfied that this resolution as well as the pronouncements of the Conference were a step forward toward the creation of a Third International. Indeed, in retrospect a drift toward the left was becoming apparent: the center had begun to use the tactics of the left, as can be seen in the revolutionary tone of the Kienthal resolutions, particularly in the vigorous criticism of the ISB; moreover, party splits, of which the center had been so fearful, were in progress or developing in Britain, Germany, and France.

[6] The belligerent governments combined with the patriotic majority socialists to try to prevent the gathering at Kienthal: the governments refused passports to socialists suspected of attending and the "social patriots" (a pejorative term coined by their opponents) attempted to pressure the minority into staying away.

DOCUMENT 1: *"The Tasks of Revolutionary Social Democracy in the European War"*

V. I. Lenin, *The Imperialist War*, "Collected Works," Vol. XVIII (New York: International Publishers, 1930). By permission. Taken from a manuscript copied by Lenin's widow N. K. Krupskaya.

RESOLUTION OF A GROUP OF SOCIAL DEMOCRATS

1. The European and World War bears the sharp marks of a bourgeois-imperialist and dynastic war. A struggle for markets, for freedom to loot foreign countries, a tendency to put an end to the revolutionary movement of the proletariat and democracy within the separate countries, a tendency to fool, to disunite, to slaughter the proletariat of all countries by inflaming the wage slaves of one nation against the wage slaves of the other for the benefit of the bourgeoisie—this is the only real meaning and significance of the war.

2. The conduct of the leaders of the German Social Democratic party, the strongest and most influential party belonging to the Second International (1889–1914), which voted for the military appropriations and which repeated the bourgeois chauvinist phrases of the Prussian Junkers and the bourgeoisie, is a direct betrayal of socialism. Under no circumstances, even assuming the absolute weakness of that party and the necessity of its submitting to the will of the bourgeois majority of the nation, can the conduct of the leaders of the German Social Democratic party be justified. This party has in fact adopted a national-liberal policy.

3. The same condemnation is deserved by the conduct of the leaders of the Belgian and French Social Democratic parties, who have betrayed socialism by entering bourgeois cabinets.

4. The betrayal of socialism by a majority of the leaders of the Second International (1889–1914) signifies an ideological and political collapse of that International. The fundamental reason for this collapse is the actual prevalence in it of petty-bourgeois opportunism, the bourgeois nature and the danger of which has long been pointed out by the best repre-

sentatives of the revolutionary proletariat of all countries. The opportunists had long been preparing the collapse of the Second International by renouncing the socialist revolution and substituting for it bourgeois reformism; by rejecting the class struggle, which at certain moments necessarily turns into civil war, and preaching instead the collaboration of classes; by preaching bourgeois chauvinism and the defense of the fatherland, under the cloak of patriotism, and rejecting the elementary truth of socialism, expressed long ago in the *Communist Manifesto,* that the workers have no fatherland; by confining themselves in the struggle against militarism to a sentimental philistine point of view instead of recognizing the necessity of a revolutionary war of the proletarians of all countries against the bourgeois of all countries; by making a fetish of the necessity of utilizing bourgeois parliamentarianism and bourgeois legality, forgetting that in times of crisis illegal forms of organization and propaganda are imperative. One of the organs of international opportunism, the *Sozialistische Monatshefte* [*Socialist Monthly*][7] which has long moved to the national-liberal position, is consistent when it celebrates its victory over European socialism. The so-called center of German social democracy and of other social democratic parties has in reality faintheartedly capitulated before the opportunists. It must be the task of the future International resolutely and irrevocably to free itself of this bourgeois trend in socialism.

5. Of the bourgeois and chauvinist sophisms by which the bourgeois parties and the governments of the two chief rival nations of the continent, the German and the French, are fooling the masses most effectively, and which are being slavishly repeated by both the open and covert socialist opportunists who are trailing at the tail end of the bourgeoisie, one must particularly note and brand the following. When the German bourgeois refers to the defense of the fatherland, to the struggle against czarism, to the fight for the freedom of cultural and national development, they lie, because Prussian Junkerdom with Wilhelm II at its head, and the big bourgeoisie of Germany, have always pursued a policy of defending the

---

[7] The periodical of the German revisionists, which during the war became the leading vehicle for the social patriots. Its leading contributors included the social imperialists Konrad Haenisch, Wolfgang Heine, and Paul Lensch.

czarist monarchy and, whatever the outcome of the war, they will not fail to direct their efforts toward its support; they lie, because, in reality, the Austrian bourgeoisie has undertaken a predatory campaign against Serbia, the German bourgeoisie oppresses Danes, Poles, and Frenchmen (in Alsace-Lorraine); it leads an aggressive war against Belgium and France for the sake of looting the richer and freer country; it organized an offensive at a moment which seemed most favorable for utilizing its latest improvements in military technique and on the eve of the introduction in Russia of the so-called great military program. Similarly, when the French bourgeois refer to the defense of the fatherland, etc., they lie, because in reality they defend countries that are backward in capitalist technique and that develop more slowly, and because they hire for their billions the Black Hundred gangs of Russian czarism for an aggressive war whose aim is to loot Austrian and German lands. Neither of the two belligerent groups of nations is behind the other as far as cruelty and barbarism in war methods are concerned.

6. It is the task of the social democracy of Russia in the first place and with particular emphasis to conduct a merciless and ruthless struggle against Great-Russian and czarist-monarchist chauvinism, and against the sophisms advanced by the Russian liberals, Constitutional Democrats, a section of the Narodniks and other bourgeois parties, for the defense of that chauvinism.

From the point of view of the working class and the laboring masses of all the peoples of Russia, by far the lesser evil would be the defeat of the Czar's armies and the Czar's monarchy, which oppress Poland, the Ukraine, and a number of other peoples of Russia, and which inflame national hatred in order to increase the pressure of Great-Russia over all the nationalities in order to strengthen the reaction of the barbarous government of the Czar's monarchy.

7. The slogans of social democracy must now be: first, an all-embracing propaganda of the socialist revolution, to be extended also to the army and the area of military activities; emphasis to be placed on the necessity of turning the weapons, not against the brother wage-slaves of other countries, but against the reaction of the bourgeois governments and parties in each country; recognition of the urgent necessity of organizing illegal nuclei and groups in the armies of all

nations to conduct such propaganda in all languages; a merciless struggle against the chauvinism and patriotism of the philistines and bourgeoisie of all countries without exception. Against the leaders of the present International who have betrayed socialism, it is imperative to appeal to the revolutionary consciousness of the working masses who bear the brunt of the war and are in most cases hostile to chauvinism and opportunism. Secondly, (as one of the immediate slogans) propaganda in favor of republics in Germany, Poland, Russia, and other countries and in favor of transforming all the separate states of Europe into united republican states of Europe. Thirdly and particularly, struggle against the czarist monarchy and the Great-Russian, Pan-Slavist chauvinism, and advocacy of a revolution in Russia as well as the liberation and self-determination of the nationalities oppressed by Russia, coupled with the immediate slogans of a democratic republic, the confiscation of the landowners' lands and an eight-hour work-day.

DOCUMENT 2: *"Manifesto of the International Socialist Conference at Zimmerwald"*

International Socialist Commission at Berne: Bulletin, No. 1 (Sept. 21, 1915). The manifesto also appeared as "French and German Delegates Put Forward a Joint Declaration," Labour Leader, No. 40 (Oct. 7, 1915).

Proletarians of Europe!

The war has lasted more than a year. Millions of corpses cover the battlefields. Millions of human beings have been crippled for the rest of their lives. *Europe is like a gigantic human slaughterhouse.* All civilization, created by the labor of many generations, is doomed to destruction. The most savage barbarism is today celebrating its triumph over all that hitherto constituted the pride of mankind.

Irrespective of the truth as to the direct responsibility for the outbreak of the war, one thing is certain: *The war which has produced this chaos is the outcome of imperialism,* of the attempt, on the part of the capitalist classes of each nation, to foster their greed for profit by the exploitation of human labor and of the natural treasures of the entire globe.

Economically backward or politically weak nations are thereby subjugated by the Great Powers who, in this war, are seeking to remake the world map with blood and iron in accord with their exploiting interests. Thus, entire nations and countries like Belgium, Poland, the Balkan states, and Armenia are threatened with the fate of being torn asunder, annexed as a whole or in part as booty in the game of compensations.

In the course of the war, its driving forces are revealed in all their vileness. Shred after shred falls the veil with which the meaning of this world catastrophe was hidden from the consciousness of the peoples. The capitalists of all countries, who are coining the red gold of war-profits out of the blood shed by the people, assert that the war is for defense of the fatherland, for democracy, and the liberation of oppressed nations! They lie. *In actual reality, they are burying the freedom of their own people together with the independence of the other nations in the places of devastation.* New fetters, new chains, new burdens are arising, and it is the proletariat of all countries, of the victorious as well as of the conquered countries, that will have to bear them. Improvement in welfare was proclaimed at the outbreak of the war—want and privation, unemployment and high prices, undernourishment and epidemics are the actual results. *The burdens of war will consume the best energies of the peoples for decades,* endanger the achievements of social reform, and hinder every step forward.

Cultural devastation, economic decline, political reaction— these are the blessings of this horrible conflict of nations.

Thus the war reveals *the naked figure of modern capitalism* which has become irreconcilable not only with the interests of the laboring masses, not only with the requirements of historical development, but also with the elementary conditions of human intercourse.

The ruling powers of capitalist society who held the fate of the nations in their hands, the monarchic as well as the republican governments, the secret diplomacy, the mighty business organizations, the bourgeois parties, the capitalist press, the Church—all these bear the full weight of responsibility for this war which arose out of the social order fostering them and protected by them, and which is being waged for their interests.

Workers!

Exploited, disfranchised, scorned, they called you brothers and comrades at the outbreak of the war when you were to be led to the slaughter, to death. And now that militarism has crippled you, mutilated you, degraded and annihilated you, the rulers demand that you surrender your interests, your aims, your ideals—in a word, *servile subordination to civil peace.* They rob you of the possibility of expressing your views, your feelings, your pains; they prohibit you from raising your demands and defending them. The press gagged, political rights and liberties trod upon—this is the way the *military dictatorship* rules today with an iron hand.

This situation, which threatens the entire future of Europe and of humanity, cannot and must not be confronted by us any longer without action. The socialist proletariat has waged a struggle against militarism for decades. With growing concern, its representatives at their national and international congresses occupied themselves with the ever more menacing danger of war growing out of imperialism. At *Stuttgart,* at *Copenhagen,* at *Basel,*[8] the international socialist congresses have indicated the course which the proletariat must follow.

Since the beginning of the war, socialist parties and labor organizations of various countries that helped to determine this course have disregarded the obligations following from this. Their representatives have called upon the working class to *give up the class struggle,* the only possible and effective method of proletarian emancipation. They have *granted credits* to the ruling classes for waging the war; they have placed themselves at the disposal of the governments for the most diverse services; through their press and their messengers, they have tried to win the *neutrals* for the government policies of their countries; they have delivered up to their governments *socialist ministers* as hostages for the preservation of civil peace, and thereby they have assumed *the responsibility before the working class, before its present and its future, for this war, for its aims and its methods.* And just as the indi-

---

[8] At the Stuttgart Congress in 1907, the Copenhagen Congress in 1910, and the Basel Congress in 1912, the Second International passed resolutions condemning war and imperialism and exhorting the working class to prevent war or to bring it to a speedy conclusion by means it considered most effective. The Congresses stopped short of recommending general strikes against wars.

vidual parties, so the highest of the appointed representative bodies of the socialists of all countries, the *International Socialist Bureau,*[9] has failed them.

These facts are equally responsible for the fact that the international working class, which did not succumb to the national panic of the first war period, or which freed itself from it, has still, in the second year of the slaughter of peoples, found no ways and means of taking up an energetic struggle for peace simultaneously in all countries.

In this unbearable situation, we, the representatives of the socialist parties, trade unions and their minorities, we Germans, French, Italians, Russians, Poles, Lets, Rumanians, Bulgarians, Swedes, Norwegians, Dutch, and Swiss, we who stand not on the ground of national solidarity with the exploiting class, but on the ground of the international solidarity of the proletariat and of the class struggle, have assembled to retie the torn threads of international relations and to call upon the working class to recover itself and to fight for peace.

This struggle is the struggle for freedom, for the reconciliation of peoples, for socialism. It is necessary to take up this struggle for peace, for a peace without annexations or war indemnities. Such a peace, however, is only possible if every thought of violating the rights and liberties of nations is condemned. Neither the occupation of entire countries nor of separate parts of countries must lead to their violent annexation. No *annexation,* whether open or concealed, and *no forcible economic attachment* made still more unbearable by political disfranchisement. The *right of self-determination of nations must be the indestructible principle in the system of national relationships of peoples.*

Proletarians!

Since the outbreak of the war, you have placed your energy, your courage, your endurance at the service of the ruling classes. Now you must stand up for your own cause, for the

---

[9] The International Socialist Bureau was established in 1900 with headquarters in Brussels. It was not a central authority with plenary powers to enforce decisions and punish breaches of discipline. Its powers were of an administrative nature including handling correspondence, issuing appeals and circulars, and making arrangements for congresses. Attempts made to convene the ISB in 1916 failed because the leadership of the various socialist parties was still stuck fast in the mire of social patriotism and national self-interest.

sacred aims of socialism, for the emancipation of the oppressed nations as well as of the enslaved classes, by means of the irreconcilable proletarian class struggle.

It is the task and the duty of the socialists of the belligerent countries to take up this struggle with full force; it is the task and the duty of the socialists of the neutral states to support their brothers in this struggle against bloody barbarism with every effective means. Never in world history was there a more urgent, a more sublime task, the fulfillment of which should be our common labor. No sacrifice is too great, no burden too heavy in order to achieve this goal: peace among the peoples.

Working men and working women! Mothers and fathers! Widows and orphans! Wounded and crippled! We call to all of you who are suffering from the war and because of the war: beyond all borders, beyond the reeking battlefields, beyond the devastated cities and villages—

Proletarians of all countries, unite!

Zimmerwald, September, 1915.

In the name of the International Socialist Conference:

For the German delegation: Georg Ledebour, Adolf Hoffmann.

For the French delegation: A. Bourderon, A. Merrheim.

For the Italian delegation: G. E. Modigliani, Constantino Lazzari.

For the Russian delegation: N. Lenin, Paul Axelrod, M. Bobrov.

For the Polish delegation: St. Lapinski, A. Warski, Cz. Hanecki.

For the Inter-Balkan Socialist Federation: In the name of the Rumanian delegation: C. Rakovsky; *In the name of the Bulgarian delegation:* Vasil Kolarov.

For the Swedish and Norwegian delegation: Z. Höglund, Ture Nerman.

For the Dutch delegation: H. Roland-Holst.

For the Swiss delegation: Robert Grimm, Charles Naine.

DOCUMENT 3: *"Draft Manifesto Introduced by the Left-Wing Delegates at the International Socialist Conference at Zimmerwald"*

V. I. Lenin, *The Imperialist War*. By permission. First appeared in *Sotsial Demokrat*, No. 45–46 (Oct. 11, 1915).

PROLETARIANS of Europe!

The war has now lasted for more than a year. The battle-fields are strewn with millions of dead, millions have been crippled and doomed to remain a burden to themselves and to others for the rest of their lives. The war has caused terrific devastations, it will result in an unheard-of increase in taxes.

The capitalists of all countries, who at the price of proletarian blood have been reaping enormous profits during the war, demand of the masses that they strain all their efforts and hold out to the end. They say: "The war is necessary for the defense of the fatherland, it is waged in the interests of democracy." They lie! In not a single country did the capitalists start the war because the independence of their country was threatened, or because they wanted to free an oppressed people. They have led the masses to slaughter because they want to oppress and to exploit other peoples. They were unable to agree between themselves as to how to divide the peoples of Asia and Africa that were still independent; they were lying in ambush for each other, watching for a chance to snatch from each other the spoils previously seized.

It is not for their own freedom, nor for the freedom of other peoples, that the masses are bleeding in all parts of the immense slaughterhouse called Europe. This war will bring the proletariat of Europe and the peoples of Asia and Africa new burdens and new chains.

There is, therefore, no reason why this fratricidal war should be waged to the end, to the last drop of blood; on the contrary, every effort must be strained to put an end to it.

The time for this has already come. What you must demand first, is that your socialist deputies, those whom you delegated to parliament to fight against capitalism, against militarism, against the exploitation of the people, do their duty. All of them, with the exception of the Russian, Serbian, and the Italian comrades, and with the exception of Comrades Liebknecht and Rühle, have trampled upon that duty;[10] they have either supported the bourgeoisie in their rapacious war, or else have vacillated and have shirked responsibility. You must demand that they either resign from their seats, or that they use the platform of parliament to make clear to the people the nature of the present war, and that outside of parliament they help the working class to resume its struggle. Your first demand must be this: *refusal of all war credits, withdrawal from the cabinets in France, Belgium, and England.*[11]

But that is not all! The deputies cannot save you from the rabid beast, the World War, that subsists on your blood. *You must act yourselves.* You must make use of all your organizations, of your entire press, to rouse the broadest masses groaning under the burden of the war to revolt against it. You must go out *into the streets* and throw into the face of the ruling classes your rallying cry: *"Enough of slaughter!"* Let the ruling classes remain deaf to it, the discontented masses will hear it, and they will join you and take a part in the struggle.

The demand must immediately and energetically be made that the war be stopped; a loud protest must be raised against the exploitation of one people by another, against the division of any people among several states. All this will take place, if any capitalist government comes out victorious and is able to dictate the terms of peace to the others. If we allow the

---

10 Five Bolshevik and six Menshevik deputies refused to vote for war credits and left the Russian Duma; the Serbian Social Democrats refused to support their government; and the socialist parties of Italy, the United States, and Portugal, and the social democratic parties of Holland, Switzerland, and the Scandinavian countries denounced the war and demanded the neutrality of their governments. Karl Liebknecht and Otto Rühle were the first German Social Democratic deputies to break party discipline and vote against war credits in the *Reichstag.* Liebknecht's first negative vote came on December 2, 1914, Rühle's on March 20, 1915.

11 Jules Guesde and Marcel Sombart became ministers in the French government of national defense; Emile Vandervelde joined the Belgian ministry; and Arthur Henderson became a minister in the British war cabinet.

capitalists to conclude peace in the same manner as they started the war, without the participation of the masses, the new conquests will not only strengthen reaction and arbitrary police rule in the victorious country, but they will sow the seeds of new wars, even more horrible.

The overthrow of the capitalist governments—this is the object which the working class in all belligerent countries must set themselves, because only then will an end be put to the exploitation of one people by another, an end put to wars, when capital has been deprived of the power of disposing of the life and death of peoples. Only peoples who shall be freed of want and misery, of the rule of capital, will be in a position to settle their mutual relations, not by war, but by friendly agreement.

Great is the goal we set ourselves, great are the efforts that will be required to attain it, great will be the sacrifices before it is attained. Long will be the road to victory. Methods of peaceful pressure will be insufficient to overcome the enemy. But it is only when you are ready to make for your own liberation, in the struggle against capital, part of those innumerable sacrifices that you have been making on the battlefield for the interests of capital, only then will you be able to put an end to the war, to lay a firm foundation for a lasting peace, which will transform you from slaves of capital into free men.

But if the deceitful phrases of the bourgeoisie and of the socialist parties that support it succeed in restraining you from energetic struggle, and if you confine yourselves to pious wishes because you are unwilling to proceed to an attack and to sacrifice your bodies and souls for the great cause, then capital will go on shedding your blood and wasting your belongings at its own discretion. In all countries the number of those who think as we do grows daily. It is by their order that we have assembled, representatives of various countries, to address to you this call to battle. We shall carry on this struggle with mutual support, as there are no interests to divide us. It is essential that the revolutionary workers of each country deem it their duty and honorable distinction to serve as a model for others, a model of energy and self-sacrifice. Not timid expectation as to whither the struggle of others will lead, but struggle in the first ranks—that is the road that leads to the formation of a powerful International which will put an end to war and capitalism.

DOCUMENT 4: *"Theses Submitted to the International Socialist Committee by the German 'Internationale' Group"*

O. H. Gankin and H. H. Fischer, *The Bolsheviks and the World War: The Origins of the Third International* (Stanford: Stanford University Press, 1960). By permission. The Theses were drafted by Rosa Luxemburg and adopted at a conference of the *Internationale* group on January 1, 1916. They were first published as "Leitsätze der Gruppe Internationale," *Spartakusbriefe*, I, No. 4 (Feb. 3, 1916).

1. The World War has brought to naught the results of the forty years of labor of European socialism, by destroying the significance of the revolutionary labor class as a factor of political power and the moral prestige of socialism, by breaking up the proletarian International, by leading its national sections into a fratricidal slaughter, and by chaining the desires and hopes of the masses in the most important capitalist countries to the galley of imperialism.

2. The official leaders of the German, French, and English socialist parties (with the exception of the Independent Labor party), by voting war credits and approving the proclamation of civil peace, have strengthened the backbone of imperialism, have induced the masses of the people to bear patiently the misery and the horrors of the war, and thereby have contributed toward a dissolute unchaining of imperialist frenzy, toward a prolongation of the massacre and an increased number of victims, and have taken upon themselves the responsibility for the war and its consequences.

3. These tactics of the official party institutions in the belligerent countries, and primarily in Germany, hitherto the leading country of the International, constitute treason against the most elementary principles of international socialism, against the vital interests of the laboring class, against all the democratic interests of the peoples. The socialist policy of those countries, where the party leaders have remained faithful to their duties—in Russia, Serbia, Italy, and, with one exception, in Bulgaria—has also been rendered impotent.

4. The official social democracy of the belligerent countries, by giving up the class struggle during the war and by postponing it until after the war, has granted to the ruling classes in all countries a respite which greatly strengthens their position economically, politically, and morally at the expense of the proletariat.

5. The World War serves neither national defense nor the economic nor the political interests of the masses of any of the peoples; it is merely a monstrous creation of imperialist rivalry between the capitalist classes of various countries for world power and for the monopoly in sucking dry and oppressing the territories not yet under the capitalist rule. In an era of unchained imperialism national wars are no longer possible. National interests serve only as a means of deception, to make the laboring masses of the people subservient to their deadly enemy, imperialism.

6. Freedom and independence for any of the oppressed nations cannot grow out of the policy of imperialist states and from the imperialist war. The small nations, whose ruling classes are hangers-on and accomplices of their class comrades in the large states, are only pawns in the imperialist game of the Great Powers and are being misused as tools in the same way as their working masses have been misused during the war, only to be sacrificed after the war to the imperialist interests.

7. Under these circumstances the present World War signifies with its every victory and its every defeat the defeat of socialism and democracy. Whatever its outcome, unless there occurs the revolutionary intervention of the international proletariat, it is driving toward the strengthening of militarism, of international antagonisms, and of the rivalries in world economy. It accelerates capitalist exploitation and domestic political reaction, weakens public control, and reduces parliaments to obedient tools of militarism. Thus the present World War also develops all the premises for new wars.

8. World peace cannot be guaranteed by means of utopian and fundamentally reactionary plans, such as international courts of arbitration of the capitalist diplomats, diplomatic treaties on "disarmament," "freedom of the seas," "the abolition of the right of capture at sea," "European state alliances," "central European custom leagues," "national buffer states," etc. Imperialism, militarism, and wars are neither to

be abolished nor to be dammed up so long as the capitalist classes uncontestedly exercise their class power. The only means to resist them effectively and the only security for world peace lies in the capacity of the international proletariat for political activity and in its revolutionary will to throw its power on the scales.

9. Imperialism as the latest phase of life and the highest stage of the political rule of world capital is the worst enemy of the proletariat of all countries. But it shares also with the earlier phases of capitalism the destiny of strengthening the forces of its worst enemy to the extent that it unfolds itself. Imperialism hastens the concentration of capital, the disintegration of the middle class, the increase of proletariat; it arouses the growing opposition of the masses and thus leads toward the intensive sharpening of class antagonism. The proletarian class struggle, during war as well as in time of peace, should first of all be concentrated against imperialism. For the proletariat the struggle against imperialism is at the same time a struggle for political power in the state, the decisive controversy between socialism and capitalism. The socialist goal can be reached only by the international proletariat making a united front against imperialism and raising the slogan "war against war" with the utmost exertion and the extreme courage of self-sacrifice as the precept of its practical policy.

10. The main problem of socialism today is directed, therefore, to gathering the proletariat of all countries into a vital revolutionary force, to making it a decisive factor in political life through a strong international organization with a unanimous understanding of its interests and tasks, with united tactics and a capacity for political action in peace as in the war —all of which history has destined it to be.

11. The Second International has been broken up by the war. Its inadequacy has been proved by its inability to erect during the war an effective dam against national disintegration and to carry on the common tactics and action of the proletariat in all countries.

12. In view of the treason committed by the official representatives of the socialist parties in the leading countries against the aims and the interests of the laboring class, in view of their deviation from the basis of the proletarian International to the basis of bourgeois imperialist policy, it is a vital

necessity for socialism to create a new Workers' International which would take it upon itself to lead and to unify the revolutionary class struggle against imperialism in all countries.

In order to fulfill its historical task the International should rest on the following principles:

1. The class struggle within the bourgeois states against the ruling classes, and the international solidarity of the proletariat of all countries are two inseparable, vital rules of the laboring class in its universal historical struggle for liberation. There is no socialism outside of the international solidarity of the proletariat, and there is no socialism outside class struggle. The socialist proletariat cannot give up either class struggle or international solidarity during peace or during war without committing suicide.

2. The class action of the proletariat of all countries must have as its main aim in peace as well as in war the conquering of imperialism and the prevention of wars. Parliamentary and trade union action as well as the entire activity of the labor movement must be subordinated to the aim of placing the proletariat in every country in sharp opposition to the national bourgeoisie, of emphasizing at every opportunity the political and spiritual differences between the two, and of advancing to the foreground and affirming the international solidarity of the proletarians in all countries.

3. The center of gravity of the proletarian class organization lies in the International. The International determines in peace the tactics of the national sections on questions of militarism, colonial policy, trade policy, the May celebration, and, furthermore, determines the general tactics to be observed in time of war.

4. The duty of executing the resolutions of the International takes precedence over all other duties of the organization. National sections which act at variance with the resolutions of the International thereby place themselves outside the latter.

5. In the struggle against imperialism and against the war, a definite authority can be established only by the consolidated masses of the proletariat of all countries. The national sections should bear in mind the importance of teaching political activity and resolute initiative to the broad masses, of assuring the international coherence of mass actions, of building up political and trade union organizations so as to bring about

at any time through their medium quick and active cooperation among all the sections and thus turn the will of the International into the deeds of the broad working masses of all
countries.

6. The next task of socialism is the spiritual liberation of
the proletariat from the guardianship of the bourgeoisie,
which manifests itself in the influence of nationalist ideology.
The national sections, in their agitation in parliaments as well
as in the press, should denounce the traditional phraseology
of nationalism as the bourgeois instrument of power. The
revolutionary class struggle against imperialism is today the
only protection of all true national freedom. The Socialist International is the fatherland of the proletarians, to the defense
of which everything else should be subordinated.

DOCUMENT 5: *"To the Peoples Who Suffer Ruin and
Death: Manifesto of the Kienthal Conference"*

Gankin and Fischer, *The Bolsheviks and the War*. By permission. First appeared as "Zweite internationale Sozialistische Zimmerwalder Konferenz. An die Völker die man
zu Grunde richtet und tötet," *Berner Tagewacht*, No. 106
(May 6, 1916).

Proletarians of all countries unite!
Two years of world war! Two years of devastation! Two
years of bloody sacrifice and of the raging of reaction!
Who is responsible? Who backs those who have thrown a
burning torch into the powder keg? Who has desired this war
and has prepared it for so long?—*The ruling classes.*
When in September 1915 we socialists of the belligerent
and the neutral countries joined hands across the bloody confusion and assembled at *Zimmerwald* amidst the unchained
war passions, we said in our manifesto:
". . . The ruling forces of capitalist society, in whose hands
were the destinies of the nations, the monarchical and the republican governments, secret diplomacy, the vast employers'
organizations, the middle-class parties, the capitalist press, the
Church—all these forces must bear the full weight of responsibility for this war, which has been produced by the social

order nurturing them and protecting them and which is being carried on for the sake of their interests. . . ."

"Every nation," said Jaurès a few days before his death "rushed with a burning torch through the streets of Europe.'

After millions of men have sunk into their graves, millions of families have been made to mourn, and millions of women and children have been turned into widows and orphans, after ruins have been piled on ruins and irreplaceable cultural achievements destroyed, the war has come to an *impasse*.

In spite of hecatombs of victims on all fronts no decisive results have been attained! In order to shake these fronts even slightly the governments would require additional millions of human sacrifices.

Neither victors, nor vanquished. Rather *all vanquished;* all bleeding, all ruined, all exhausted—such will be the outcome of this gruesome war. The ruling classes will thus realize the vanity of their dreams of imperialistic world dominance.

Thus it has once more become manifest that only those socialists who, in spite of calumnies, have opposed the nationalist delusion and have demanded *immediate peace without annexations* have served the interests of their peoples.

Therefore, join us in our war cry: *"Down with the war. Hail peace!"*

WORKERS IN TOWNS AND FIELDS!

The governments, the imperialist cliques, and their press tell you that it is imperative to hold out in order that the oppressed nations may be freed. Of all methods of deception which have been used in this war, this is the crudest. The true aim of this general slaughter lies, for some, in *making secure that which they have scraped together during centuries or conquered in many wars, and for others in a repartitioning of the world,* in order to increase their possessions; these wish to annex new territories, subdivide and tear apart whole nations, and degrade them to ordinary servants and helots.

Your governments and your press tell you that the war must be continued in order that militarism may be abolished.

Don't be misled! A *nation's militarism can be abolished only by the nation itself,* and, moreover, this must be done in *all* countries.

Furthermore, your governments and your press tell you that

the war must be extended in order that it should be the last
war.

This also is a deception. *Never has war done away with
war.* On the contrary, it arouses desire for revenge, since violence provokes violence!

So after each sacrifice your torturers will demand further
sacrifices. Even the road of the bourgeois pacifist revilers does
not lead you out of this infernal circle.

*There is but one effective means of preventing future wars:
the seizure of political power and the abolition of capitalist
property by the working class.*

Lasting peace can result only from victorious socialism.

PROLETARIANS!

Who are they who preach to you the policy of "endurance
until victory"?—They are the responsible authors of the war,
the mercenary press, the army purveyors, the war profiteers;
the social patriots, who repeat the bourgeois war slogans;
these are the reactionaries who rejoice secretly over the death
on the battlefields of the socialists, of the trade unionists, of
all those who planted the seed of socialism in towns and villages and who were but yesterday a menace to the privileges
of the rulers.

They are the endurance politicians!

They control the government, *they* dominate the press, they
are allowed to agitate in favor of continuing the war, of adding to the number of bloody sacrifices and devastations.

Whereas, you, the victims, are allowed only to starve, to
keep silent and to endure the chains of the state of siege, the
shackles of censorship and the close atmosphere of prisons.

You, the people, the working masses, are sacrifices in a war
which is not your war.

You, the toilers from towns and villages, are now in the
trenches, in the foremost lines, whereas the rich and their accomplices, the poltroons, may be seen *behind the lines* in security.

For them war means the death of others.

At the same time as they accentuate as never before *their*
class struggle against you, and preach civil peace to you—as
they ruthlessly exploit your misery—they endeavor to incite

you to commit treason against your class duty, and they thus deprive you of your best strength—the hope for socialism.

Social injustice and class dominance are even plainer in war than in peace.

In peace the capitalist system robs the worker of the joy of living; *in war* it takes everything from him, even his life.

Enough of assassination! Enough of suffering!

Likewise, enough of devastations! For it is upon you workers that today and in the future those accumulations of ruins will fall.

Hundreds of billions are thrown today into the jaws of the war god and thus are lost to the people's welfare, to the cultural aims, and to the carrying out of such social reforms as would ameliorate their lot, promote public education, and lessen misery.

Tomorrow, new heavy taxes will descend upon your bowed shoulders.

Therefore, let us put an end to the wasting of your labor, your money, your vital strength! *Join the struggle in favor of an immediate* peace without annexations!

In all belligerent countries workingmen and women should rise against the war and its consequences, against the misery and deprivations, against the unemployment and the high cost of living. Let them raise their voices in favor of restoring the civil liberties of which they have been deprived and in favor of social legislation and the demands of the working class in towns and villages.

Let the *proletarians of the neutral countries* aid the socialists of the belligerent states in their difficult struggle and oppose to their utmost a further expansion of this war.

Let the *socialists of all countries act according* to the decisions of the international congresses, which made it the duty of the working class to put forth every effort so as to bring about an early peace.

Exercise the maximum pressure possible upon your deputies, your parliaments, your governments.

Demand that the representatives of the socialist parties deny at once every support to the government's war policy. Demand from the socialist parliamentarians that they vote from now on against all war credits.

Every means at your disposal should be used to end quickly this slaughter!

Your slogan should be: immediate armistice! Rise up and fight, you people, led to ruin and death!

Courage! Behold that you are a majority, and that the power could be yours if you so wished.

The governments should be told that the hatred against the war and the will to social retaliation is growing in all countries and that the hour of peace between the peoples is inevitably approaching.

Down with the war!

Hail peace, immediate peace without annexations!

Hail international socialism!

THE SECOND INTERNATIONAL

May 1, 1916   SOCIALIST ZIMMERWALD CONFERENCE

DOCUMENT 6: *"The Attitude of the Proletariat toward the Question of Peace: Resolution of the Kienthal Conference"*

Gankin and Fischer, *The Bolsheviks and the War*. By permission. First appeared in *Berner Tagewacht*, No. 107 (May 8, 1916).

I

1. The modern development of bourgeois property relations gave rise to *imperialist antagonisms*. The present *World War* is one of the *consequences* of these antagonisms in the interest of which unsolved national problems, dynastic aspirations, and all the historical relics of feudalism are being utilized. The *aim* of this war is the repartitioning of former colonial possessions and the subjugation of economically backward countries to the power of finance capital.

2. The war eliminates neither capitalist economy nor its imperialist form; therefore, it cannot do away with the *causes* of future wars. It reinforces finance capital, leaves unsolved the old national and world power problems, complicates them, and creates new antagonisms. This leads to the increase of economic and political reaction, to new armaments, and the danger of further military complications.

3. Therefore, if the governments and their bourgeois and social-patriotic agents assert that the purpose of the war is

to create a *lasting peace,* they lie or they ignore the conditions which are necessary for the realization of this purpose. Annexations, economic and political alliances of imperialist states, can contribute as little to the realization of a lasting peace on a capitalistic basis as can the compulsory courts of arbitration, the limitation of armaments, the so-called democratization of foreign policy, etc.

4. Annexations, i.e., the forcible annexing of foreign nations, stirs up *national hatred* and increases the *areas of friction* between states. *The political alliances* and the *economic treaties* of the imperialist powers are a direct method of *extending the economic wars*—a method which leads to *new world conflicts.*

5. The plans to eliminate the dangers of wars through a *general* limitation of armaments and compulsory courts of arbitration are mere utopias. They presuppose a generally recognized authority and a material force which would stand above the opposed interests of the states. Such an authority, such a force, does not exist, and capitalism with its tendency to sharpen the antagonisms between the bourgeoisie of various countries or of their coalitions prevents its appearance. Democratic control over foreign policy presupposes a complete democratization of the state. This control may be a *weapon in the hands of the proletariat* in its struggle against imperialism, but cannot be a means for turning democracy into an instrument of peace.

6. Because of these considerations the laboring class must reject the *utopian demands of the bourgeois or socialist pacifism.* In place of the old illusions the pacifists evoke new ones and attempt to force the proletariat to serve these illusions, which in the end only mislead the masses and divert them from the revolutionary class struggle and favor the game of the see-it-through policy in the war.

II

7. If a capitalist society cannot provide the conditions for a lasting peace, then these conditions will be provided by socialism. By abolishing capitalist private property, together with the exploitation of the masses by the propertied classes and together with national oppression, socialism eliminates the

cause of wars. *The struggle for lasting peace can, therefore, be only a struggle for the realization of socialism.*

8. Every action of the workers which renounces class struggle and subordinates proletarian aims to those of the bourgeois classes and of their governments and is in solidarity with the exploiting class of the proletariat—every such action works against the conditions necessary for a lasting peace, entrusts the capitalist classes and the bourgeois governments with a task which they cannot fulfill; moreover, it places on the shambles the best forces of the working class. The strongest and most capable elements of the proletariat, which both in time of war and in time of peace would be the first to be called upon to lead the struggle for socialism, are now destined to collapse and destruction.

III

9. As has already been stated in the resolutions of the Stuttgart, Copenhagen, and Basel international congresses, the attitude of the proletariat toward war cannot depend upon a given military and strategic situation. *Therefore, it is a vital commandment of the proletariat to raise the call for an immediate truce and an opening of peace negotiations.*

10. The laboring class will succeed in hastening the end of the war and in gaining influence over the character of the imminent peace only to the extent to which this call finds a response in the ranks of the international proletariat and leads to forceful action directed toward the overthrowing of the capitalist class. Any other attitude leaves the establishment of the peace conditions to the fiat of governments, diplomacy, and the ruling classes.

11. In the revolutionary mass struggle for the aims of socialism—the liberation of mankind from the whip of militarism and of war—the proletariat should struggle against all *lust of the belligerents for annexations.* Likewise it should reject all attempts at establishing, under the pretext of liberating oppressed peoples, pseudo-independent states. The proletariat struggles against annexations not because it considers that the map of the world in its prewar conditions corresponds with the peoples' interests and therefore requires no changes, but because socialism strives to eliminate all national oppression by means of an economic and political unification of the peo-

ples on a democratic basis, something which cannot be realized within the limits of capitalist states. Annexations, in whatever form they occur, make the attainment of this aim more
difficult, because a forcible partitioning of nations, the arbitrary subdividing and incorporation of them by foreign states,
makes worse the conditions of the proletarian class struggle.

12. So long as socialism has not achieved the freedom and
equality of rights of all nations, the proletariat's unfailing duty
is to take part in the class struggle *against all national oppression,* to oppose any violation of weaker nations, to promote
the *protection of national minorities* and the *autonomy of the
peoples* on the *basis of real democracy.*

13. The demand for war indemnities on behalf of the imperialist powers is incompatible with the interests of the proletariat, as are annexations. Just as the ruling classes in every
country try to put the burden of war costs upon the shoulders
of the working class, so the war indemnities in the end will
be borne by the laboring class of the country in question. This
transfer of the burden of indemnities is harmful also to the
laboring class of the *victorious* country, because the deterioration of economic and social conditions of the laboring class
of one country affects the laboring class of other countries and
thereby makes more difficult the conditions for the international class struggle. Not the transfer of the economic consequences of the war from one people to the other, but a *general transfer of these consequences to the propertied classes*
by means of an annulment of state debts brought about by
the war—such is our demand.

14. The struggle against the war and against imperialism,
originating in the misery of human slaughter, will in the future grow with increasing force out of the calamities with
which the imperialist era scourges the masses of the people.
The International will expand and deepen the mass movements against the high cost of living and unemployment and
in favor of the agrarian demands of the rural workers, against
new taxation and political reaction, until all these movements
unite into one general international struggle for socialism.

III : Creation of the Third International

From the Kienthal Conference to the founding of the Communist International in March 1919 the regrouping of socialist factions, splinters, and parties continued, leading to the establishment of two fairly well-defined camps. These were the patriotic and reformist party majority of most national sections represented by the ISB, and party minorities and dissident groups, pacifist and increasingly more revolutionary in outlook, represented by the Zimmerwald movement. The outcome of their struggle decided the fate of the Second International. If one event can be said to have tipped the balance, it was certainly the Russian Revolution. It not only brought the outspoken leaders of the Zimmerwald left to state power, but by virtue of its accomplishments for a brief time made revolutionary socialism much more than academic in socialist circles everywhere.

Between Kienthal and the Russian Revolution the ISB Executive followed two policy lines: to check the growing influence of Zimmerwaldians and to convince the Allied majority socialists—especially the French—of the need for convoking a full meeting of the ISB at the earliest opportunity to forestall a split in the International. The Executive Committee of the ISB played a waiting game. It refused to antagonize the French party still dominated by its right wing and hoped that a change in French intransigence would come about through an internal party power realignment. The Executive Committee feared that the Zimmerwaldians under pressure of their own left might disown the ISB and set up their own International, taking other opposition groups and even moderate forces dissatisfied with the Executive's wait-and-see policy with them.

As the war wore on the conditions leading to popular discontent naturally grew worse and significant sectors of the proletariat, longing for peace, withdrew their support from the patriotic socialists and transferred it to those who demanded an end to hostilities. Consequently, in virtually every national party the pacifist minority with its revolutionary fringe elements grew stronger. So serious was the conflict between the majority and the minority in the German party, that a split brought the Independent Social Democratic party into being in April 1917. Splits also occurred in Bulgaria, Sweden, and Switzerland. By 1917, because of bitter antagonism, the majority and minority of the French party met separately, and in Italy, Britain, and the United States the majority in the parties opposed the war. After Kienthal the various governments attempted to crush the left and its dangerous doctrine of civil war. Repressive measures included: imprisonment of the German leaders Luxemburg, Liebknecht, Franz Mehring, and Clara Zetkin as well as of the Rumanian leader Christian Rakovsky, the Swedish leader Carl Höglund, and the British leader John MacLean; drafting into the army of the French leaders Pierre Monatte and Alfred Rosmer; and expulsion of Trotsky from France and suppression of *Nashe Slovo*, which was edited by him.

In spite of repressions the Zimmerwald left carried on a vigorous underground propaganda campaign and increased its strength. In Germany it comprised the Spartacists, the Bremen left radicals led by Paul Frölich, and the International Socialists of Germany led by Julian Borchardt. In France the revolutionary socialists were much less significant, consisting mainly of those associated with the Committee for the Resumption of International Relations. The left was also strong in Sweden, Norway, Denmark, and in Switzerland, where the Russian exiles were influential. The Zimmerwald left had its own Bureau staffed by Lenin, Zinoviev, and Radek. Its publications included: *Internationale Flugblätter* and *Vorbote: Internationale Marxistische Rundschau*.[1] In spite of these signs of activity and growth, the left was still fragmented and

[1] Other publications which followed the Zimmerwald left line included: *Die Jugend Internationale* of the Socialist Youth International; in Germany *Lichtstrahlen, Spartakus Briefe, Arbeiter Politik,* and *Bremer-Bürgerzeitung;* by Russian Bolsheviks in exile *Sotsial Demokrat, Sbornik Sotsial Demokrata,* and *Kommunist;* in Switzerland *Berner Tagewacht, La Sentinelle, La Voix des Jeunes,* and *Freie Jugend;* in Sweden *Politicken* and *Stormklockan;* in Holland *De Tribune;* in Norway *Klassenkampen;* in the United States *The Internationalist;* in Poland *Gazeta Robotnicza;* and in Italy *Avanti.*

very much a minority in the international movement. Lenin appears to have concluded that a new International could emerge only from a purified left and that, therefore, a split was necessary with the social patriots of the right and with the pacifists of the center. But the situation continued to be ambiguous; whether the Second International could be revived or a Third International would be created seemed to depend on the future commitment of the center socialists.

The Russian Revolution of March 1917 left its mark on the development of every socialist party and precipitated a realignment of forces upsetting all previous calculations. The success of the March Revolution released a popular yearning for peace and strengthened the hand and resolve of socialist pacifists. Under the impact of the tremendous popular enthusiasm which it aroused, socialist leaders of all complexions were prompted to adopt a more militant tone. It gave an impetus to the calling of an international socialist conference at Stockholm. The proposal for such a conference came from three sources: from neutral socialists affiliated with the ISB; from the Petrograd Soviet; and from the Zimmerwaldist ISC. On July 11, 1917 a joint Russian-Dutch-Scandinavian Committee was formed, representing a merger of the ISB and Petrograd Soviet proposals. This committee held extensive and numerous separate conferences with representatives of socialist and labor organizations of the belligerent countries. Its attempts to convene an international conference at Stockholm failed mainly because of the opposition of the Entente governments and the continued patriotic stance of certain socialist groups. The collapse of negotiations for a broad-based international conference was a serious setback for the revival of the Second International and for healing the breach between the center and right which the left had opened at Zimmerwald and Kienthal. The ISC made its own plans and, despite official and other opposition, arranged a Third Zimmerwald Conference in Stockholm on September 5–12, 1917.[2] The Conference was much less significant than its predecessors. The absence of British, French, and Italian delegates who had been refused passports by their governments also made it less representative than earlier ones. Finally, its resolutions merely

[2] The ISC was transferred from Berne to Stockholm so as to be nearer to Russian events.

repeated the proclamation which had been issued at Zimmer-wald and Kienthal.

The successful October Revolution transformed the Bolsheviks from exile revolutionists who had led the Zimmerwald left into the most dynamic force in the international movement. Given the disunity, obstructionism, and sluggishness of the established socialist parties in reviving international relations, the Bolsheviks by their revolutionary success were now in a position to realize their goal of creating a Third International. Theoretically, the Zimmerwald movement continued to exist, but in practice only a secretariat remained, which was largely an instrument of the Bolsheviks. The Bolsheviks were committed to world revolution and revolutionary socialists everywhere looked to them for guidance and leadership. In spite of the short-lived specter of revolution on the horizon following the conclusion of armistice in November 1918 (to be discussed more fully in Part II) and the founding of communist parties in several countries, the leaders of the world proletariat generally did not support the Bolshevik appeal for revolutionary mass action. Fear of the Bolsheviks led to a gradual rapprochement between the right and center of the socialist movement in working for a revival of the Second International. The most important step in that direction was the Berne Conference of February 1919, even though it was boycotted by elements of the right, center, and left.[3] The most significant question before the Conference was the attitude to be adopted toward revolutionary movements in central and eastern Europe. The resolution passed on this question virtually declared war on the Bolsheviks and leftist forces elsewhere by proclaiming reformism rather than revolution to be the proper path to socialism. The Berne Conference succeeded in reviving the Second International; it also made final the split, which originated before the war, between evolutionary and revolutionary socialists.

The left, now largely dominated by the Bolsheviks, decided to seek mass support by calling for the creation of a Third

---

[3] The Belgian Labor party and American Federation of Labor refused to sit at the same table with "enemy" socialists. Those who considered the conference too reactionary included: the Russian Bolsheviks, the Spartacists, the "narrow" Bulgarian Social Democrats, and the official parties of Italy, Switzerland, Serbia, and Rumania.

International. The appeal to thirty-eight party groups affiliated or identified with the left was issued from Moscow three days before the scheduled opening of the Berne Conference. In taking this step the Bolsheviks and their cohorts were prompted by a belief in the possibility of world revolution; by the fear that the Russian Revolution would be reversed by the intervention of capitalist states;[4] and by the threatened revival of the Second International by the Berne Conference.

The founding congress of the Communist International met in Moscow from March 2–6, 1919. The delegates who assembled at the Kremlin were far from representative of the forces of the revolutionary left. This can be explained in part by the haste with which the conference was called and the difficulties in traveling to Russia at the time. The nineteen delegates with voting rights represented groups mainly from eastern and central Europe; delegates with a consultative voice came from France, Britain, Czechoslovakia, the United States, Switzerland, Yugoslavia, Holland, Bulgaria, Turkey, and parts of Asia. The important Italian party was not represented. The representation was much weaker than a mere enumeration of delegates would indicate, for some of the delegates lacked official credentials from their parties and others were simply party members who were in Russia at the time. Furthermore, among delegations with full powers, votes were not distributed in accordance with actual party strength, so that the negligible Hungarian party, for instance, had five votes while the German party had three. The Russian Bolsheviks controlled nearly half the votes.[5]

The major issue before the delegates involved the purpose

[4] The Bolsheviks had good reason to fear for the revolution in the early months of 1919: a "cordon sanitaire" isolated Russia from trade with the outside world; there were Allied forces in Archangel, Murmansk, and Vladivostok; and counter revolutionary armies with Allied assistance were a formidable threat to the revolutionary government. In this climate of uncertainty either a revolution spreading throughout Europe or an organization of revolutionary socialists of all nations working to foil the counter-revolutionary activities of their governments must have appeared at the time to hold out the promise of salvation.

[5] The Armenians, Estonians, Finns, Latvians, Hungarians, Lithuanians, Ukrainians, Germans in Russia, and Oriental Nationalities in Russia together with the Bolsheviks had 23 out of 55 votes.

of the conference. The Bolsheviks and their followers maintained that the assemblage constituted the founding congress of a new revolutionary international. Others, particularly the German delegate Max Albert (Hugo Eberlein), called such an interpretation premature, and considered the purpose of the conference to be a discussion of possibilities and an assessment of forces for the creation of a Third International at some future date (Document 1). The lengthy argument on this subject was interrupted by the late arrival of Gruber (Steinhardt), an Austrian delegate, who breathlessly described the revolutionary wave which he had seen rising during his difficult journey to Moscow. His enthusiasm seems to have been infectious, for when the question designating the meeting as a founding congress was called all but Eberlein voted for it. He merely abstained, in spite of his instructions from the leaders of the German Communist party to vote in the negative. Had he followed his instructions, the weight of the German vote might well have delayed the creation of the Third International and thereby altered some features of its subsequent history. With the Communist International (Comintern) an accomplished fact, the delegates elected an Executive Committee (ECCI) of seven and the ECCI elected an inner Bureau of five.[6] The main task before what had turned into the First Congress of the Comintern was now the framing of a statement of principles. What came to be called the New Communist Manifesto was written by Trotsky and issued by the Bureau on March 10th (Document 2). The Manifesto characterized the war as a symptom of the inherent contradictions of capitalism; prescribed proletarian revolution rather than self-determination as the proper course for small states; called for revolution in the colonies; distinguished between liberty and democracy as an instrument of class rule and as a product of proletarian dictatorship; and rallied proletarians of all lands to the "International of Action." With the creation of the Comintern the split in the international labor movement was formalized; during the next four years it was to become irreparable.

[6] The ECCI included the parties of Russia, Germany, Austria, Hungary, the Balkan Federation, Switzerland, and Scandinavia. Zinoviev was elected chairman and Balabanoff secretary. The Bureau consisted of Zinoviev, Lenin, Rakovsky, and Platten.

DOCUMENT 1: *"German Reservations about the Founding of the Comintern"*

Der 1. Kongress der Kommunistischen Internationale. Protokoll der Verhandlungen in Moskau vom 2. bis zum 19. [6.] März 1919 (Hamburg, 1921).

Comrade Albert [Hugo Eberlein] (Germany). Comrades! We have already discussed at length at the beginning of the conference the question as to whether this conference should become a congress at which the Third International is to be founded or whether we ought to first prepare for its founding. We agree at the urging of the German delegation, which was not authorized to vote for immediate founding, that this should be a conference preparing the founding of the Third International, which act would occur later. Since in spite of that decision, some comrades are again attempting to establish the Third International immediately, I feel compelled to briefly explain to you what motivated us to advise against going on with the founding now. When it is stated that the founding of the Third International is an absolute necessity, we venture to dispute this. If it is said that the proletariat needs in its struggle above all an intellectual center, it can also be said that such a center already exists, and that all those elements which have come together on the basis of the council system[7] have thereby already separated themselves from all the other elements in the working class who are still inclined toward bourgeois democracy; we see this separation taking place everywhere. But a Third International cannot merely be an intellectual center, not merely an institution in which theoreticians deliver heated speeches to each other; it must be the basis for organizational power. If we want to make a useful instrument of the Third International, if we

[7] The Council Movement arose spontaneously in 1918, particularly in Germany and Austria. The workers' and soldiers' councils were moderate rather than revolutionary, and in general filled the administrative gap created by the collapse of the old regimes. Eberlein is referring here to a minority of radical councils which wanted to follow the Russian system of politically all-powerful soviets.

want to forge this International into a weapon, then the preconditions for it must obtain. This question cannot be raised or judged alone from an intellectual standpoint; rather we must ask ourselves objectively if the organizational bases exist. I always have the feeling that the comrades pressing for founding are letting themselves be very much influenced by the development of the Second International, and that they wish to start an organization in competition with the Berne Conference. That seems less important to us, and when it is said that a clarification is necessary or else all doubtful elements will go over to the Yellow [Second International], then I say that the founding of the Third International will not stop those who today still are going over to the other side. If they are still going over, then they belong there. But the most important question concerning the founding of a Third International is, what do we want, what platform makes it possible for us to join with one another? The reports of the comrades from the different countries showed that the ideas as to activity, as to the means toward the end, were unknown to them, and when the delegations from the different countries came here, they could not have come with the decision to participate at the founding of the Third International. It is their task to inform their memberships first, and even the invitation assumes this, as it reads on the first page. "All these circumstances compel us to take the initiative in order to bring on the agenda for discussion the question of calling together an international congress of revolutionary proletarian parties." Hence, already in the invitation it is said that we must first examine the question here whether it is possible to call all the comrades together to a founding congress. That the ignorance concerning the goals and directions of the individual parties was great as long as there was no discussion here is shown by the letter from Longuet, a comrade active in political life who sympathizes with the center but who still thinks it is possible for us to participate in the Berne Conference. We in Germany did not know either how great the contradictions among the parties were, and when we left Germany I was prepared for deep disagreements on the various issues. I must say that we are unanimous on most questions, but we did not know that beforehand. If we want to proceed with the founding of the Third International, then we must first tell the world where we stand, first explain

which path it is upon which we can and want to unite. It is
not true to say that the Third International was already
founded at Zimmerwald. The Zimmerwald Movement fell
apart a long time ago, and only the small part of it left can
be considered for cooperation later on. On the one hand, all
these things advise against establishing the Third International now, but it is organizational issues which warn us
against it on the other. For what do we have? There are real
communist parties in only a few countries; in most others,
they have been created within the last few weeks, and in
several countries communists have as yet no organizations. I
am astonished to hear the delegate from Sweden propose the
founding of the Third International when he must admit that
there is as yet no purely communist organization in Sweden, but merely a large communist group within the Swedish Social Democratic party. We know that in Switzerland
and other countries real parties do not exist and still have to
be created, so that the comrades there can only speak in the
name of groups. Can they really say who stands behind them
today: Finland, Russia, Sweden, Austria-Hungary, and from
the Balkans not even the whole Federation? The delegates
from Greece and Serbia do not recognize Rakovsky as their
representative. All of western Europe is missing: Belgium and
Italy are not represented; the Swiss delegates cannot speak
in the name of one party; France, England, Spain, and Portugal are missing; and America is also not in a position to say
which parties would stand with us. There are so few organizations participating in the founding of the Third International that it is even difficult to make it all public. It is therefore necessary that we make our platform known to the
world before we go on with the founding, and then call
upon the communist organizations to declare their willingness
to create the Third International with us.

Communist organizations must be promoted, for it is no
longer possible to work with Kautsky and Scheidemann. I
strongly urge you not to establish the Third International
today and beg you not to act too quickly, but to call together
in the shortest possible time a congress at which the new international will be founded, an international which will really
have power behind it.

Those are the reservations which my organization has about
the immediate establishment of the Third International, and

I beg you to consider in a mature fashion if it is advisable to proceed with the founding on such a weak basis.

DOCUMENT 2: *"Manifesto of the Communist International to the Proletariat of the Entire World"*

Jane Degras, *The Communist International 1919–1943: Documents,* Vol. I (London: Oxford University Press, 1956). By permission. First appeared in *Manifest, Richtlinien, Beschlüsse des ersten Kongresses: Aufrufe und offene Schreiben des Exekutivkomitees bis zum zweiten Kongress* (Hamburg, 1920).

Seventy-two years have passed since the Communist party announced its program to the world in the form of a manifesto written by the greatest teachers of the proletarian revolution, Karl Marx and Friedrich Engels. Even at that time communism, which had barely entered the arena of struggle, was beset by the baiting, lies, hatred, and persecution of the possessing classes, who rightly sensed it their mortal enemy. In the course of those seven decades communism developed along complex paths, periods of stormy advance alternating with periods of decline; it has known successes, but also severe defeats. But essentially the movement proceeded along the path indicated in advance by the Manifesto of the Communist party. The epoch of final, decisive struggle came later than the apostles of social revolution had expected and hoped. But it has come. We communists, the representatives of the revolutionary proletariat of various countries of Europe, America, and Asia, who have gathered in Soviet Moscow, feel and consider themselves to be the heirs and executors of the cause whose program was announced seventy-two years ago. Our task is to generalize the revolutionary experience of the working class, to cleanse the movement of the disintegrating admixtures of opportunism and social patriotism, to mobilize the forces of all genuinely revolutionary parties of the world proletariat and thereby facilitate and hasten the victory of the communist revolution throughout the world.

Today, when Europe is covered with debris and smoking ruins, the most infamous incendiarists are busy seeking out the criminals responsible for the war. Behind them stand their professors, members of parliament, journalists, social patriots, and other political pimps of the bourgeoisie.

For many years socialism predicted the inevitability of imperialist war, seeing its causes in the insatiable greed of the possessing classes of the two chief camps and, in general, of all capitalist countries. At the Basel Congress, two years before the outbreak of the war, responsible socialist leaders of all countries branded imperialism as the originator of the impending war and threatened the bourgeoisie with socialist revolution as the proletarian retribution for the crimes of militarism. Today, after the experience of the last five years, after history has laid bare the predatory appetites of Germany, and the no less criminal acts of the Entente, the state-socialists of the Entente countries continue together with their governments to expose the overthrown German Kaiser. On top of this, the German social patriots, who in August 1914 proclaimed the Hohenzollern diplomatic *White Book* to be the most sacred gospel of the peoples, are now, like vile toadies, following in the footsteps of the Entente socialists and accusing the overthrown German monarchy, which they had once slavishly served, as the chief criminal. They hope in this way that their own guilt will be forgotten and at the same time to earn the goodwill of the victors. But the light cast by unfolding events and diplomatic revelations shows up, alongside the toppled dynasties of the Romanovs, the Hohenzollerns, and the Hapsburgs, and the capitalist cliques of their countries, the ruling classes of France, England, Italy, and the United States in all their boundless infamy.

English diplomacy did not raise its veil of secrecy up to the very moment when war broke out. The government of the financiers took care to make no unambiguous statement of its intention of entering the war on the side of the Entente in order not to frighten the Berlin government. In London they wanted war. That is why they behaved in such a way that Berlin and Vienna counted on England's neutrality, while Paris and Petrograd relied firmly on England's intervention.

Matured by the entire course of events over decades, the war was unleashed through the direct and deliberate provocation of Great Britain. The English government calculated on extending just enough aid to Russia and France to keep them going until, themselves exhausted, England's mortal enemy, Germany, was also crippled. But the power of the

German military machine proved too formidable and demanded of England not token but actual intervention in the war. The role of *tertius gaudens* [third party] to which Great Britain, following ancient tradition, aspired, fell to the United States. The Washington government reconciled itself the more easily to the English blockade, which unilaterally restricted American stock-exchange speculation in European blood, since the countries of the Entente compensated the American bourgeoisie with fat profits for violations of "international law." But Germany's enormous military superiority compelled the Washington government to abandon its fictitious neutrality. In relation to Europe as a whole, the United States assumed the role which England had taken in relation to the Continent in previous wars and tried to take in the last war, namely, weakening one camp by helping the other, intervening in military operations only so far as to secure for itself all the advantages of the situation. According to American standards of gambling, Wilson's stake was not very high, but it was the final stake, and it secured him the prize.

The war has made mankind aware of the contradictions of the capitalist system in the shape of primitive sufferings, hunger and cold, epidemics, and moral savagery. This had settled once and for all the academic controversy within the socialist movement over the theory of impoverishment and the gradual undermining of capitalism by socialism. Statisticians and pedants of the theory that contradictions were being smoothed out have for decades been trying to dig out from every corner of the globe real or alleged facts testifying to the greater well-being of various groups and categories of the working class. It was assumed that the theory of impoverishment had been buried to the accompaniment of contemptuous jeers of the eunuchs of bourgeois professordom and the mandarins of socialist opportunism. Today this impoverishment, no longer only of a social kind, but also physiological and biological, confronts us in all its shocking reality.

The catastrophe of the imperialist war has swept away all the gains of the trade union and parliamentary struggle. For this war itself was just as much a product of the inherent tendencies of capitalism as were those economic agreements and parliamentary compromises which the war buried in blood and mud.

Finance capital, which plunged mankind into the abyss of war, has itself suffered catastrophic changes in the course of war. The relation between paper money and the material foundation of production has been completely disrupted. Steadily losing significance as the means and regulator of capitalist commodity circulation, paper money has become an instrument of requisition, of robbery, and of military-economic violence in general. The complete debasement of paper money reflects the general mortal crisis of capitalist commodity exchange. In the decades preceding the war, free competition, as the regulator of production and distribution, had already been supplanted in the major fields of economic life by the system of trusts and monopolies; but the course of events during the war tore this role from the hands of these economic associations and transferred it directly to the military state power. The distribution of raw materials, the utilization of Baku or Rumanian oil, of Donetz coal or Ukrainian wheat, the fate of German locomotives, trucks, and automobiles, the provisioning of starving Europe with bread and meat—all these fundamental questions of the world's economic life are being settled not by free competition, nor by associations of national and international trusts and consortiums, but by the direct application of military power in the interests of its continued preservation. If the complete subjection of state power to the power of finance capital led mankind into the imperialist shambles, then through this mass slaughter finance capital has completely militarized not only the state but also itself, and is no longer capable of fulfilling its cardinal economic functions otherwise than by means of blood and iron.

The opportunists, who before the World War appealed to the workers to practice moderation for the sake of the gradual transition to socialism, and who during the war demanded class docility in the name of civil peace and national defense, are now again demanding self-denial of the proletariat in order to overcome the frightful consequences of the war. If this sermon were to be obeyed by the working masses, capitalist development would celebrate its restoration in new, more concentrated and more monstrous forms on the bones of many generations, with the prospect of a new and inevitable world war. Fortunately for mankind this is no longer possible.

State control of economic life, which capitalist liberalism resisted so strongly, has become a fact. There is no return to free competition, nor even to the domination of trusts, syndicates, and other economic monsters. There is only one question: Who shall henceforth take charge of nationalized production—the imperialist state or the state of the victorious proletariat?

In other words: Shall all toiling mankind become the bond slaves of a victorious world clique who, under the name of the League of Nations and aided by an "international" army and "international" navy, will plunder and strangle in one place and cast crumbs elsewhere, while everywhere shackling the proletariat, with the sole object of maintaining their own rule; or shall the working class of Europe and of the advanced countries in other parts of the world themselves take in hand the disrupted and ruined economy in order to assure its reconstruction on socialist foundations?

It is possible to shorten the present epoch of crisis only by means of the proletarian dictatorship, which does not look back to the past, which respects neither hereditary privileges nor property rights, but takes as its starting point the need of saving the starving masses, and to this end mobilizes all forces and resources, introduces universal labor conscription, establishes the regime of labor discipline, in order in the course of a few years not only to heal the gaping wounds inflicted by war but also to raise mankind to new and unimagined heights.

The national state, which imparted a mighty impulse to capitalist development, has become too narrow for the further development of productive forces. This makes still more untenable the position of the small states hemmed in by the major powers of Europe and other continents. These small states, which arose at different times as fragments chipped from larger ones, as small change in payment for various services rendered, or as strategic buffers, have their own dynasties, their own ruling cliques, their own imperialist pretensions, their own diplomatic intrigues. Their illusory independence rested, before the war, on the same foundations as the European balance of power—the uninterrupted antagonism between the two imperialist camps. The war has disrupted this equilibrium. By giving an enormous preponderance to Germany in its early stages, the war forced the small states to seek salvation in the magnanimity of German militarism. When Germany was defeated, the bourgeoisie of the small states, together with their patriotic "socialists," turned to the victorious Allied imperialists and began to seek guarantees for their continued independent existence in the hypocritical provisions of the Wilsonian program. At the same time the number of small states increased; out of the Austro-Hungarian monarchy, out of parts of the former Czarist empire, new state entities have been carved, which were no sooner born than they sprang at one another's throats over the question of state frontiers. Meanwhile the Allied imperialists are constructing combinations of small powers, both old and new, bound to themselves by the pledge of mutual hatreds and common impotence.

While oppressing and coercing the small and weak peoples, condemning them to hunger and degradation, the Allied imperialists, like the imperialists of the Central Powers a short while ago, do not stop talking about the right of national self-determination, which is today trampled underfoot in Europe as in all other parts of the world.

The small peoples can be assured of a free existence only by the proletarian revolution, which will liberate the productive forces of all countries from the constraint of the national state, unite the peoples in closest economic collaboration on the basis of a common economic plan, and afford even the smallest and weakest people the opportunity of conducting their national cultural affairs freely and independently, without detriment to the unified and centralized European and world economy.

The last war, which was not least a war for colonies, was at the same time a war fought with the help of colonies. The colonial populations were drawn into the European war on an unprecedented scale. Indians, Negroes, Arabs, and Madagascans fought on the European continent—for what? For their right to remain the slaves of England and France. Never before has the infamy of capitalist rule been shown up so clearly; never before has the problem of colonial slavery been posed so sharply as it is today.

Consequently there has been a series of open insurrections, revolutionary ferment in all the colonies. In Europe itself Ireland reminded us by bloody street battles that it still remains and still feels itself an enslaved country. In Madagascar, Annam, and other countries, the troops of the bourgeois republic had more than one revolt of colonial slaves to repress during the war. In India the revolutionary movement has not subsided for a single day, and has lately led to the greatest workers' strike in Asia, which the British government met by ordering its armored cars into action in Bombay.

Thus the colonial question in its fullest extent has been placed on the agenda, not only on the order papers of the diplomats in congress in Paris, but also in the colonies themselves. Wilson's program, at its best, is meant only to change the commercial label of colonial slavery. The emancipation of the colonies is possible only in conjunction with the emancipation of the metropolitan working class. The workers and peasants, not only of Annam, Algiers, and Bengal, but also of Persia and Armenia, will gain their opportunity of independent existence only when the workers in England and France have overthrown Lloyd George and Clemenceau and taken state power into their own hands. Even now the struggle in the more developed colonies is more than the struggle for national liberation; it is assuming an explicitly social character. If capitalist Europe forcibly dragged the backward sections of the world into the capitalist whirlpool, then socialist Europe will come to the aid of the liberated colonies with its technology, its organization, its spiritual forces, in order to facilitate their transition to a planned and organized socialist economy.

Colonial slaves of Africa and Asia! The hour of proletarian dictatorship in Europe will also be the hour of your own liberation!

The entire bourgeois world accuses the communists of abolishing freedom and political democracy. That is not true. Having taken power, the proletariat merely asserts the utter impossibility of employing the methods of bourgeois democracy, and creates the conditions and forms of a new and higher workers' democracy. The whole course of capitalist development, especially during its final imperialist epoch, has undermined political democracy not only by splitting nations into two irreconcilable classes, but also by condemning the numerous petty-bourgeois and semi-proletarian strata, as well as the lowest strata of the proletariat, to permanent economic deprivation and political impotence.

In those countries where history provided the opportunity, the working class utilized the regime of political democracy in order to organize the fight against capital. The same thing will happen in those countries where conditions for the workers' revolution have not yet matured. But the broad intermediate strata in the countryside as well as the town are being hampered by capitalism, and are behindhand in their historical development. The peasant in Baden and Bavaria who still cannot see beyond the spire of his village church, the small French wine producer who is being ruined by the large-scale capitalists who adulterate wine, and the small American farmer fleeced and cheated by bankers and Congressmen—all these social strata, thrust by capitalism out of the mainstream of development, are ostensibly called on, under the regime of political democracy, to run the state. But in reality, on all the important questions which determine the destiny of the peoples, the financial oligarchy makes the decision behind the back of parliamentary democracy. That was true above all on the question of war; it is true now on the question of peace.

When the financial oligarchy thinks it advisable to get parliamentary cover for its acts of violence, the bourgeois state has at its disposal for this purpose all the manifold instruments inherited from centuries of class rule and multiplied by all the miracles of capitalist technology—lies, demagogy, baiting, calumny, bribery, and terror.

To demand of the proletariat that like meek lambs they comply with the requirements of bourgeois democracy in the final life-and-death struggle with capitalism is like asking a man fighting for his life against cutthroats to observe the artificial and restrictive rules of French wrestling, drawn up but not observed by his enemy.

In this realm of destruction, where not only the means of production and exchange but also the institutions of political democracy lie in bloody ruins, the proletariat must create its own apparatus, designed first and foremost to bind together the working class and to ensure the possibility of its revolutionary intervention in the further development of mankind. This apparatus is the workers' soviets. The old parties, the old trade unions, have in the person of their leaders proved incapable of carrying out, even of understanding, the tasks presented by the new epoch. The proletariat has created a new kind of apparatus, which embraces the entire working class regardless of occupation or political maturity; a flexible apparatus capable of continual renewal and extension, of drawing broader and broader strata into its orbit, opening its doors to the working people in town and country who stand close to the proletariat. This irreplaceable organization of working-class self-government, of its struggle, and later of its conquest of state power, has been tested in the experience of various countries and represents the greatest achievement and mightiest weapon of the proletariat of our time.

In all countries where the masses have wakened to consciousness, soviets of workers', soldiers', and peasants' deputies will continue to be built. To strengthen the soviets, to raise their authority, to put them up in opposition to the state apparatus of the bourgeoisie—this is today the most important task of the class-conscious and honest workers of all countries. Through the soviets the working class can save itself from the disintegration introduced into its midst by the hellish sufferings of war and of hunger, by the violence of the possessing classes, and by the treachery of its former leaders. Through the soviets the working class will be able most surely and easily to come to power in all those countries where the soviets are able to rally the majority of the working people. Through the soviets, the working class, having conquered power, will manage all spheres of economic and cultural life, as is the case at present in Russia.

The collapse of the imperialist state, from the Czarist to the most democratic, is proceeding simultaneously with the collapse of the imperialist military system. The multimillioned armies mobilized by imperialism could stand firm only so long as the proletariat remained obediently under the yoke of the bourgeoisie. The breakdown of national unity means also an inevitable breakdown of the army. This is what happened first in Russia, then in Austria-Hungary and Germany. The same thing may be expected to occur in other imperialist states. The revolt of the peasant against the landlord, of the worker against the capitalist, and of both against the monarchical or democratic bureaucracy, inevitably brings in its train the revolt of soldiers against the army command, and subsequently a sharp split between the proletarian and bourgeois elements of the army. The imperialist war, which pitted one nation against the other, has passed and is passing over into civil war which pits one class against another.

The outcry of the bourgeois world against civil war and red terror is the most monstrous hypocrisy yet known in the history of political struggle. There would be no civil war if the clique of exploiters who have brought mankind to the very brink of ruin had not resisted every forward step of the working masses, if they had not instigated conspiracies and assassinations, and summoned armed assistance from without in order to maintain or restore their thievish privileges.

Civil war is forced on the working class by its arch-enemies. Unless it renounces itself and its own future, which is also the future of all mankind, the working class must give blow for blow. The communist parties, which never conjure up civil war artificially, try to shorten it as much as possible whenever with iron necessity it does break out, to reduce to a minimum the number of victims and, above all, to assure victory to the proletariat. Hence arises the necessity of disarming the bourgeoisie in time, of arming the workers, of creating a communist army to defend the proletarian power and the inviolability of its socialist construction. Such is the Red Army of Soviet Russia which arose to defend the conquests of the working class against all attacks from within and without. The Soviet army is inseparable from the Soviet state.

Conscious of the world-historical character of their tasks, the enlightened workers, from the very beginning of their organized socialist movement, strove for an association on an international scale. The foundation stone was laid in London in 1864 in the shape of the First International. The Franco-Prussian War, from which the Germany of the Hohenzollerns emerged, undermined the First International, while at the same time it gave an impetus to the development of national workers' parties. In 1889 these parties came together at a congress in Paris and created the organization of the Second International. But the center of gravity of the workers' movement during this period remained wholly on national soil, wholly within the framework of national states, founded upon national industry and confined within the sphere of national parliamentarianism. Decades of reformist organizational activity created a generation of leaders the majority of whom recognized in words the program of social revolution but denied it by their actions; they were bogged down in reformism and in adaptation to the bourgeois state. The opportunist character of the leading parties of the Second International was finally revealed, and it led to the greatest collapse in world history, at a moment when the march of events demanded revolutionary methods of struggle from the working-class parties. If the war of 1870 dealt a blow to the First International, disclosing that there was as yet no resolute mass power behind its socialist-revolutionary program, then the war of 1914 killed the Second International, disclosing that the working masses, though welded together, were dominated by parties which had become transformed into subsidiary organs of the bourgeois state!

This applies not only to the social patriots who have today gone over openly to the camp of the bourgeoisie, who have become their favorite agents and the most reliable hangmen of the working class; it also applies to the amorphous, unstable socialist center, which is now trying to reestablish the Second International, that is, to reestablish the narrowness, the opportunism, and the revolutionary impotence of its leading élites. The Independent party of Germany, the present majority of the Socialist party of France, the Menshevik group of Russia, the independent Labour party of England, and other such groups are actually trying to fill the place occupied before the war by the old official parties of the Second International by coming forward, as before, with ideas of compromise and unity, using all the means at their disposal to paralyze the energies of the proletariat, to prolong the crisis, and thus make Europe's calamities even greater. The struggle against the socialist center is the indispensable premise for the successful struggle against imperialism.

In rejecting the timidity, the lies, and the corruption of the obsolete official socialist parties, we communists, united in the Third International, consider that we are carrying on in direct succession the heroic endeavors and martyrdom of a long line of revolutionary generations from Babeuf to Karl Liebknecht and Rosa Luxemburg.

If the First International predicted the future course of development and indicated the roads it would take, if the Second International rallied and organized millions of proletarians, then the Third International is the International of open mass struggle, the International of revolutionary realization, the International of action.

The bourgeois world order has been sufficiently lashed by socialist criticism. The task of the international communist party consists in overthrowing that order and erecting in its place the edifice of the socialist order.

We summon the working men and women of all countries to unite under the communist banner under which the first great victories have already been won.

Proletarians of all countries! In the struggle against imperialist savagery, against monarchy, against the privileged estates, against the bourgeois state and bourgeois property, against all kinds and forms of social and national oppression —Unite!

Under the banner of workers' soviets, under the banner of revolutionary struggle for power and the dictatorship of the proletariat, under the banner of the Third International— proletarians of all countries, unite!

Further Reading

The two best introductions to Marx and Marxism are George Lichtheim's *Marxism: An Historical and Critical Study* (New York/London, 1961) and Franz Mehring's *Karl Marx: The Story of His Life* (Ann Arbor, 1962). The first imaginatively relates Marxist theory to the historical circumstances in which it arose and developed; the second, although marred by a clumsy translation, is still the best biography and intellectual overview. The First International has still to find its historian. For a brief account of the diverse elements comprising it and its complex struggles, see Jacques Freymond and Miklos Molnar, "The First International: Why Did It Rise? Why Did It Fall?," *One Hundred Years of Revolutionary Internationals*, ed. Milorad Drachkowitch (Stanford, 1965).

The Second International also lacks a comprehensive and interpretive study. The most recent work by James Joll, *The Second International 1889–1914* (London, 1955), is a brief and sketchy survey lacking a discussion of theoretical issues and serious analysis. An earlier but still serviceable introduction is R. W. Postgate's *The Workers' International* (London,

1920), dealing with the First and Second International and the beginnings of the Third. The most detailed account of the subject and of labor and socialist organizations before the First World War is G. D. H. Cole's *The Second International 1889–1914* (London/New York, 1956), 2 vols. Revisionism is given careful exposition in two exceptional works whose main focus is on other subjects. Peter Gay's *Dilemma of Democratic Socialism: Eduard Bernstein's Challenge to Marx* (New York, 1962) is an excellent intellectual biography, and Carl E. Schorske's *German Social Democracy 1905–1917: The Development of the Great Schism* (Cambridge, 1955), is a brilliant monograph on the German party's development and internal struggles. For the two leading rebutters of revisionism, see Karl Kautsky, *Bernstein und das sozialdemokratische Programm: Eine Antikritik* (Stuttgart, 1899) and Rosa Luxemburg, *Gesammelte Werke*, ed. Paul Frölich (Berlin, 1928), Vol. III. Two other works which shed light on socialism in the Second International era, especially on the position of the center and the left, are Harvey Goldberg's magisterial *The Life of Jean Jaurès* (Madison, 1962) and Leopold H. Haimson's penetrating *The Russian Marxists and the Origins of Bolshevism* (Cambridge, 1955).

The most useful book on the reaction of social democracy to the outbreak of war is William E. Walling's *The Socialists and the War* (New York, 1915), which contains excerpts from statements by leading socialists and from resolutions and proclamations by the national parties. For a more specialized treatment of the German party's orientation, see William Maehl, "The Triumph of Nationalism in the German Socialist Party on the Eve of the First World War," *Journal of Modern History*, XXIV (1952), and Richard Hostetter, "The S. P. D. and the General Strike as an Anti-War Weapon," *The Historian*, XIII (1950–51). An excellent treatment of socialism during the war and the various attempts to revive international socialist relations can be found in Olga H. Gankin and H. H. Fischer, *The Bolsheviks and the World War* (Stanford, 1940). The authors present a wide range of pertinent documents together with succinct scholarly commentary. An interesting though colored firsthand account of that era by a leading figure of the Zimmerwald left is Angelica Balabanoff's *Memoirs of a Zimmerwaldian* (Leningrad, 1925). For the Russian Revolution of 1917 and its impact, the most comprehensive, though implicitly Leninist work is E. H. Carr's *The Bolshevik Revolution* (New York, 1951–1952), *Vols. I and II*. Merle Fainsod's introductory *International Socialism and the World War* (Cambridge, Mass., 1935), though written more than thirty years ago, contains the best account of the founding of the Third International and the conflicts within the socialist movement preceding it.

PART TWO

1919—WORLD REVOLUTION ON
THE HORIZON:
BERLIN, BUDAPEST, MUNICH, VIENNA

Looking backward, it has become customary to conclude that the communists' belief in a growing revolutionary wave on the heels of the armistice in November 1918 reflected a myopic inability to see the larger European frame of reference and to appreciate the staying power of reformist and revisionist socialism. Instead of practicing hindsight, however, it is more important to reconstruct the historical conditions of the period, particularly the political, intellectual, and emotional climate in which difficult choices had to be made. No doubt the communists' expectations were in some respects unrealistic, but there was also justification for them. It is therefore instructive to review the possibilities for world revolution immediately after the war as they appeared to the leaders of the revolutionary left.

The dislocation of established political order after the armistice and the relatively easy success of the October Revolution prompted the Russian Bolsheviks and other Zimmerwaldian leftists to view and interpret certain developments in Europe as signals of an approaching world revolution. The collapse of the two remaining European empires, the Austro-Hungarian and the German, left a power vacuum quickly filled by less backward forces, among which socialists held commanding positions. Legions of weary soldiers and war prisoners returned to their homelands and, in central Europe particularly, constituted an unstable element by contributing to existing unemployment, food and housing shortages. Hampered in easy adjustments to civilian life and in many instances infected with leftist propaganda, these returning veterans seemed to represent the raw material of anticipated revolutions.

Strikes which on the home front of the Central Powers had had political anti-war overtones as early as 1917, by October/November 1918 became more blatantly political and proto-revolutionary. The quite sudden appearance of work-ers', peasants', and soldiers' councils acting as grass-roots ad-ministrative agencies during the power interregnum in Ber-lin, Munich, Vienna, Budapest, and other urban centers was interpreted by the radical left as further proof of the masses' readiness for far-reaching revolution. These masses, it was believed by those who stood at the commanding heights of the Comintern early in 1919, had the instruments of power all but in their hands, and only the directive skill of trained revolutionists was needed to plunge all of central and eastern Europe into revolution.

Indeed, even the cadres of "true" revolutionaries seemed to have grown in number and had established themselves within national socialist movements or created clear-cut com-munist parties. By the spring of 1919 communist parties had been created in Austria, Hungary, Germany, and the Netherlands. In addition, various established socialist parties or segments of them took a big step to the left. These in-cluded: the Italian Socialist party, the "narrow" Bulgarian Socialist party, the Serbian Social Democratic party, the Norwegian Labor party, the French Socialist party (par-ticularly its extreme left under Fernand Loriot), the Swedish Left Social Democratic party, the Young Guards of the Bel-gian Labor party, and the British Socialist party.

Before 1919 drew to a close, and more decisively during the following two years, these revolutionary harbingers turned out to be frail straws in the wind. Soviet Russia's pre-carious existence under the pressure of civil war and Allied intervention on the side of the Whites to overthrow or at least contain Bolshevism probably largely accounts for the Bolshevik leaders' tendency to anticipate the world revolu-tion—for their desire to almost will it into being. To this ex-cessive optimism stemming from the fear of isolation and the desire for communist allies (there was as yet no thought of socialism in one country) must be added a less than pro-found understanding of conditions in central and western Europe and the tendency to view all developments as homologues of the Russian Revolution. Consequently, the Bolsheviks failed to appreciate that mass strikes and street demonstrations by workers and soldiers were not preludes to civil war but demands for civil order and peace; that the citadel of power of even vanquished states could not be stormed by a handful of resolute revolutionists alone; that the councils were not soviets but rather instruments of the reformist socialists; and that ultimately the masses were content to accept the bloodless political revolution in place of a fratricidal social one.

Reality and illusion were both put to the test in revolutionary fires that burned in Berlin, Budapest, Munich and Vienna.

I : Spartacus in Berlin

The abortive strike of some half million workers of Berlin in January 1918 was the prelude to serious popular discontent which came to full expression that November and continued to flare up on a diminished scale in the following January. The strike organized by the rank and file over the heads of their trade union leaders was in large measure a political protest against German policies in the peace negotiations at Brest-Litovsk and against the harsh official attitude toward peace feelers by the Allies. At that juncture popular pressure to call a halt to almost four years of slaughter and privation and to redress some of the most serious political grievances was no match for the authoritarian control exercised by the General Staff. It was the failure of the German summer offensive on the Western front which forced Hindenburg and Ludendorff to demand that the civil authorities take steps to negotiate an armistice.

In October, a revolution from above, virtually ordered to specifications by Ludendorff, established parliamentary government in Germany under Reich Chancellor Prince Max von Baden. The Prince proceeded to broaden the base of his government and invited the Majority Socialists to join the ruling coalition. Although the parliamentary monarchy promulgated a new constitution and carried out other reforms, the public remained largely unaffected. Indeed to the man in the street a prince at the head of the government, a general as minister of war, the perpetuation of imperial military discipline, and the continuance of martial law which, for instance, left the General commanding in Berlin free to prohibit political meetings and censor the press, were if anything proof that the old order had not changed. By the end of October the new government bore the further onus of having failed to make peace. A revolt of the sailors in Kiel early in November developed into a revolutionary wave, spawning workers' and soldiers' councils, which assumed political power as it swelled and spread throughout Germany. When it reached Berlin on November 9th, Prince Max was swept from office, William II was forced to abdicate, and the Majority Socialists came to power in the person of Friedrich Ebert.

During this critical period social democracy in Germany was divided against itself. Signs of disunity appeared soon after the outbreak of the war over the issues of civil peace, war aims, and support for war appropriations between the patriotic socialist majority and the pacifistic and the revolutionary minorities. An open split occurred in April 1917, and the left centrists and Spartacists founded the Independent Social Democratic party (USPD, or Independents). From the beginning this union was a misalliance of forces in which the Spartacists, committed to revolution, were much more radical than their admittedly Marxist but generally moderate left-centrist confreres. The Independents were primarily an anti-war association and as such attracted a broad spectrum of socialists who during the revolutionary period gravitated to the two extremes—Majority Socialists or Spartacists.

Para-political organizations such as the workers' and soldiers' councils and the Revolutionary Shop Stewards were another source of confusion and division within the left. The councils, which arose spontaneously during October and November 1918, attempted to fill the administrative gap created by the collapse of the Empire. The Spartacists and other radicals hoped that the councils could be developed into Bolshevik-styled soviets which would constitute the basis for a governmental alternative to Ebert's provisional rule. The Revolutionary Shop Stewards were a radical offshoot of the trade unions in Berlin, first organized as an anti-war movement in 1914 and radicalized during the mass strikes of 1916 and 1917. Unlike the Spartacists, they did not believe in mass action as the means to revolution, but in conspiratorial actions of small groups of militants, and, therefore, considered the shops rather than parties the marshaling center for revolution. Another practice which tended to blur political alignments in this period was simultaneous membership in a number of parties and organizations. Thus, members of the Shop Stewards were also active trade unionists and were affiliated with the Independents, and those comprising the councils might also be inscribed in the rolls of the Majority Socialists, the Independents, or the Spartacists.

Although Ebert took the reins of government under unstable and uncertain conditions, particularly in Berlin, he quickly managed to disperse and repress those forces which desired to drive the revolution to the left. One of the first acts of his provisional republican government was to form a coalition with the right wing of the Independents and to declare that a soon-to-be-elected National Assembly would decide on the final political form of the state. In preparing the way for a legitimate government in which the Majority Socialists would be predominant, Ebert correctly assessed the outlook of most Germans, including the workers. The public was simply tired of strife and hardship; November 9th was regarded as "the" revolution which would usher in an era in which social democracy would quietly but steadily add to its successes. The only obstacle to the development of a democratic republican government was the council movement. Ebert realized that if the councils fell under the sway of the Spartacists or left Independents, an alternative form of government might well emerge, and he mobilized his party's forces in the councils to prevent a takeover by the left. When the crucial vote in the First National Congress of Councils came on December 19th, the councils declared their powers to be transitional and surrendered them to the future National Assembly.

This vote by the Congress of Councils was a severe blow to the revolutionary left, which had hoped to dominate an anti-parliamentary alliance and thereby to complete the "unfinished" revolution. Ironically, only five days before the councils rejected further revolution for the Republic, Rosa Luxemburg had outlined in the Spartacist organ *Die Rote Fahne* a program for a soviet republic resting largely on the councils (Document 1). She opened with an idealistic sketch of the socialist future with peace, plenty, and a new freedom for all. Her tone regarding the present was cautious, and she stressed the long, hard road ahead rather than the final goal. The proletariat, she insisted, faced incessant struggles on all levels of capitalist society and could expect no easy or automatic victory, for the bourgeoisie would not surrender its power; it would sooner destroy the country than yield. Her practical proposals for the present were both offensive and defensive: measures to safeguard the revolution, including disarming the police and army and replacing them with a workers' militia; measures in the political and social field, including a detailed scheme for local and national administration by the councils; and measures for the economy, including nationalization of all large industrial, commercial, and financial establishments. The Spartacists, she concluded, would neither enter a coalition with the social democrats nor take over the government simply because the social democrats had reached the end of their rope and wanted to surrender their power. The Spartacists would take power only with a mandate from the majority of the proletariat.

The Spartacists possessed a program but lacked a political base. Their fragile ties to the Independents had worn thin, and by the end of December the Spartacists made the final break. They met with the Bremen Left Radicals under the tutelage of Karl Radek between December 30th and January 1st and founded the German Communist party (KPD). This move was clearly a retrenchment because the possibilities for revolutionary action with mass support appeared to have passed.

Strangely enough, neither Ebert's success nor the Spartacists' rejection by the councils had dampened all the revolutionary fires. What has gone down in history as the Spartacist Putsch of January 1919 was a spontaneous outburst which was fanned and nurtured by the Independents and the Revolutionary Shop Stewards and received only secondary support from the Spartacists. The second phase of the German revolution began with the resignation of the Independents from the provisional government and from the Prussian cabinet.[1] Emil Eichhorn, the left-wing Independent Berlin Police President, refused to follow suit and remained at his post in spite of official government demands for his resignation. He received strong support from his own party and the Revolutionary Shop Stewards, who were joined by the KPD leadership. The three organizations called for a mass demonstration for January 5th (Document 2). The demonstration was well-attended, and the sponsors formed a provisional revolu-

[1] The dispute between Independents and Majority Socialists involved the latter's suppression of the *Volksmarinedivision*. This division of sailors had mutinied and participated in the street fighting during the Christmas season of 1918.

tionary committee. In a proclamation of January 6th, they called for the overthrow of the government (Document 3). On the evening of January 5th undisciplined and leaderless bands, the unstable elements of the three organizations, occupied various city districts, skirmished with the police, and took over some of the leading newspapers.

The KPD leadership was sharply divided over support of this uprising. The party's *Zentrale* was almost prepared to disavow Liebknecht, who had acted on the provisional revolutionary committee in the name of the party. But even though Luxemburg realized the dangers of this adventure, she was loath to leave fighting workers in the lurch, and the party ambiguously criticized and encouraged the insurgents. Within a week's time the full force of the government had been mobilized and the revolt crushed. In the wave of repression that followed, Luxemburg and Liebknecht were arrested and murdered by officers and men of a Berlin cavalry regiment. The German revolution remained stabilized at the level of November 9th.

DOCUMENT 1: *The German Spartacists: Their Aims and Objects*

"International Socialist Library II" [of the British Socialist party], (London, 1919). First appeared as "Was will der Spartakusbund?," *Die Rote Fahne,* No. 29 (Dec. 14, 1918). Rosa Luxemburg's draft program was adopted in full by the founding congress of the German Communist party. See *Bericht über den Gründungsparteitag der Kommunistischen Partei Deutschlands (Spartakusbund) vom 30. Dezember 1918 bis 1. Januar 1919* (Berlin, 1919).

On the 9th of November, 1918, the workers and soldiers of Germany overthrew the old regime. The bloody dream of subjecting the world to the domination of militarism vanished like smoke on the battlefields of France. The band of criminals who kindled the world conflagration and drove Germany into the sea of blood reached on that day the end of their career. The people, who were deceived for four years, and, in the service of Moloch, forgot their duties as cultured people, lost all sense of honor and humanity, and allowed themselves to be used in connection with any base act, finding themselves on the brink of an abyss, awakened from the stupor in which they were for more than four years.

On the 9th of November the German workers arose to throw off the disgraceful yoke. The Hohenzollerns were driven out; soviets of workers' and soldiers' deputies were elected.

But the Hohenzollerns were never more than the agents of the imperialist capitalists and junkers. The class rule of the capitalists—that was the real cause of the World War in Germany and France, in Russia and England, in Europe and America. The capitalists of all countries—these are the real initiators of the slaughter of peoples. International capitalism is the insatiate Moloch into whose bloody jaws are thrown millions upon millions of fresh human sacrifices.

The World War confronted society with a choice of two alternatives: either the continued existence of capitalism, with its consequent new wars and inevitable and speedy destruction due to chaos and anarchy, or the abolition of capitalist exploitation.

With the end of the World War the class rule of the capitalists lost its right to existence. It is no longer capable of leading society out of the terrible economic chaos which the imperialist orgy has left in its wake.

The means of production were destroyed to a frightful extent. Millions of workers, the best and the soundest element of the working class, were slaughtered. Those left alive, upon returning home, will receive the mock welcome of poverty and unemployment. Starvation and disease threaten to sap the remaining strength of the people. Financial bankruptcy, as a consequence of the crushing burden of war debts, is inevitable.

Only socialism can save the people from this bloody chaos, this gaping abyss. There is no other way. Only the world-wide proletarian revolution can establish order in place of this anarchy, put an end to the mutual extermination of the peoples, provide work and bread for all, and bring peace, freedom, and true culture to tortured humanity. "Down with wage labor!" Such is the battle cry of the day. Wage labor and class rule must give way to work on a cooperative basis. The means of production must cease to be the monopoly of a class; they must become the common property of all. The present system of production, which is nothing but exploitation and robbery, must be abolished. No more exploiters or exploited. Production and the distribution of products must be regulated in the interests of the nation as a whole.

Instead of masters and wage slaves there will be free fellow workers! Labor will cease to be a burden for anybody when it becomes the duty of all. An existence worthy of men will be assured to all who fulfill their duty toward society. Hunger will cease to be the curse of workers; it will be the punishment for idlers.

Only in such a society can slavery and mutual hatred among nations be destroyed. Only when such a society is established will the earth cease to be outraged by fratricidal conflicts. Only then shall we be able to say: "We have seen the end of war."

II

The establishment of the socialist order of society is the greatest task that ever fell to the lot of a class and of a revolution in the course of human history. This task involves the complete reconstruction of the state and an entire change in the social and economic foundation of society.

This change and this reconstruction cannot be accomplished by a decree issued by some officials, committee, or parliament. They can only be accomplished by the mass of the people themselves.

In all preceding revolutions it was a small minority of people who conducted the revolutionary struggle. This minority determined the goal, gave direction to the fight, and used the masses only as tools to secure victory for their own interests, the interests of the minority. The socialist revolution is the first revolution which can secure victory for and through the great majority of the workers themselves.

It is the task of the proletarian mass not only clearly and consciously to determine the aim and direction of the revolution. It must also establish socialism step by step through its own activity.

The main feature of the socialist society is to be found in the fact that the great mass of workers will cease to be a governed mass, but, on the contrary, will itself live the full political and economic life and direct that life in conscious and free self-determination.

Therefore the proletarian mass must substitute its own class organs—the workers' and soldiers' councils—for the inherited organs of capitalist class rule—the federal councils, municipal councils, parliaments—applying this principle from the highest authority in the state to the smallest community. The proletarian mass must fill all governmental positions, must control all functions, must test all requirements of the state on the touchstone of socialist aims and the interests of its own class.

Only by means of a constant, mutual action upon each other on the part of the masses and their organs—the soviets of workers' and soldiers' deputies—can their activity fill the state with a socialist spirit.

Likewise, economic reconstruction can go only as a process carried on by the mass action of the working class.

Mere decrees on socialization issued by high revolutionary authorities are of no more value than empty sounds. Only the working class, by its own efforts, can change these sounds into actuality. Only in a stubborn fight with capital, face to face in every enterprise, by their own direct pressure, by means of strikes, and by creating their permanent representative organs, can the workers secure control and, finally, the actual administration of production.

The workers must learn to transform themselves from mere machines, which the capitalist employs in the process of production, into free, active, thinking leaders of this process. They must acquire the sense of responsibility of active members of the commonwealth, which alone is the owner of all social wealth. They must develop zeal at work, without the whip of the employer, the highest productivity without the spur of capitalist drivers, discipline without yoke, and order without domination. Highest idealism in the peoples' interest, strictest self-discipline, true civic spirit of the masses —these constitute the moral basis of a socialist society, just as stupidity, egotism, and corruption are the moral basis of capitalism.

These socialist civic virtues, as also knowledge and the ability to conduct socialist industries, can be acquired by the workers only by personal activity and personal experience.

The socialization of society can be accomplished to the fullest extent only by the persistent and uninterrupted struggle of the workers at all points where labor and capital, the people and the class rule of the bourgeoisie, meet face to face.

The emancipation of the working class must be the work of the workers themselves.[2]

III

In bourgeois revolutions bloodshed, terror, and political murder were the indispensable weapons of the rising classes.

The proletarian revolution requires no terror for the realization of its aims; it looks upon manslaughter with hatred and aversion. It has no need for such means because the struggle it conducts is not against individuals but against institutions. It enters the arena with no naïve illusions, the dispersal of which would prompt it to have recourse to revenge. The proletarian revolution is not the desperate attempt of a minority forcibly to transform the world in accordance with its own ideal. On the contrary, it is the action of great masses, of millions of people, called upon to carry out their historic mission and to make a reality of what has become an historic necessity.

But the proletarian revolution is at the same time also the death knell of all slavery and oppression. This is the reason why the capitalists, Junkers, petty bourgeoisie and officers, and the beneficiaries and parasites of exploitation and class rule, are rising like one man to fight to the death against the proletarian revolution.

It is madness to suppose that the capitalists will submit voluntarily to the socialist verdict of a parliament or a national assembly, that they will calmly surrender their property, their profits, their privileges of exploitation. All ruling classes have fought obstinately to the end for their privileges. The Roman patricians, as well as the feudal barons of the Middle Ages, the English nobles and the American slave owners, the boyars (large estate owners) of Wallachia and the silk manufacturers of Lyons—all shed rivers of blood. They trampled upon corpses, they committed murder, ar-

---

[2] Here, and in the following paragraph, Luxemburg once again emphasized her position on the need for working-class consciousness and direct participation, which she used to attack Lenin's notion of revolution from above in 1903.

son, and state treason, they precipitated civil war for the purpose of defending their privileges and power.

The imperialist capitalist class, as the last offspring of the caste of exploiters, surpasses all its predecessors as far as brutality, open cynicism, and rascality are concerned.

It will defend its "holy of holies"—its profits and privileges of exploitation—tooth and nail. It will defend them with the cold-blooded viciousness which it manifested during the history of its colonial policy and during the last World War. It will move heaven and hell against the workers. It will mobilize the peasantry against the industrial workers. It will set the backward elements of the proletariat against the vanguard of socialism. It will get its officers to commit massacres. It will attempt to nullify socialist measures by a hundred and one methods of passive resistance. It will put in the way of the revolution twenty uprisings à la Vandée. To save itself it will invoke the assistance of the foreign enemy, the murderous armed force of a Clemenceau, a Lloyd George, or a Wilson. It will sooner turn the country into a smoking heap of ruins than voluntarily relinquish its power to exploit the working class.

This resistance must be put down with an iron hand, with the utmost energy. The power of the bourgeois counterrevolution must be met by the revolutionary power of the working class. The plots, schemes, and intrigues of the capitalist class must be countered by the ceaseless vigilance, clearness of vision, and readiness of the proletarian mass for action at any moment. The threatening dangers of counterrevolution must be met by the arming of the people and the disarming of the ruling classes. The obstructionist maneuvers in Parliament on behalf of the capitalist class must be met by the active organization of the workers and soldiers. The presence of the bourgeoisie everywhere and the thousands of means at its command must be overcome by the concentrated compact power of the working class developed to the highest possible degree. Only the united front of the entire German proletariat—the South German with the North German, the city workers with the agricultural workers, the working men with the soldiers—and the living spiritual bond of the German revolution with the International, the elevation of the German revolution to the height of the world revolution of the proletariat, can create the granite foundation upon which the structure of the future must be based.

The struggle for socialism is the greatest civil war in history, and the proletarian revolution must prepare for this civil war the necessary weapons; it must learn to use them—to fight and to conquer.

By arming the compact mass of working people with full political power for the purposes of the revolution, the dictatorship of the proletariat is established and therefore the true democracy. True democracy, democracy that does not defraud the people, does not exist where the wage slave sits in would-be equality with the capitalist, or the farmhand with the landowner, in order to debate in parliamentary manner over questions most vital to them—true democracy is to be found only where the mass of the workers take the entire power of government into their toil-hardened hands in order to wield it over the heads of the ruling classes as the god Thor wielded his hammer.

To enable the proletariat to solve this problem the Spartacus Union demands:

I. As Immediate Means for Making the Revolution Secure.

1. The disarming of the entire police force, of all officers, as well as of the non-proletarian soldiers.

2. The seizure of all supplies of arms and ammunition, as well as of all war industries, by the workers' and soldiers' councils.

3. The arming of the entire adult male population as the workers' militia. The formation of a red guard of the workers, as the active part of the militia, for the effective protection of the revolution against counter-revolutionary plots and risings.

4. Abolition of the commanding power of the officers and non-commissioned officers. The substitution of the voluntary discipline of the soldiers for the old brutal barrack discipline. Election of all superiors by the rank and file, with the right to recall these superiors at any time. Abolition of courts-martial.

5. The removal of all officers and ex-officers from the soldiers' councils.

6. Substitution of authorized representatives (Vertrauensmaenner) of the workers' and soldiers' councils for all political organs and authorities of the old regime.

7. Creation of a revolutionary tribunal to try the men chiefly responsible for the war and its prolongation, namely, the two Hohenzollerns, Ludendorff, Hindenburg, Tirpitz, and their fellow-criminals, as well as all conspirators of the counterrevolution.

8. Immediate seizure of all means of subsistence to secure provisions for the people.

II. On the Political and Social Field.

1. Abolition of all separate states; a united German Socialist Republic.

2. Removal of all parliaments and municipal councils, their functions to be taken over by the workers' and soldiers' councils and by the committees and organs of the latter bodies.

3. Election of workers' councils all over Germany by the entire adult population of working people of both sexes in cities and rural districts, along the lines of industries, and election of soldiers' councils by the soldiers, excluding the officers and ex-officers. The right of workers and soldiers to recall their representatives at any time.

4. Election all over Germany of delegates from the workers' and soldiers' councils to the Central Council of the w. and s. councils; the Central Council to elect the Executive Council as the highest organ of legislative and executive power. For the present the Central Council is to be convened at least every three months—the delegates to be reelected each time—for the constant control of the activity of the Executive Council and for the establishment of a living contact of the bulk of the workers' and soldiers' councils in the country with their highest organ of government. The right of local w. and s. councils at any time to recall their representatives on the Central Council and send new ones in their stead in case the former do not act in accordance with the will of their constituents. The right of the Executive Council to appoint or remove the people's representatives as well as the central authorities of the land.

5. Abolition of all class distinctions, titles, and orders; complete legal and social equality of the sexes.

6. Radical social legislation, reduction of working hours to avoid unemployment and to conform to the physi-

cal exhaustion of the working class occasioned by the World War; limitation of the working day to six hours.

7. Immediate, thorough change of the policy with regard to food, housing, health, and education in the spirit of the proletarian revolution.

III. Further Economic Demands.

1. Confiscation of all crown estates and revenues for the benefit of the people.

2. Annulment of the state debts and other public debts, as well as all war loans, except those subscribed within a certain limited amount, this limit to be fixed by the Central Council of the w. and s. councils.

3. Expropriation of the land held by all large and medium-sized agricultural concerns; establishment of socialist agricultural cooperatives under a uniform central administration all over the country. Small peasant holdings to remain in possession of their present owners, until they voluntarily decide to join the socialist agricultural cooperatives.

4. Nationalization by the Republic of Councils of all banks, ore mines, coal mines, as well as all large industrial and commercial establishments.

5. Confiscation of all property exceeding a certain limit, the limit to be fixed by the Central Council.

6. The Republic of Councils to take over all public means of transport and communication.

7. Election of administrative councils in all enterprises, such councils to regulate the internal affairs of the enterprises in agreement with the workers' councils, regulate the conditions of labor, control production, and, finally, take over the administration of the enterprise.

8. Establishment of a Central Strike Committee which, in constant cooperation with the industrial councils, shall secure for the strike movement throughout the country uniform administration, socialist direction, and most effective support by the political power of the w. and s. councils.

IV. International Problems.

Immediate establishment of connections with the sister parties abroad in order to place the socialist revolution upon an international basis and to secure and maintain peace through international brotherhood and the revolutionary rising of the international working class.

IV

This is what the Spartacus Union stands for!

And because it wants this, because it calls for it, struggles for it, because it is the socialist conscience of the revolution —it is hated, persecuted, and slandered by all open and secret enemies of the revolution and of the working class.

"Crucify him!" call the capitalists, trembling for fear of losing their moneybags.

"Crucify him!" call the petty bourgeoisie, the officers, the anti-Semites, the press lackeys of the capitalist class, trembling for the fleshpots of capitalist class rule.

"Crucify him!" call men like Scheidemann who, like Judas Iscariot, have sold the workers to the capitalist class and are trembling for the shekels of their political power.

"Crucify him!" repeat, like an echo, the duped, the deceived, the misled elements of workers and soldiers, who do not know that they are attacking their own flesh and blood when they attack the Spartacus Union.

In hatred and slander are united against the Spartacus Union all who are counterrevolutionists, enemies of the people, anti-socialists, all who are ambiguous, confused, afraid of light. This only proves that the heart of the revolution is beating in the Spartacus Union, that the future belongs to us.

The Spartacus Union is no party wanting to climb into power on the shoulders of the mass of workers. The Spartacus Union is only the conscious party of the proletariat. At every turn it calls the attention of the general body of workers to their historic duties. At every stage of the revolution it fights for the final goal of socialism, and in all national questions it represents the interests of the international revolutionary working class.

The Spartacus Union refuses to share government power with the lackeys of the capitalist class, the Scheidemann-Ebert element, because it sees in such cooperation an act of treason against the basic principles of socialism, an act calculated to paralyze the revolution and strengthen its enemies.

The Spartacus Union will also refuse to take over the

power of government merely because the Scheidemann-Ebert element have completely discredited themselves and the Independent Socialist party, through cooperation with them, has reached a blind alley.

The Spartacus Union will never take over the power of government otherwise than by a clear manifestation of the unquestionable will of the great majority of the proletarian mass of Germany. It will only take over the power of government by the conscious approval by the mass of the workers of the principles, aims, and tactics of the Spartacus Union.

The proletarian revolution can reach full clearness and ripeness only by struggling gradually, step by step, along the Golgotha path of the workers' own bitter experiences through defeats and victories.

The victory of the Spartacus Union is not in the beginning but at the end of the revolution: it is identical with the victory of the great mass of the socialist working class.

Arise, proletarians! To the battle! We have to struggle against a world, to conquer a world.

In this last class struggle of history for the highest aims of humanity our motto toward the enemy is: "Hand on throat and knee on the breast!"

DOCUMENT 2: *"Joint Declaration by the Independent Socialist Party (USPD) and the Communist Party (KPD) of January 5, 1919"*

Eric Waldman, *The Spartacist Uprising of 1919 and the German Socialist Movement* (Milwaukee: Marquette University Press, 1958) pp. 169–170. By permission. First appeared in the respective parties' newspapers *Freiheit* and *Die Rote Fahne* on January 5th.

Attention! Workers! Party Comrades!

The Ebert-Scheidemann government has heightened its counterrevolutionary activities with a new *contemptible conspiracy* directed against the revolutionary workers of Greater Berlin: it tried *maliciously to oust Chief of Police Eichhorn from his office.* It wished to replace Eichhorn with its willing tool, the present Prussian minister of police, Ernst.

By this action the Ebert-Scheidemann government wishes not only to remove the last trusted man of the revolutionary Berlin workers, but primarily it intends to *establish in Berlin a despotic rule antagonistic to the revolutionary workers.*

Workers! Party Comrades! The person of Eichhorn is not the main issue; you yourselves will lose the last remnants of your revolutionary achievements through this major blow.

The Ebert government with its accomplices in the Prussian ministry intends to support its power through bayonets and *to secure* for itself the *grace of the capitalist bourgeoisie,* whose disguised representative it was from the very beginning.

By this blow directed against the Berlin police headquarters, the entire German proletariat, the entire German revolution is to be struck.

Workers! Party Comrades! *This you cannot and must not permit!* Therefore, turn out for powerful *mass demonstrations.* Prove your power to the autocrats of today; prove that the revolutionary spirit of the November days has not been extinguished.

Come today, Sunday, at 2 p.m. to the impressive mass demonstrations in the Siegesallee!

Come in masses! Your freedom, your future, the fate of the revolution is at stake! Down with the despotism of Ebert, Scheidemann, Hirsch, and Ernst! Long live revolutionary, international socialism!

Berlin, January 5, 1919

The Revolutionary Shop Stewards of the large factories of Greater Berlin.

The Central Committee of Greater Berlin Social Democratic Election Association of the Independent Social Democratic Party.

The Central Committee of the Communist Party of Germany (Spartacist League).

DOCUMENT 3: *"Proclamation by the Revolutionary Committee Representing the Revolutionary Shop Stewards, the Central Committee of the Berlin USPD, and the Central Committee of the KPD of January 6, 1919"*

Waldman, *Spartacist Uprising of 1919* pp. 175–176. By permission.

Workers! Soldiers! Comrades!

On Sunday you demonstrated with overwhelming force your intention to destroy the latest malicious assault by the bloodstained Ebert-Scheidemann government.

Now there are more important things in the offing! It is necessary to stop all counterrevolutionary intrigues!

Therefore, come out of your factories! Appear in masses this morning at 11 a.m. in the Siegesallee!

Our task is to strengthen the revolution and bring it to fulfillment! Forward to the fight for socialism. Forward to the fight for the power of the revolutionary proletariat!

Down with the Ebert-Scheidemann government!

II : Béla Kun's 133 Days

The Bulgarians' suit for peace on September 29, 1918, which was taken up by the Turks several days later, signaled to the rulers in Vienna that the old Austro-Hungarian imperial order could no longer hold. On October 16th Emperor Karl issued a manifesto which turned Austria into a federated state of independent nationalities but significantly exempted Hungary from all of its provisions. At a time when the multinational empire was dissolving into its component parts—the National Councils of Czechoslovakia and Yugoslavia had declared their independence and Rumania was preparing to do the same—the die-hards of the old Kingdom in Budapest were still insisting on the territorial integrity of "historic" Hungary under Magyar hegemony.

The unrealistic Hungarian aristocracy, blinded by the perennial national disease of cultural chauvinism, was unprepared to deal with either the victorious Allies abroad or the increasing popular discontent at home. War-weariness coupled with political and economic grievances led to a series of bitter strikes in Budapest in 1917 and 1918 culminating in the general strike of June 1918, which radiated from the capital to all parts of the nation. Revolutionary propaganda found a ready audience in the ranks of the strikers. Even more receptive to radical slogans and manifestoes were the unemployed, whose numbers were swelled by some 680,000 prisoners of war, who returned from Russia and Rumania often still in possession of their weapons. As the gulf between the disintegrating government and the restive populace widened, one man, the liberal Count Michael Károlyi, appeared to fulfill the aspirations of contending forces: to the nationalists he seemed to be the man to get a sympathetic hearing from the victorious Allies; to the intellectuals and liberals he stood for peace and democracy; and to the leaders of social democracy he represented the means to the first stage of the revolution —a constitutional bourgeois democracy.

Károlyi quickly demonstrated his ineptness as a man of action, for even his appointment as Prime Minister on October 31st was wrested from the Hapsburg dynasty by the demonstrating population of Budapest. On November 16th Károlyi's government proclaimed a Republic, emphasizing its separation from the Hapsburg dynasty and the old Empire. For four and a half months a hapless coalition of Radicals, Social Democrats, and Károlyi's followers ruled like an interim committee without constitution or legislature. The fate of the new regime was sealed by its inability to make peace on favorable terms and to carry out agrarian reform. In the first task it was hampered by the Allies, who allowed the succession states (Czechoslovakia, Rumania, and Yugoslavia) to occupy some of the rich lands inhabited by a Magyar majority and traditionally subject to the Hungarian crown. It failed to achieve the second because both social democrats and communists opposed parceling out the land of the great estates to the peasants, on the ground that it would decrease output and make nationalization of the land more difficult. Károlyi's government, unable to rule or to find a willing substitute for itself, was given the *coup de grâce* by the Allies on March 20th, when Lieutenant-Colonel Vix, the French chief of the Armistice Commission at Budapest, demanded that the government withdraw from Magyar-populated communities on the Eastern frontier, including the major city of Debrecen. The political void which for less than five months had been filled so ineffectually by Károlyi was now reopened to invite and ultimately entrap the left.

As in Germany, the left in Hungary had been a significant movement before the old order had given way. The Social Democratic party, which was dependent on the trade unions, was reformist before 1914 and, even though all political rights were denied to the Hungarian workers, remained loyal to the government during the war. Only toward the end of the war, and partly in response to the Russian Revolution, did more radical organizations make their appearance in Budapest, which was the political arena of the nation. Until Károlyi came to power the radical left included an opposition group within the Social Democratic party, the Revolutionary Shop Stewards who had led the "spontaneous" strikes, the Hungarian Revolutionary Socialists who believed in terror and assassination, and the workers' and soldiers' councils. Of these the first three maintained their affiliation with the Social Democratic party, to which segments of the fourth also belonged.

To these groups must be added the Hungarian Communist party, founded on November 24, 1918, which as a catalytic agent radicalized the entire Hungarian left. As early as March 1918, Béla Kun and a group of Hungarian prisoners of war in Russia had founded the Russian Communist (Bolshevik) Party's Hungarian Group, which carried on Bolshevik propaganda among Hungarian war prisoners and trained leadership cadres to constitute a revolutionary nucleus at home. Kun and his fellow hot-house leaders returned to Hungary armed with the prestige of the Bolsheviks and the personal commendations of Lenin.[1] Kun and the Communist party directed their criticism not only against the ineffectual Károlyi regime but also against the social democrats, who defended themselves by moving to the left and joining the attacks on Károlyi and by turning against the communists. It is therefore not surprising that when the Károlyi interregnum came to an end on March 20th, the communist leadership was in prison.

From the outset the merger of socialists and communists into the Socialist party of Hungary on March 21st was a misalliance.[2] The proclamation of a Soviet Republic conveniently filled the existing political vacuum. In this coalition of convenience, which took power when all other parties dared not, each partner hoped to make significant gains: the socialists hoped that the violent attacks against them, particularly in the trade unions, would cease; the communists looked forward to being able to permeate the machinery of the mass

[1] The communists found it difficult to obtain a base among the organized workers who remained loyal to the Social Democratic party. Their support then and later came from the streets of Budapest—from the unemployed and discharged soldiers. Thus, whereas they were excellent agitators, they failed to develop a cohesive rank-and-file organization.

[2] Soon after the Soviet Republic was established, Kun made radio contact with Lenin and Zinoviev. Both wanted to know whether the communists were in control and expressed concern over the fact that the new party called itself "socialist" rather than communist. Kun allayed their fears and avowed the new regime's loyalty to the Comintern. It proved more difficult to change the party's name, which the Hungarian communists were able to do in June by agreeing to the compromise title Hungarian Party of Socialist-Communist Workers.

movement. During the Soviet Republic's 133 days of continual emergency the socialists proved to be the stronger contestants. They neutralized the communists, who as a governing party could no longer rely on the politics of the streets, by strengthening their hold on the trade unions and through them on the new fusion party, by controlling the leading positions in the Red Army, and by secretly negotiating with the Allies for complete power.

As bitter as this power struggle was to become in the latter period of the Soviet Republic, the first weeks were filled with optimism as the nation, feeling itself betrayed by the Wilsonian West, took heart in the military victories of the Russian Red Army and showed a willingness to participate in a Leninist experiment. The cornerstone of the Soviet Republic was an instrument of government largely patterned on the Russian model of July 1918. *The Constitution of the Hungarian Socialist Federated Soviet Republic* (Document 1), sketched a federated form governed by a National Congress of Federated Soviets and its executive arm, the Central Committee. The power of the National Congress was derived in an indirect and hierarchical manner from the local soviets. Power was wielded, however, by the People's Deputies or Commissars elected by the Central Committee. In short, the Republic of Workers', Soldiers', and Peasants' Councils subscribed to a federated structure overlaid with a highly centralized administration. Among numerous provisions the Constitution guaranteed freedom of speech, assembly, and religion; provided for the formation of a proletarian Red Army; guaranteed free education; and explicitly established the equality and cultural autonomy of national minorities. On the nature of the economy —a central issue of any socialist regime—the Constitution was decidedly vague, simply providing that all the means of production above the retail level would be nationalized.

As an instrument of government the Constitution was at best a rough outline that was filled in by hundreds of executive orders emanating from the various commissariats. In spite of tremendous confusion resulting from the inexperience of Kun and his fellow commissars, the invasion of Hungary by her neighbors, and the lack of trained and experienced administrators to carry out policy on the local level, important reforms succeeded in bringing education, medical care and public health facilities, and other social services to large segments of the population. It is not surprising that an inexperienced leadership should have made serious mistakes, for instance, the issuance of so-called "white" paper money which the population, particularly the peasants who controlled the food supply of the cities, considered unreliable. It is astonishing that a policy of wholesale nationalization was adopted. It appears as though Kun was attempting to prove that he could more effectively carry out the policy of war communism than his mentor Lenin. The effect of nationalization was seriously to curtail industrial production, causing commodity shortages that turned both workers and peasants against the government. The nationalization of large estates, which were converted into collectives generally managed by the local gentry and their agents, who were the most experienced administrators, automatically made many peasants enemies of the regime.

If the domestic policy of the Kun government was chaotic and given to fostering popular resistance rather than support, the foreign policy, by failing to satisfy Magyar national aspirations, doomed the Soviet Republic. The popular mandate in March was for a revolutionary government of national defense that would secure the old national boundaries against the power politics of the Allies and the expansionism of the succession states. In taking a hard line in foreign policy Kun and his cohorts counted on Russian troops, which in March stood virtually at the Polish border, and on a possible alliance with a Soviet Austria. By April the Russians, on the first leg of a general retreat, were already back in Kiev, and the Austrian Social Democrats resisted both a Leninist revolution and Hungarian entanglements. The Soviet regime was forced to face Rumanian and Czech invaders and a hostile Allied Commission in isolation. To mount such a defense while carrying on a full program of economic nationalization proved impossible, and the revolutionary government was forced to abdicate. The failure of the revolutionary experiment and a violent counterrevolutionary terror which followed in August emasculated Hungarian social democracy and the labor movement.

This failure was even more significant for the international communist movement. It was a clearer sign than the abortive Spartacist uprising in Berlin had been that other European states were not about to follow in Russia's revolutionary footsteps. Before the traces of events could be blurred by the passage of time, leading communists began a postmortem analysis to determine why the revolution had misfired. Of the many revolutionary leaders-in-exile who rushed into print with self-serving justifications, the most unbiased analysis was by Béla Szántó, former Commissar of War. Szántó enumerated (Document 2) what he believed were the causes for the failures of the Soviet Republic: the lack of loyal communist cadres to carry out local administration; the printing of untrustworthy currency; the appointment of former officers to commanding positions in the Red Army; the obstructionism of social democratic and trade union bosses. The cardinal error, he maintained, was the merger of the Social Democratic and the Communist parties in March 1919.

This last charge, which struck at the theoretical foundations of the Hungarian revolution, occupied the critics and defenders of the Soviet experiment, who regarded it as a lesson in principle and practice for the whole communist movement. Karl Radek, a leading figure of and troubleshooter for the Comintern ECCI, denied that the Hungarian Soviet Republic was an artificial creation resulting from the compromise of party leaders, and that the communists had merely inherited power from their exhausted opponents without struggle (Document 3). The Hungarian masses, he claimed, were on the march, and the communists had either to lead or desert them. He dubbed the revolution a "self-sacrificing battle of a revolutionary outpost on an advanced redoubt," which by creating a diversion had aided Soviet Russia against the worldwide counterrevolution.[3] The lesson to be learned by the Hungarian proletariat was that social democracy was its enemy and communism its only friend. The lesson for communists everywhere was to avoid uniting with anyone but communists.[4]

Paul Levi, leader of the German Communist party, attacked Radek's attempt to whitewash the Hungarian communists

[3] This was the first instance in which a revolutionary setback and proletarian sacrifice were interpreted as valuable because they benefited Soviet Russia. In the post-Leninist era of the Comintern this generally became the first consideration.

[4] This view anticipated measures taken at the Second World Congress of the Comintern to tighten discipline and to insure communist purity in the various national parties.

(Document 4). In his capitulation speech of August 1st Béla Kun had attributed his government's collapse to the abandonment of the leaders by the masses, who lacked revolutionary class-consciousness. Levi went much further by insisting that the Hungarian communists had fallen into the very pitfalls Rosa Luxemburg had warned about in the Spartacist Program: they had seized power simply because social democracy was at its wits' end and had thereby pulled its chestnuts out of the fire; they had engaged in a mechanical merger without the support of a revolutionized proletariat and were therefore at the mercy of the better-organized social democrats.

Although the Comintern virtually had no influence on events in Hungary, the setback there had a profound effect on its future course. The failure of the Hungarian Soviet Republic was in fact the fourth reversal for world revolution, for by August 1st the revolutionary sparks in Munich and Vienna already had been extinguished.

DOCUMENT 1: *"The Constitution of the Hungarian Socialist Federated Soviet Republic"*

The Class Struggle, III, No. 3 (Aug., 1919). First appeared in Jenö Pongrácz, *A Forradalmi Kormányzótanács és a Népbiztosságok Rendeletei* [The Revolutionary Governing Soviet and the Orders of the Commissariats] (Budapest, 1919), Vol. II.

Fundamental Principles

Sec. 1. In establishing the Soviet Republic the proletariat has taken into its hands full liberty, full right, and full power for the purpose of doing away with the capitalistic order and the rule of the bourgeoisie and putting in its place the socialistic system of production and society. The dictatorship of the proletariat is, however, only a means to the destruction of all exploitation and class rule of whatever kind, and the preparation for the social order which knows no classes and in which also the most important instrument of class rule, the power of the state, ceases to exist.

Sec. 2. The Hungarian Soviet Republic is the Republic of the Workers', Soldiers' and Peasants' Councils. The Soviet

Republic will not grant to the exploiters a place in any council. In the Workers', Soldiers' and Peasants' Councils the working people shall create the laws, execute them, and pass judgment upon all who transgress against these laws. The proletariat exercises all central and local authority in the Councils.

Sec. 3. The Soviet Republic is a free league of free nations. In its foreign policy the Soviet Republic shall aim, with the aid of the world revolution, to bring about the peace of the workers' world. It desires peace without conquest and without indemnities, based upon the right of self-determination of the workers.

In place of imperialism, which caused the World War, the Soviet Republic desires the union, the federation of the proletarians of all lands, the international Soviet Republic of the workers. Hence it is opposed to war as a mode of exploitation, opposed to all forms of oppression and subjugation of the people. It condemns the means employed by class governments in their foreign relations, particularly secret diplomacy.

The Rights and Duties of the Workers in the Hungarian Federated Soviet Republic

Sec. 4. For the sake of checking exploitation and organizing and increasing production the Soviet Republic aims to transmit all the means of production into the possession of the society of the workers. To this end it shall take over as public property all industrial, mining, and transportation establishments exceeding retail dimensions.

Sec. 5. The domination of financial capital shall be checked in the Hungarian Soviet Republic by turning all financial institutions and insurance companies into public property.

Sec. 6. In the Hungarian Soviet Republic only those who work shall have the right to live. The Soviet Republic prescribes general compulsory labor and, on the other hand, insures the right to work. Those who are incapacitated for work, or to whom the state cannot offer employment, shall be supported by the state.

Sec. 7. In order to insure the power of the toiling masses, and in order to thwart the reestablishment of the power of the exploiters, the Soviet Republic shall arm the workers and disarm the exploiters. The Red Army shall form the class-army of the proletariat.

Sec. 8. In the Soviet Republic the workers shall be able to express their opinion freely in speech and writing, for that power of capital which enabled it to degrade the press to an agency for disseminating the capitalistic ideologies and obscuring the self-consciousness of the proletarians, the dependency of the press upon capital, has ceased. The right to publish literature of every kind belongs to the workers, and the Soviet Republic shall see to it that the ideas of socialism shall be propagated freely throughout the country.

Sec. 9. In the Soviet Republic freedom of assemblage of the workers shall be absolutely guaranteed. All proletarians shall have the right to meet freely or organize processions. With the overthrow of the rule of the bourgeoisie all obstacles to the right of organization of the workers are removed, and the Soviet Republic shall not only bestow upon the workers and peasants the fullest freedom of union and organization, but shall also, in order to secure the development and permanency of their freedom of organization, extend to them every material and moral support.

Sec. 10. The Soviet Republic shall do away with the cultural privilege of the bourgeoisie and extend to the workers the opportunity for the positive appropriation of culture. It shall guarantee to the working class and the peasants free instruction, offering a high degree of education.

Sec. 11. The Soviet Republic shall preserve the true freedom of conscience of the workers by complete separation of church and state and of church and school. Everyone may exercise his own religion freely.

Sec. 12. The Soviet Republic proclaims the proposition of the unification of the proletarians of all lands and, therefore, grants to every foreign proletarian the same rights that are due to the proletarians of Hungary.

Sec. 13. In the Hungarian Soviet Republic every foreign revolutionist shall possess the right of asylum.

Sec. 14. The Hungarian Soviet Republic recognizes no differences of race or nationality. It shall not permit any form of oppression of national minorities nor any abridgment of the use of their language. Everyone shall be permitted to use his mother tongue freely, and it shall be the duty of all officials to accept any document written in any language in use in Hungary, to hear everyone in his native tongue, and to deal with him in that tongue.

The Central Organization of the Soviet Government

Sec. 15. In the Soviet Republic the supreme authority shall be vested in the National Congress of Federated Soviets.

Sec. 16. The jurisdiction of the National Congress of Soviets shall extend over all state affairs of high importance, in particular (1) the establishment and amendment of the Constitution of the Hungarian Socialist Federated Soviet Republic; (2) the establishment and modification of the boundaries of the country; (3) the declaring of war and the negotiating of peace; (4) the closing of international agreements; (5) the raising of state loans; (6) the supreme direction of external and internal policies; (7) the division of the country into districts; (8) the definition of the jurisdiction of the local councils; (9) the general direction of the economic life of the country, in its entirety as well as in its separate branches; (10) the establishment and modifications of the monetary system and the system of weights and measures; (11) the drawing up of the budget of the Soviet Republic; (12) the determination of the public burden; (13) the determination of the system of defense; (14) the regulation of the right of state citizenship; (15) state, civil, and criminal legislation; (16) the determination of the structure of the judicial system; (17) general or partial amnesty; (18) the supreme direction of cultural affairs.

All questions relating to the affairs over which the National Congress of Federated Soviets has established its authority shall be brought up in the National Congress of Soviets. During the time that the National Congress of Federated Soviets is not in session its jurisdiction shall be exercised by the Directing Federal Central Committee.

The following, however, shall come unconditionally and solely under the jurisdiction of the National Congress of Federated Soviets:

a) the establishment and amendment of the Constitution;

b) the declaring of war and the negotiation of peace;

c) the determination of the boundaries of the country.

Sec. 17. The National Congress of Soviets shall be convened by the Directing Federal Central Committee at least twice in each year.

Sec. 18. The National Congress of Soviets must be convened by the Federal Central Committee upon demand of the Councils of districts and cities whose population totals at least one-third of the population of the country.

Sec. 19. The Directing Federal Central Committee, which is to be elected by the National Congress of Federated Soviets, shall consist of not more than 150 members. All nationalities living in the country shall be represented in the Central Committee in proportion to their population.

Sec. 20. The Directing Central Committee shall, during the time that the National Congress of Councils is not in session, assume the conduct of state affairs; it shall exercise supreme legislative and executive power. During the other time it shall always participate directly in the control of state affairs. From among its members shall be chosen, besides the People's Deputies, all committees assigned to the People's Commissariats and supplementing the work of the People's Deputies.

Sec. 21. The Directing Central Committee directs the activities of the Workers', Soldiers' and Peasants' Councils as well as of all representative publications of the Councils. It shall care for the practical working out of the Soviet Constitution and carry out the decisions of the National Congress of Soviets.

Sec. 22. The Directing Central Committee shall report to the National Congress of Soviets concerning its operations. It shall keep the Congress informed of the general political and economic situation, as also concerning definite questions of greater importance.

Sec. 23. The Directing Central Committee shall be responsible for its actions to the National Congress of Soviets.

Sec. 24. The Directing Central Committee shall elect the Revolutionary Soviet Government and its President.

Sec. 25. The members of the Revolutionary Soviet Government are the People's Deputies. The Revolutionary Soviet Government shall appoint the People's Deputies to the heads of the various People's Commissariats and of the main sections of the People's Council for Political Economy.

Sec. 26. It shall be the duty of the Revolutionary Soviet Government to transact the affairs of the Soviet Republic in accordance with the injunctions of the National Congress of Soviets, as well as of the Federal Central Committee.

Sec. 27. The Revolutionary Soviet Government shall have the power to issue decrees. In general it may order all that is necessary for the speedy transaction of state business.

Sec. 28. The Revolutionary Soviet Government shall inform the Directing Central Committee forthwith of its decrees, decisions and any measures taken in important affairs.

Sec. 29. The Directing Central Committee shall examine the decrees, decisions, and measures of the Revolutionary Soviet Government, the People's Council for Political Economy, and all other People's Commissariats, and shall have power to amend them.

Sec. 30. The Soviet Government may take steps in state matters of decisive importance without previous dispensation of the Directing Central Committee only in case of extraordinary urgency.

Sec. 31. The members of the Revolutionary Soviet Government are responsible to the National Congress of Soviets and the Directing Federal Central Committee.

Sec. 32. The various People's Commissariats shall be, as follows: (1) the People's Council for Political Economy; (2) the People's Commissariat for Foreign Affairs; (3) for Military Affairs; (4) for the Interior; (5) for Justice; (6) for Public Welfare and Health; (7) for Education; (8) the German; (9) the Russian People's Commissariat.

Sec. 33. The various People's Deputies may, within the jurisdiction of their respective People's Commissariats, and the People's Council for Political Economy in questions coming under its jurisdiction, issue decrees and injunctions. The Revolutionary Soviet Government shall have power to amend the decrees of the People's Council for Political Economy as well as those of the various People's Commissariats.

Sec. 34. The jurisdiction of the People's Council for Political Economy shall extend over the uniform control of production and the distribution of goods, the issuing and executing of decrees affecting the national economy, and the technical and economic control of the agencies of production and distribution.

Sec. 35. The main divisions of the People's Council for Political Economy are as follows:

a) general administration of production, husbandry of raw materials, and foreign trade; b) agriculture and cattle-raising; c) technical direction of industrial production and channels of distribution; d) finance; e) public relief; f) traffic; g) economic organization and control; h) labor.

Organization of the Local Soviets

[Sections 38 to 65 concern the structure of the local system of councils, the prescriptions for suffrage, the powers and the mutual relations of the councils, which hold all political power in their hands. On account of lack of space we can reproduce only a few of the most important dispositions.]

The working rural population sends one member to the village council for each 100 inhabitants, the working urban population sends only one member for each 500 inhabitants to the city council. The village and city councils of a district elect the District Workers', Peasants' and Soldiers' Councils, in which the delegates of the cities may not comprise more than one half. For every 1000 inhabitants there is one member. The district councils of each county (comitat) elect the county councils, one delegate being elected for each 5000 inhabitants.

Sec. 48. The function of the village, city, district, and county councils shall be to promote in every way the economic and cultural welfare of the working people living within the borders of their respective territorial units. To this end they shall decide all matters of local significance and execute all decrees referred to them by their superior councils and People's Commissariats.

Sec. 49. The previously existing machinery of local administration herewith ceases to exist. The personnel taken over by the councils with the public offices and public works shall be at the disposal of the councils. The administration and other public buildings that have heretofore served the purposes of local government shall be transferred, together with their equipment, into the hands of the councils.

Sec. 52. The councils shall constantly observe whether the ordinances of their superior administrative bodies prove satisfactory. They shall direct the attention of the latter or of the appropriate People's Commissariat to any shortcomings and may present suggestions, if in their opinion any measure of the higher administration or of any other body seems necessary.

Sec. 53. The councils shall receive all the public works and institutions serving the dietary, hygienic, economic, cultural, and similar needs of the population, may create new ones and recommend the establishment of others to their superior councils.

Sec. 54. The villages, cities, districts, and counties shall conduct their financial affairs independently, within the limits ordained by the People's Council for Political Economy.

Sec. 55. The councils shall have power to choose and discharge officials and other trained workers, including the transferred personnel of the former administration. Any trust conferred upon an officer of the Hungarian Soviet Republic may be revoked at any time.

Sec. 58. In counties, cities, and districts special committees of experts (subcommittees) shall be regularly formed for the following affairs: (1) economic, financial, and industrial; (2) roads and public traffic; (3) public welfare and health; (4) housing; (5) public relief; (6) cultural affairs.

Sec. 62. The councils shall see to it that disputing parties receive prompt and accurate advice in regard to their cases without any formalities and in their mother tongue; that appropriate agencies exist for receiving oral complaints and requests; that, after the hearing of the interested parties and after a complete disposition of the case—based, wherever possible, upon direct observation of the circumstances—the requests be discharged within the shortest time possible, without awaiting solicitation, and the parties be notified thereof in appropriate form.

Suffrage

Sec. 66. In the Hungarian Socialist Federated Soviet Republic only the working people shall have the right to vote. All those are voters and eligible for election to membership in the councils, regardless of sex, who have passed their eighteenth year and as workers or employees, etc., live by work that is useful to society, or occupy themselves with household labor which makes possible the labor of the above-mentioned workers or employees, etc. Further, soldiers of the Red Army are voters and eligible for election, as well as those workers and soldiers who have formerly lived by useful labor, but have entirely or partially lost their capacity for labor.

Sec. 67. Citizens of other states shall also be voters and eligible for election, provided they fulfill the conditions contained in preceding sections.

Sec. 68. The following may not vote and are not eligible for election: a) all those who employ wage-workers for the purpose of obtaining profit; b) those who live off unearned income; c) merchants; d) clergymen and members of religious orders; e) those mentally deranged and those living under guardianship; f) those whose political rights have been suspended because of a crime committed from base motives, for the period of time stipulated in the conviction.

The Budget Privilege

Sec. 78. The Hungarian Soviet Government shall be guided in its financial policy exclusively from the point of view of the satisfaction of the needs of its workers. It shall show no consideration for unearned income.

Sec. 79. The branches of the Soviet Republic may collect receipts and defray expenditures only within the limits of an approved budget.

Sec. 80. The estimate of costs for the village, district, city, and county shall be determined by the appropriate local council upon the suggestion of the directing committee, the estimate of costs for the Soviet Republic by the National Congress of Soviets upon the suggestion of the Revolutionary Soviet Government or of the Directing Central Committee.

The Rights of Nationalities in the Hungarian Socialist Federated Soviet Republic

Sec. 84. All nationalities living in the Hungarian Socialist Federated Soviet Republic may use their language freely and foster and promote their own culture. To this end any national group, even if it does not live in a continuous territory, may create a federal council for the promotion of its culture.

Sec. 85. As a result of the Soviet system the local administration will be conducted by the workers of those nationalities whose workers form the majority in their respective local unit. This sort of local administration will naturally find expression in the matter of language. The national minorities may, nevertheless, use their own speech in dealing with the agents of the Soviets. This system cannot disturb the Soviet organization based upon territorial principles.

Sec. 86. Wherever the workers of any particular nationality in a continuous territory extending over several districts find themselves in the majority, independent counties shall be created.

Where any particular national group in a continuous territory extending over several counties finds itself in the majority, the districts may unite into one national county.

The counties united in this manner are, through the national county, parts of the Hungarian Socialist Federated Soviet Republic.

Sec. 87. The Hungarian continuous counties with German majority or Russian majority are herewith recognized under the Constitution of the Federated Soviet Republic as German and Russian national counties. In matters affecting the universal interests of the Soviet Republic the decisions of the Federated Soviet Republic extend to the national counties.

Sec. 88. The Hungarian Socialist Federated Soviet Republic shall interpose no obstacle if the national groups of the increasingly independent territories, empowered by their population and their economic strength, decide to form a separate Soviet Republic allied with the Hungarian Soviet Republic.

Sec. 89. The provisions of the Constitution relating to the rights of nationalities may be amended only with the consent of the Federal Council of the workers of the participating national groups.

DOCUMENT 2: Béla Szántó, *"The Real Reason for the Collapse of the Federal Hungarian Soviet Republic"*

Die Internationale: Eine Zeitschrift für Praxis und Theorie des Marxismus, I, No. 15/16 (Nov. 1, 1919).

. . . Since I have not yet come face to face with an even approximately faithful and authentic newspaper report reflecting the actual situation, I feel it incumbent upon myself to take the opportunity of my flight through Germany to explain to the German comrades the reasons why the existence of the Hungarian Soviet Republic had become an impossibility. May the German comrades learn from it in order to avoid those errors which have unhappily been committed in Hungary.

When we founded under the leadership of Béla Kun the Hungarian Communist party during the last days of November 1918, nobody, not even the greatest optimists among us, thought that we would after only five months' existence establish the dictatorship of the proletariat on that memorable March 21, 1919. Nobody thought of it chiefly because of the strong resistance on the part of the Social Democrats and the

bourgeoisie. Shortly prior to the proclamation of the Soviet
Republic Béla Kun was nearly beaten to death in prison by
the *Tisza* hussars, as the police and constables are generally
called in Hungary. The fact that he did not afterward revenge
himself when he had become the holder of real power, but
instead gave the simple answer to a question referring to this
matter: "They did not know what they were doing. They did
not know what I wish to do for them!" is a lasting testimony
to his magnanimity.

When Béla Kun and all the other imprisoned communists
were fetched from prison on March 21, 1919, his first step
was to advocate a merger of the Social Democratic and Communist parties under the name: "Hungarian Socialist party."

At this moment the seed for the decline of the dictatorship
of the proletariat was planted!

May this sentence forever resound in the ears of the German comrades, though it may appear quite peculiar to some
of them.

Only a few among us could already at that time anticipate
the fateful significance of this merger. Most comrades, including comrade Béla Kun, called us either overly cautious or
overly radical. But the course of events revealed in ghastly lu-
cidity how right I had been in my objections to the merger.

Strictly speaking, no differences had yet made their appearance when the government was being formed; no obstacles
were raised by the social democrats, and the former social
democrats entering the government honestly strove in the
beginning to cooperate along our lines.

But Budapest was not Hungary!

Many of the secretaries, leaders, and functionaries of the
former Social Democratic party and the trade unions suddenly
began to oppose us in secret, because in part they felt themselves crowded in the positions of power formerly occupied by
them. The local soviets—that is, the workers' and peasants'
councils—elected a directory from their midst performing the
functions of the magistrate, mayor, judge, presiding judge, or
the county committee, depending upon the size of the administrative unit concerned. Since other qualified candidates were
lacking, the very same leaders and secretaries of the old party
and the trade unions were frequently elected to the Executive
Committee of the Directory. Everybody has to admit that the

administrative work performed by these soviets was not of a communist nature.

We then proceeded by force of necessity with the establishment of the *"politika megbizot,"* called in German political commissars. A political commissar with extensive power, appointed by the People's Commissariat of the Interior, was thus attached to every executive committee of the county and district directories. It was the function of these political commissars to supervise the faithful execution of all decrees issued by the Soviet government. In by far too many cases these political commissars were viewed as troublesome rivals and controllers by the leaders of the local soviets. Instead of summoning all forces against the common enemy during this critical period, these former party and trade union bosses made it their task to combat the political commissars and often to slander them in a most foul manner. Travels back and forth to Budapest for every trifle were an everyday occurrence. The brawls of these people deserve a chapter of their own. To complicate matters, the office of the Commissariat of the Interior committed numerous blunders in that it seemed to view everyone who had demonstrably been a Russian prisoner of war as politically reliable and as serviceable in the department for political administration; due to the operation of this system totally incompetent and politically immature people were often dispatched as political commissars.

The second error lies in a situation which will possibly not occur with the German comrades.

Since my earliest youth I have been a radical socialist and never an anti-Semite. I want to preface the following description in this manner, so as not to pour oil on the enemies' fires and to give cause to their stupid racist propaganda. But if I as an honest politician record the causes of the collapse, I am obliged to ruthlessly illuminate all defects.

Due to the fact that in Hungary the most eminent communist leaders are of Jewish descent, a mass of politically indifferent Jews considered themselves entitled to crowd into all sorts of offices; to be sure, only into such where they expected to gain something for themselves. The local soviets, frequently completely unaware as to the state of affairs or the nature of the International, thought that by hiring preferably people of Jewish descent they pleased the government in Budapest. The business acumen inborn in these Jewish mercenary creatures

(I am consciously not saying Jews because a large number of my political friends are Jews and far superior to a number of so-called good Christians) caused in individual districts and departments corruption the nature of which defies description. This prevalent corruption, in which not only Jewish grocers participated but generally all those elements who had been brought to the surface by the revolutionary wave and for whom the description "hyenas of the revolution" is still an endearment, had made the confidence of the farmers illusory to the point where they spoke among themselves only of the Jewish government.

This, combined with the criminal, amateurish financial policies, was our deathblow. Instead of producing banknotes clearly identified as its own from the start, the office of the commissariat of finances proceeded with the production of reprints of the 1, 2, 25, and 200 crown-notes issued by the Austro-Hungarian Bank. These reprints were very crudely produced and immediately branded by Vienna as counterfeits. The farmer blatantly refused to accept this so-called "white money" in place of [regular] money, in spite of a legal rate of exchange and strict prosecution for non-acceptance of it. Imagine the situation: all members of the Red Guard, civil servants of the Soviet Republic, teachers, railway employees, postal clerks, in fact everybody else received their salaries in this so-called white money, but could obtain nothing for it in the countryside.

Woe to the government which has the peasantry against it. It leads but a shadow existence.

However, it was the office of the Commissariat of Military Affairs which perpetrated the most outrageous act. It, so to speak, killed the bird in the egg and built the casket for the dictatorship of the proletariat by issuing the most incomprehensible of all decrees, which restored the former officers to their positions as commandants. Comrade Béla Szántó will never be able to answer for that![5] Imagine: the officers are no longer called Lieutenant, Commander, etc., but

[5] Although Szántó was a member of the Commissariat of War, he did not become Commissar until June 24th, when it was too late to alter the conditions he complained about. Earlier the Commissariat had been led first by Jóseph Pogány and later by Kun, whom Szántó blames for the errors committed without naming them.

Company-Commandant, Battalion-Commandant, Regiment-Commandant, Division-Commandant, etc. This, together with the removal of all marks of distinction and the address "Comrade Commandant" was supposed to make instruments of the dictatorship of the proletariat out of this reactionary rabble. *Sancta Simplicitas!*

We saw how these ragamuffins work during the Pentecost revolution of the white scoundrels in the county of Eisenach; in unison with the clergy they did what was humanly possible to instigate the unarmed masses and to drive the deluded farmers with their antediluvian weapons (flail and pitchforks) by the hundreds in front of the devastating fire of our machine guns. I called this pack slave dealers at that time, but I was not yet believed. When the putsch by the tutors and students of the Ludovika Academy at Pest took place, people began to pay attention. But by then it was too late; the Red Army had already become infected, was already in a state of disintegration and had ceased to be an instrument of the class struggle. A few weeks later the final collapse took place.

Now to turn to the collapse itself. When comrade Béla Kun declared with a quivering voice the resignation of the Soviet government at the memorable meeting of the Council of 500, the Socialist ministry of Peidel was born. Haubrich as Minister of War took care that no disturbances occurred until the Rumanians and the turncoat, the arch-hypocrite Joseph the perjurer, arrived. On instruction of the Peidel ministry all local soviets and political commissariats were ordered to remain at their posts until further notice. In the interest of the general welfare this order was generally but reluctantly followed. These conscientious comrades were, a few days later, amidst horrible outrage and abuse, arrested by the officers' camarilla or tortured to death. But these assassinated comrades live on in the idea, and the seed which was sown during the four and one half months will sprout magnificently, and it will bear fruit a thousandfold when the time of the harvest comes. Then the proletariat will settle accounts on the basis of the principle: *vae victis!* An eye for an eye! A tooth for a tooth!

If one draws the quintessence of the foregoing the result is the following:

1. Unprepared assumption of the government;
2. Too few politically reliable comrades;

3. Merger with the social democracy;
4. Sabotage on the part of the former social democrats;
5. Blunders on the part of the office of the Commissariat of the Interior through its indiscriminate placement of former Russian prisoners of war;
6. Corruption;
7. Enmity on the part of the farmers;
8. Amateurish finance policies;
9. Appointment of former officers;
10. Superior military strength on the part of imperialist hordes of mercenaries . . .

DOCUMENT 3: Karl Radek, *"The Lessons of the Hungarian Revolution"*

Die Internationale, II, No. 21 (Feb. 25, 1920).

Comrade *Béla Szántó*, one of the Hungarian People's Commissars, relates in the pamphlet before us the short history of the rise to power of the Hungarian working class and the history of its defeat.[6] This first authentic account deserves to be read with the greatest attention by the international proletariat so that none of the experiences gathered by the Hungarian proletariat in its struggle and purchased at an enormous cost in suffering will be lost to the proletariat of other countries. Its victories and defeats were fought and suffered for not only by the Hungarian proletariat, but they are of great significance for the whole world proletariat.

The Hungarian revolution yields up before all else two lessons. It illuminates the question of the *seizure of power* and throws light on the *question of our relation to the other working class parties* who, without being communist, are forced by the course of events to seize power together with the Communist party.

When on March 21 a telegram brought news of the seizure of power by the Hungarian proletariat, many Western communists had the feeling that the Hungarian Soviet Republic

[6] This pamphlet, *Klassenkampfe und Diktatur des Proletariats in Ungarn* (Berlin, 1920), is an expanded version of the article reprinted above.

was an *artificial* creature, created as a result of an agreement between the Communist and Social Democratic parties, without a struggle against the bourgeoisie on the part of the proletariat. And because born without struggle, it had to perish; for only in the heat of battle would the proletariat develop those resources required for the preservation of the Soviet government. This opinion was also expressed here in the German press, and when the Hungarian Republic was actually crushed, various circles took this as a confirmation of the correctness of their apprehensions uttered in March. They appealed in this connection to a sentence contained in the program of the *Spartacus League,* written by Rosa Luxemburg, which said that the Communist party should not seize power simply because the Scheidemann government had ruined itself. This interpretation of the origin of the Hungarian Soviet Republic was in conflict with the facts as known already during the birthdays of the Hungarian Soviet Republic. Even those who, like the author, are not in command of the Hungarian language and thus could not follow all the phases of the struggle in Hungary must have known that a period of increasingly more intense class struggles against the social democratic-bourgeois coalition preceded this seizure of power. The article by Vargas, published in the *Wiener Arbeiterzeitung* immediately after the establishment of the Hungarian Soviet Republic, confirmed this. Károlyi as well testified that the social democratic-bourgeois government only resigned because its downfall was imminent due to pressure not only from without but also from within. Szántós' pamphlet provides a detailed picture of the disintegration of the social democratic-bourgeois coalition and the growth of the pressure by the working class. It is laughable to view the Hungarian Soviet government as the simple result of a compromise among party leaders. It was a *result of the revolutionary class struggle of the proletariat.* Whoever, in view of these facts, obstinately insists in depicting the establishment of the Hungarian Soviet government as a deterrent example is simply stuck on the sentence from the pamphlet "What does the Spartacus League want?" which reads: *"The Communist party is unwilling to seize power simply because the Ebert-Scheidemann government is stuck in a blind alley or because it has ruined itself."* This sentence was absolutely justified as a rejection of the putschist elements within the German Communist party

who, in December 1918, when the decisive majority of the
working class stood behind the Scheidemann people, thought
in terms of a quick seizure of power. But the born dialectician
Rosa Luxemburg would certainly have rejected having this
sentence recited like a surah of the Koran.

The idea of a simple collapse of the bourgeois-social democratic coalition, without the process of the collapse of the
bourgeois state at the same time being a process of the gathering of the proletarian forces, is entirely unhistorical. The capitalist state falls apart when it fails in the task of organizing
capitalist production to the point where the misery of the
masses increases and they become revolutionary. If under
such conditions the Communist party is not able to influence
these masses intellectually, to unite them and to weld them
into a factor of reconstruction, it would only mean that the
Communist party did not exist. If one inclines toward taking
Rosa Luxemburg's sentence literally, it would simply mean
that the Communist party cannot seize power even following
the collapse of the capitalist state, in which case the Communist party does not exist. But for such obvious insights Rosa
Luxemburg's mind was too profound. The cited sentence was
only a warning not to attempt to reap where one had not
sown; it was not a historical analysis or a historical perspective. The Hungarian communists have sown; they have
fought, organized, propagandized, and the fact that the Hungarian social democrats, having arrived at the end of their wits,
had to turn to the communists constitutes proof that the communists represented a force. What should the communists
have done when the collapse of the bourgeois-social democratic coalition became obvious, when the bourgeois members
resigned and the social democracy turned to the communists
with the suggestion of the creation of a Soviet government?
The enormous difficulties which awaited the Hungarian Soviet
government both in its external and internal relations were
certainly clear to the Hungarian communists. The Hungarian
sources of raw material, the Hungarian food warehouses were
under foreign occupation, and the Hungarian communists certainly knew that they would have to deal with a world of
enemies. Béla Kun wrote in his letter to Ignaz Bogar, dated
March 11, 1919: "*I can't help it, but I look forward to the
events with a certain incredulity. The present state of the
whole international working class movement compels me to.*"

If the Hungarian communists nevertheless refused to remain idle and instead took to the sword, they did so because they were revolutionaries, not political disputants. Marxian analysis indicated to them the enormous difficulties with which they were faced. But the same analysis told them that Europe was in the process of distinct dissolution and that one could not know what the next day might bring.

In the article written from prison, upon hearing the tidings of the collapse of Soviet Hungary, in order to oppose the dogmatic evaluation of the Hungarian revolution, I already referred to the *Times* of July 19 which characterized the world situation as follows: "The spectre of unrest haunts the whole world, from the Western United States to China, from the Black to the Baltic Seas; no society or civilization is so secure, no constitution so democratic that it is able to withstand this evil influence. The symptoms are everywhere present that the elementary bonds of society are torn and decayed as a result of the long exertion." Such was the real situation; to evade in this situation the struggle which cannot be evaded because the masses are surging toward it meant desertion, meant to leave the working masses in the lurch. For these masses would have fought nevertheless—but without leadership—making much larger sacrifices and gaining for it a much smaller result. It redounds to the honor of the Hungarian communists that in the face of these difficult circumstances they took up the fight, and there cannot exist the least doubt that this fight had much deeper consequences than the credulous critics of the Hungarian revolution assume. It has not only given expression to the will to freedom on the part of the Hungarian working class, but it has strengthened and deepened it. And if the momentary result is the suppression of the Hungarian working class, the time will come when the Hungarian proletariat will from a comparison between the Red and the White dictatorship derive the iron will for the victorious battle. The Hungarian revolution has done much toward revolutionizing the workers of other countries and it has improved the conditions of resistance of the Russian Soviet Republic— the first citadel of the world revolution—facilitating its victory over Kolchak, by placing for months obstacles in the path of the worldwide counterrevolution. Whoever views the world revolution as an entity, as a process, will not speak of the Hungarian Republic as an example of a wretched revolutionary policy, but rather as an *example of a self-sacrificing fight, of a revolutionary outpost on an advanced redoubt.*

Those who died in this battle will enter the pages of history not only as martyrs of the proletarian cause, but as its brave, courageous, and prudent pioneers. And the lesson taught us—opponents of the attempt to seize power on the part of a small minority—by their wounds, that their martyrdom lies in the following: that we have to place ourselves *where the working class fights its battle whether we triumph or suffer a defeat.* This lesson of the Hungarian revolution is also the lesson of the *second Munich Soviet Republic,* whose history was recently eloquently related by Paul Werner. And *Béla Kun* will stand forth in the history of the proletarian struggle, like Leviné, not as a revolutionary adventurer, but as a revolutionary leader; that is, as a leader in the sense in which Karl Marx understood the role of the leader of the revolution; as a leader to whom Marxism in fact reveals to the full extent the difficulties of the battle, without turning him into the disputant who believes fighting is only then justified when history assures him of victory by means of a notary public.

With the same determination with which Szántó described the collapse of the Károlyi regime, he describes the fight and defeat of the Soviet government, and reveals as one of its main causes the *tactical* error committed by Béla Kun and his friends. He relates that Kun said during the consultation with the communists on the day following the formation of the Soviet government: "It *went too smoothly,* I couldn't go to sleep. I spent the whole night figuring out where our error lay, for there must be an error somewhere. The whole thing was too smooth; we will stumble upon it but, I fear, only when it is too late." The error is obvious. The Hungarian social democracy, belonging to the most politically corrupt creatures of the Second International, was bankrupt. The masses escaped from its leadership. The left elements of the party decided on a desperate step, the formation of the Soviet Republic. A part of the right leadership resigned. But the mass of small trade union and party bureaucrats stood behind the left leaders when these turned to the Communist party with the suggestion of the formation of the joint government. If the Communist party did not want to leave the masses in the lurch it had to agree to the formation of the Soviet government jointly with the social democrats. But the error took shape at the point at which the communists helped to cover up the reality. Reality was the fact of the bankruptcy of the social democracy, not its conversion to communism. One does not become a communist by accepting the communist program. Weltner, Kunfy, or whatever the names of the leaders of social democracy are, may well have been honest in their intentions to realize the communist program; but it should be clear that they could not have developed overnight the measure of revolutionary energy and insight which is the mark of communism. For this reason it was necessary to keep alive in the masses the awareness that the leaders of social democracy —in accepting the basis of communism only by force of circumstance—would only fight when pressed by the situation and threatened by the masses. The Communist party should not have permitted the dissolution of its separate organization; it should not have declined to operate as the big stick, ready at any moment to move into action against Garbay, Weltner, and Kunfy. The coalition with social democracy was necessary; but the communists should have maintained the gallows next to the government buildings in order, if necessary, to demonstrate to their dear allies the concrete meaning of proletarian dictatorship. By dropping the necessary caution, the Communist party was in the hands of the vacillating elements of social democracy.

It is for that reason that the fate of the Hungarian Soviet government is of such significance to the West European proletariat. *Wherever in the West the Communist party is still in the process of formation, social democracy will be increasingly forced to accept the basis of communism. Communists everywhere might by the course of events be confronted with the necessity of a coalition and they will then everywhere be pressured by the proletarian masses—yearning for unity—not only toward coalition but toward unity.* And here the Hungarian experience teaches: unity only with communists. Communist is not he who embraces on paper the dictatorship of the proletariat, but he whose blood has already mingled with that of communists in a common battle, only he who has suffered in prison with us communists—in sum, only he who has proven by his deeds that his hands do not shake, nor his feet waver in the battle for life or death. What followed the downfall of the Hungarian Soviet Republic, the cowardly and vile betrayal on the part of social democracy which now serves as window dressing for the Horty government, without Kunfy and Weltner breaking with it in full publicity, will cure the Hungarian proletariat once and for all of all its illusions regarding the Hungarian social democracy. It will demonstrate to it that there exists only *one* party willing to fight till the last drop of blood: the party of communism. And like the error of the Hungarian communists which Szántó plainly presents here, the betrayal by Hungarian social democracy is equally suited in spreading the lesson of the Hungarian revolution far beyond the frontiers of Hungary. The lesson teaches us that this new epoch, no longer concerned with parliaments and discussions but with the question of life and death, requires united and strong communist parties capable of remaining at the helm of a ship in a strong gale. Szántó's book will not only relate to the proletariat of the world the fate of the Hungarian revolution, but thanks to its veracity will also serve it as a guide. This veracity in the exploration of their own mistakes which distinguishes Szántó's book is an offspring of the same determination which put the sword of dictatorship into the hands of the Hungarian communists on March 22; it is in fact the continuation of their struggles. This veracity is worth no less than the self-sacrificing devotion of the best who died for the Hungarian Soviet Republic. And the fighting world proletariat will be indebted to the Hungarian communists as much for their veracity as it owes them thanks for their courage . . .

DOCUMENT 4: Paul Levi, *"The Lessons of the Hungarian Revolution"*

Die Internationale, II, No. 24 (June 24, 1920).

In No. 21 of the *Internationale* comrade Radek has bequeathed to us what he has learned from the Hungarian revolution. His pleasure herein is twofold: firstly—*discendi voluptas*—to show that *he* has learned something from it, secondly—*docendi voluptas*—to show that *others* have not learned as much as he. He enjoys this second pleasure with the same frigid superiority with which the mountains of eternal snow look down upon the lower peaks. The lesser minds are "credulous critics"—in which case honest belief is presumably contrasted with the poor understanding—and "political disputants," etc. Since according to my knowledge no one except myself has "reasoned" in Germany in this manner, I have the honorable task to bring this "dispute" to a conclusion, with due consideration to what comrade Radek had to say about it.

First the facts.

On March 22, 1919 the Soviet government was proclaimed in Budapest. On March 24, 1919 I wrote in the Hanau *Freiheit*—the *Rote Fahne* had again become an object on which Gustav Noske tested the freedom of the press[7]—an article on the Hungarian events which read in part as follows (after the bankruptcy of the Hungarian bourgeoisie had first been described):

> In this situation the proletariat enters the stage, summoned by Count Károlyi and the Hungarian bourgeoisie itself. The Soviet Republic is proclaimed in Hungary and the proletariat seizes power. The call resounds to the proletariat of the world but particularly to those who are today's shock troops of the world revolution, the Russian brothers.
>
> This is actually a moment of impressive greatness. A low-bent and broken people, deprived of all light and air, all prospects and hope, hurls itself into the arms of the International, sounding the tocsin so that its shrill sound rings throughout the world.
>
> And yet, in the face of all the might and majesty of these events, we should not disregard the historical context, the *manner* in which this was all brought about. And here it must be said: the new revolution in Hungary, replacing the bourgeois democracy with the Soviet government, is not the immediate result of a battle given by the Hungarian proletariat to the Hungarian bourgeoisie and the Hungarian Junkers. It is not the result of a struggle between the proletariat and the bourgeoisie in which the latter has been vanquished, but is simply the result of the fact that the

[7] Noske was given a ministerial post by the Ebert government and made responsible for internal security. He succeeded in crushing the Spartacist uprising of January 1919 in Berlin and subsequently outlawed the Communist party and its chief paper *Die Rote Fahne*.

Hungarian bourgeoisie—another expression is hardly more appropriate—kicked the bucket. It perished in shame and dishonor and the only force which remained was the proletariat.

This is precisely the case we had in mind in the framing of our program [of the Spartacists, see above] when we said "that the Communist party is unwilling to seize power simply because—speaking of Germany—the Ebert-Scheidemann government is stuck in a blind alley or because it has ruined itself."

This case has just now materialized in Hungary and it almost seems to us as if the first moves of this new Hungarian revolution already demonstrate the correctness of our views. As far as we are concerned, the possibility for the dictatorship of the proletariat does not exist when the bourgeoisie collapses but when the proletariat ascends—when, in other words, it has acquired in the process of a constant revolutionary struggle the intellectual maturity, the determination and the insight to realize that salvation lies in its dictatorship alone; it will become possible when the last proletarian is filled with the belief in socialism.

To illustrate: the German proletariat held power on November 9th. It was the strongest factor contending for power in the Reich; before its determination everything bent low. Why did it not hold on to this position of power? Because its power too did not rest on a victory but on the bankruptcy of November 9th; because the proletariat as a whole, as a mass lacked the insight on that day that it had to establish the dictatorship. The will of the German proletariat was excluded because it had ceased already on November 10th to possess a will, because it had begun already on November 10th to return to the bourgeoisie by way of the "unity of all socialists"—meaning by way of Ebert-Scheidemann—that power which had just slipped from its hands.

And what about the present events in Hungary? The proletariat gains power as a result of the collapse of the bourgeoisie. Does it have the intellectual maturity nevertheless? We are seeing only one thing; in the beginning of this revolution too stands the "unity of all socialists"; the same scoundrels who betrayed the Hungarian proletariat as Ebert-Scheidemann betrayed the German proletariat

now rave for the Soviet Republic and the dictatorship of
the proletariat.

That is the danger which is awaiting the Hungarian
revolution already today and which we have to point to for
the sake of our brothers in Hungary and for the sake of the
German movement.

I do not think that there exist many today who will find
this analysis, made two days after the events, faulty in its
main outline. I further think that all subsequent critics—in
the best sense of the word, naturally—are able to diagnose
nothing more than what had been said at that time. Even
Radek does no more. For when he writes in his article: "What
followed the downfall of the Hungarian Soviet Republic, the
cowardly and vile betrayal on the part of the social democracy . . . will cure the Hungarian proletariat once and for
all of all its illusions regarding the Hungarian social democracy," it is nothing more than the assertion that such traitors
had been included in the foundation of the Soviet fortress.
Radek in fact speaks freely about the "tactical error" committed in this connection by Béla Kun and his friends.

It should thus be possible to admit that what I wrote has
been justified by the course of events and that my skepticism
on March 24, 1919 was not just general "defeatism"—saying
"I told you so" when things went wrong—but rather pointed
up the heel of Achilles of the Hungarian revolution.

I find myself thus in the curious situation of having to
defend myself against having been correct, and I will therefore address myself to the reasons adduced by comrade
Radek to show why right has been wrong and wrong been
right.

To begin with, I am even in polemics against my friend
Radek a friend of clarity. And clarity in this case means to
assert that the proletariat of Hungary and thus the proletariat
of the world suffered a defeat in Hungary. One should
not conceal this fact by explanations like the following:
". . . there cannot exist the least doubt that this fight had
much deeper consequences than the credulous critics of the
Hungarian revolution assume." This is on the same plane as
when certain German professors and literati assert that the
German defeat has strengthened the "inner nature" of the
Germans, etc. It is nothing more than the assertion that every

evil, even the worst, has its propitious side. Since, however, we communists can solve our critical and leading task only if we decline to participate in such comforting nonsense, it is incumbent upon us to recognize the fact of defeat.

Having recognized this fact we have to examine the following questions:

1. Could the coming defeat of March 22nd be anticipated?
2. Is it the duty of communists to join in tactics which presumably were bound to lead to defeat?

II

I am proceeding with the answer to the first question not without a feeling of uneasiness. For I know that to judge badly an action after it has gone badly easily invites the impression of "self-righteousness" and of "knowing-all" at the expense of others, and nothing is more alien to me than that. In fact I go even further and admit that I do not even know whether I would have acted differently, had I been any one of the Hungarian friends, than they did; for it is a known fact that the judgment of any politician in the midst of the action is not the result of a sober evaluation but is dependent in varying degrees on intangibles, such as the intellectual atmosphere of the given moment, which deflect purely theoretical judgment and either weaken or strengthen the acuity of judgment. What I am saying here is thus not "cleverness," though comrade Radek would love to have it viewed as such, but a critical examination of what happened in Hungary; it has equally nothing to do with putting on airs, for I do not place *myself* in relation to the proclamation of the Soviet Republic in Hungary, but our party program and its author.

But to come to the point, the key to my criticism lies in the sentence of the Spartacus program "The Communist party is unwilling to seize power simply because Ebert-Scheidemann are stuck in a blind alley or have ruined themselves."

According to Radek this sentence had been wholly justified as a rejection of the putschist elements of the German Communist party, but "Rosa Luxemburg would certainly have rejected having this sentence recited like a surah of the Koran."

In this view I am in agreement with comrade Radek. I too think little of the sacerdotal inclinations of Rosa Luxemburg, in fact as little as of his own or my own. On the other hand I value the political qualifications of Rosa Luxemburg too highly to believe that she was here simply engaged in political casuistry, in drawing up at a moment of opportunist caprice a sentence designed for Germany, December 1918. I rather assume that this sentence in the party program constitutes a deduction from a political principle. We would thus proceed logically, in my view, if we attempt to locate this principle; if this succeeds we have to explore further whether it is applicable to Hungary and to decide the Hungarian case accordingly. This logical procedure should have been all the more obvious since it only involved comrade Radek's reading of the following sentence in which Rosa Luxemburg outlined the positive presuppositions for the assumption of power by the communists:

The Spartacus League will never assume governmental power unless by means of the clear, unequivocal will of the large majority of the proletarian masses in Germany, never otherwise than by means of their conscious consent to the prospects, aims, and fighting methods of the Spartacus League.

Thus the principle guiding Rosa Luxemburg has been fairly satisfactorily expressed: that is, that the positive criterion, so to speak, for the seizure of power by the proletariat lies within the *proletariat* and is expressed in the revolutionary stage of development in which the proletariat finds itself.

On the basis of this principle Rosa Luxemburg came to a conclusion about the November and December situation in Germany in 1918. What is decisive is not the negative action on the part of the bourgeoisie but the positive action on the part of the proletariat.

In reply comrade Radek has ready a simple recipe. He writes: "The idea of a simple collapse of the bourgeois-social democratic coalition, without the collapse of the bourgeois state at the same time being a process of the gathering of the proletarian forces, is entirely unhistorical."

In that case I dare to have this unhistorical idea. Comrade Radek's concept involves simply the following: the bourgeoisie on the one hand and the proletariat on the other constitute in a sense a system of communication tubes in which the outflow of one is the inflow of the other, or a minus in the one *mechanically* calls forth a plus in the other. I on the other hand believe that all thinking along mechanical lines is especially unhistorical and I am moreover of the particular opinion that there is not necessarily a correlation between the degree of purpose and determination of the proletariat and the degree of carelessness and disorganization of the bourgeoisie. I think we have evidence for this in the above-cited example of Germany in November 1918, where a momentary total powerlessness and carelessness of the bourgeois was not balanced by a corresponding degree of clarity and determination but an equally great powerlessness and carelessness on the part of the proletariat. The case cited by comrade Radek in which the downfall of the bourgeoisie involves at the same time a consolidation of the proletariat in such a manner that the moment of cessation of bourgeois power coincides with the ascent of the proletariat to it is *perhaps possible* but *not at all inevitable;* it might indeed be more appropriate to say that normally—as far as it is at all possible to speak of norms in history—a twilight zone interpolates itself between the bourgeois night and the proletarian day. It is in the condition of such twilight, in which the power of the bourgeoisie in certain cases is already so diminished that the seizure of power by a small minority becomes conceivable, that the first great and positive task devolves upon us communists: the organization of the proletariat as a class in the soviets. I maintain that the result of this phase of the organization of the proletarian class—which cannot proceed either according to some formula along a "soviet system," but will be an up-and-down movement of battles, demonstrations, actions, etc.—will be decisive in determining the moment of the seizure of power by the communists, and that Rosa Luxemburg said nothing more nor less.

All Hungarian comrades as well as Radek and myself are after all agreed on the fact and the manner of the mistake of the Hungarian comrades.

This error, [says Radek] is obvious. Hungarian social democracy, belonging to the most corrupt creatures of the Second International, was bankrupt. The masses escaped from its leadership. The left elements of the party decided on a desperate step, the formation of the Soviet Republic. . . . If the Communist party did not want to leave the masses in the lurch it had to agree to the formation of the Soviet government jointly with the social democrats.

Comrade Radek establishes in this sentence two facts which ought to be treated separately. Firstly he refers to the fact that Hungarian social democracy had failed and that the masses were moving leftward in the direction of communism. The process of organization and consolidation of the proletarian class on the basis of communism had thus entered a particularly crucial stage and even I readily admit that the firmness and determination of the masses in such a stage may grow in a very short time, perhaps within days, to the point where it provides a sound foundation for a soviet republic. At such a time everything depends on the *manner* in which this process of consolidation proceeds, and what we communists have to do in order to make it as lasting and as thorough as possible.

The Hungarian comrades now had taken the road toward an alliance with the social democrats, who declared themselves in agreement with the communist program—that is, they accepted the "basis of the given situation"—and who became with almost all their leaders at their head communists overnight. Radek fundamentally approves of this approach and this is his second assertion in the sentence quoted above. He adds:

The coalition with social democracy was necessary; but the communists should have maintained the gallows next to the government buildings in order, if necessary, to demonstrate to their dear allies the concrete meaning of proletarian dictatorship. By dropping the necessary caution, the Communist party was in the hands of the vacillating elements of the social democracy.

I realize quite well that the allusion to the gallows as an instrument of government makes an unusually strong and manly impression, and that all those who doubt the omnipotent effect of this instrument of power easily provoke the contrary impression. As much as I am thus aware of the resulting danger I have to say this: I think that under the dictatorship of the proletariat thorough and drastic measures against the bourgeoisie are necessary; I can even imagine difficult situations in which the proletariat is forced to maintain its own power in the face of the fainthearted or traitors in its own ranks by means of drastic measures. But to propose the gallows, at the moment of the establishment of Soviet power, as the method of unifying and amalgamating the proletariat; to undertake the organization and consolidation of the proletariat not on the basis of the "clear, unequivocal will of the large majority of the proletariat," "its conscious consent to the prospects, aims, and fighting methods" of the communists (according to Rosa Luxemburg), but on the basis of mutual hangings, all this strikes me—I don't want to use strong words—as a very unfortunate method for the unification of the proletariat. Neither do I think that this method has ever been practiced, nor that there exist prospects for its use. I am not aware that for example the Russian Soviet Republic adopted to the hammer and sickle the gallows as the third link of their emblem; I do not think that this omission is due to accident or to shamefacedness, but simply to the fact that the Russian Soviet Republic has been erected on the basis of different foundations than those proposed for Hungary by comrade Radek. The bond holding the proletarian class as such together perhaps cannot be a garland of roses, but it certainly cannot be the noose of the executioner.

I therefore think that the approach suggested by comrade Radek does not need to be discussed seriously. I consider it fundamentally wrong and believe that in all similar cases no other approach is possible than that carried out by the Munich comrades [see the next chapter below] under the leadership of Leviné, which corresponds to the spirit of the Spartacus program. And this spirit involves the questioning of the working class itself through elections of factory councils, or better yet, through election of workers' councils, and the direction of these elections under such slogans as stand in the sharpest possible contrast to the current "socialist" leadership of the working class. The more trenchantly these slogans are formulated, the more effective they will be. If the working class adopts these slogans then the ditch which it builds against its present leadership is correspondingly deep; it becomes conscious of stepping across the Rubicon. If the proletariat on the other hand rejects such slogans formulated by us, if it hesitates in the crossing of the Rubicon, then we communists should not act as if it were ready to cross the Rubicon. Naturally I lack the precise knowledge of Hungarian conditions to indicate what slogans the communists should have raised in a concrete situation. But I can easily imagine that demands, such as for example the arrest of Garbay, Weltner, and Kunfy could have been raised. With this method it seems to me the error might have been avoided that no one else recognized and expressed as clearly as Béla Kun himself when he said, "It went too smoothly." And on the basis of this sentiment of Béla Kun, on the basis of the present exposition, together with what I wrote on March 24, 1919 as an application of these thoughts, I answer to the question as to whether the coming defeat in Hungary could be anticipated with a Yes. . . .

III: The Bavarian Soviet Republic

Bavaria was one of the German states least likely to experience a revolution. Not only was it a Roman Catholic and monarchical society largely of peasant proprietors, but even its Social Democratic party under the leadership of Georg von Vollmar, a champion of reformism, desired nothing more than the gradual transition toward political democracy. Yet, revolution did come and, though at first it consisted of little more than a changing of the guard, its momentum and intensity grew, and Munich, its focal point, appeared to the communist movement as another telltale of world revolution.

War-weariness, the anachronism of the Wittelsbach dynasty, and news of the collapse of the Hapsburg monarchy and the naval mutiny in Kiel created a sense of expectancy at the beginning of November 1918, but the forces for a political, not to speak of a social, revolution appeared to be lacking. The revolution of November 7th, which began as a demonstration by social democrats against the war and which ended with Kurt Eisner leading the soldiers of the Munich garrison in taking over the state, came as a surprise to everyone. Eisner, who was the leader of the Independent Socialists, may well have planned that demonstration with the Majority Socialists in the hope of delivering a fatal blow to the old regime, but he could not have anticipated the enthusiastic support of the soldiers nor the capitulation of the chief of police and other authorities.

On November 8th a republic was proclaimed with Eisner as the head of a coalition government of Independent and Majority Socialists, which ostensibly derived its power from the hurriedly organized soldiers' and workers' councils. Eisner and his Council government found itself ill-prepared and isolated: lacking administrative experience, it relied on the existing bureaucracy; in the absence of a firm base among the population, it was forced to collaborate with the Majority Socialists and peasant organizations at the price of postponing the social revolution until an indefinite future time. Eisner's need to compromise led him to surrender the important Ministry of the Interior to Erhard Auer, the conservative leader of the Majority Socialists, who had no intention of letting the councils become a political force. Had Eisner wanted to establish the supremacy of the councils it would have been imperative to keep their executive supervision in his own hands, but his fear of Bolshevism prompted him to search for a balance between the parliamentary and council systems. The Majority Socialists considered the councils a threat to their authority within the working class and gave their support to parliamentary government in which they would be bound to play an important role.

Compromise and equivocation led Eisner to agree to elections of the Bavarian State Assembly, which demonstrated that in a democratic republic he had no mandate at all. The crushing electoral defeat for Eisner and his Independent Socialist party on January 12, 1919 was accompanied by a serious economic crisis which had been developing since the armistice. High unemployment, a coal shortage, and a housing shortage in Munich coupled with inflation throughout Bavaria fanned radicalism in the councils and threatened to make the streets the arena for political settlement. Eisner still nominally retained their leadership, although he had lost all control of the political situation: he had neither the mandate to remain the leader of a parliamentary government, nor was he prepared to use force in establishing a soviet system. He had decided to step down and was in fact on the way to inform the State Assembly, meeting for the first time on February 21st, of his decision, when he was struck down by the bullets of the monarchist fanatic Count Anton von Arco-Valley.

Eisner's assassination threw Bavaria into a state of anarchy and reestablished that power vacuum which the *ad hoc* Republic of the previous four months seemingly had filled;[1] it also ushered in the second and third stages of the Bavarian

---

[1] It seems more than likely that had Eisner been permitted to tender his resignation on February 21st, the Bavarian revolution would have ended then and there. A legally elected parliamentary government consisting of a Majority Socialist and Democratic coalition would have constituted a legitimate and viable regime able to withstand almost any opposition.

revolution at a time when elsewhere in Germany Noske and the Free Corps already had triumphed. After weeks of jockeying for power by the councils and the Majority Socialists, the State Assembly was convened on March 18th and gave full legal authority to a cabinet under Majority Socialist Johannes Hoffmann. But the time for parliamentary government had passed; a deepening of the economic crisis, which in Munich brought the economy to a virtual standstill, perpetuated the climate of expectancy. On April 7th a rump of an *ad hoc* central committee of the left seized power in Munich and proclaimed the Soviet Republic of Bavaria. The Hoffmann ministry went into exile at Bamberg in the North.

The creation of the Soviet Republic failed to clear the air, since no one seemed certain of where the new locus of power lay. The leaders of the new government including the pacifist scholar Gustav Landauer, the Expressionist playwright Ernst Toller, and the anarchist poet Erich Mühsam, were an odd conglomeration of political novices who had come to the fore in the last few months and who lacked a political base anywhere. The relationship between these leaders and the organization of the left—the workers' and soldiers' councils, the Shop Stewards, and the former followers of Eisner—was tenuous at best. The opponents of the Soviet Republic were easier to identify than its supporters. The Hoffmann government-in-exile considered itself the only legitimate authority in Bavaria and entered into consultations with Ebert's government in Berlin about means of realizing its claims. At the other end of the political spectrum, the Communist party under the leadership of Eugen Leviné dubbed the new regime the "pseudo-Soviet Republic" and claimed that it was the artificial creation of romantic adventurers. Ironically, due to fragmentary information, the Comintern and the Hungarian Soviet Republic were dazzled by the new government's name and welcomed it to the family of communist nations.

The proclamation announcing the creation of the Soviet Republic (Document 1), broadly sketched the outlines of the new order. It was to be based on the councils, led by People's Commissars, and administered by leftists of all persuasions aided by the lower and middle echelons of the old bureaucracy. The press was to be nationalized, a Red Army and Revolutionary Tribunal were to be created, and friendly relations were to be established with Soviet Russia and Soviet Hungary, but not with Berlin. In a matter of days this proclamation was amended by hundreds of decrees providing for the economic and social transformation of Bavaria. The Communist party immediately declared war on the new regime (Document 2). It denied the existence of a true soviet republic, which could only be created by the revolutionary masses, called for the election of a new revolutionary council, which alone could determine the tempo of the revolution, and directed the working class to follow only the directives of the Communist party.

An unsuccessful coup on April 13th engineered by Ernst Schneppenhorst, Minister of Military Affairs of the government-in-exile, among the Republican Soldiers Corps in Munich swept away the first Soviet Republic. The communist leaders Eugen Leviné and Max Levien now took command of the second, even though its prospects were hopeless. Hoffmann, who until now had been opposed to using outside forces to settle Bavaria's internal problems, gave way to Ebert's demands that military means be used. Isolated in the South, without hope of aid from Hungary, Austria, or Russia, and with North Germany subdued by the Free Corps, the end of the second Soviet Republic was only a matter of time. On May Day advanced units of the Free Corps troops commanded by the Prussian General von Oven entered Munich, and the white terror began.

Since the Bavarian communist leaders were either murdered, imprisoned, or dispersed during the counterrevolution, the task of assessing the revolutionary experience was left to leaders of the KPD in Berlin. The discussion of the Soviet Republic in the pages of the party's theoretical journal revealed two opposite directions with: the KPD in the tendency to view actions involving only fragments of the proletariat as mass actions which the party had to lead; and the inclination to husband the resources of the party, in view of recent reverses, and to build a base among the masses through specific but limited activities uniting various segments of the proletariat.

The KPD functionary Paul Frölich defended the Bavarian communists in general and in every particular (Document 3). The Bavarian comrades, he maintained, knew immediately that the pseudo-Soviet Republic was nothing more than a distribution of ministerial posts and criticized it accordingly. But the situation called for more, demanded that the communists put forward positive slogans for the organization of the masses. This they did until April 13th when the abortive putsch forced the party to take power. In doing so the communists not only responded to the dynamics of the situation but received justification for their decision from the victorious action of the masses in putting down the counterrevolutionary coup.

Paul Levi branded Frölich's notion of revolutionary politics deterministic (Document 4). Since the pseudo-Soviet Republic was not revolutionary, said Levi, the KPD should have stood by and seen it go to the devil and let it make room for some other government which did not arouse illusions among the proletariat. The KPD had acted correctly by fighting against the putsch attempt of April 13th because it threatened the positions of power attained by the proletariat of Munich. But these did not constitute a sufficient base for a soviet republic. The main error of the Munich comrades, Levi concluded, stemmed from their faulty political psychology: if the masses take action which is useless or injurious to the revolution and leads only to reverses, the party must warn and criticize; it must not lead.

Writing in August 1919, Levi had already concluded that an era of retrenchment had begun, and his postmortem of the Munich failure was intended to dampen the optimism and to dispel the illusions still prevalent at Comintern headquarters.

DOCUMENT 1: *The Revolutionary Central Council of Bavaria, "Proclamation of the Soviet Republic on April 6, 1919"*

Paul Werner [Paul Frölich], *Die bayerische Räte-Republik: Tatsachen und Kritik*, 2nd enl. ed. (Leipzig, 1920).

To the People of Bavaria:
The decision has been made. Bavaria has become a Soviet Republic. The working people have become master of their

own destiny. No longer separated from each other by parties, the revolutionary working class and peasantry of Bavaria, including all our soldier brothers as well, are united in the understanding that all exploitation and oppression must henceforth come to an end. The dictatorship of the proletariat, having now become a reality aims at the realization of a genuinely socialist republic, requiring of every working person participation in public affairs, and an equitable socialist-communist economy.

The Bavarian State Assembly, that sterile creation of the vanquished bourgeois-capitalist era, has been dissolved, and the ministry created by it has resigned. Shop stewards chosen by the councils of the working people and responsible to the people will receive as People's Commissars extraordinary powers within certain fields of jurisdiction. They will be assisted by trustworthy men from all the tendencies of revolutionary socialism and communism; the numerous capable forces of the civil service, particularly of the lower and middle echelons, are summoned to an active cooperation in the new Bavaria. The system of bureaucracy, however, will be promptly done away with.

The press will be nationalized.

A Red Army will be formed immediately for the protection of the Bavarian Soviet Republic against reactionary moves both from within and without. A Revolutionary Tribunal will speedily and ruthlessly punish all attacks against the Soviet Republic.

The Bavarian Soviet Republic follows the example of the Russian and Hungarian peoples. She establishes at once fraternal relations with these nations. She refuses on the other hand any cooperation with the contemptible government of Ebert, Scheidemann, Noske, Erzberger because it continues, under cover of a socialist republic, the imperialist-capitalist dealings of the German Empire which collapsed in disgrace.

It calls upon all German brother nations to proceed along the same road. The Bavarian Soviet Republic offers greetings to all proletarians, wherever they fight for freedom and justice and for revolutionary socialism, whether in Wurttemberg, in the Ruhr, or in the whole world.

As an expression of the joyous hope for a happy future for all of mankind we are herewith declaring April 7 as a national holiday. In appreciation of the departure from the accursed era of capitalism, work will come to a standstill throughout Bavaria on Monday, so far as it is not necessary to the life of the working people, about which more detailed regulations are published simultaneously.

Long live free Bavaria! Long live the Soviet Republic! Long live the world revolution!

DOCUMENT 2: *"Declaration of the Communist Party Regarding the 'Pseudo'-Soviet Republic"*

Werner, *Die bayerische Räte-Republik*. First appeared in *Münchener Rote Fahne,* April 11, 1919.

Workers! Follow only the Directions of the Communist party!

Workers! Soldiers! Working Peasants of Bavaria!

A Soviet Republic has been proclaimed by the party of the "dependents" and "independents," the Central Council as well as the so-called "Revolutionary Workers' Council."

As yet not a hair has been touched on the head of capitalism, but already bragging and lying proclamations are broadcast to the world which claim "the working people have become master of their own destiny."

As yet persists unchanged the exploitation of man by man —but in the proclamation the "departure from the accursed era of capitalism" is already planned.

We protest vehemently against these attempts to dilute or strangle the concept of a soviet republic through the proclamation of a *pseudo*-Soviet Republic.

The soviet republic has to emanate from the will of the working masses themselves if it is to be a genuinely proletarian one. Only the masses are authorized to proclaim the soviet republic by means of revolutionary councils specifically elected by them for this purpose.

The presently existing so-called "revolutionary" council can in no way be considered as such a representation of the working classes. It has not been elected by the masses. This *pseudo*-revolutionary council will not become an iota more revolutionary if it enlarges itself through the addition of any number of "dependent" and "independent" party delegates.

No single parties, comprising only a part of the proletariat, are in any way entitled to proclaim the soviet republic in place of the whole proletariat. Least of all are the "dependents"—the party comrades of Ebert and Noske, of Schneppenhorst and Durr—entitled to it.

Equally ill-suited are the "independents," those "independents" who are sharing the same party with the worst enemies of the soviet system.

We are now as much as ever filled by the unshakable conviction that only the establishment of a communist soviet republic will deliver the working class from want and misery. But we continue to be equally convinced that the establishment of this soviet republic can only be the work of the revolutionary masses.

Workers! Soldiers! Working Peasants of Bavaria!

We therefore call upon you to proceed at once with the election of such a body, which alone will be entitled to formulate your will and to put it into effect. Only this genuinely revolutionary council is competent and authorized to make the decision when to proclaim the proletarian soviet republic, when to begin the struggle for it.

Even the workers' committees are not entitled to make this decision, for they were elected for different purposes. The workers elected to these bodies were expected to have knowledge of the national insurance system, of the laws governing the auxiliary labor service, and similar snares of the capitalist slave era. From the members of the new revolutionary workers' council different qualities will be expected: those necessary in a stubborn revolutionary struggle against the citadels of the bourgeoisie and of capitalism and their *pseudo*-socialist accomplices.

Workers! Soldiers! Working Peasants of Bavaria!

Elect such a body!

If the "dependent" murderers of proletarians, the "independent" *pseudo*-socialists, and the anarchist counselors of confusion now proclaim a *pseudo*-Soviet Republic, do not believe this would make the election of a revolutionary political body superfluous. It makes it necessary more than ever before!

Like a soap bubble bursts or a house of cards collapses, in the same manner will that creation collapse which was spawned over the heads of the masses with an advertising skill and self-flattery fit for *pseudo*-socialist leaders—because it lacks inner strength.

Your representatives will have to watch closely in order to choose the proper moment for the release of the slogan: all power to the W[orkers]', P[easants]' and S[oldiers]' Council!

Workers! Soldiers! Working Peasants of Bavaria!

We call upon you to elect a Revolutionary Shop Steward in every factory; in plants with more than 1,000 workers, one for every thousand.

You should not confuse these elections with the elections to the factory councils and workers' councils, either. The workers' council, to be composed of representatives of the factory councils, is expected to carry out administrative functions following the conquest of power by the proletariat. It will perform all those tasks which evolve upon the proletariat after the seizure of political power.

In contrast, the new, yet-to-be-elected revolutionary council is to decide on the preparations for the seizure of political power. Moreover, it alone decides when the time has come for the proclamation of a communist soviet republic.

Accordingly, you will make your choice from among your comrades. If you elect to the workers' committees people familiar with the law and to the workers' councils delegates with knowledge and understanding of economic and administrative tasks, to the revolutionary workers' council you will have to elect men consumed by the fire of revolution, filled with energy and pugnacity, capable of rapid decision-making, while at the same time possessing a clear view of the real power relations, thus enabling them to act boldly as true revolutionaries and to choose soberly and cautiously the moment for action.

Workers! Soldiers! Working Peasants of Bavaria!

We urge you at the same time: Elect communists as Revolutionary Shop Stewards of your factories, elect communists as delegates to the revolutionary workers' council.

Workers! Soldiers! Working Peasants of Bavaria!

The need for political parties cannot be disposed of by decree on the part of some confused and enthusiastic political chieftains. We communists will as usual unite within the Communist party (Spartacus League) all our supporters seeking to struggle for the same goals by the same means. We will carry our ideas into the masses as before, drawing a sharp demarcation line between ourselves on the one hand, and all traitors to the revolution who have fought against the soviet system up to now and those ever-vacillating "independents" who have watered down the soviet system on the other.

We call upon you to maintain the profoundest distrust toward all steps taken by the founders of the *pseudo*-Soviet Republic. We request that you do everything necessary toward the winning and realization of the communist soviet republic!

Avoid demonstrations and celebrations in honor of the *pseudo*-Soviet Republic.

Workers! Follow only the directives of the Communist party!

DOCUMENT 3: P. Werner [Paul Frölich], *"The Munich Experience"*

Die Internationale, I, No. 9/10 (Aug. 4, 1919).

The Attitude of the Party.

It is impossible to render a historical account of the Bavarian Soviet Republic in the pages of this journal. But it is necessary already at this time to draw lessons from the mighty class struggle which shook Bavaria in April. We hope we are correct in the assumption that our readers are at least in broad outline familiar with these events.

At the time, the policies of the Communist party in Munich were violently attacked by the right; at present, objections against those policies are raised from within the party. Since the lips of the most qualified persons are forever sealed and since others are prevented from speaking at the present time, the task of the defense of these policies devolves upon me. In doing so, I trust to be able to render a service to the party in its future struggles.

It is a known fact that the proclamation of the Bavarian Soviet Republic in the first week of April was a treacherous act of demagogy on the part of the right socialists, and that the anarchists and "independents" were thoroughly taken in. We communists considered a soviet republic consisting of

Bavaria alone an absurdity. Bavaria is not economically self-sufficient, its industries are extremely backward, and the strongly preponderant agricultural population, while a factor in favor of the counterrevolution, cannot at all be viewed as pro-revolutionary. A soviet republic without areas of large-scale industry and coal fields is impossible in Germany. Moreover, the Bavarian proletariat is only in a few industrial giant plants genuinely disposed toward revolution and un-hampered by petty-bourgeois traditions, illusions, and weak-nesses. A Bavarian Soviet Republic appeared to us for this reason from the beginning a mistaken undertaking.

The Soviet Republic did not arise at this time from the immediate needs of the working class; its proclamation was rather to give the capitalists and their henchmen, the Major-ity Socialists, the longed-for opportunity to attain real politi-cal power. To drive the working class forward to an unten-able position, to use this as a pretext for the gathering of mercenary armies in order to crush the revolutionary move-ment—that was the program of Hoffmann and Schneppen-horst. The Communist party saw through the demagogic machinations from the beginning, even though it did not yet recognize in the rabble around Schneppenhorst the criminal element which later revealed themselves. To the communists, the avant-garde of the revolution, fell thus the task of apply-ing the brakes, of warning the masses in the most urgent manner of the snares set up by Schneppenhorst. This task the communists have fulfilled.

The aim and nature of the creators of this first Soviet Re-public also determined the manner in which they gave birth to their creature. They were not concerned with producing anything lasting. And the "independents," as well as the anarchists, lacked as much in historical sense as the right so-cialists in good will. The establishment of a Soviet republic was to them a reshuffling of political offices, the conse-quence of which was of little concern to them. For this hand-ful of people the Soviet Republic was established when their bargain at the green table had been closed, resulting in a neat distribution of ministerial positions among themselves. The masses on the outside were to them little more than be-lievers about to receive the gift of salvation from the hands of these little gods. The thought that the Soviet Republic could only arise out of a mass movement, and that the management of the affairs of state could not be the result of horse trading between individual party leaders, was far removed from them. While they achieved the Soviet Republic, they lacked its most important component: the councils.

The KPD in Munich fought this ridiculous dabbling in revolution with every critical weapon. But the action of Schneppenhorst, Toller, and Landauer nonetheless had a substantial result: the government disappeared and the so-called Soviet government took control of the state. At the same time this gave the revolutionary parties completely unlimited opportunities for action. This mere possibility made action imperative; if there ever really exist conditions under which the Communist party should confine itself to negative criticism alone, the present situation called for the supplementation of criticism by positive slogans. But these slogans compellingly demanded their own realization. The party criticized the deceptive maneuvers by the Majority Socialists, pointed to the absence of any mass movement, and declared that only the will of the masses themselves could be decisive in the installation of a government. In the first instance it could confine itself to enlightening the masses about the knavery of the Majority Socialists. But in the second instance, it was already compelled to summon all its forces to bring about the mass movement and to see to it that this mass movement was activated by a conscious revolutionary will. The KPD used the time, which the other parties spent bargaining at the green table, toward achieving this end by holding huge outdoor rallies and by agitating in the army barracks and factories. It endeavored with every means to channel the confused enthusiasm which the mere idea of a soviet republic had aroused in the masses back to a realistic evaluation of the facts. As a result, the workers of large-scale industry above all else came to show the necessary skepticism toward the adventurers of the Cafe Stephani. The KPD went further, carrying out the demands which derived directly from the action program of the party. It armed the workers in large-scale industry, as much as this was possible, in the face of the failure of the *pseudo*-Soviet Republic on all practical questions. The tension existing from the beginning between the working class and the Republican Guards, led by that miserable creature Aschenbrenner, led at once to the early creation of a military organization of the workers, to the placing of workers' guards at the approaches to factories, etc.

The organizational structure of the party had already been set up some weeks earlier under the energetic leadership of Leviné and was now being vigorously enlarged. In this manner the party gained the strongest influence over the whole activist part of the proletariat, particularly in large-scale industry. This was indicated by the fact that the shop stewards, elected as a result of our appeal, acknowledged our line.

This, in brief outline, is a description of the achievements of the party, which, it may be assumed, are generally approved by the membership.

Now the question must be raised whether one could stop with the criticism of the infantile play with revolution on the part of the great men of the Wittelsbach Palace, and with the consolidation of the party organization and the whole proletariat. The answer is: No! To make communist politics means to act in accordance with a clear, well-defined revolutionary will. *But the will of a party is as unfree as the will of an individual human being. It is not solely determined by general tactical precepts and guiding principles, but is dependent upon the situation.* It does not help us at all to say that the situation has been created by conscious or unconscious political criminals. Admittedly, the party could have declared: you prepared the stew, now eat it; I won't move a finger! But such an attitude would have meant its demise as a party. *It had to act beyond mere criticism in order to gain as much as possible from the muddled situation for the proletariat and the revolution.*

What were the facts? The Hoffmann government had fled and exercised no power either in Munich or in all of Upper Bavaria. It was positively impossible for us to recall it in order thereby to undo the putsch. The *pseudo*-Soviet Republic did not expire as a result of our criticism. However weak, it constituted a real government. A mollusc it might be, but it was not a phantom. The only factor which gave it a treacherous appearance was that it called itself a Soviet Republic.

We were compelled forward precisely because it did not dare oppose us. In due time we might have been forced to declare open war against it, with all its consequences, such as a civil war among the proletariat and the assumption of power which we ourselves considered altogether too narrowly based. We were spared the first consequence thanks to the Hoffmann government; the second consequence, the taking over of power, was forced upon us, though happily for us not under the worst possible circumstances, that is, following a victory over the pseudo-Soviet government and its supporters.

Why we were forced into the assumption of power will be explained at once. The opponents of our conception now object: in that case our actions and destiny are shaped by the activities of the Independent Socialists and other putschists! Up to a certain point this is in fact the case. What enables these putschists to engage in actions of great political significance is the lack of political education on the part of the proletariat. This lack in turn takes revenge on the working class and above all else on our party, which is the most energetic in combating it. This has been our misfortune, our tragic fate since the January days.

That we are not deceiving ourselves about the situation is proven by our words and deeds up to the moment of our actual entry into the government. What about weakness of character? We stood firm in the face of the enemies' wooing, though it constituted both a genuine and flattering—if grudgingly given—recognition of our political capabilities. We defied the hatred of the remote masses, demagogically whipped up against us, who, dully perceiving the incompetence of their leaders and the approach of a dreadful doom, were not yet ready for our line. We were coerced by the dynamics of the situation.

Not much was done by the pseudo-Soviet government, but what it did was sufficient for the counterrevolution. For it played around with the slogans of the dictatorship of the proletariat, which had become the bogey of the bourgeoisie because with us they had significance. That was precisely what Schneppenhorst had been waiting for, and together with Commander von Epp he organized the white terror against Munich. This danger compelled us to make concessions to the pseudo-Soviet Republic. On the order of the Revolutionary Shop Stewards we proffered our advice about resistance against the counterrevolution. We did not go any further. We did not intervene in the affairs of state outside these limits. We decided nothing, but simply made suggestions. We placed the forces of our party at their complete disposal for the purpose mentioned, refusing, however, any responsibility; not because we were afraid of responsibility, but because we wanted to keep alive the critical faculty of the working class and to concentrate its determination on the resistance against the counterrevolution. We quickly recognized the impotence of the government which greedily accepted our suggestions without, however, being able to carry them out. The premature birth of the Soviet Republic claimed its toll; death was knocking on the door. We were already debating whether to give up our useless activity as advisor to the government and to apply all our forces to party organization, when the situation changed through the counterrevolutionary putsch of the Republican Guards on April 13.

By means of this putsch the *status quo ante* should have been restored, but in this political carnival the putsch itself was a farce. Its actors on and behind the stage believed, as had the pseudo-Soviet government, that a wall poster constituted a political fact and a handful of conspirators political power. And as if by instinct they wanted to employ that power immediately against the communists. They attacked one of our party locals, where they received their first bloody noses. This was the signal for the best part of the working class and the troops to enter into the battle. Having at first prepared itself for a purely propagandistic exploitation of the situation, the party leadership now assumed the direction of the battle.

It resulted in a victory, and this victory had to be carried to its logical conclusion. There was no longer a turning back. The most essential prerequisite existed: the victorious action of the masses. The Soviet Republic had become the only alternative. We placed ourselves without reservation at the disposal of the working class.

The *Rote Fahne,* the central organ of the party, laid down during the days prior to our entry into the government the following principles governing the conduct of the KPD:

1. the most trenchant criticism of the weaknesses, inadequacies, and obscurities of the movement and its present exponents is required;
2. however, it is the task of the communists to point out positive goals to the movement, to formulate the slogans suitable to the situation; in short, to do everything pos-

sible to overcome the shortcomings of the movement. *If the movement is not on the level of the platform of communism, it should be raised up to this level.*

At no time did we go beyond these principles. We were even more cautious than was called for. When the decision had to be made we acted without hesitation and with energy, in spite of our awareness of the dangers and of the enormous responsibility. Even now in the wake of the conclusion of the great tragedy we see no cause for regret.

The manner in which we functioned within the Soviet government has not been challenged in the party. It is therefore merely necessary to describe our practical experiences and to draw from them the lessons for the future.

DOCUMENT 4: Paul Levi, *"The Munich Experience: an Opposing View"*

Die Internationale, I, No. 9/10 (Aug. 4, 1919).

I believe that before one begins a discussion it is best to focus on the facts that one discusses with somewhat greater precision than comrade Werner has done. The history of the Munich Soviet Republic may be concisely rendered in the following manner: Majority Socialists, "independents," and anarchists determine on a "Soviet Republic" in the Cafe Stephani and surrounding environs, whose sovereign *Reich* reaches from Schwabing to Pasing and from Laim to Freimaring [four suburbs of Munich]. The communists oppose this Soviet Republic with the most trenchant criticism. This Soviet Republic did not suffer from premature birth, as comrade Werner claims, but was rather a *prodigiosum aliquid,* that is, a freak; as a human child cannot issue from the womb of a female gorilla, as little can a Soviet Republic issue from the womb of a majoritarian-independent-anarchist coffeehouse clique.

This Soviet Republic is just in the process of passing over into the Elysian fields—meaning into the memoirs and *feuilletons* of its generally poetically gifted leaders—when the Hoffmann government stages a putsch against it on April 13. The purpose of this putsch was less concerned with giving the *coup de grâce* to the mortally sick than with its revival, in order to give Schneppenhorst and others a just opportunity for a blood bath. This was the second phase. The position of our party during this *second* phase involved the taking over and direction of the defense against the putsch. Out of this defensive action grew without special restraint the third phase: the Communist Soviet Republic.

How could the party comport itself in relation to these three phases?

I trust that we are all agreed on the first phase. This "Soviet Republic" was the result of a putsch, a very clumsy one at that, not staged by the working masses, but by a handful of literati who are now appealing for a full measure of mercy on the part of the tribunals. They deserve it in accordance with the proverb: Forgive him who does not know what he does.

Confronted with this situation, comrade Werner believes that it was incumbent upon the communists to "apply the brakes." I don't share that opinion. A communist never holds back. When he calls a spade a spade, a putschist a putschist, when he exposes illusions for what they are, when he reveals the impotence, incompetence, and the immaturity of political actions—he does not "retard" but *leads* the revolution. Only people who believe that wherever there is noise there must also be a revolution will call this applying the brakes.

Accordingly, our party stood with its trenchant criticism in the forefront of the revolution; so far there existed everywhere complete agreement on the conduct of our Munich comrades, or rather it existed until comrade Werner began to defend the Munich action.

Until now we had all been of the opinion that the Munich comrades had viewed the Soviet Republic of Toller, Mühsam, etc. as one of those comedies whose rapid collapse was required in the interest of the progress of the revolution. The Munich comrades themselves clearly recognized that this Munich Republic lacked any relationship with the Bavarian and particularly with the German proletarian revolution.

In his reflections on the question of free will, comrade Werner embraces a personal and political determinism. I do not touch this question here as a philosophical speculation: in everyday business I can manage without it. "To make revolutionary politics means to act in accordance with a clear, well-defined revolutionary will," says comrade Werner. My formulation is shorter: to make revolutionary politics means to act rationally in the interest of the revolution. In this manner I skip around Werner's problem of the will. When comrade Werner then continues to say that "the 'firmly defined will' is not solely determined by general tactical precepts and guiding principles, but is dependent upon the situation," he is actually quite correct. But it is not the "will" which is dependent upon the situation, but the *decision*. Thus things fall into place even without determinism.

Back to the situation. As outlined above, we have on the one hand a dying Soviet Republic, and deficient maturity on the part of the whole German proletariat for the task of the seizure of power, and, on the other hand, the impossibility of establishing a soviet republic in Munich. Out of this situation developed with a physical necessity the politics pursued by the Munich [comrades] until April 13. Comrade Werner believes that the existence of the pseudo-Soviet Republic imposed certain obligations on us. Not that I know of. "The pseudo-Soviet Republic did not expire as a result of our criticism." This may be true, but what our criticism did not accomplish, Toller, Mühsam, Landauer, etc. accomplished of their own accord. "However weak, it constituted a real government." True but what kind of government! If it was revolutionary, we had to be part of it; if it was not it might as well go to the devil and make room for another that at least did not arouse illusions in the proletariat.

"The only factor which gave it a treacherous appearance was that it called itself a Soviet Republic." This "only" of comrade Werner speaks volumes, for behind this "only" hides the most important fact: it just was not a soviet government.

This Munich Soviet government was actually a nothing, not fish nor meat, not roast nor salad. But from the nothingness of this government comrade Werner infers that we were compelled to take up the open fight against it, with all its consequences, culminating in the "seizure of power which we ourselves considered altogether too narrowly based." What does that mean? It means to replace an independent-majoritarian-anarchist "Soviet Republic," established with insufficient support among the masses, by a communist soviet republic with the same shortcoming—and according to comrade Werner's own description inevitably so—as the other.

This means to replace one nothing with another. Comrade Werner calls that "to act in accordance with a clear, well-defined revolutionary will." Others call it something else, call it in fact an aimless drifting in the political whirlpool. I do not believe in fate in politics, in a fate inflicted on us by mighty gods, let alone in a fate concocted by six bar cronies in a corner of the Cafe Luitpold.

But I am looking ahead, and I do not want to have the Munich comrades suffer for the defense which comrade Werner inflicts on them. Considering the unequivocal attitude of Leviné it cannot be assumed that the Munich comrades vacillated to the point indicated in Werner's description; in fact the really difficult situation arises for them during the second phase, with the Hoffmann putsch.

I distinguish in this second phase two alternatives. One is the defense of the "pseudo-Soviet republic." As has been generally agreed, the Toller-Mühsam Soviet Republic was a nothing, from which I draw the conclusion that one does not defend a nothing. The fatherland of Toller-Mühsam distinguishes itself only in degree, not in principle, from that of the [House of] Wittelsbach. If the action of the Munich comrades had been nothing but a defensive gesture on behalf of the ungracefully dying Toller Republic, it would be in my opinion inadmissible both from a logical and tactical point of view.

The comrades who describe it simply as such a defensive action of the Soviet Republic do it, however, injustice. It was a trifle more. It was a defensive action in behalf of certain real positions of power attained by the proletariat during the months of the revolution, particularly in Munich. Should the Munich proletariat have defended them with gun in hand? In view of the unfinished state of revolutionary development at that time we followed the tactic of evading an armed struggle throughout Germany even in the face of an offensive act by advance of the counter-revolution, because a victorious conclusion of an armed struggle appeared impossible. This tactic was applied with all our consent in Bremen, in Braunschweig, in Leipzig, in Gotha, Erfurt, indeed everywhere. But, I admit, matters in Munich were different. As far as I can judge the situation from a distance, the position of the Munich proletariat was such that it did not have to stand by while its rights created by the revolution were being wrested from its hands. The Bavarian government on the basis of its own strength was unable to move against it. Waiting before the gates, however, were Noske, Haase, etc., eager to move in. But here the Hoffmann government was limited as well. In view of certain Bavarian peculiarities it could not afford to open the gates willy-nilly to the "Prussians" and other foreigners. In addition, the mere fact that the Munich proletariat held on to its revolutionary position might not have been a sufficient reason for the Hoffmann people to take refuge with the "Prussians." The Hoffmann government might well have been obliged to come to terms with the Munich proletariat.

Accordingly, I believe that the Munich comrades made the correct decisions during the second phase as well.

Then came the third phase.

The defense "resulted in a victory and this victory had to be liquidated. There was no longer a turning back." What does comrade Werner mean by the liquidation of the victory? Does he mean by "liquidation of the victory" that one lays hold of everything delivered up by the moment without consideration as to whether one can hold on to it? . . . But should the liquidation of the victory not have meant instead the determination of what corresponded to the inner development of the revolution? In that case the result would have been different.

"There was no longer a turning back. The most essential prerequisite existed; the victorious action of the masses. The Soviet Republic had become the only alternative." Well, comrade Werner. Indeed! At the end of his exposition comrade Werner states that the action of the masses constitutes the essential prerequisite not only for the establishment of a Munich but of a Bavarian Soviet Republic. At the beginning of his exposition comrade Werner spoke differently. "We communists considered a soviet republic consisting of Bavaria alone an absurdity. . . . A soviet republic without the areas of large-scale industry and the coal fields is impossible in Germany. Besides, the Bavarian proletariat is only in a few industrial giant plants genuinely disposed toward revolution. . . . A Bavarian Soviet Republic appeared to us for this reason from the beginning a mistaken undertaking." Thus spoke comrade Werner at the beginning. He seems to belong to that category of people who are wiser before entering a discussion than after. Too much meditation does not agree with him. For the time being I side with comrade Werner's earlier view and raise the question: Has anything happened between April 6–13 which changed *these* true prognoses of a Bavarian Soviet Republic? No, nothing at all. The Bavarian Soviet Republic was on April 13th as much an absurdity as on April 6th, and the "victorious action" at the large plants of Maffei, Krupp, etc., was not a sufficient basis, constituted no "essential prerequisite" for a Bavarian Soviet Republic, on April 13th as little as on April 6th.

But I repeat: injustice is being done to the Munich comrades if one judges them on the basis of comrade Werner's defense. Their decision was not as blatantly wrong as it must appear from comrade Werner's defense. The difficulty of their decision did not lie in the sphere of political calculation —here the case was as clear as daylight—but in that of political psychology. We are often required to tread along different paths from those of the masses. The masses have as yet not completely comprehended our program—otherwise we would already have reached our goal. They often continue along other paths than those desired by us, in which case we have recourse to criticism. No one among us has any scruples on this score, because the difference between us and the masses usually consists of our wish for action, while the masses remain passive.

It is for this reason that it is particularly hard for us when the reverse is the case, when the masses proceed with action while we have to tell them that the action is useless or injurious to the interest of the revolution. Before we declare ourselves opposed to the action, we have to make doubly and triply sure whether we cannot turn it to our advantage. But there can be no serious doubt that this must be our position. If the masses proceed with actions which are only pseudo-revolutionary and in reality can only lead to setbacks, it is our duty to step forward with warnings and criticism, as was done by the Munich comrades. To place ourselves, however, at the head of the movement, if the masses move ahead nevertheless, though it can only lead to trouble—that obligation we do not have. Not only for our own sake, but also for the sake of the masses who will thus be enabled, in the face of the setback and the disappointment, to seek support in the derided critics of yesterday. . . .

The Munich comrades failed to take into account one additional factor. The grievous denouement of the Munich action involved essentially no setback for us in Germany, aside from the terrible loss of some of our best comrades-in-arms. The German revolutionary working class movement hardly suffered as a result of the Munich events. For unknown reasons, however, it appears that Munich has stirred up abroad, particularly in Russia and Hungary, illusions about the possibilities for revolution in Germany, which fail to be substantiated by the conditions of the whole German revolutionary movement, but which could actually become highly dangerous for Hungary, Austria, and even Russia. We are presently involved not only in a German but in a worldwide revolution, and in viewing every possibility for action we should not lose sight of the possibility of a reaction not only at home but against the world revolution.

Was it necessary to say all this? Yes, for the sake of clarity and our future. Is it possible to reproach anyone? No, I do not lift a stone against any person.

IV: Vienna: Window to the West?

To the radical forces which expected Bolshevik revolutions to sweep central and eastern Europe in 1919 the small Austrian state, which emerged from the ruins of the old empire, represented a key in linking revolutionary Germany with Hungary and Russia. But Vienna refused to become a communist window to the west, and its resistance to Bolshevism resembles that of Berlin earlier in the year. Whereas communism in Germany had been crushed by military force employed by the Majority Socialists in Berlin, Munich, and other urban centers, communism in Austria was adroitly neutralized by the socialists without resort to armed repression. The abortive communist bid for power in Vienna became the fourth in a series of reversals which by the end of 1919 marked the recession of the revolutionary wave, with a soviet republic established nowhere save in Russia.

On October 21, 1918, less than a week after Emperor Karl's manifesto turning Austria into a federated state of independent nationalities, the Social Democrats of the Austrian parliament constituted themselves as a Provisional National Assembly and carried out a parliamentary revolution by which they announced the creation of an independent German-Austrian state, claimed all the territories populated by Germans,[1] and proposed that a Constituent National Assembly be elected and empowered to draft a constitution. On November 12th the Provisional Assembly adopted a law proclaiming the republic. Elections for the Constituent National Assembly were set for February 1919, and the new German-Austrian republic was declared a part of Germany.[2] Follow-

[1] Even at this point the new state was envisaged as including the German-speaking areas of the Bohemian Sudeten districts in newly created Czechoslovakia and of western Hungary.

[2] The desire for annexation to a socialist Germany was strong within the Austrian Social Democratic party. The Versailles Treaty of June 1919, which expressly forbade such a union, together with

ing the February elections the Social Democrats, who emerged as the strongest party, formed a coalition government with the Christian Socials, a middle-class and peasant party, in which they held the key positions (chancellorship and ministries of foreign affairs, interior, and war). By April 1919 the Social Democrats had succeeded in carrying out and directing a political revolution that left them in control, but all the forces of discontent within the new republic had not been satisfied, and a decided threat from the left continued. This threat became all the more real and ominous as news of the Hungarian and Bavarian revolutions reached Vienna.

Social democracy was well established in Austria before the war, being based on a highly developed trade union structure and a large, politically enlightened, and socially conscious working class, concentrated in Vienna and its environs. Toward the end of the war the old revisionist and reformist leadership of the Social Democratic party (SPÖ), symbolized by Max Adler, was yielding to younger men, including Friedrich Adler, the popular assassin of Prime Minister Karl von Stürgkh, and Otto Bauer, a theorist of seemingly revolutionary tendencies. The new look of the SPÖ, intimating a more revolutionary direction at the time of the empire's collapse, corresponded to the radicalization of the rank and file by the course of the war, by the Russian October Revolution, and by Bolshevik propaganda brought back by returning prisoners of war. By the winter of 1918 the SPÖ contained, therefore, a noteworthy minority which appeared ready to use the means necessary to create a soviet-style republic.

The impetus for the creation of the Austrian Communist party (KPÖ) came from Franz Koritschoner, a staunch SPÖ member who had attended the Kienthal Conference, and Elfriede Friedländer, an SPÖ intellectual.[3] The main organizing talent, however, was Karl Tomann, who had won his revolutionary spurs as a prisoner of war in Russia and

---

the waning power of German socialists soon thereafter ended the desire for *Anschluss* of Austrian socialists. After Hitler's success in Germany annexationism was revived, but this time by the Austrian right.

[3] By 1920 Elfriede Friedländer appeared in Germany, where she quickly assumed a position of prominence in the KPD under the name of Ruth Fischer.

who, like Kun, had been part of the cadres trained by the Bolsheviks for domestic action. At the KPÖ's founding congress on February 9, 1919, it went on record as opposed to the elections for a Constituent Assembly later that month. Similar to the stand of the KPD in Berlin, the KPÖ refused to be associated with bourgeois and social democratic parliamentarianism; it decided to gain control of the council movement and to convert it into a soviet republic.[4]

The councils had their origins in popular discontent at war's end: the workers' councils grew out of the bitter January strike in Vienna, and the soldiers' councils arose among returning veterans during the armistice period. Other parapolitical organizations included a radical Red Guard in Vienna, which attempted to storm the parliament building on the day the republic was proclaimed, and radicalized shop stewards in the Viennese factories and workshops. One feature not to be found in any of the revolutions discussed so far was a Republican army. From November 1918 onward Julius Deutsch, later to become SPÖ minister of war, organized the *Volkswehr* or People's Militia from working class elements of the old imperial army. The soldiers' councils, as well as the Red Guard, were incorporated into this unique organization, and at least one of its major battalions was predominantly communist.

Conditions in Austria, especially a working class army, certainly more so than anywhere else, favored the creation of a soviet republic. But neither Adler nor Bauer wanted it; their tone was revolutionary, but their actions were not. Not only had they mastered the parliamentary revolution, but they also succeeded in using the generally moderate councils in hamstringing the KPÖ. At a time when the political situation appeared to be in flux, Adler and Bauer convinced the communists to join the councils and thereby to subordinate themselves to a National Executive Committee, which would act as a "parliament of the working class." In fact the SPÖ, because it controlled a majority in the councils, was able to make the communists toe its line on the ground that the councils' decisions were "a judgment of the proletarian

[4] The party also declared itself part of the International Communist movement and, as we have seen in the previous chapter, was accepted as a member of the Comintern after its formation in March.

democracy." It is within this shackling frame of reference that the communists carried out several abortive actions and through which they were ultimately outmaneuvered.

This is not to say that there were no embarrassing moments for the Social Democrats. One of the first came shortly after the creation of the Hungarian Soviet Republic, with Béla Kun's appeal "To All, To All, To All," requesting that others follow the example of the Hungarian workers. The Executive Committee of the workers' councils agreed with the Hungarians that the Entente powers had become the main enemy of the working class and indicated its willingness to follow in the footsteps of the Hungarians, but "not at this time," lest the Entente cut off food supplies and starve the population (Document 1).[5] This masterful stroke of circumvention seems to have escaped the Austrian communists, who continued to act as if the balance of power in the councils was not against them. Communist propaganda continued to be successful in the streets among the unemployed, war invalids, and homecoming war prisoners. A series of demonstrations organized by the KPÖ led to the storming of the parliament building on April 17th, resulting in dead and wounded. The municipal police was unable to cope with the situation, and Julius Deutsch called out units of the People's Militia which, in the name of safeguarding the Republic, crushed the uprising. The Militia showed itself to be an instrument against revolution and thereby upheld the outlook of its parent organization, the councils. Nevertheless, the KPÖ in spite of the reversal remained convinced the workers' councils were the means for attaining the dictatorship of the proletariat (Document 2).

If it was not clear to the KPÖ that any future revolutionary activity would have to be carried on outside and ultimately in opposition to the councils, Béla Kun had come to that conclusion. In May he dispatched a Dr. Ernst Bettelheim to Vienna, apparently with the mandate to galvanize radical forces for action. Bettelheim used his ample financial resources to circumvent the KPÖ leadership in establishing

[5] That this answer was a refusal was soon understood in Budapest. Kun's ambassador was received, however, and a trade treaty was concluded, under the terms of which Hungary received valuable Austrian industrial products.

anonymous action committees. The opportunity for testing his clandestine activities came in June, when the Entente demanded that the popular People's Militia be reduced by twenty-five percent. Bettelheim mobilized aroused workers and soldiers in a series of demonstrations, and the Social Democrats, alarmed by rumors of a Hungarian troop concentration on the Austro-Hungarian frontier, convinced the Entente to rescind its order. But Bettelheim was not to be stopped; plans continued for a mass action on June 15th. A communist broadside of June 14 called on members of the People's Militia to demonstrate for a soviet republic with weapons in hand (Document 3). On the same day a directive of the Action Committee told members of the People's Militia how to act in the revolutionary struggles of the morrow (Document 4). The Vienna Workers' Council responded by calling the planned action a putsch over the heads of the workers (Document 5). The Social Democrats followed their words with deeds: that night the Minister of the Interior arrested 115 leaders of the KPÖ. The uprising of the 15th ended in a rout of the communists. A subsequent general strike, called for July 21st by the Comintern as a sympathetic action on behalf of the dying Hungarian Soviet Republic, failed to materialize.

On the whole Adler, Bauer, and Austrian social democracy proved themselves much better tacticians than the communists. They made themselves masters of the mass movement and used the threat from the left to make the Christian Socials willing and grateful junior partners of their coalition government and as a weapon to carry out social and economic reforms (such as the eight-hour day). They talked about their desire to carry the revolution further but claimed to be prisoners of the Entente, which threatened to cut off deliveries of food and fuel to Vienna, and of the peasant provinces Tyrol and Voralberg, which threatened to secede and starve out the capital. Revolutions, of course, always involve risks and cannot be planned with the accuracy of the accountant's ledger. Intervention by the Entente, against a united regime drawing its strength from a large and well-organized working class and with a popular army at its command, was by no means a certainty. Furthermore, the potentially loyal provinces of Austria produced much more food than the possible defectors. Behind the official explanation for inaction lay the unwillingness of the leaders of Austrian social democracy to risk a republican government, in which their gradual reforms could be carried out, for revolution and possibly armed conflict which, if successful, would lead to a social upheaval in which they had ceased to believe. Against this determination the communists could do little. They influenced the streets but lacked an organized following, and heaped only discredit upon themselves by their impulsive actions.

The Austrian party had suffered a serious defeat with which the communist movement had to come to terms. Karl Radek, who was later to insist that the Hungarian communists' bid for power was not premature, was not so charitable in analyzing the Austrian situation at the end of 1919 (Document 6). He exonerated the Austrian communists for the fiasco of June 14th by blaming Bettelheim and other "Hungarian adventurers" for having driven the KPÖ into a wild putsch. Bettelheim, he claimed, had no mandate from anyone—not from the Hungarians and certainly not from the Comintern, because both hewed to the principle that world revolution could not be made by emissaries but only by the proletariat of each country, which alone could determine the tempo of its activities.[6] The weak KPÖ, he concluded, should have devoted itself to organizing the masses under its leadership. Its error was to be carried away by the electrifying news from Budapest and Vienna and to be instigated by adventurers.

Bettelheim was permitted to have the final word in an official Comintern publication (Document 7).[7] He blamed the collapse of the June 14th action on the Hungarians' failure to make a strong declaration in favor of the KPÖ and the obstructionism of certain "careerist" communist leaders who had left the masses in the lurch. His mandate, he protested, had come from Kun, and he had used it to make those

[6] It is interesting that Radek's plea for recognition of nationally unique conditions as determinants of revolution was the very argument adopted by various leaders of national parties (the German in 1921 and the Bulgarian in 1923) against the ECCI's attempt to impose formulas later on.

[7] The practice of opening the pages of Comintern publications for rejoinders by those who had been officially criticized was abandoned within the next few years.

preparations which, in view of the disintegration of Austrian social democracy and the favorable international situation, could have ushered in a new Soviet Republic. He mixed truth with hyperbole when he claimed that Austria had been the key to the salvation of the Hungarian revolution and to the prospects for world revolution.

DOCUMENT 1: *"Declaration by the Executive Committee of Workers' Councils to the Proletariat of Hungary on March 23, 1919"*

Julius Braunthal, *Die Arbeiterräte in Deutschösterreich* (Vienna: Wiener Volksbuchhandlung, 1919). By permission. First appeared in *Die Arbeiterzeitung,* March 23, 1919.

Comrades!

Your appeal "To Everyone" has reached us at the meeting of the National Executive Committee of the Workers' Councils of German Austria.

You have taken state power in your hands and posed the fearlessness and fighting spirit of the united Hungarian proletariat against the imperialism of the Entente. We believe with you that today, after the collapse of German and Austro-Hungarian imperialism, *the main enemy is the imperialist victor.* The conference of the victors at Paris will meet with the determined resistance of the workers if it intends to rape whole nations and assault the right of nations to self-determination.

You have appealed to us to follow your example. We would do this wholeheartedly *but we cannot do so at this time.* There is no more food in our country. Even our scarce bread rations depend entirely on the food trains sent by the Entente. For this reason, we are enslaved to the Entente. If we were to follow your advice today, the Entente capitalists would cut off our last provisions with cruel mercilessness, and leave us to starvation. We are convinced that the Russian Soviet Republic would try to help us in every way possible. But before it could help us, we would starve to death. We are therefore in a much more difficult position than you. *Our dependence on the Entente is total.*

But our most sacred duty is to be prepared for any event. That is why the national conference of our workers' councils resolved three weeks ago to build up the council organizations. We have directed an appeal to working people to set up workers' councils everywhere, to promote the building of peasants' councils, as well as to unite the peasants', workers', and soldiers' councils with existing reliable organizations in order to prepare for anything the moment demands.

At the moment we are calling on workers from all areas to build up the council organization rapidly. We have also asked that the central council which was called for in the resolutions of the national conference meet within the next few days.

All our best wishes are with you. We are following events with ardent hearts and hope that *the cause of socialism will win.* We also stand ready to fight, determined to carry out what historical necessity demands.

Long live international workers' solidarity!

For the National Executive Committee of the Workers' Councils of German Austria, Joseph Benisch—Secretary, Friedrich Adler—Chairman.

DOCUMENT 2: *"Declaration of the Communist Workers' Councilors"*

Beschlüsse der ersten Delegiertenkonferenz der Kommunistischen Arbeiterräte Deutschösterreichs (Vienna, 1919).

The National Conference of the Communist Workers' Councilors of German Austria, held May 4–5 1919, declares:

The National Assembly, the *Landtag,* and Communal Council are all organs of bourgeois society. The proletariat realizes that it will not achieve its complete political and economic emancipation through bourgeois-democratic bodies, whether it is in a majority or minority within them. The history of the class struggle shows us that a ruling class never gave up its power through an act of parliament or voluntarily. On the contrary, the bourgeoisie has always proven that it knows how to secure its interests through the application of all means of power and force outside of legislative bodies.

The proletariat must therefore reject *bourgeois parliamentarianism* in order to carry through the transformation of the capitalist economic system into a communist one, and create an organization for itself in order to consolidate all economic and political power in its hands. The only suitable form which makes this possible is the *workers'* and *soldiers' councils* and *the councils of small peasants and proprietors.*

It is therefore the duty of every communist workers' and soldiers' council and the councils of small peasants and proprietors to make this uniquely suitable institution completely acceptable through untiring, systematic struggle and tenacious endurance.

The struggle must be waged against capitalism and for the dictatorship of the proletariat, which must be exercised in the transitional period and through which the communist state must be established. For us communists the only correct principle remains, "The emancipation of the working class can only be the work of the workers themselves."

Thus we are stating once again that the workers' councils are the only road to the dictatorship of the proletariat.

DOCUMENT 3: *"Austrian Communist Broadside of June 14, 1919"*

Julius Deutsch, *Aus Österreichs Revolution: Militärpolitische Erinnerungen* (Vienna: Wiener Volksbuchhandlung, n.d.). By permission.

Soldiers!

The hour for the emancipation of the proletariat has come!

Our comrades in the International are fighting against our enslavement by the Entente bourgeoisie in every way. Our Hungarian and Russian brothers have triumphed over Entente militarism! The victory of the world revolution depends on us.

Comrades!

We have nothing to lose! Exploited and starved by the bourgeoisie, we are now to crawl under a new yoke and again tie ourselves to the machines for the use and profit of our enemies, the capitalists! Comrades, this cannot be allowed! Either we crush our opponents or we will perish! We have no choice!

On Sunday the 15th of June at 10 a.m., the revolutionary workers will demonstrate for the setting up of a soviet dictatorship, against hunger and exploitation, for social revolution!

Every member of the People's Militia has the duty to participate in this demonstration with his weapon in hand.

Militiamen, come out!

Come out into the streets for the liberation of the proletariat! Come out into the streets for the future of the working class, for the world revolution!

!!Long live the Soviet Republic of German Austria!!

DOCUMENT 4: *"Directive of the Action Committee of Austrian Communists, June 14, 1919"*

Deutsch, *Aus Österreichs Revolution*. By permission.

. . . a) If the soldiers come upon fighting between proletarians and police, etc., the comrade already selected for the job by the Action Committee will unfurl the red flag and cheer for the dictatorship, etc. The others will join in enthusiastically and do everything to get the whole company to come along and join the workers. Side by side with their brothers in work clothes, the militiamen will fight their common enemy, whether it be police, officers' lackeys, or reactionary students.

b) And if the soldiers come upon proletarians storming buildings, they will unfurl the red banner (as in point "a"), set up cheers, join the workers, and take the building hand in hand with them. The company will occupy the particular building and act according to point "c".

c) If the company which has the job of occupying some building does not come upon fighting, it will raise the red banner on the building and the soldiers will demand that the command of the building be placed in the hands of a building committee, to be made up of social democrats and communists in equal parts (soldier-councilors or men from the company, but no officers!).

Send continuous reports!!!

Particularly after every sort of action.

DOCUMENT 5: *"Declaration of the Viennese Workers' Councilors"*

Braunthal, Die Arbeiterräte in Deutschösterreich. By permission.

June 14, 1919

Workers!

The fears expressed in yesterday's appeal by the Workers' Council of Vienna have proven completely justified. From thousands of posters and leaflets it is quite clear that *a putsch is being more or less openly planned for Sunday morning.* Not only the Communist party itself, but a "Central Committee of Organizations of the Unemployed" and a "Central Committee of the Free Union of Soldiers Returning from the Front," that is, *anonymous committees,* are calling a demonstration "for the establishment of a soviet republic."

We are for complete freedom of opinion and do not want to obstruct anyone's right to assemble. But what is being planned for this Sunday is no popular forum for the exchange of opinions, but *a rousing of the rabble for violence.*

This emerges clearly from the communist leaflet to the People's Militia. It is said there, "Every militiaman has the duty to participate in this demonstration with his weapon in hand."

Tomorrow's demonstration is no meeting in the usual sense. But in spite of this, we do not want any force used to prevent this attempted putsch. It must become quite clear *who will bear the real responsibility* if there are any incidents.

It is an act of violence which is being planned by this "Committee of Four" with the Hungarian lieutenant Bettelheim (or Bernstein) as leader, a man completely unknown to the Viennese workers.

And that is why we are holding this "Committee of Four" and its agents responsible from the start for any harm that can occur today.

The overwhelming majority of Viennese workers do not want to let themselves be misused for any unscrupulous putsch attempts and will, therefore, keep away from today's demonstration.

Workers!

Do not let yourselves be used for an attempted putsch!

Do not believe the senseless rumors that will certainly be spread today!

Remain aloof from the unscrupulous demonstrations of the communists!

Follow the orders of the Workers' Council only!

For the Executive of the Vienna District Workers' Council, Franz Ziegler.

For the National Board of Executives of the Vienna Workers' Councils, Joseph Benisch, Friedrich Adler.

DOCUMENT 6: Karl Radek, *"The Lessons of an Attempted Putsch: The Crisis in the German-Austrian Communist Party"*

Kommunistische Räte-Korrespondenz, I (Nov. 20, 1919)

. . . 2. The Origin of the German-Austrian Communist Party.

In order to comprehend the crisis during the months May to August, it must be borne in mind that the German-Austrian Communist party is much weaker than the German one. In Germany the left-radical tendency within social democracy existed already before the war and created in its struggle against the open and hidden opportunism of the Kautsky-Haase tendency the intellectual foundations for the future German Communist party. During the war this tendency deepened its independent ideology; it trained cadres of disciples in spite of all obstacles and with the greatest of sacrifices, and formed illegal organizations which became legal at the outbreak of the revolution and soon comprised large masses. This task was facilitated by the split within social democracy in 1917. The foundation of the independent German Communist party in December 1918 was the result of an eight-year-long intellectual and a four-year-long organizational activity of hundreds of experienced comrades. In German-Austria prior to the war there existed no Marxist opposition within social democracy at all. With the exception of the Reichenbach editor, Joseph Strasser, the Austrian Marxists under the leadership of Otto Bauer and Fritz Adler did not consider the struggle against opportunism their task, but rather its avowal. The fact that the German Austrian party never had a chance to approve the war credits because the Austrian Parliament was not convened at all permitted the leaders of social democracy, which possessed in the person of Victor Adler great and deserved moral authority and in the person of Renner a cunning leadership, to obscure and obliterate the differences within the party. The sense of weakness experienced by the moderate opposition developed during the war is best illustrated by the assassination by Victor Adler [of Prime Minister Karl Stürgkh on October 21, 1916], who reached for his gun in the absence of mass support and because he felt incapable of political action. The left-radical opposition around comrade Franz Koritschoner, which developed during the war, counted only very few supporters.

When the revolution broke out, the elements which soon coalesced into the German-Austrian Communist party consisted of a very small group of very young intellectuals shaken up by the war and filled with the will toward revolutionary proletarian politics, but devoid of all political experience. They were joined by prisoners of war returned from Russia who were naturally alienated from the German-Austrian conditions. It should be clear that a party thus composed and not developed organically could become only slowly the center of the revolutionary aspirations developing in the proletariat when the German-Austrian social democracy under the leadership of Renner and Seitz and with the aid of Fritz Adler (who revealed himself during the revolution as a tame petty bourgeois gone mad in 1916 under the impact of the war) entered an alliance with the bourgeoisie. The infant German-Austrian party had to commit many errors before it could discover the appropriate means of struggle. *Communist politics does not consist in the application of principles discovered and patented in Moscow, but consists in the leadership of the revolutionary mass struggle, the conditions of which vary widely with each country.* Only through the gathering and digestion of experience in their spontaneous struggle will the working masses themselves pave the road toward communism. The more educated and experienced the vanguard of the proletariat, the more quickly it realizes the lessons of the struggle and helps the proletariat in its orientation. In view of the youth and composition of the German-Austrian Communist leadership, the Communist party could make, during its first months of existence, only a few steps in the direction of agitation and organization. The length of the road ahead or its many turns it could hardly have imagined. The stormy character of the German movement during the period from January until April and the strikes in England seemed to indicate to it an early victory of the world revolution. The proclamation of the Hungarian and shortly thereafter of the Munich Soviet Republics occurred in an atmosphere engendered by these expectations.

3. The Hungarian Putschist Tactic in Vienna.

The revolutionary workers of Vienna—not only the communist but the social democratic as well—were electrified by the course of these events. The communist leaders felt themselves obliged to agitate for the proclamation of a Soviet Republic with full force. They were totally correct in arguing against the social democrats that the establishment of a Soviet Republic in Vienna would extend the arena of battle and would thus also provide the possibility of overcoming the very substantial shortage of foodstuffs which the Adlers used as a main argument against the establishment of the Soviet Republic in German Austria. The establishment of a German-Austrian Soviet Republic did not only involve the necessity of feeding so-and-so many people which the social democrats considered impossible; it also meant that the impetuous Hungarian proletariat would be joined by hundreds of thousands of organizationally trained German-Austrian workers, thus giving the allied Soviet Republics an altogether different military potential and with it the possibility of occupying the Hungarian territories abounding in grain. The eye-opening effect of the victory of the Austrian and Hungarian proletariat on the technicians and the intimidation of the Entente would have had a different significance under those circumstances than was the case in the isolation of Budapest. The communists for this reason did nothing but their duty in trying with all their power to win the German-Austrian proletariat for the dictatorship of the Soviets.

The "realists" around Fritz Adler and Bauer, by warning the proletariat with all their power against the "experiment," in effect betrayed the proletariat. They aided Renner and Ellenbogen in surrendering the proletariat to the bourgeoisie, and if they are now in turn surrendered to the bourgeoisie by Renner and Ellenbogen it is solely the result of their tactics designed to avoid all struggle. Their fate represents a repetition of the fate of Haase and Dittman, whose brothers they are. But the agitation for a soviet dictatorship seemed to a number of Hungarian comrades insufficient aid on the part of the German-Austrians. It should be mentioned that in Hungary too, the Communist party disposed of very few experienced and trained leaders; following its easy victory it was obliged to staff many important positions with totally inexperienced comrades, not to mention the fact that as the victorious party it was infiltrated by adventurous elements intent on furthering their own interests. *From a distance it is difficult to distinguish to what degree the inexperienced, the adventurers, and the vultures participated in the foreign propaganda of the Hungarian Soviet Republic. The fact is that these elements began to drive the young Communist party in Vienna toward a putsch.* In the middle of May Dr. Bettelheim arrived as Hungarian emissary in Vienna. He posed as a plenipotentiary of the Third International, with the alleged order to proclaim the Soviet Republic as soon as possible. In reality the Executive of the Communist International knew of Dr. Bettelheim—a fellow altogether new to the movement—as much as Dr. Bettelheim knew of the Communist International—that is, nothing. We do not know whether the mandate was a figment of Dr. Bettelheim's own imagination in order to be in a better position to drive the inexperienced Viennese comrades toward a putsch, or whether some propaganda department of the Hungarian Soviet Republic played him this practical joke to give him courage in his messianic role. The fact, however, is that Dr. Bettelheim's "Moscow mandate" is either the product of the imagination of a young comrade unfamiliar with communism or the swindle of an adventurer. The Russian Communist party has never either before or after the foundation of the Communist International given mandates to some comrade for the purpose of traveling to a given country in order to proclaim a Soviet Republic there at a given moment. The Russian Communist party aided materially—though modestly—those Russian comrades who had lived for long periods in certain countries or those comrades from these countries who lived as prisoners of war in Russia and decided to leave Russia in order to work in Austria, Germany, France, or some other country, in the same manner as it aided foreign socialist groups and parties turning to it for help. Its sole and obvious compensation consisted in the dissemination of the teachings of communism and of information on the proletarian revolution. The Russian Communist Party and later the Executive of the Communist International dominated by it never imagined that *they could determine from Moscow the concrete policies of the foreign communist parties or set the pace of the foreign movement.* As the writer of these lines, in charge of the foreign propaganda of the Bolsheviks until December 1918, mentioned in his letters, written in February 1919 and published in November 1919 by the *Kommunistische Räte-Korrespondenz* on the occasion of the debates on parliamentarism, in the name of the Russian Communist party he had warned the German, Hungarian, Czech, and South Slav comrades returning illegally to Austria-Hungary in October 1918 not to attempt to apply the results of the Russian Revolution to the early stages of the Austrian-Hungarian revolution. He even advised them to take a position on the National Constituent Assembly only on the spot, depending upon the degree of opposition and the maturity of the movement.

The Executive of the Communist International, in the hands of such cautious tacticians as Zinoviev and Worovsky, both educated Marxists in the service of the movement for seventeen and twenty-five years respectively, naturally pursues no other policy. The Russian Communist party knows that the Russian Revolution can ultimately only be victorious with the help of the victory of the world revolution. But the world revolution can develop as a movement only if made by the proletariat of every country, not by "emissaries." If the proletarian revolution does not advance sufficiently in the other countries in the foreseeable future, thereby paralyzing the imperialism of the Entente, then the Russian Soviet Republic will be threatened by the fate of bleeding to death; for its defensive war against the Entente paralyzes all of its forces aimed at the reorganization of the economy. Soviet Hungary with its narrow revolutionary base succumbed to this fate. But the awareness of this danger should not becloud the fact that the endangered Soviet Republics *can only be helped by the development of the proletarian revolution, not by the artificial promotion of putsches which can only lead to the weakening of the movement in other countries, harming Soviet*

Russia and every other revolutionary center, not to mention
the compromise which the idea of communism would suffer.
Had the German-Austrian proletariat in its majority adopted
and realized the idea of the Soviet Republic, it would have
strengthened the Hungarian Soviet Republic. Had the
German-Austrian Communist party on the other hand usurped
"power" by means of a putsch—which would have been possible considering the weakness of the German Austrian government—without the support of the majority of the proletariat, this "victory" would merely have weakened the Hungarian
Soviet Republic. A German Austrian Soviet Republic à la Bettelheim would not have been a soviet republic at all. The
councils were after all opposed to its proclamation. The trade
unions were opposed to it; on whom could it have based itself?
On enlisted Red Guards who would have been obliged to apply force against the majority of the working class? From
where would it have taken the surplus of forces to aid the
Hungarian brother republic? These simple reflections should
have indicated to the Bettelheim people the madness of a
putschist tactic, if they had known more about the Soviet
Republic than its name. But this is precisely the crux of the
matter: the messiah of the Budapest bureau of propaganda
did not have a glimmer of the meaning of communism; every
word of his charge against the German-Austrian Communist
party proves this.

4. The Putsch of June 15.

What did Bettelheim report about the strength of the Communist party when he arrived in Vienna in mid-May with his
fantastic mandate in his pocket? "The party leadership could
not name to the delegated comrade a single deed worthy of
its name [we will see what this good fellow calls a "deed"]
or one success worth mentioning. It could not produce a listing of the factories, nor give the number of comrades employed in a given factory, nor locate the shop stewards working within the factories. There were no organized agitators
nor a regular system of contributions. The huge mass of unemployed was without any organization whatever. Communications with the provinces were completely neglected." If this
was the situation, then the only possible conclusion to be
drawn from it by any person other than a crackpot was simple: it is a long way to Tiperary. All the work still lay ahead:

the party had to be organized, the factories had to be opened up to our influence and organized, relations with the provinces had to be established, and an agitational campaign had to be initiated; every opportunity provided by the socio-political situation had to be utilized for actions which would mobilize and organize the working class and eventually lead it slowly onto the field of battle. But a messiah carts no manure, works on no fields, and digs no wells. He possesses a magic wand and produces miracles. Dr. Bettelheim, the pseudo-messiah, could, however, only cast pseudo-spells. Instead of organizing the party he disorganized it by undermining the leadership and replacing it with a "directorate." *And since he, like all miracle workers, desired to reap where he had not sown, he resolved on June 15—that is, a month after the beginning of his blessed stay in Vienna—to free the proletariat from the yoke of capitalism and to proclaim the Soviet Republic.* He could not do it on a smaller scale because he wrote literally in his unequaled justification, "I understand by action the proclamation of the Soviet Republic." How could the miracle be made to occur? For the time being Dr. Bettelheim had achieved only one thing: to drive out the intellectually most reliable Austrian Communist, Josef Strasser, and to name the "directorate." That was sufficient. "Week by week we moved ahead. The organization made its appearance in the factories. Strong movements developed in the military barracks; the unemployed, the enlisted men, and the disabled demonstrated. The might of the proletarian revolution manifested itself, as if called forth by magic, in Vienna and in the countryside to such a degree that the proclamation of the Soviet Republic could be expected by June 15." The extent of the power of the "proletarian revolution" will be seen shortly. The miracle of Dr. Bettelheim's anticipation of the date of the revolution is easily explained, for he continues in his statement that the revolution was fixed for the state, that in fact "all details of the planned revolution" had been fixed. In short, a regular putsch was to take place on June 15. Accordingly, the magic, which had made the organizations "apparent" like signs in the sky and created strong movements prior to the date of the "action," is devoid of all sorcery. Dr. Bettelheim let loose on Vienna a cohort of agitators who spent thousand-crown bills quite freely and who actually organized the putsch. It was to come off on June 15, but on June 14 the directorate was arrested. (Bettelheim maintains, without proof, that it was arrested at its own request).

The hastily summoned unemployed and demobilized demonstrate and attempt to free the leaders. Some people are killed. Why does the "proletarian revolution" not triumph? "The proletariat freed its leaders and demanded of its leaders to actually realize the revolution." That means the "proletarian revolution," come about "as if by magic," declares to its leaders: "You made me, now you should also realize me." The proletarian revolution has to be realized by men such as Tomann and Koritschoner. There is no other way. The time-honored insight that the emancipation of the working class can only be the work of that class is transformed by newly fledged "communists" into the doctrine: the proletariat can only be emancipated and saved by its leaders. The close resemblance between Bettelheim and his antipode, Renner, becomes apparent here: people like Renner "save" the proletariat by begging for bread for the starving; people like Bettelheim save it by "proclaiming" the Republic. In the first instance the proletarians are supposed to remain quiet; in the second instance they are supposed to smash windows, but in both cases they are supernumeraries. The leaders are the saviors. But—and here begins the farce—the leaders designated by Bettelheim as leaders failed. "The leaders promised to realize the revolution but then again dissembled and did not dare to appear before the masses. They did not think of emancipating the proletariat." Really ghastly people these, who could have emancipated the proletariat but who would not even think of it. In Vienna lived, however, on June 15th a Dr. Bettelheim who, according to his own contention, had been sent to Vienna by the International in order to initiate the reign of the proletariat. Why then did he not put into effect his "mandate" and free the proletariat? No one could suspect him of lack of courage, considering the nonsense this brave man has been capable of! He may well have refrained from "the emancipation of the proletariat" out of fear that the Viennese revolution, not knowing that he had created it "by magic," might tell him: "Excuse us, Mr. Bettelheim, but we do not know you, we cannot be emancipated by you; that has to be the work of Tomann and Koritschoner personally." One could actually die of laughter at the reading of this "report," if the story had not resulted in casualties. Bettelheim, the poor wretch, has in part done penance for his sin by writing a priceless report demonstrating unconsciously to every sound thinking worker the cretinism of the putschist tactic. The fact that he did not recognize this cretinism of his action even after the experience of June 15, that he put up for election recently radicalized leaders whom he accuses of having "recoiled from the revolution on the first day of their election," indicates that we are dealing here with an incurably sick Rinaldo Rinaldino. But the communist workers do not suffer from a deranged mind; Bettelheim's report will fill them with the deepest distrust for the rotten putschist magic. The vanguard of the German-Austrian proletariat, the communists, frustrated during the June days the putschist tactic of the Bettelheims. They did not plunge themselves into the adventure of the "proclamation" of the Soviet Republic without soviets. Their present task consists not only in learning to understand completely the harmfulness of the putschist tactic but also in overcoming it in practice.

5. The Road of Communism and the Social Democratic Struggle.

But it should be clear that the crises of a movement are not overcome by historical investigations, however fruitful they may be, but by proletarian action. Naturally, I am not referring to "proclamations" à la Bettelheim. To the contrary, I am referring to diligent organizational work, to the building up of appropriate organizations, and to the daily struggle of the masses against increasing misery in order to develop the dormant power of the German-Austrian proletariat, until the day arrives when the proclamation of the Soviet Republic does not constitute a putsch but only the expression of what the reality, of what life has given birth to. . . .

DOCUMENT 7: Ernst Bettelheim, *"The 'Bettelheimerei': A Contribution to the History of the Austrian CP and at the Same Time an Answer to Radek's Criticism of the Events of June 15th"*

Kommunismus, II, No. 29/30 (Aug. 15, 1921).

. . . The directorate met on the evening of June 12th for the decisive consultation. Present were members of the RSK [Revolutionary Soldiers' Committee], representatives of the unemployed, the demobilized and the disabled, the delegates from Floridsdorf, from the larger factories and from the provinces, all invested with a vote. One member of the directorate, Melcher, left demonstratively immediately after the start of the meeting, with, however, no further effect on the course of the deliberations. I especially called the attention of the comrades giving reports to the fact that they should report truthfully and that they should subject the facts to the most searching and objective criticism. The first report was given by a member of the RSK on the situation in the barracks. The result: the active participation of the majority of the soldiers on the side of the CP is secured. Not one battalion is against us. All military units view us with sympathy.

Next a report by the head of the section for factory agitation and organization. The result: undivided sympathy along the whole line. The dissatisfaction with social democracy has reached its culmination point. The active participation in the fight of thousands upon thousands is secured. Floridsdorf and the representatives of the larger factories confirm this report. The leaders of the unemployed, etc., report in a similar vein. The activity of some communities in the provinces was even higher than in Vienna. Final result: the active participation or at least the sympathy of the vast majority of the proletariat and the military in the struggle for the dictatorship of the proletariat is secured.

The bourgeoisie, on the other hand, was totally disorganized and in a state of panic. Its only hope, the Social Democratic party, began to disintegrate in the course of events. The only possible resistance against us could have come from the police force. But the previous day a *notice from the Police Commissioner of Vienna* had fallen into our hands which read essentially as follows: *"The militia is on the side of the communists, the railroad constabulary sympathizes with them, a part of the urban police is on the side of the communists, another part is unreliable. Only a few could be counted on. The younger elements of the police force unreliable, with the others the discipline is undermined, the rest is powerless against the masses."* The peasantry was as yet unorganized. The battalions of the militia in the provinces were sufficiently strong to keep them in check. Telephone and telegraph were in our hands. Within the Austrian-Hungarian bank preparations had been made for its surrender.

In back of us we had Soviet Hungary. The Red troops had smashed the Czech imperialists, and stood now in the North near the frontier of old Bohemia. In the West, near Pressburg, Red troops were ready. In some parts of Czechoslovakia the proletariat was only waiting for the entry of the Red troops. In Transdanubia, along the Austrian border, a Red corps was awaiting the command to act.

News from Italy was most encouraging. In Russia Kolchak's armies were withdrawing. The unification of the [Russian] Bolsheviks with the Hungarian Red Guards could be expected shortly. In England and France there were strikes and soldier revolts. In Yugoslavia and Bulgaria tremendous growth of the communist parties. In Bosnia the revolutionary peasants had seized the land.

Never before was the bourgeois weaker, the proletariat in greater misery, more desperate, and more ready for action than at this time. This was the historic moment at which the proletariat had to seize power.

As far as the relationship between Austria and Soviet Hungary was concerned and the impact of an Austrian proletarian revolution on the world revolution, the following was decisive:

a) The territory of Soviet Hungary was very small and extended only in a radius of 50 to 250 km around Budapest. The fights in April had already indicated that even insignificant successes of the enemy could greatly endanger Budapest. The continuation of the war would have been impossible following the loss of Budapest, since the weapons and ammunition factories were concentrated in and around Budapest. This strategic situation imposed on the Hungarian Soviet Republic the duty to secure for itself an area of retreat in case Budapest were to be lost. In view of the then existing situation, such an area was only offered by Austria. There the whole military equipment of the past monarchy was stored. With Vienna and its mighty weapon and ammunition factories, the Hungarian troops could have withdrawn behind the Danube and beyond even after the loss of Budapest. And the same would have been possible in the opposite direction.

b) But Austria was connected with Hungary not only strategically and geographically but for four hundred years economically as well. They complemented each other; the one was an industrial, the other an agricultural nation. The Bank of Issue of the old monarchy was located in Austria with all the technical equipment. The counterrevolutionary curse of the "white money" would have been removed at one blow and the Hungarian peasantry would have been inseparably tied to the dictatorship by Austrian industrial goods. At the same time the provisioning of the Austrian proletariat would have been secured.

c) Following the dissolution of the Hungarian Communist party the Social Democratic party bureaucrats spread themselves out over all the revolutionary institutions. They made no secret of their opposition to the dictatorship. The renewed build-up of the CP during the dictatorship became impossible due to the opportunism of a few communist leaders. For this reason there existed no prospect of rebuilding the old Communist party in time. It became clear that the days of the dictatorship were numbered without the CP. If the proletariat had seized power in Austria under the leadership of the CP alone, then the resistance of the sabotaging Hungarian comrades could have been broken, and the Hungarian CP and through it the Hungarian dictatorship would have been given a new lease on life.

d) In view of the international situation of that time Austria was not only the key to the salvation of the Hungarian dictatorship but to the extension of the world revolution. If the Hungarian Red troops crossed the border of Czechoslovakia and at the same time declared the dictatorship in Austria, then a Czech revolution could safely be expected. The Hungarian, Austrian, and Czech Red troops would have established contact with Soviet Russia through Rumania and possibly Galicia. This would have decided the fate of Italy and the proletarian revolution in the Balkan states. It would have meant the collapse of the peace negotiations at Versailles, the revolutionary effects of which would have been immense.

The most serious problem concerned the provisioning of Austria. The Entente at that time purposely supplied provisions for only three or four days to Austria. This constituted the sole weapon of the social democratic press against the proletariat. "The Entente will cut off the supply of foodstuffs." "Soviet Hungary is even less able to provision its own proletariat than Austria." "Any change of system in Austria means certain starvation."

We knew that the sympathy of the masses was with us. But all of us also had to face the fact of food shortages, of the counterrevolutionary agitation of social democracy as well as the fact that not a single voice could be heard in Soviet Hungary openly in favor of the Austrian proletariat. There were negotiations on this question between representatives of Hungary and delegates of the Austrian Social Democrats, the results of which were published only in the social democratic press, naturally totally distorted: "Soviet Hungary goes hungry, they have nothing to eat either." This was the sole break on the wheel of the revolution.

We were able to establish on the basis of data at our disposal that the provisioning of Austria out of reserves was secured for four weeks even after the discontinuance of the supplies by the Entente. In Soviet Hungary the harvest had already begun. Four weeks later that of Austria would have begun. According to information by the army corps this side of the Danube, the barns of the rich farmers of Hungary contained vast supplies of foodstuffs. In the case of our victory the united Red troops could have reconquered the granaries of Bacska and of the Banates; in short, the provisioning of the Austrian proletariat would have been secured under any circumstances for at least three-quarters of the year, even without an extension of the world revolution.

The Social Democratic party knew that too. Its State Secretary of the Army expressed the hope before a delegation of demonstrators on June 5th that this demonstration was directed against the Entente and the dictated peace, and he called upon the delegation to show the highest degree of resistance. He revealed, however, in this foolish manner the baseness of his party. "If we move, the supply of foodstuffs will be cut off." Nevertheless he now summoned the proletariat to fight against the Entente—the same Entente which supplied the foodstuffs. The CP naturally exploited the confession of the State Secretary to the fullest.

Then the debate began on the reports and the situation. In the course of the debate a member of the RSK fainted. *In the early-morning hours this meeting adopted unanimously the following resolution:* The counterrevolutionary government has to be dispersed by force and the dictatorship proclaimed by the CP in the name of the proletariat. An armed demonstration of the proletariat and the military must be called for this purpose for June 15. The directorate and the RSK declare themselves to be in a permanent session.

The details of the preparation were discussed immediately, as follows: I asked my superior [Béla Kun] to forward immediately to the CP a declaration of the Hungarian proletariat for publication, to the effect that sufficient foodstuffs were at the disposal of the Hungarian proletariat, that the Austrian press lied when it asserted the contrary, and that in case of the proclamation of the dictatorship the Hungarian proletariat would consider the provisioning of its Austrian brothers to at least the same extent as that of its own working class as its duty. The attack on Pressburg was to take place early on June 14. The Transdanubian army corps was to march up near the Austrian border in a mighty demonstration.

Comrade *Koritschoner* traveled early on June 13th to the industrial area of Neunkirchen and entered into association with the workers of Ternitz, Neunkirchen, and Wiener-Neustadt with the aim of having the workers there seize power on June 14th under the leadership of the CP. (This province was the focal point of the January strike of 1918, and the CP commanded a large following there. Comrade Koritschoner, the leader of the January strike, was very popular.) In the afternoon of June 14th a plenary session took place in Floridsdorf, paralleled in certain places by continuous sessions of the unemployed and the disabled. In the course of the evening designated battalions were to carry out military tasks which remain secret to this day.

These instructions had the following purpose: The proclamation of the Hungarian proletariat would have dispelled, in view of the temper of that time, all reservations regarding the difficulty of the food situation. The siege of Pressburg and the demonstrative deployment of the Red corps on the border would have heightened to the utmost, in the atmosphere of that time, the aggressiveness of the Austrian proletariat. And the proclamation of the proletarian dictatorship in the industrial area of Neunkirchen would have been decisive. Naturally, once the dictatorship had been proclaimed, a vast network had been prepared to announce it throughout Vienna. These events, the afternoon plenary session at Floridsdorf, and the meetings of the unemployed and the disabled in conjunction with the military tasks during the evening, would have decided the fate of the armed demonstration on June 15. The meeting did not, however, preclude the possibility that the whole proletariat would rise and seize power as a result of the events expected for June 14 with an irresistible and elementary force on the same day; the demonstration of June 15 would then have been little more than the weak tremor of a mighty proletarian uprising.

Budapest was appraised of all our activity. On June 13th Koritschoner traveled to Ternitz. The details for the military operation were fixed on the same afternoon and for the evening a mass meeting was arranged in the people's hall of the town hall. Rosa Luxemburg was buried on the same evening. Such a huge mass appeared that it flowed over from the people's hall out into the town-hall square, where two speakers discussed the agenda. The masses tempestuously demanded the dictatorship of the proletariat. The decision of the party was spread abroad with great speed already in the early-morning hours. Assured of its victory, the party made all its preparations openly.

On the evening of June 13th the government "temporarily" withdrew the ordinance [concerning freedom of assembly]. The district workers' council of Vienna at the same time opposed the action of the CP. Fritz Adler, the lackey of the bourgeoisie, announced: "I will show no mercy." Melcher, the former member of the directorate who had left demonstratively the meeting of June 12th appeared in the barracks on the Selzergasse demanding that I call off the action, lest he announce early in the morning in the name of the CP that the demonstration of June 15th had been called off. I made it clear to him that only the hitherto existing body was entitled to decide on this question. Meanwhile it was announced that the founder of the party, [Ruth Fischer] together with a few outmaneuvered careerists, was waiting downstairs for an answer. Melcher had become their spokesman.

The Secretary for Military Affairs issued an order in the morning hours of the 14th canceling all leave for members of the militia during June 14–16. Three members of the RSK, headed by Gruber—the one who had fainted—*called upon the militia in the name of the party to strictly abide by the order.* Simultaneously, comrade Koritschoner was called back in my name but without my knowledge. Instead of meeting in permanent session, the members of the directorate dispersed. Until noon of June 14th there was no news from Hungary. The shop stewards in Floridsdorf bided their time until the afternoon mass meeting. The three members of the RSK declared their withdrawal from the military operation. In the afternoon someone declared in the most widely circulated evening paper of Vienna, *Der Abend*, in the name of the CP, that the demonstration of June 15th would not take place. All the careerists of the party, under the leadership of the founding lady, toured the military quarters in order to instigate the crowds against the demonstration. They appeared in some places as representatives of the directorate, in order to be able to do a more "thorough job." The Workers' Council and the executive committee of the Social Democratic party appealed to the proletariat and the militia in a proclamation. *In the midst of it—at the last moment—a telegram arrived from Budapest: "I have prepared everything! Proceed cleverly and courageously! Its success is a vital matter!"* (Nothing, absolutely nothing had been prepared.) Not a single one of the agreed-upon precautions had been taken.

I had hardly received the telegram when a comrade appeared breathlessly with the urgent plea for me not to appear at the conference of the shop stewards that evening, since the police had been informed of everything and had decided to arrest everyone of the participants. I learned at that time that a new conference of shop stewards had been called for that evening at a completely unguarded place, although the barracks on the Selzergasse were at the complete disposal of the CP. I had some comrades immediately informed of the danger of arrest as well as of the content of the telegram. The conference met nevertheless at the designated place. It had hardly begun when the police appeared and arrested all participants—one hundred and forty shop stewards. (Even the police could not have arranged it better!).

The proletariat, weakened in its revolutionary discipline and resolution and ignorant of these events, appeared nonetheless in masses for the demonstration in the forenoon of June 15th. It learned immediately that its leaders had been arrested. In its revolutionary fever it proceeded to liberate them. The police opened fire, with dead and wounded as the result. The first police barrier was broken through with renewed volleys of fire. More dead and wounded. Ever new barriers were broken through; the masses liberated their leaders.

The militia, locked up in the barracks, heard about the events and wanted to rush out, *but was prevented by the RSK from turning against the police.* The RSK hindered its alliance with the proletariat in the revolutionary struggle. *In their impotent rage the soldiers tore the red buttons off their caps while cursing their leaders.*

In the streets, meanwhile, the liberated "leaders" appealed to the masses for law and order. They sent them home with the understanding they would come together again in the afternoon. Hundreds of thousands of provocative leaflets were distributed among the masses in the name of the military barracks. *While the masses returned in the afternoon, none of the leaders returned.* The confused masses surged like an immense sea back and forth in the streets until dawn. Vienna was in the throes of the red fever of the revolution. In this situation the leadership did nothing more than to ascertain during a newly called evening conference that "the Social Democratic party has ceased to exist as of today." This was the revolutionary deed of which the leadership of the CP was capable. . . .

V: Voices of Orthodoxy——Critics and Jeremiahs

The revolutionary sparks of 1919 flared up and died, with the newly formed Comintern standing by as a spectator rather than acting as a director of events. To be sure, there were messages exchanged between the Comintern and communist leaders in Budapest, Munich, and Vienna, but these were largely congratulatory, informational, or programmatic. Communications were so poor, and the Bolshevik leaders were so occupied with the civil war and intervention in their own country, that they often received full details about revolutions only after they had failed. Because the Bolsheviks were cut off from the outside world and had a rather limited understanding of conditions in central and western Europe, they viewed the revolutionary outbursts there as milestones of an ongoing world revolution. But the sister soviet republics did not materialize or last; the Comintern had to find a new orientation to the world situation at the end of 1919, in which it would have to coordinate activities leading to revolution rather than direct the relations of communist states. In Petersburg-Moscow and in various European communist parties, the 1919 experience had to be evaluated and assimilated and a new set of tactics devised.

A syndicalist-anarchist Left, anti-parliamentary and anti-trade union in nature, had appeared in the communist movement, influenced the revolutionary experiments in Berlin, Budapest, Munich, and Vienna, and gained considerable prominence in the German, British, American, and Dutch parties. It became clear to the Comintern leaders that under the influence of the Left there had been too great a dependence during the revolutions of 1919 on the activation of the streets through agitation, and not enough on the permeation of existing working class associations and the building of communist organizations. In a larger sense, 1919 demonstrated that the capitalist Jericho would not crumble before a few loud communist trumpet blasts. Democratic parliaments could not simply be bypassed in favor of the councils, nor could the latter be relied upon in a revolutionary situation.

"Into the trade unions and the parliaments!" was Lenin's remedy for the "infantile disease" of the Left which had infected the international movement in its first year. Lenin condemned the "doctrinairism" of the left wing of the communist movement and the "opportunism" of the right wing. This attempt to steer a middle course in a period of retrenchment was made the orthodox line of the Comintern at its Second World Congress in July 1920. On that occasion, the Twenty-One Conditions for Admission to the Comintern sought to outlaw deviations to the right and left. Lenin, writing his famous attack on the Left several months prior to the Congress, took as his keynote the position that the road to world revolution would be difficult and long (Document 1). The Lefts, he lectured, had become intoxicated with questions of ideological and organizational purity and failed to understand that in the protracted war to overthrow the international bourgeoisie communists had to maneuver and compromise. Communists, he insisted, must work wherever the masses are to be found—must struggle within the trade unions against their reactionary leaders and thus educate the workers, and must act within parliaments against reactionary politicians and thus promote consciousness among backward workers and ignorant and downtrodden peasants.

Deviations, however, could not be checked by Lenin's prestige or extirpated by Comintern decree. As we shall see in the next chapter, the controversy about orthodoxy and deviation split several major communist parties. Lenin's polemic did not go unanswered. Hermann Gorter, a leading Dutch communist, took up the cudgels in defense of the Left (Document 2). Lenin and the Comintern were guilty of opportunism, he charged, in trying to build mass parties by attracting middle-class elements and in working through the bankrupt trade unions. The Left, however, was concerned with building a sound and loyal nucleus of communists first, to which other proletarian elements, and only those, would be added in time. The trade unions he characterized as outworn evolutionary instruments that had to be replaced by industrial organizations commanded at the grass-roots level by shop stewards and merged into one big union. Parliaments likewise ought to be disregarded as bourgeois horse-trading institutions and boycotted in favor of direct action among the masses. Gorter simply dismissed Lenin's recommendations for western Europe as meaningless, since they were based on Russian conditions and experience. He warned that in following opportunistically in Russian footsteps western European parties would go blindly to defeat, and that the Russian Soviet Republic would go down with them.

The Lenin-Gorter controversy marked the end of international communism's heroic period, before the Comintern was really an organization and while feelings of individual and party equality ran high. The Second World Congress ushered in the institutionalization of the Comintern and of its members.

DOCUMENT 1: V. I. Lenin, *"'Left-Wing' Communism, an Infantile Disorder"*

(New York: International Publishers, 1940). By permission. Although the basic part of this work was finished by the end of April, 1920, it did not become well-known until the Second World Congress of the Comintern met in July.

. . . We can (and must) begin to build socialism not with imaginary human material, not with human material invented by us, but with the human material bequeathed to us by capitalism. That is very "difficult," it goes without saying, but no other approach to this task is serious enough to warrant discussion.

The trade unions were a tremendous progressive step for the working class at the beginning of the development of capitalism, inasmuch as they represented a transition from the disunity and helplessness of the workers to the *rudiments* of class organization. When the *highest* form of proletarian class organization began to arise, *viz.*, the *revolutionary party of the proletariat* (which will not deserve the name until it learns to bind the leaders with the class and the masses into one single indissoluble whole), the trade unions inevitably began to reveal *certain* reactionary features, a certain craft narrowness, a certain tendency to be non-political, a certain inertness, etc. But the development of the proletariat did not, and could not, proceed anywhere in the world otherwise than through the trade unions, through their interaction with the party of the working class. The conquest of political power by the proletariat is a gigantic forward step for the proletariat as a class, and the party must more than ever, and not merely in the old way but in a new way, educate and guide the trade unions, at the same time not forgetting that they are and will long remain an indispensable "school of communism" and a preparatory school for training the proletarians to exercise their dictatorship, an indispensable organization of the workers for the gradual transfer of the management of the whole economic life of the country to the working *class* (and not to the separate trades), and later to all the toilers.

A *certain* amount of "reactionariness" in trade unions, in the sense mentioned, is *inevitable* under the dictatorship of the proletariat. He who does not understand this utterly fails to understand the fundamental conditions of the *transition* from capitalism to socialism. To fear *this* "reactionariness," to try to *avoid* it, to skip it, would be the greatest folly, for it would mean fearing that function of the proletarian vanguard which consists in training, educating, enlightening, and drawing into the new life the most backward strata and masses of the working class and the peasantry. . . .

Further: in countries which are more advanced than Russia, a certain amount of reactionariness in the trade unions has been manifested, and was undoubtedly bound to be manifested, to a much stronger degree than in our country. Our Mensheviks found (and in a very few trade unions to some extent still find) support in the trade unions precisely because of the narrow craft spirit, craft selfishness, and opportunism. The Mensheviks of the West have acquired a much firmer "footing" in the trade unions; there the *craft-union, narrowminded, selfish, unfeeling, covetous, petty bourgeois "labor aristocracy," imperialistically minded and bribed and corrupted by imperialism,* represents a much stronger stratum than in our country. That is incontestable. The struggle against the Gomperses, against Messrs. Jouhaux, Henderson, Merrheim, Legien and Co. in western Europe is much more difficult than the struggle against our Mensheviks, who represent an *absolutely homogeneous* social and political type. This struggle must be waged ruthlessly and must be waged absolutely to the very end, just as we waged it, until all the incorrigible leaders of opportunism and social-chauvinism have been completely discredited and driven out of the trade unions. *It is impossible to capture* political power (and the attempt to capture it should not be made) until this struggle has reached a *certain* stage. This "certain stage" will be different in different countries and in different circumstances; it can be correctly gauged only by thoughtful, experienced, and well-informed political leaders of the proletariat in each separate country. . . .

But we wage the struggle against the "labor aristocracy" in the name of the masses of the workers and in order to attract them to our side; we wage the struggle against the opportunist and social-chauvinist leaders in order to attract the working class to our side. To forget this most elementary and self-evident truth would be stupid. But it is just this stupidity the German "Left" communists[1] are guilty of when, *because* of the reactionary and counterrevolutionary character of the *heads* of the trade unions, they jump to the conclusion that . . . we must leave the trade unions!! that we must refuse to work in them!! that we must create new and *artificial* forms of labor organization!! This is such an unpardonable blunder as to be equivalent to the greatest service the communists could render the bourgeoisie. For our Mensheviks, like all the opportunists, social-chauvinist, Kautskian trade union leaders, are nothing but "agents of the bourgeoisie in the labor movement" (as we have always said the Mensheviks were), or "labor lieutenants of the capitalist class," to use the splendid and absolutely true expression of the followers of Daniel DeLeon in America. To refuse to work in the reactionary trade unions means leaving the insufficiently developed or backward masses of the workers under the influence of the reactionary leaders, the agents of the bourgeoisie, the labor aristocrats,

[1] The "German 'Left' communists" Lenin referred to were an influential group within the KPD, under the leadership of Heinrich Laufenberg and Fritz Wolffheim, which had been largely responsible for the abortive Berlin Spartacist uprising in January 1919. They desired to replace existing unions with "one big union," believed that the revolution must develop and be fought (by general strikes) only on an economic plane, and were unwilling to consider the party the vanguard of the revolution. This faction was forced out of the KPD in 1919 and formed the German Communist Workers party (KAPD) the following year.

or the workers who have "become completely bourgeois" (*cf.* Engels' letter to Marx in 1852 on the British workers) [*Selected Correspondence* of Marx and Engels, p. 60].

It is just this absurd "theory" that the communists must not belong to reactionary trade unions that most clearly shows how frivolous is the attitude of the "Left" communists toward the question of influencing "the masses," and how they abuse their vociferations about "the masses." If you want to help "the masses" and to win the sympathy, confidence, and support of "the masses," you must not fear difficulties, you must not fear the pinpricks, chicanery, insults, and persecution of the "leaders" (who, being opportunists and social-chauvinists, are in most cases directly or indirectly connected with the bourgeoisie and the police), but must imperatively *work wherever the masses are to be found*. You must be capable of every sacrifice, of overcoming the greatest obstacles in order to carry on agitation and propaganda systematically, perseveringly, persistently, and patiently precisely in those institutions, societies, and associations—even the most reactionary —in which proletarian or semi-proletarian masses are to be found. And the trade unions and workers' cooperatives (the latter at least sometimes) are precisely the organizations where the masses are to be found. . . .

The Executive Committee of the Third International must, in my opinion, positively condemn, and call upon the next congress of the Communist International to condemn, both the policy of refusing to join reactionary trade unions in general (explaining in detail why such refusal is unwise, and what extreme harm it does to the cause of the proletarian revolution) and, in particular, the line of conduct of several members of the Dutch Communist party, who—whether directly or indirectly, openly or covertly, wholly or partly does not matter—supported this erroneous policy. The Third International must break with the tactics of the Second International; it must not evade nor gloss over sore points, but must put them bluntly. The whole truth has been put squarely to the "Independents" (the Independent Social Democratic party of Germany); the whole truth must likewise be put squarely to the "Left" communists. . . .

Even if not "millions" and "legions" but only a fairly large *minority* of industrial workers follow the Catholic priests—and rural workers the landlords and kulaks (*Grossbauern*)—it *un-*

doubtedly follows that parliamentarism in Germany is *not yet* politically obsolete, that participation in parliamentary elections and in the struggle on the platform of parliament is *obligatory* for the party of the *revolutionary* proletariat *precisely* for the purpose of educating the backward strata *of its own class,* precisely for the purpose of awakening and enlightening the undeveloped, downtrodden, ignorant peasant *masses.* As long as you are unable to disperse the bourgeois parliament and every other type of reactionary institution, you must work inside them, *precisely* because there you will still find workers who are stupefied by the priests and by the dreariness of rural life; otherwise you risk becoming mere babblers.

Thirdly, the "Left" communists have a great deal to say in praise of us Bolsheviks. One sometimes feels like telling them to praise us less and try to understand the tactics of the Bolsheviks more; to make themselves more familiar with them! We took part in the elections to the Russian bourgeois parliament, the Constituent Assembly, in September–November 1917. Were our tactics correct or not? If not, then it should be clearly stated and proved, for this is essential in working out correct tactics for international communism. If they were correct, certain conclusions must be drawn. Of course, no parallel can be drawn between conditions in Russia and conditions in western Europe. But as regards the special question of the meaning of the concept "parliamentarianism has become politically obsolete," our experience must absolutely be taken into account, for unless definite experience is taken into account such concepts are very easily transformed into empty phrases. Did not we, the Russian Bolsheviks, have more right in September–November 1917 than any Western communists to consider that parliamentarianism was politically obsolete in Russia? Of course we did, for the point is not whether bourgeois parliaments have existed for a long or a short time, but to what extent the broad mass of the toilers are *prepared* (ideologically, politically, and practically) to accept the soviet system and to disperse the bourgeois-democratic parliament (or to allow it to be dispersed). That, owing to a number of special conditions, the urban working class and the soldiers and peasants of Russia were in September–November 1917 exceptionally well-prepared for the acceptance of the soviet system and for the dispersal of the most democratic of bourgeois parliaments is an absolutely incontestable and fully established historical fact. Nevertheless, the Bolsheviks did *not* boycott the Constituent Assembly, but took part in the elections both before and *after* the proletariat conquered political power. That these elections yielded exceedingly valuable (and for the proletariat, highly useful) political results I have proved. . . .

The conclusion which follows from this is absolutely incontrovertible; it has been proved that participation in a bourgeois-democratic parliament even a few weeks before the victory of a soviet republic, and even *after* such a victory, not only does not harm the revolutionary proletariat, but actually helps it to *prove* to the backward masses why such parliaments deserve to be dispersed; it *helps* their successful dispersal, and *helps* bourgeois parliamentarism to become "politically obsolete." To refuse to take this experience into account and at the same time to claim affiliation to the Communist *International,* which must work out its tactics *internationally* (not narrow or onesided national tactics, but international tactics), is to commit the gravest blunder and actually to retreat from real internationalism while paying lip service to it. . . .

In western Europe and America parliament has become an object of particular hatred to the advanced revolutionary members of the working class. This is incontestable. It is quite comprehensible, for it is difficult to imagine anything more vile, abominable, and treacherous than the behavior of the vast majority of the socialist and social democratic parliamentary deputies during and after the war. But it would be not only unreasonable but actually criminal to yield to this mood when deciding *how* this generally recognized evil should be fought. In many countries of western Europe the revolutionary mood, we might say, is at present a "novelty," or a "rarity," which had been too long waited for vainly and impatiently; and perhaps that is why the mood is so easily succumbed to. Of course, without a revolutionary mood among the masses, and without conditions favoring the growth of this mood, revolutionary tactics would never be converted into action; but we in Russia have been convinced by long, painful, and bloody experience of the truth that revolutionary tactics cannot be built up on revolutionary moods alone. Tactics must be based on a sober and strictly objective estimation of *all* the class forces in a given state (and in neighboring states, and in all states the world over) as well as of the experience of revolutionary movements. Expressing one's "revolutionariness" solely by hurling abuse at parliamentary opportunism, solely by repudiating participation in parliaments, is very easy; but just because it is too easy, it is not the solution for a difficult, a very difficult, problem. It is much more difficult to create a really revolutionary parliamentary fraction in a European parliament than it was in Russia. Of course. But this is only a particular expression of the general truth that it was easy for Russia in the specific, historically very unique situation of 1917 to *start* a socialist revolution, but that it will be more difficult for Russia than for the European countries to *continue* it and consummate it. I had occasion to point this out even in the beginning of 1918, and our experience of the past two years has entirely confirmed the correctness of this view. Certain specific conditions, viz., (1) the possibility of linking up the Soviet revolution with the ending (as a consequence of this revolution) of the imperialist war, which had exhausted the workers and peasants to an incredible degree; (2) the possibility of taking advantage for a certain time of the mortal conflict between two world-powerful groups of imperialist robbers, who were unable to unite against their Soviet enemy; (3) the possibility of enduring a comparatively lengthy civil war, partly owing to the enormous size of the country and to the poor means of communication; (4) the existence of such a profound bourgeois-democratic revolutionary movement among the peasantry that the party of the proletariat was able to adopt the revolutionary demands of the peasant party (the Socialist-Revolutionary party, the majority of the members of which were definitely hostile to bolshevism) and to realize them at once, thanks to the conquest of political power by the proletariat—these specific conditions do not exist in western Europe at present; and a repetition of such or similar conditions will not come about easily. That is why, apart from a number of other causes, it will be more difficult to *start* a socialist revolution in western Europe than it was for us. To attempt to "circumvent" this difficulty by "skipping" the difficult job of utilizing reactionary parliaments for revolutionary purposes is absolutely childish. You want to create a new society, yet you fear the difficulties involved in forming a good parliamentary fraction, consisting of convinced, devoted, heroic communists, in a reactionary parliament! Is that not childish? . . .

It is a wonder that, holding such views, these "Lefts" do not emphatically condemn bolshevism! For, the German "Lefts" must know that the whole history of bolshevism, both before and after the October Revolution, is *full* of instances of maneuvering, temporizing and compromising with other parties, bourgeois parties included!

To carry on a war for the overthrow of the international bourgeoisie, a war which is a hundred times more difficult, prolonged and complicated than the most stubborn or ordinary wars between states, and to refuse beforehand to maneuver, to utilize the conflict of interests (even though temporary) among one's enemies, to refuse to temporize and compromise with possible (even though transitory, unstable, vacillating, and conditional) allies—is not this ridiculous in the extreme? . . .

After the first socialist revolution of the proletariat, after the overthrow of the bourgeoisie in one country, the proletariat of that country *for a long time* remains weaker than the bourgeoisie, simply because of the latter's extensive international connections, and also because of the spontaneous and continuous restoration and regeneration of capitalism and the bourgeoisie by the small commodity-producers of the country which has overthrown the bourgeoisie. The more powerful enemy can be conquered only by exerting the utmost effort, and by *necessarily*, thoroughly, carefully, attentively, and skillfully taking advantage of every, even the smallest, "rift" among the enemies, of every antagonism of interest among the bourgeoisie of the various countries and among the various groups or types of bourgeoisie within the various countries, by taking advantage of every, even the smallest, opportunity of gaining a mass ally, even though this ally be temporary, vacillating, unstable, unreliable, and conditional. Those who do not understand this do not understand even a particle of Marxism, or of scientific, modern socialism *in general*. Those who have not proved by deeds over a fairly considerable period of time, and in fairly varied political situations, their ability to apply this truth in practice have not yet learned to assist the revolutionary class in its struggle for the emancipation of toiling humanity from the exploiters. And this applies equally to the period before and to the period after the conquest of political power by the proletariat. . . .

Capitalism would not be capitalism if the "pure" proletariat were not surrounded by a large number of exceedingly mixed transitional types, from the proletarian to the semi-proletarian (who earns half of his livelihood by the sale of labor power), from the semi-proletarian to the small peasant (and petty artisan, handicraft worker, and small proprietor in general), from the small peasant to the middle peasant, and so on, and if the proletariat itself were not divided into more or less developed strata, if it were not divided according to territorial origin, trade, sometimes according to religion, and so on. And all this makes it necessary, absolutely necessary, for the vanguard of the proletariat, its class-conscious section, the Communist party, to resort to maneuvers, arrangements, and compromises with the various groups of proletarians, with the various parties of the workers and small proprietors. The whole point lies in *knowing how* to apply these tactics in such a way as to *raise*, and not lower, the *general* level of proletarian class consciousness, revolutionary spirit, and ability to fight and to conquer. Incidentally, it should be noted that the victory of the Bolsheviks over the Mensheviks demanded the application of tactics of maneuvers, arrangements, and compromises not only before *but also after* the October Revolution of 1917, but such maneuvers and compromises, of course, as would facilitate, accelerate, consolidate, and strengthen the Bolsheviks at the expense of the Mensheviks. . . .

. . . As long as national and state differences exist among peoples and countries—and these differences will continue to exist for a very long time, even after the dictatorship of the proletariat has been established on a world scale—the unity of international tactics of the communist working class movement of all countries demands, not the elimination of variety, not the abolition of national differences (that is a foolish dream at the present moment), but such an application of the *fundamental* principles of communism (soviet power and the dictatorship of the proletariat) as will *correctly modify* these principles in *certain particulars*, correctly adapt and apply them to national and national state differences. The main task of the historical period through which all the advanced countries (and not only the advanced countries) are now passing to investigate, study, seek, divine, grasp that which is peculiarly national, specifically national in the *concrete manner* in which each country *approaches* the fulfillment of the *single* international task, the victory over opportunism and "Left" doctrinairism within the working class movement, the overthrow of the bourgeoisie, and the establishment of a soviet republic and a proletarian dictatorship. The main thing—not everything by a very long way, of course, but the main thing —has already been achieved in that the vanguard of the working class has been won over, in that it has ranged itself on the side of the soviet power against parliamentarism, on the side of the dictatorship of the proletariat against bourgeois democracy. Now all efforts, all attention, must be concentrated on the *next* step—which seems, and from a certain standpoint really is, less fundamental, but which, on the other hand, is actually much closer to the practical carrying out of the task—namely, on seeking the forms of *transition* or *approach* to the proletarian revolution. . . .

The immediate task that confronts the class-conscious vanguard of the international labor movement, i.e., the communist parties, groups and trends, is to be able to *lead* the broad masses (now, for the most part, slumbering, apathetic, hidebound, inert, and dormant) to their new position, or, rather, to be able to lead *not only* their own party, but also these masses in their approach, their transition to the new position. While the first historical task (*viz.*, that of winning over the class-conscious vanguard of the proletariat to the side of the soviet power and the dictatorship of the working class) could not be accomplished without a complete ideological and political victory over opportunism and social-chauvinism, the second task, which now becomes the immediate task, and which consists in being able to lead *the masses* to the new position that will ensure the victory of the vanguard in the revolution, this immediate task cannot be accomplished without the liquidation of "Left" doctrinairism, without completely overcoming and getting rid of its mistakes. . . .

Inexperienced revolutionaries often think that legal methods of struggle are opportunist because in this field the bourgeoisie has most frequently (especially in "peaceful," nonrevolutionary times) deceived and fooled the workers, and that illegal methods of struggle are revolutionary. But that is not true. What is true is that those parties and leaders are opportunists and traitors to the working class who are unable or unwilling (don't say you cannot, say you won't!) to adopt illegal methods of struggle in conditions such as those which prevailed, for example, during the imperialist war of 1914–1918, when the bourgeoisie of the freest democratic countries deceived the workers in the most insolent and brutal manner, forbidding the truth to be told about the predatory character of the war. But revolutionaries who are unable to combine illegal forms of struggle with *every* form of legal struggle are poor revolutionaries indeed. It is not difficult to be a revolutionary when the revolution has already flared up and is raging, when everybody is joining the revolution just from infatuation, because it is the fashion, and sometimes even from careerist motives. After its victory, the proletariat has to make most strenuous efforts, to suffer the pains of martyrdom, one might say, to "liberate" itself from such pseudo-revolutionaries. It is far more difficult—and far more useful—to be a revolutionary when the conditions for direct, open, really mass and really revolutionary struggle *do not yet exist*, to defend the interests of the revolution (by propaganda, agitation, and organization) in non-revolutionary bodies and even in downright reactionary bodies, in non-revolutionary circumstances, among the masses who are incapable of immediately appreciating the need for revolutionary methods of action. The main task of contemporary communism in western Europe and America is to learn to seek, to find, to correctly determine the specific path or the particular turn of events that will bring the masses *right up against* the real, last, decisive, and great revolutionary struggle. . . .

. . . The communist in western Europe and America must learn to create a new, unusual, non-opportunist, non-careerist parliamentarism; the communist parties must issue their slogans; real proletarians, with the help of the unorganized and downtrodden poor, should scatter and distribute leaflets, canvass workers' houses and the cottages of the rural proletarians and peasants in the remote villages (fortunately there are not nearly so many remote villages in Europe as there are in Russia, and in England there are very few); they should go into the most common taverns, penetrate into the unions, societies, and casual meetings where the common people gather, and talk to the people, not in scientific (and not in very parliamentary) language; they should not at all strive to "get seats" in parliament, but should everywhere strive to rouse the minds of the masses and to draw them into the struggle, to catch the bourgeois on their own statements, to utilize the apparatus they have set up, the elections they have appointed, the appeals to the country they have made, and to tell the people what bolshevism is in a way that has never been possible (under bourgeois rule) outside of election times (not counting, of course, times of big strikes, when, in Russia, a *similar* apparatus for widespread popular agitation worked even more intensively). It is very difficult to do this in western Europe and America, very, very difficult; but it can and must be done, because the tasks of communism cannot be fulfilled without effort; and every effort must be made to fulfill *practical* tasks, ever more varied, ever more closely connected with all branches of social life, *winning* branch after branch and sphere after sphere *from the bourgeoisie*. . . .

DOCUMENT 2: Hermann Gorter, *Open Letter to Comrade Lenin: An Answer to Lenin's Pamphlet "'Left-Wing' Communism, an Infantile Disorder"*

(Berlin, 1920).

. . . *When we West European Marxists read your pamphlets, essays, and books, while admiring and agreeing with almost everything you wrote, we would nevertheless always come to a point when we would have to read more cautiously and when we would begin to expect more elaboration. Upon finding none, we would accept what you wrote with great reserve. This point was when you spoke of the workers and the poor peasantry.* You do that very, very often. And everywhere you speak of these two categories as revolutionary factors throughout the world. And nowhere, at least not in what I have read, do you emphasize *the very great difference that exists on this question between Russia* (and some of the East European countries) and *West Europe* (that is, Germany, France, England, Belgium, Holland, Switzerland, and the Scandinavian countries, perhaps even Italy). In my opinion, the reason for the difference between your viewpoint about tactics on the trade union and parliamentary questions and that of the so-called Left in West Europe lies precisely in the difference between West Europe and Russia.

Of course, you know this difference as well as I, but you have not drawn the conclusions from it in regard to tactics in West Europe, at least not in the works I have read. You have neglected these conclusions and because of this, your judgment about West European tactics is wrong. This was and is all the more dangerous, because everywhere in West Europe this notion of yours [that the majority of peasants in every capitalist country desires the overthrow of the regime] is being parroted mindlessly, in all the communist parties, even by Marxists. The impression gotten from all communist newspapers, magazines, and pamphlets and from public meetings is that a revolt of poor peasants is approaching in West Europe. The great difference with Russia is not mentioned. This leads to erroneous conclusions, even on the part of the proletariat. Because you had a great mass of poor peasantry in Russia and won with their help, you think that we will have such aid here in West Europe. Because you were victorious in Russia *only* by virtue of this help, you think that victory will be won here with that help as well. That you think so is plain from your silence on this question and its import in West Europe, and your whole tactic arises from this view.

This point of view, however, is not correct. There is a great difference between Russia and West Europe. In general, the significance of the poor peasantry as a revolutionary factor lessens from east to west. In parts of Asia, China, India, this class would be absolutely crucial if a revolution broke out there; in Russia it is an indispensable, main factor; in Poland and some states of southeast and central Europe it is still significant for the revolution. But the more one goes westward, the more hostile it is toward the revolution. . . .

From this difference between Russia and West Europe, arise the following consequences:

1. When you or the Executive in Moscow, or the opportunist communists in West Europe, or of the *Spartakusbund,* or of the English Communist party, say to us that the struggle over the question of leadership and masses is nonsense, this is not only wrong in regard to us because we are still looking for leadership, but also because this question has a completely different meaning for you.

2. When you tell us that leadership and masses must be an indivisible whole, this is not only absurd because we too

are seeking such a unity, but also because this question means to us something completely different from what it means to you.

3. When you say there should be an iron discipline and absolute military centralization in the Communist party, this is not only wrong because we also want iron discipline and strong centralization, but because this issue means to us something different from what it means to you.

4. When you say you did thus and such in Russia (for instance, after the Kornilov offensive or some other episode), or you entered parliament in this or that period, or you remained in the trade unions and therefore the German proletariat should do the same, it does not mean very much and therefore neither is nor has to be correct. For West European class relations in the revolutionary struggle are entirely different from those in Russia.

5. If you or the Executive or the opportunist communists in West Europe want to force upon us a tactic which was right in Russia—as, for instance, the tactic consciously or unconsciously dependent on and based upon the idea that poor peasants or other working classes will soon join us; in other words, that the proletariat does not stand alone—then the tactic which you describe and which is followed here will lead the West European proletariat into ruin and terrible defeats.

6. If you or the Executive in Moscow, or the opportunist elements in West Europe, as for instance the Central Committee of the *German Spartakusbund* and the BSP in England, think you can force us into an opportunist tactic (opportunism always leans on alien elements who abandon the proletariat), you are wrong.

And this: that the proletariat stands alone, that there can be no expectation of help, that the importance of the masses is relatively greater, that of the leadership relatively less—all these form the general basis from which a West European tactic must be derived. . . .

By their nature, the trade unions are not a good weapon of the West European revolution! Apart from the fact that they have become instruments of capitalism and are in the hands of traitors, apart from the fact that these organizations, no matter who its leaders are, by their very nature must make slaves and instruments out of their members, they are also useless in every other way.

The trade unions are too weak for the revolutionary struggle against highly organized West European capital and its state. The latter is too strong for them. For they are still in part craft associations and for that reason alone cannot make a revolution. And so far as they are industrial associations, they are not based in the factories, the shops themselves, and are therefore weak. They are also more like mutual aid societies rather than combat organizations, and came into being in the petty bourgeois era. Their organizational structure was inadequate for combat already before the revolution and in West Europe is completely unfit for the revolution itself. For the factories, the workers in the factories, do not make revolution in their professions and industries, but rather in the workshops. Besides, these unions are slow-moving, complicated instruments, good only for the evolutionary period. If the revolution did not come immediately and we had to resort to peaceful struggle for a while, even then, the trade unions would have to be destroyed and replaced by industrial associations based on factory and workshop organizations. And with these miserable trade unions which in any case would have to be destroyed, you want to make a revolution!!! The workers need weapons for the revolution in West Europe. The only weapons are the factory organizations, merged into a large unit! . . .

It is the curse of the workers' movement that as soon as it has attained some "power," it seeks to extend it through unprincipled means. Even social democracy was in almost all countries "pure" in the beginning. Most of today's social patriots were real Marxists. The masses were won with Marxist propaganda. As soon as some "power" was won, the masses were left in the lurch.

You and the Third International are acting now as the social democrats did then. Now it is on an international, not on a national, scale. The Russian Revolution won through "purity," through adhering to firm principles. Now it has power and through it, the international proletariat has power. This power is now to be extended over Europe, and the old tactic immediately is abandoned!!

Instead of applying the same tested tactic in all countries, thereby making the Third International internally strong, we are now once again turning to opportunism, just as social democracy once did. Now everything must be included: the trade unions, [German] Independents, the French center, parts of the [British] Labour party. In order to preserve Marxist appearances conditions are set which must be *signed* (!!) and Kautsky, Hilfering, Thomas, etc., are excluded. The masses, the middle-class masses are, however, included and pulled in by every means. *The best revolutionaries*, such as the KAPD, *are excluded!*

And once this great mass has been unified on a middling political line, then we are to march forward together, in iron discipline and under leaders who have been so extraordinarily tempered. And where to? Into the abyss.

Of what use are the impressive principles, the brilliant theses of the Third International, if we are actually practicing opportunism. The Second International also had the most beautiful principles, but it failed because of its deeds.

But we of the Left want no part of opportunism. We want to build in West Europe, just as the Bolsheviks did in Russia, very solid, very homogeneous, and very strong parties—nuclei, even if they have to be small in the beginning. When we have them, we will make them bigger. But they will still be very solid, very strong, and very "pure." Only thus can we win in West Europe. That is why we reject your tactic totally, comrade. . . .

You use in your fight against us, comrade Lenin, only three arguments which come up time and again, either combined or singly, throughout your pamphlet.

They are the following:

1. The advantage of propaganda in parliament in winning the proletarian and petty bourgeois elements.

2. The advantage of parliamentary action for making use of the "rifts" among the parties, and for making compromises with some of them.

3. The example of Russia, where this propaganda and these compromises worked so well.

You have no further arguments. I will now answer these in that order.

First of all, the argument about propaganda in parliament. This is an insignificant argument, for the non-communist workers, that is the social-democratic, christian, or other bourgeois-oriented workers, usually do not hear anything about our parliamentary speeches from their newspapers. The speeches are mostly distorted. We therefore do not reach them with these parliamentary speeches. We only reach them through meetings, pamphlets, newspapers.

We—and I speak frequently in the name of the KAPD—are reaching them (and we speak now of the period of revolution) particularly through actions. In all larger cities and villages, they see us act: our strikes, our street-fights, our councils. They hear our slogans. They see us go forward. That is the best propaganda and it does the most convincing. Such actions do not occur in parliament!

The as yet non-communist workers, petty bourgeois, and small peasant elements are reached quite well without parliamentary activity. . . .

The second argument: The advantage in parliamentary action of making use of rifts among the parties and for compromises with some of them. . . .

Making use of "rifts" in parliament is meaningless, because the "rifts" have for so many years, so many decades, been insignificant: among the big bourgeois parties as well as between them and the petty bourgeois parties; in West Europe, in Germany, and in England. This does not date from the revolution, either; it was true already much earlier, in the period of slow development. All parties, the petty bourgeois and the small peasant parties as well, have stood *against* the workers for a long time already, and the differences among them on issues concerning the workers (and therefore on all other issues as well) have become very small and have even disappeared entirely. . . .

The big bourgeoisie and large landholders, the middle classes and the middle peasantry, the lower sections of the bourgeoisie and peasantry in West Europe and particularly in Germany and England are, because of the monopolies, trusts, banks, war, and imperialism, and because of the revolution against the workers. They stand together on this.[2] And because the question of the workers dominates everything they are united on all questions. . . .

I am not denying that there still can be rifts. I am only saying that the general trend, which will remain so for a long

[2] It is true that because of the war proletarianization has advanced enormously. But everyone (or nearly everyone) who is not proletarian is hostile to communism, clings tenaciously to capitalism, and is prepared to defend it with weapons if necessary.

time during the revolution is: unification of these classes. And I say that it is better for the workers in West Europe to direct their attention to this unity rather than to the rifts. For they are the ones who will have to make the revolution here, and not their leaders, their representatives in parliament.

I am also not saying that, as narrow minds will construe from my words, the real interests of these classes are the same as those of big capital.

What I am saying is only this:

These classes are joined with big capital more than ever because now they see the additional danger of the proletarian revolution before them.

The domination of capitalism in West Europe means for them a certain security in life, the possibility or at least the belief in the possibility of rising in the world and bettering their lives. Now chaos and revolution, which at first would mean even greater chaos, threatens them. For that reason they support the capitalists in their attempts to end the chaos at all costs, to revive production, and to drive the workers longer hours and into bearing their privation passively. The proletarian revolution in West Europe means for them the collapse of all order and security, no matter how tenuous it really is. That is why they support big capital and will continue to do so for a long time, even during the revolution.

I ought to say that here I am again speaking about tactics for the beginning and the course of the revolution. I know that at the very end of the revolution, when victory is near and capitalism shattered, these classes will come to us. But it is our job to define a tactic for the beginning and the course of the revolution. . . .

I now come to your third argument about the Russian examples. You refer to them repeatedly (they appear continually from pages 1 to 97). I read them with the greatest attention and just as I admired them then, I admire them now. I was always with you from 1903 on. Even when I did not as yet know your reasons—communications were cut off—at the time of the Brest-Litovsk Treaty, I defended you with your own reasons. Your tactics were brilliant for Russia, and the Russians were victorious because of them. But what does that prove for West Europe? In my opinion, nothing, or very little. The soviets, the dictatorship of the proletariat, the means toward revolution and reconstruction, all this we accept. Your international tactic, at least up until now, was also an example for us. But this is not the case with your tactics for the West European countries; that is quite natural.

How can a tactic be the same for East and West Europe? Russia is a country in which agriculture predominates and where an industrial capitalism was only partially developed and minute in comparison with the rural sector. Even this [infant capitalism] was nurtured to a very large extent by foreign capital. In West Europe, and particularly Germany and England, this is exactly reversed. In your country: old-fashioned forms of capital, beginning with usury. In our countries: almost exclusively highly developed bank capital. In yours: enormous vestiges of the feudal and pre-feudal era and even of tribal and barbarian times. Here, especially in England and Germany: all agriculture, commerce, transport, industry, is under the control of the most developed capitalism. In your country: great vestiges of serfdom, poor peasantry, and stagnated middle classes in the villages. In our countries, even the poor peasants are connected with modern production, transport, technology, and trade. In the cities and in the countryside the middle classes, even the lowest, are in direct contact with big capitalists. . . .

Comrade, there are few more loyal than we, your old friends Pannekoek, Roland-Holst, Rutgers, and myself.[3] When we learned of your West European tactic we asked ourselves what could be the reason for it. There were many different opinions. Someone said that the economic condition of Russia is so bad that it needs peace more than anything else; that is why comrade Lenin wants as much power as possible. This power he hopes to gain by gathering the Independents, the Labour Party, etc., in Europe, who will help obtain peace. Another said he wants to accelerate the general European revolution and that therefore the millions must be made to cooperate. Hence the opportunism.

I personally believe, comrade, that you misunderstand the conditions in West Europe.

[3] Anton Pannekoek, Henrietta Roland-Holst, and Gorter were leaders of the Dutch Communist party who held strong anarchist-syndicalist views. In October 1919 the Comintern dispatched S. J. Rutgers to Amsterdam to open a West European Bureau. Almost immediately Rutgers was converted to the anti-parliamentarianism and anti-trade unionism of the three leftist leaders.

But whatever your reasons you will suffer a terrible defeat and lead the proletariat to the most horrible defeats if you persist in this tactic.

For if you want to rescue Russia and the Russian revolution, then you are gathering with this tactic the non-communist elements as well. They are uniting with us real communists at a time when we do not even have a strong nucleus! With this motley crowd of dead trade unions, with a mass of one-half, one-quarter, or one-eighth or even non-communists, without a strong nucleus, you want to fight the best-organized capitalists in the world, with whom the non-proletarian classes are allied. It is obvious that in the moment of battle this motley crew will fall apart and the masses will flee.

Comrade, a smashing defeat, for instance, that of the German proletariat, will be the signal for a general attack on Russia.

If you want to make the revolution here, with this stew containing the Labour Party, the Independents, the French center, the Italian party, etc., and the trade unions, it will not end otherwise. . . .

The Third International believes that the West European revolution will proceed according to the laws and tactics of the Russian Revolution.

The Left believes that West European revolution will have its own laws and will follow them.

The Third International believes that the West European revolution will be able to make compromises and alliances with small peasant, petty bourgeois, and even big bourgeois parties.

The Left believes that this is impossible.

The Third International believes that there will be in West Europe "rifts" and splits between bourgeois, petty bourgeois, and small peasant forces.

The Left believes that the bourgeoisie and the petty bourgeoisie will form a united front until the very end of the revolution.

The Third International underestimates the power of West European and North American capital.

The Left constructs its tactics according to this great power.

The Third International does not recognize the ability of large-scale and finance capital to unite all bourgeois classes.

The Left, however, constructs its tactics according to this unifying power.

As the Third International does not believe that the proletariat stands alone in West Europe, it neglects the intellectual development of this proletariat—which still lives deeply under the influence of bourgeois ideology—and chooses a tactic which allows slavery and subordination to the ideas of the bourgeoisie to continue.

The Left chooses its tactics above all with the aim of freeing the mind of the proletariat.

Since the Third International neither focuses its tactics on liberating the mind of the proletariat nor upon the [dangerous] unity of all bourgeois parties, but upon the compromises and "rifts," it allows the old trade unions to continue and tries to admit them into the Third International.

As the Left wants above all the liberation of the mind and believes in the unity of the bourgeois forces, it realizes that the trade unions must be destroyed and that the proletariat needs better weapons.

For the same reasons, the Third International allows parliamentarianism to remain.

For the same reasons, the Left annuls parliamentarianism.

The Third International allows the condition of slavery to continue as it was at the time of the Second International.

The Left wants to change it completely. It grasps the evil by the root.

As the Third International does not believe that the liberation of minds is above all necessary in West Europe and does not believe in the unity of all bourgeois forces in the period of revolution, it gathers the masses about it without asking whether they are real communists, without coordinating its tactics as if they were communists, because all that counts is that they are masses.

The Left will build parties in all countries containing only communists, and will aim for this in its tactics. By virtue of the example of these initially small parties, the Left hopes to make communists out of the majority of the proletariat, that is, out of the masses.

For the Third International, the masses of West Europe are a means.

For the Left they are the end.

Throughout this whole tactic (which was correct in

Russia), the Third International has been conducting a leadership-oriented policy.

The Left, on the other hand, conducts a policy for the masses.

With this tactic the Third International is leading not only the West European but particularly the Russian Revolution as well, toward its ruin.

The Left, on the other hand, is leading the West European proletariat with its tactic to victory. . . .

Further Reading

Historians have not viewed 1919 primarily as a revolutionary year and, consequently, there exists no work which treats his subject from that special vantage point. A recent work which comes near to filling this gap in scholarship is James W. Hulse's *The Forming of the Communist International* (Stanford, 1964). This valuable survey of the first two years of the Comintern and of the birth pains of several communist parties also contains an excellent analysis of left-wing communism.

The most recent monograph of the Spartacist uprising, Eric Waldman's *The Spartacist Uprising of 1919 and the Crisis of the Socialist Movement: A Study of the Relation of Political Theory and Party Practice* (Milwaukee, 1958), carefully delineates the divisions within the left and lays bare the hostility arising from them. Discounting the notion that the uprising was premeditated, Waldman attributes it to a combination of his hostility and fortuitous circumstances. Perhaps the most important contribution to the history of the German revolution in recent years is Eberhard Kolb's *Die Arbeiterräte in der deutschen Innenpolitik 1918–1919* (Düsseldorf, 1962). Based on a wealth of published and unpublished sources, it examines the outlook, composition, and activity of the councils and demonstrates that they certainly were not the foundation upon which a soviet republic could be built. For the activities of the Spartacist leaders Luxemburg and Liebknecht there are two biographies of unequal quality. J. P. Nettl's *Rosa Luxemburg* (London, 1966), 2 vols., is a work of careful scholarship particularly useful in tracing Luxemburg's ideas and activities against the background of the revolutionary period. Karl W. Meyer's *Karl Liebknecht: Man Without a Country* (Washington, D.C., 1957), contains a just assessment of Liebknecht's role in the November Revolution and the January Uprising, but is simplistic in its treatment of the revolution and he reasons for its failure. Although written more than thirty

years ago, still the most satisfactory account of the genesi
and unfolding of the German revolution is to be found in Ar
thur Rosenberg's pioneering studies *The Birth of the Germa
Republic* (London, 1931) and *History of the German Repub
lic* (London, 1936).

A full-length biography of Béla Kun and a comprehensiv
history of the Hungarian Soviet Republic are still to be wri
ten. The most recent study of the Soviet regime, Fran
Eckelt's "The Rise and Fall of the Béla Kun Regime in 1919
(dissertation, New York University, 1965), based on unpul
lished material in Hungarian archives, attributes the failur
of the communists primarily to the duplicity of the socia
democrats and secondarily to mismanagement, inexperienc
and foreign pressure. An interesting collection of translate
documents from the Soviet Republic can be found in th
biased work of Elemér Mályusz, *The Fugitive Bolshevi*
(London, 1931). An interesting account of Béla Kun's a
tempt to create a soviet republic in Slovakia for force of arn
can be found in Peter A. Toma, "The Slovak Soviet Republi
of 1919," *American Slavic and East European Review*, XV
(Apr., 1958). For an analysis of the Soviet Republic's foreig
political position in relation to the Entente powers and th
Succession States, see Alfred D. Low, "The Soviet Hungaria
Republic and the Paris Peace Conference," *Transactions* o
the American Philosophic Society (Philadelphia, 1963). A
appraisal of the theoretical and tactical implications of th
Hungarian defeat for the communist movement can be foun
in David T. Cattell, "The Hungarian Revolution of 1919 an
the Reorganization of the Comintern in 1920," *Journal* o
Central European Affairs, XI (Jan.–Apr., 1951).

The most authoritative history of Bavaria's revolutiona:
period is Allan Mitchell's *Revolution in Bavaria 1918–191*
The Eisner Regime and the Soviet Republic (Princeto
1965). Mitchell concentrates on Eisner's attempt to steer
middle course between a parliamentary and a council gover
ment, but also reveals the real conditions and fortuitous ci
cumstances which drove the revolution further to the Sovi
phase. For a discussion of the Bavarian councils, see Kolb
magisterial account above. A well-documented history of th
Bavarian KPD can be found in John Raatjes; "The Role o
Communism during the Munich Revolutionary Period, N
vember 1918–May 1919" (dissertation, University of Illino

1958). For an analysis of the relationship between the Bavarian Soviet Republic and the Russian Soviet Republic and the Comintern see Helmut Neubauer, *München and Moskau 1918/1919: Zur Geschichte der Rätebewegung in Bayern* (Munich, 1958). Neubauer's careful study reveals that the Bolshevik leaders were poorly informed about Bavarian events and exercised no influence on them. Fascinating firsthand accounts by two writer-revolutionists of the first Soviet Republic are Ernst Toller's *I Was a German,* trans. Edward Crankshaw (New York, 1934) and Erich Mühsam's *Von Eisner bis Leviné: Die Entstehung der Bayerischen Räterpublik* (Berlin, 1929). Both works clearly portray the anarchism, idealism, confusion, inexperience, and improvisation which prevailed during the short existence of the pseudo-Soviet Republic. A succinct discussion of the Free Corps' role in giving the *coup de grâce* to the Soviet regime and in carrying out a white terror can be found in Robert G. L. Waite, *Vanguard of Nazism: The Free Corps Movement in Postwar Germany 1918–1923* (Cambridge, Mass., 1952).

A balanced and detailed history of Austria's revolutionary period is still to be written. The most scholarly treatment of the subject is by Charles A. Gulick, *Austria: From Hapsburg to Hitler* (Berkeley, 1948), Vol. I. There the events of 1919 are related against a background of working class and social democratic development and the transition from a monarchical to a republican regime. Far less objective is the more personal history by Otto Bauer, *Die österreichische Revolution* (Vienna, 1923), for it invariably interprets the events of the revolution and the alternatives of action to justify the behavior of the social democratic leadership. The council movement in Austria has yet to receive serious attention from scholars. For an early episodic work rich in documentary reproductions, see Julius Braunthal, *Die Arbeiterräte in Deutschösterreich* (Vienna, 1919). A valuable analysis of Bauer's Marxism and its significance for the revolution can be found in Adam Wandruszka's "Otto Bauer und der 'Austromarxismus'," *Geschichte der Republik Österreich,* ed. by Heinrich Benedikt (Vienna, 1954).

PART THREE

ORIGIN OF
BOLSHEVIK HEGEMONY:
ITALIAN SPLIT AND
GERMAN OFFENSIVE

Bolshevization of the Comintern and of its members began in 1920 and not, as is commonly assumed, after the death of Lenin. On the eve of the Second World Congress in July 1920, the Comintern's leaders pursued two aims that indirectly increased the influence of the Bolsheviks and fostered their eventual hegemony over the movement. They sought to promote the organization of truly communist parties resting on a mass base drawn from other left-wing parties but excluding their leaders. They also hoped to subordinate all national communist parties to the Comintern, which as parent body would formulate the theory and plan the strategy of the entire movement and assign to each member party the tasks necessary to enhance its position nationally and the role it would play in furthering the growth and consolidation of international communism. Both of these goals required a tightening of party structures including the neutralization of factional pressures on the leadership, the application of Lenin's principle of democratic centralism to the activities of central committees, and a general remodeling of parties along Russian Bolshevik lines.

Bolshevization was not the product of a conspiracy by Russian leaders to dominate the members of the Comintern and to subordinate their individual interests to the needs of the Soviet Union. Bolshevization developed slowly but steadily from 1920 onward because of historical conditions involving the Russian leaders, the status of the world revolution, and the relative strength of communist parties within the move-

ment. The Bolsheviks who had captured state power were naturally in a position to tell those who had not done so how
to proceed. Revolutionary failures in 1919 from Berlin to
Vienna indicated that the world revolution would be postponed, at the very least. An even more realistic appraisal of
the situation foresaw a period in which communists would
have to educate and organize the masses preparatory to revolutionary action. The Bolsheviks' success in November 1917
and the subsequent revolutionary failures in the West under-
standably prompted the Bolsheviks to consider themselves the
only qualified teachers in this phase of development. Russian
preeminence in the movement was strengthened further by
the location of Comintern headquarters in Moscow, where
conditions and developments within the Russian setting and
decisions taken at Russian party congresses were bound to af-
fect the course of the International.

From its inception the Comintern attempted to avoid the
shortcomings of the Second International, specifically its inability to make its decisions binding on its members. To do
so the Comintern developed a centralized structure with co-
ercive powers wielded by its Executive. Within such a structure the strongest member was bound to exert a disproportion-
ate influence on the policies of the organization and through
it ultimately to dominate the activities of individual parties.
Against these bolshevizing currents the theoretical brilliance,
tactical skill, or personal dynamism of national communist
leaders failed to serve as a countervailing force. The peership
of communist leaders within the movement was forced to give
way to the centralizing drive of the international organization.
To be sure, there were test cases in which distinguished national leaders tilted lances with the Comintern ECCI over domestic issues on which their knowledge and experience were
superior, but only to discover that they were not masters in
their own house. By the Third World Congress in 1921 the
Comintern demonstrated that it had learned from its errors,
but it would not assume responsibility for them or permit individuals, no matter how well justified, to challenge its authority. At this early date it was already indicated that bolshevization precluded the existence of strong national leaders who
desired to initiate rather than implement policy.

In the short run bolshevization produced a violent upheaval
in the movement, characterized by splits, factional fights, open

and vitriolic polemics, and defections. These violent growth pains, by which most member parties were shaken to their foundations, threatened the existence of the Communist International itself. In the long run this ordeal by fire produced an organization unique in the annals of international socialism: single-minded in purpose, unitary in structure, and based on a practical inequality of members that would have been unthinkable in the previous two internationals.

Such a bolshevized Third International certainly was not predictable early in 1920. The movement was still recovering from the revolutionary reverses of 1919, and Lenin was just launching his critique of the syndicalist-anarchist Left, which was offering truculent resistance to its would-be mentor. The Comintern ECCI, out of touch with European events, was hardly in a position to provide firm leadership, and the various parties and groups arrayed under the aegis of the Comintern suffered from isolation or an uncertain status within the mass movements of their own countries. At this point Lenin's strategy was to anchor the nascent communist parties in the mass movement through parliamentary and trade union activity and to make the communist nucleus attractive to the left wing of social democracy in various countries. But leading the masses, of, say, the German Independents or the French Socialists, into the communist camp and thus giving the Comintern a broader base was fraught with dangers, particularly of watering down the communists' revolutionary *élan*. If the Third International was to avoid the mistakes of its predecessors it would have to combine growth in numbers with the development of statutes that would safeguard the character and goal of the organization. The Second World Congress, during which the seeds of bolshevization were planted, faced the difficult task of providing the Comintern with a mass base and of enforcing a rigid discipline at the same time.

I: The Twenty-One Conditions and Communist Discipline: The Italian Example

The more than two hundred delegates representing thirty-five countries who assembled in Petrograd on July 19, 1920 for the opening of the Second World Congress were received by the Russian hosts with pomp and circumstance. The festive mood created by the hosts, which overlay the serious deliberation of the congress in Moscow from July 23 to August 7th, stemmed from successes of the Red Army in the Russo-Polish War. The Russians' optimism over their apparent advance on Warsaw could not disguise the fact that the Comintern had gathered to appraise the revolutionary reverses of the previous year and chart a new course for the immediate future.

The composition and relative power of the delegations revealed much about the problems facing the Congress and the ultimate decisions that had to be made. As in the founding congress, the Bolsheviks had a commanding influence guaranteed by their representatives, who constituted forty percent of the 167 delegates with voting rights. Moreover, the size or voting strength of delegations did not correspond to the actual strength or size of national communist parties, so that Germany, Britain, and the United States each had five votes and the negligible parties of Finland and Georgia had the same number. Similarly, the formidable Italian Socialist party (PSI) had four votes and so did the Austrian party, which had virtually ceased to exist after its abortive uprisings in June and July 1919. In spite of the appearance of broad representation and evenly divided power, the Congress was actually under the control of the Bolsheviks and those who subscribed to their position. Some of the major delegations were divided seriously along political lines drawn with respect to willingness to participate in parliamentary and trade union activity and to the degree of authority to be invested in the Comintern. Thus the German delegation included representatives of the KPD with voting rights and of the Independents (USPD) and expelled leftists (KAPD) with consultative status; the three directions of the PSI were represented, although the right and left wings had only a consultative voice. In the French Socialist party delegation the left had voting rights and the center was without real voice.

Zinoviev's opening speech at the Congress was a restatement of Lenin's *"Left-Wing" Communism* and singled out for criticism the British Shop Stewards, the French Syndicalists, and the American IWW, who opposed parliamentary and trade union activity. The British anti-parliamentarians reacted violently to Zinoviev's admonitions and attempt to lay down a policy line. In the ensuing debate Jack Tanner of the British Shop Stewards crossed swords with Zinoviev and challenged the authority of the Bolsheviks. "Let me ask the Russians and other representatives if there is nothing more for them to learn from the economic struggles and revolutionary movement of other countries or if they have come here only to teach?"[1] The British question generated so much heat that it was referred to a special commission and only returned to the plenum on the last day, when Lenin succeeded in forcing the adoption of the decision to affiliate the British Communist party with the Labor party. Other attempts to foster model communist parties by playing national factions off against each other failed. Attempts by the Bolsheviks and their closest followers to intimidate G. M. Serrati by casting him in the role of obstructionist and centrist did not convince him of the need to purge the right wing of the PSI. Bolshevik maneuvers to woo both the German USPD and the KAPD failed, for although the Independents were drawn closer to the Comintern, the Leftists left the Congress in disgust after firing off charges of opportunism, and Levi, representing the KPD, became incensed by the pandering to the Leftists, who had, after all, been expelled from the party.

Other issues, including the national and colonial question, were peripheral to the main business of the Congress, which was to frame statutes governing membership in the Comintern. The first nineteen of what came to be known as The Twenty-One Conditions for Admission to the Communist In-

[1] *Protokoll des II. Weltkongresses der Kommunistischen Internationale* (Hamburg, 1921), p. 79.

ternational, circulated by the ECCI at the beginning of the Congress, represented the fruits of the Comintern's experience in its first fifteen months of existence (Document 1). The document stressed the means of creating disciplined parties rather than revolutions. Indeed, the complete absence of calls to arms distinguished it from proclamations of the Left going back to the Zimmerwald Conference. Parties desiring to obtain or maintain membership in the Third International were instructed to: create a reliable communist press; remove reformists and centrists from all party offices; carry on systematic propaganda in the army and in rural areas; create an illegal as well as a legal apparatus; split with reformism and the policy of the center; oppose colonialism and imperialism; form communist cells within trade unions; tighten control over parliamentary representatives and newspapers and periodically purge petty bourgeois elements; accept all resolutions of the Comintern and ECCI as binding; and quickly call special congresses to discuss these obligations.

The discussions of the nineteen points were stormy and tended to expose the contradiction in the ECCI's attempt to eliminate some social democrats while hoping to add large numbers of others to the communist parties. The French centrist delegates Marcel Cachin and L. O. Frossard objected to the demand for expulsion of their party's right wing. Zinoviev placated them and obtained their promise to fight for the adoption of the conditions by their party. The Comintern leaders' accommodation to Cachin and Frossard angered leftist delegates, who questioned the spirit in which these two had accepted the conditions. It was pointed out, and immediately underlined by Serrati, that the French Socialists whom the Comintern was ready to embrace had been guilty of the worst treacheries during the war, whereas the right wing of the PSI, which the Comintern was ready to expel, had behaved "properly" at the time. Serrati ultimately voted for the conditions, but explained that the right wing of the PSI would be expelled only when it had demonstrated anti-revolutionary intentions.

Later in the discussion, after Cachin and Frossard had left the Congress, two more conditions were introduced which aggravated the dissatisfaction of delegates who rejected a mechanical discipline (Document 1). The first stipulated that all communist parties be reorganized so that two-thirds of the membership of central committees was drawn from those who had endorsed the Comintern before the Second World Congress. The second called for the expulsion of all those who refused to vote for the Twenty-One Conditions. The Congress ended with a revision of ECCI membership that gave the Russian party five members and allowed one each to other major parties.[2] In spite of spirited opposition on certain issues and occasionally heated discussions, the Bolsheviks prevailed in the end. It remained to be seen how the parties would implement the Twenty-One Conditions and whether the tactic of opposites—purifying the parties by expulsion and increasing their mass base by cooperation—could be carried out simultaneously.

The first test of Comintern policy came in Germany, where the Independents with a membership of 800,000 were to be brought into the fold on the basis of the Twenty-One Conditions. Under the influence of Levi's skillful management and Zinoviev's fiery oratory and revolutionary prestige, a majority of the delegates at the USPD party congress at Halle in October voted to join the Comintern on its terms. This was a victory for the Comintern and for the KPD, which increased its membership from 50,000 to 350,000 and became a mass party, even though one-third of the split USPD, including its trade union core, remained in the old party and many members left the socialist movement altogether. The Comintern registered a similar success at the congress of the French Socialist party at Tours in December. There the Twenty-One Conditions were ratified by a two-to-one vote; the party adopted the name "communist" and became affiliated with the Comintern. All but a small right wing made the conversion to the new party, including reformists and centrists who should have been expelled if the Twenty-One Conditions had

[2] It is apparent that of the twenty-five members elected to the second ECCI those from Austria, Yugoslavia, Finland, Latvia, and Hungary did not represent "major" parties. The ECCI designated by the First World Congress to include representatives from the parties of Russia, Germany, Austria, Hungary, the Balkan Communist Federation, Switzerland, and Scandinavia, had been dominated by the Russians because none of the other parties save the Hungarian had been able to send a permanent delegate. The planning for the Second World Congress including the Twenty-One Conditions was therefore almost exclusively the Bolsheviks' handiwork.

been interpreted strictly. By the end of 1920 the Comintern's strategy, executed tactfully and compromisingly, had met with considerable success, witnessed by the two sizable reconstructed parties it commanded. In Italy, the same strategy, applied with considerably less finesse, only served to aggravate the differences within the party without producing the desired result.

The PSI, the strongest party in Italy and one of the earliest affiliates of the Comintern, had been the star in the diadem of international communism until the Second World Congress. As long as revolution in western Europe still loomed large, the Bolsheviks had paid little attention to the fact that the PSI represented a spectrum from reformism to syndicalism. When the emphasis shifted from agitation to organization, the absence of communist orthodoxy with its implicit lack of discipline was not to be tolerated by the Comintern. At the Second World Congress attempts had been made to intimidate Serrati and to force him in principle to acquiesce in the splitting of his party, but he had parried them. Back in Italy he took stock of what had transpired in Moscow, and indicated how he thought the Twenty-One Conditions ought to be implemented (Document 2). Two points stand out in Serrati's report to the readers of his journal *Comunismo:* that those who had been the worst nationalists and chauvinists during the war, even if they now were ready instantaneously to convert to communism, should not be trusted, and, implicitly, that those who had been good socialists during the war and were now reticent about becoming communists ought to be; and that every party be given time to work out the purging of its ranks in its own way.

Serrati was not to waver from this position in the following months, just as his opponents were not to falter in their quest for a "pure" communist party. The deep cleavages in the PSI were brought fully into the open at the congress of Livorno (Leghorn), which convened in January 1921 to take up the Twenty-One Conditions. Shortly before the congress opened two emissaries of the ECCI, Mátyás Rákosi and Khristo Kabakchiev, arrived and acted as fervent advocates of the left wing of the party (Document 3). The Socialist Concentration or right wing under Filippo Turati were traitors, they maintained, who surreptitiously undermined the party and had to be expelled. These traitors, they continued, were being shielded by the centrists or Unitary Communists under Serrati, who covered up the right wing's present crimes by references to its past virtues. Under the guise of unity Serrati was prepared to bring "bourgeois agents" into the Comintern and to deceive the rank and file of the PSI into believing that communists and enemies of the world revolution should be allied. The lesson of the Hungarian Soviet Republic and of the Soviet dictatorship in Munich and Finland taught, they concluded, that a union with reformists spelled disaster. The Unitary Communists responded with a plea for party unity and an affirmation of their adherence to the Comintern (Document 4). They accepted the Twenty-One Conditions, but argued that their implementation should be left to individual parties, which would be guided by conditions prevailing in their countries. The Socialist Concentration endorsed the position of the Unitarians, but its resistance to discipline imposed from without was stated much more clearly (Document 5). Although it accepted the dictatorship of the proletariat as a transitional stage leading to socialism, it refused to be guided by the Russian experience in this respect. When the conditions for such a development were right, it conceded, the party might conquer political power by means consistent with the times.

The right wing simply refused to be driven out of the PSI on grounds of rejection of the Twenty-One Conditions. And since it accepted them—in its own non-conformist way, to be sure—Serrati was unwilling to demand the expulsion of Turati and his followers. The congress was forced to choose between two extreme positions: Serrati's desire to keep the Right in the party until it had given proof of its disloyalty and refusal to come to grips with the reformism of its leaders, and the ruthless purification demanded by the Left and the Comintern delegates, by which not only Turati but also by implication his protector Serrati would be removed from the party. When the expulsion of the Socialist Concentration was brought to a vote, the Left lost by a margin of two to one, and withdrew to found the Italian Communist party (PCI).

The Comintern's support of this split in the Italian party fragmented one of its most significant sections and created a variety of anomalies. Both the PSI and the PCI declared their loyalty to the Comintern and agreed to abide by the Twenty-One Conditions. Neither of them conformed to the standards for communist parties of the Comintern: the former retained the reformists in its ranks and the latter was dominated by Amadeo Bordiga, who was close to the Dutch anarcho-syndicalists and opposed parliamentary participation. The Comintern had intensified the conflicts within the PSI and had encouraged the split, but the communist party which emerged suffered from the left-wing infantilism that along with right-wing opportunism Lenin was attempting to excise from the movement.[3]

The repercussions of the Italian experience were serious, and the postmortem by defenders and opponents of the Comintern's stand was carried on uncompromisingly and with bitterness. Paul Levi, who had been the KPD's representative at Livorno, agreed with the Comintern's policy in principle, but objected to the means by which it was applied in Italy. Parties, he insisted, could not simply be created by splits; their growth must be organic, with the members themselves responsible for purification (Document 6). Resorting to continual splits in the various parties could only lead to terrible reverses in western Europe. The purpose of the split in Italy, he continued, had been to exclude Turati, but the Italian communists and Comintern delegates had handled the matter mechanically and clumsily. They erred grievously in not realizing that the masses of the PSI could be kept within the communist movement only if Serrati was taken along in the bargain. Until the end of 1920, he pointed out, Serrati had been a respected leader of the PSI and even had been a member of the Presidium of the Second World Congress. Three months later the masses could not simply be told that he was a traitor who had to be expelled; they could accept the need for such a split only if it arose out of their daily experience.

[3] The ECCI tried to sponsor the Turin group under the leadership of Antonio Gramsci, who stood close to the Bolsheviks, for leadership in the PCI, but Bordiga and his Abstentionist faction were too well entrenched. The ECCI was clearly unhappy about the split in Italy and invited both the PCI and the PSI to send delegates to the Third World Congress in 1921. When the PSI expelled the Turati faction in 1922, the Comintern directed the PCI to fuse with Serrati and his followers. The Comintern victory was hollow at this point, because the struggle of the previous year had led to numerous defections from the PSI, and only a rump remained to make the conversion.

Radek, secretary of the ECCI, directed his counterattack against Serrati and Levi (Document 7). Not only Turati, he charged, was responsible for the non-revolutionary bearing of the PSI, but also such "semi-centrists" as Serrati. After equivocating about his position at the Second World Congress, Serrati had finally unmasked himself by refusing to exclude the reformists and by deviously offering to expel them individually for breaches of discipline. The Italian situation, Radek explained, had been a test case for the Comintern. At stake was whether it would permit the infiltration of centrist elements that would attempt to steer their party into quiet reformist waters in a non-revolutionary period, when the revolution had to be prepared intellectually and organizationally. Lastly, he turned on Levi, whose attack on the split at Livorno, he said, revealed that he was in the camp of those sabotaging the resolutions of the Second World Congress.

The Italian split was more than a local failure for the Comintern; it had a grave epilogue in Germany, where developing bolshevization encountered its first significant opponent.

DOCUMENT 1: *Conditions of Admission into the Communist International*

(New York, 1934). First appeared in *Der Zweite Kongress der Kommunistischen Internationale: Protokoll der Verhandlungen vom 19 Juli in Petrograd und vom 23 Juli bis 7 August 1920 in Moskau* (Hamburg, 1921).

The Second Congress of the Communist International resolves that the conditions for membership in the Communist International shall be as follows:

1. The daily propaganda and agitation must bear a truly communist character and correspond to the program and all the decisions of the Third International. All the organs of the press that are in the hands of the party must be edited by reliable communists who have proved their loyalty to the cause of the proletarian revolution. The dictatorship of the proletariat should not be spoken of simply as a current hackneyed formula; it should be advocated in such a way that its necessity should be apparent to every rank-and-file working

man and woman, each soldier and peasant, and should emanate from the facts of everyday life systematically recorded by our press day after day.

The periodical and non-periodical press and all party publishing organizations must be wholly subordinate to the Central Committee of the party, irrespective of whether the party as a whole, at the given moment, is legal or illegal. That publishing organizations, abusing their autonomy, should pursue a policy that does not completely correspond to the policy of the party cannot be tolerated.

In the columns of the newspapers, at public meetings, in the trade unions, in the cooperative societies—wherever the adherents of the Third International gain access, they must systematically and mercilessly denounce not only the bourgeoisie, but also its assistants, the reformists of every shade.

2. Every organization desiring to belong to the Communist International must steadily and systematically *remove* from all responsible posts in the labor movement, in the party organization, editorial boards, trade unions, parliamentary fractions, cooperative societies, municipalities, etc., all reformists and followers of the "center," and have them replaced by communists, even at the cost of replacing, at the beginning, "experienced" leaders by rank-and-file workingmen.

3. The class struggle in almost all of the countries of Europe and America is entering the phase of civil war. Under such conditions the communists can have no confidence in bourgeois law. They must *everywhere* create a parallel illegal apparatus, which at the decisive moment could assist the party in performing its duty to the revolution. In all countries where, in consequence of martial law or exceptional laws, the communists are unable to carry on all their work legally, a combination of legal and illegal work is absolutely necessary.

4. The obligation to spread communist ideas included the particular necessity of persistent, systematic propaganda in the army. Wherever such propaganda is forbidden by exceptional laws, it must be carried on illegally. The abandonment of such work would be equivalent to the betrayal of revolutionary duty and is incompatible with membership in the Third International.

5. It is necessary to carry on systematic and steady agitation in the rural districts. The working class cannot consolidate its victory without the backing of at least part of the

agricultural laborers and the poorest peasants, and without having neutralized, by its policy, a part of the rest of the rural population. Communist work in the rural districts is acquiring a predominant importance during the present period. It should be carried on, in the main, by revolutionary communist workers of both city and country only, who have connections with the rural districts. To refuse to do this work or to transfer such work to untrustworthy half-reformists is equal to renouncing the proletarian revolution.

6. Every party that desires to belong to the Third International must expose, not only open social patriotism, but also the falsity and hypocrisy of social pacifism; it must systematically demonstrate to the workers that without the revolutionary overthrow of capitalism, no international arbitration courts, no disarmament, no "democratic" reorganization of the League of Nations will save mankind from new imperialist wars.

7. The parties desiring to belong to the Communist International must recognize the necessity of a complete and absolute rupture with reformism and the policy of the "center," and they must carry on propaganda in favor of this rupture among the broadest circles of the party membership. Otherwise a consistent communist policy is impossible.

The Communist International unconditionally and peremptorily demands that this split be brought about *with the least delay*. The Communist International cannot reconcile itself to the fact that such avowed reformists as Turati, Kautsky, Hilferding, Hillquit, Longuet, MacDonald, Modigliani, and others should be entitled to consider themselves members of the Third International. This would make the Third International resemble, to a considerable degree, the late Second International.

8. On the question of the colonies and oppressed nationalities, an especially distinct and clear line must be taken by the parties in those countries where the bourgeoisie possesses colonies or oppresses other nations. Every party desirous of belonging to the Third International must ruthlessly denounce the methods of "their own" imperialists in the colonies, supporting, not in words, but in deeds, every independence movement in the colonies. It should demand the expulsion of their own imperialists from such colonies, and cultivate among the workers of their own country a truly fraternal attitude toward

the toiling population of the colonies and oppressed nationalities, and carry on systematic agitation in its own army against every kind of oppression of the colonial population.

9. Every party that desires to belong to the Communist International must carry on systematic and persistent communist work in the trade unions, in workers' and industrial councils, in the cooperative societies, and in other mass organizations. Within these organizations it is necessary to create communist groups, which by means of practical and stubborn work must win over the trade unions, etc., for the cause of communism. These cells should constantly denounce the treachery of the social patriots and the vacillations of the "center," at every step. These communist groups should be completely subordinate to the party as a whole.

10. Every party that belongs to the Communist International must carry on a stubborn struggle against the Amsterdam "International" of yellow trade unions. It must persistently propagate among the organized workers the necessity of a rupture with the yellow Amsterdam International. It must give all the support in its power to the incipient international alliance of the red trade unions affiliated to the Communist International.

11. The parties desiring to belong to the Third International must overhaul the membership of their parliamentary fractions, eliminate all unreliable elements from them, to control these fractions, not only verbally but in reality, to subordinate them to the central committee of the party, and demand from every communist member of parliament that he devote his entire activities to the interests of really revolutionary propaganda and agitation.

12. Parties belonging to the Communist International must be built up on the principle of democratic *centralism.* At the present time of acute civil war, the communist party will only be able fully to do its duty when it is organized in the most centralized manner, if it has iron discipline, bordering on military discipline, and if the party center is a powerful, authoritative organ with wide powers, possessing the general trust of the party membership.

13. The communist parties of those countries where the communists' activity is legal shall make periodical cleanings (re-registration) of the members of the party organizations,

so as to systematically cleanse the party from the petty bourgeois elements who inevitably attach themselves to it.

14. Every party that desires to belong to the Communist International must give every possible support to the Soviet Republics in their struggle against all counterrevolutionary forces. The communist parties should carry on a precise and definite propaganda to induce the workers to refuse to transport munitions of war intended for enemies of the Soviet Republic, carry on legal or illegal propaganda among the troops, which are sent to crush the workers' republic, etc.

15. The parties which up to the present have retained their old social democratic programs must in the shortest possible time overhaul these programs and draw up a new communist program in conformity with the special conditions of their respective countries and in accordance with resolutions of the Communist International. As a rule, the program of every party that belongs to the Communist International must be ratified by the next congress of the Communist International or by the Executive Committee. In the event of the Executive Committee of the Communist International failing to ratify the program of a particular party, that party has the right to appeal to the congress of the Communist International.

16. All decisions of the congresses of the Communist International, as well as the decisions of its Executive Committee, are binding on all parties affiliated to the Communist International. The Communist International, operating in the midst of a most acute civil war, must have a far more centralized form of organization than that of the Second International. At the same time, the Communist International and its executive committee must, of course, in all their activities, take into consideration the diversity of the conditions under which the various parties have to work and fight, and should issue universally binding decisions only on questions on which the passing of such decisions is possible.

17. In connection with all this, all parties desiring to join the Communist International must change their names. Every party that wishes to join the Communist International must bear the name: *Communist party* of such-and-such country (Section of the Third Communist International). This question as to name is not merely a formal one, but a political one of great importance. The Communist International has declared a decisive war against the entire bourgeois world and

all the yellow, social democratic parties. Every rank-and-file worker must clearly understand the difference between the communist parties and the old official "social democratic" or "socialist" parties which have betrayed the cause of the working class.

18. All the leading party organs of the press in all countries must publish all the chief documents of the Executive Committee of the Communist International.

19. All parties belonging to the Communist International, or having made an application to join it, must, in the shortest possible period, but not later than four months after the Second Congress of the Communist International, call special party congresses, for the purpose of discussing these obligations. In this connection, the central committees must take measures to enable all the local organizations to become acquainted with the decisions of the Second Congress of the Communist International.

20. The parties that would now like to join the Third International but which have not yet radically changed their former tactics, must, before joining, take steps to ensure that their central committees and all most important central bodies of the respective parties shall be composed, to the extent of at least two-thirds, of such comrades as even prior to the Second Congress of the Communist International have openly and definitely declared for joining the Third International. Exceptions may be made with approval of the Executive Committee of the Third International. The Executive Committee of the Communist International also has the right to make exceptions in the case of representatives of the "center" mentioned in point 7.

21. Members of the party who reject the conditions and theses of the Communist International, on principle, must be expelled from the party.

This applies also to the delegates to the special party congresses.

DOCUMENT 2: G. M. Serrati, *"The Second Congress of the Third International"*

Comunismo: Revista della Terza Internazionale, I, No. 24 (Sept., 1920).

Some Preliminary Observations

. . . The Second Congress started under the following circumstances:

1. The majority of the delegates had left for Russia before their respective countries had an idea of the convoking of the Congress, and thus they were only representatives in a broad sense and with a personal trust.

2. No discussions had been held previously by the individual parties with regard to the diverse items on the agenda so that, for some delegates, many theses of more than secondary importance were completely unknown.

3. The distance between the Congress and the countries of the proletarian movement, the difficulty of communications, the blockade which lasted for such a long time, the almost total absence of control on the part of a working class public which could be present at discussions of newspapers which could publish the discussions quickly, made the meeting a closed assembly which lacked communication with and from the outside.

4. The delegates of the Congress knew each other only imperfectly and did not know their respective movements, the effective power represented by this one and by that one, the means it had at its disposal, the influences which could be brought into play in international politics.

5. The Congress was held under the auspices of a great revolutionary government at the same time in which its military forces were deeply engaged in a mortal duel with the forces of reaction, and while the communist government was obliged—as it still is—to construct its own politics of offense and defense in the world of international and internationalistic capitalism. These politics, being helpful to the Republic of Soviets, must indubitably be of help to the world proletariat. All the same, they may not conform to the tactical necessities

of another country which finds itself in a critical period of its own as yet unerupted revolution.

6. There was an evident disproportion between the representative quality of the various delegates; such a disproportion as was never before seen at an international congress. And this was a notable cause of very understandable embarrassments, hesitations, and talking down in the discussions.

7. The distribution of votes of the individual countries was made not according to the real and effective political and moral forces of the different parties, but above all with consideration of the capitalistic importance of the country represented, in such a way that France, which was represented only by a very small minority of the party and of the [Trade Union] Confederation, had as many votes as Italy. England, represented by the British Socialist party, which has not even 10,000 members, and by the dissident and diverse organizations of Shop Steward Committees, Scottish Autonomous Communist Groups, etc., had the same votes as the very powerful Russian Communist party. Of the workers' organizations the Italian General Confederation of Labor, which had signed in those days a clear pact of alliance with the Russian trade union organizations and which really counts for something in the international movement, independently, if you will, of its leaders, was not represented. Instead, Spain and Georgia were represented.

8. Just as the distance of the location of the Congress and the difficulties of communication had hampered preparations, it hampered equally and perhaps even more the dissemination of the deliberations. It is enough to point out that two months after the Congress the individual parties have not been able to obtain full reports on it; that the theses voted in their definitive form were not known until more than a month after the closing; that in France and elsewhere discussions were held before the participants were able to find out if there were 9, 18, or 21 conditions for adherence; and they are still discussing this as I write. . . .

We accept the Twenty-One Conditions, which were placed before the socialists of all countries in an exceedingly rough way. But we accept them with two conditions:

1. that overwhelming leniency is not shown toward those who, after having shamefully betrayed the proletariat by getting caught up in the nationalistic infatuation during the war,

today, with equal facility, declare themselves ready to submit to the rigid discipline imposed by Moscow. These people will betray us again tomorrow. There are too many St. Pauls on the road of the proletariat for us to believe that they are all of perfectly good faith; and, if moral judgment on men's pasts has little value in the revolutionary struggle, there is however a political judgment on the immorality of certain conversions. This judgment must be made inexorably by the proletariat if it does not wish to create traitors in its own breast;

2. that time be given to the various parties who adhere to the Third International—under their own responsibility—to proceed to the necessary work of purging their ranks, without it having a harmful effect on the solidarity of the proletarian movement and without it damaging that same revolution which Moscow believes to be so near.

Let us note only one circumstance with regard to this. In these days we are winning municipalities and provinces by the hundreds, by the thousands. We have thousands of co-operatives in our hands and thousands of other proletarian institutions have been conquered or are being conquered. The Third International is not issuing any excommunications against such conquests; on the contrary, it is for them. Meanwhile, everywhere in our party we are looking for men to run municipalities, cooperatives, the Chambers of Labor, etc. There is a frightening crisis of ability in Italy and in all other countries. And here is the Second Congress of the Third International ordering us to place communists in all of these positions without worrying about their ability. Here, we are in the kingdom of the unlikely. Can you imagine the municipality of Milan directed by a group of incompetents, new arrivals, people pretending at the last minute to be fervent communists?

In order not to destroy all of the proletarian institutions created by so much effort, in order not to compromise the work of revolutionary reconstruction—which will be so much quicker and greater the more we have learned, even in the pre-revolutionary period, how to fortify it with our institutions—it is indispensable that the work of purging be accomplished with political discernment, without distasteful impositions, and without harmful violence, as without thoughtless improvisations.

DOCUMENT 3: *"Declaration of the Representative of the Communist International"*

Il Partito Socialista Italiano e L'Internazionale Comunista (Petrograd, 1921).

Documents of the Congress of Livorno

The two representatives of the Moscow Executive Committee present at this congress, comrade Kabakchiev and comrade Rákosi, in the name of that Committee declare that, as representatives of the Communist International, they accept and subscribe to the motion proposed by the Communist faction. This motion corresponds to the principle and to the tactics of the Third International and represents the only way in which this congress can accept and apply the conditions and the proposals of the Second World Communist Congress. The Communist International categorically and absolutely insists upon the exclusion from the party of the entire reformist group. We declare that according to the principle and the program of the Communist International the group which should be excluded appears in the so-called faction of Socialist Concentration. A centrist tendency exists which, in its actions and its motions, rejects this precise application of the decisions of the Second World Communist Congress. They are Unitary Communists. They insist that there is no reformist tendency, but at the most only some reformists. These are, however, much better than the social traitors in other countries, because they voted against the war, did not collaborate with the bourgeoisie, and are so inoffensive as not even to constitute a faction.

Instead we affirm that it is a question of reformists and social democrats, who are much more dangerous than their opportunistic counterparts in other countries.

These people do not betray in the open and crude way that the Noskes, the Scheidemanns, the Martovs, and Co., did. But they work instead in ways which are more dangerous because less obvious. They deny that we are in the presence of a revolutionary crisis. Therefore, all their actions have the effect of disturbing the clarity of direction of the Italian proletariat, of distracting its attention from the real danger, and thus they render the proletariat harmless in the face of the already organized counter-revolution. The function which the Mensheviks in other countries exercise openly and visibly here is hidden under hypocritical revolutionary phrases, but at bottom it is the same thing. The Communist International, on the eve of the revolution, while the White Guard has already begun the first skirmishes of civil war, points out clearly, sharply, and categorically the immense dangers to which the Italian proletariat is subject due to its reformist elements and shows that the only way to salvation is the immediate and inexorable exclusion of these elements. At the same time, here are the leaders of the centrists trying to cover up the cancerous plague in the party. They remind us of the past merits of the reformists, they conceal the danger, and they want to lead the imminent grand struggle against the bourgeoisie while keeping in the heart of the militant party conscious and unconscious enemies of the working class.

They do more. The leaders of the centrists want to bring the Turatis and the D'Aragonas into the Communist International, where these people will be able to continue their work for the bourgeoisie. They are making all possible efforts to save them. They appear on the platforms of the reformists and they appear as communists. To those comrades who say that they accept the Twenty-One Points without reservation we wish to observe that to accept them means also to put them into immediate execution. In the present situation in Italy this immediate execution is an absolute necessity and is the first and inevitable step toward the creation of a healthy and strong Communist party. This must come to pass with the resolution of the congress.

Here, we would like to recall some experiences of the Hungarian Soviet Republic which correspond in a singular manner to our situation.

Comrades! The Hungarian communists too found themselves face to face with this same problem. They also had to decide whether to collaborate with the reformists or whether to exclude the reformist leaders. They too received an admonitory letter from Lenin and the Third International and they too, as many comrades here today wish to do, in spite of the admonition, decided for the unity of the party, for the retention of the reformists. The motives which pushed

them to unity are the same ones which today move the reformists and the centrists in Livorno. There also they spoke
of special Hungarian conditions; there also they yielded to
the sentimental part of the working class and formed the party
of unity. The Hungarian communists, too, postponed the expulsion of the reformists until such time as these reformists
had given them the opportunity to justify their removal in
the eyes of the unenlightened masses. They thought, precisely
as do the followers of Serrati today, that they would be able
to accomplish the great tasks of the proletarian revolution
more easily if they entered the fight without any schisms. The
similarity is made complete by the fact that the right-wing
Hungarians also wanted, at the most, only to speak about a
"Socialist Communist party".

The results show that in every respect the Third International was right. None of these hopes bore fruit.

The rightists knew that they would be thrown out of the
party if they acted openly against the proletariat and thus
they acted underhandedly, exercising every form of sabotage.
They knew that every victory of the Russian army, every reinforcement of the power of the Soviet, brought closer the moment in which they would be placed outside the proletarian
movement. Thus they stayed on the defensive, they held together, and they tried in every way to pull down the unwelcome dictatorship. As the difficulties in the Soviet dictatorship
grew, it became increasingly harder to exclude them.

On the contrary, the more obscure the situation became,
the more brazenly and openly they intrigued. It was impossible to do anything against them as they were, after all, as
communists, members and functionaries of the party. Many
times it happened that the Hungarian D'Aragonas, as members of the party, would have needed to act against themselves, as heads of organizations. Finally they became the
fulcrum of the counterrevolution, and their strongest support
came precisely from those sentimental masses who had lost
heart when confronted with the grave duties that the power
of the councils inevitably imposed on every single worker. Unfortunately, they succeeded in undermining from the inside
the power of the workers. And when the dictatorship of the
councils fell, these gentlemen became ministers, if only for
five days, as payment for services rendered in the work of
strangling the Soviet. With great pain and with the lives of

thousands of its best sons, the Hungarian proletariat is paying for the error that today the followers of Serrati want the Italian proletariat to commit.

The story of the Soviet dictatorships in Finland and in Bavaria offers the same lesson. It would be a very grave sin if the Communist International did not make every effort to stop Serrati and Company from profiting, either consciously or unconsciously, from the inexperience and the sentimentality of certain sections of the working class and by offering them the mirage of a false unity, from leading the Italian proletariat to that same Calvary on which the proletariat of Hungary, of Finland, and of Bavaria suffer the infernal torments of the white terror.

The Communist International must use all means, even the most energetic and painful, to stop this ambiguous unitarian solution which would become the ruin of the Italian proletariat.

All the same, in the train of the trade union leaders, of the exponents of the current of unity, there are many good, simple workingmen to whom I would like to address some words. Comrades, you who with sincere devotion and with a spirit of sacrifice serve the cause of the emancipation of the Italian workers, you who have unshakable faith in the victory of the world revolution and who with every heartbeat follow the heroic fight of our Russian brothers, we tell you that in the name of the proletarian revolution they are asking you to march against the proletarian revolution.

They tell you that the Italian party can defend and sustain the Russian and the world revolution only if it remains unified. But do you not see that with unity they mean only to obtain the retention in your ranks of a current which is against the Russian Revolution and against the world revolution?

The Communist International has discovered this danger in time, and has put you on guard against it. The proletariat and the bourgeoisie of all countries are looking with bated breath at Livorno, where the reformists are trying to set a part of the revolutionary Italian workers against the revolution, against Moscow.

Comrades, workers, communists! You must now show that you really are for the Communist International, that you desire the true, the only unity, that is to say, the unification of all those revolutionary working forces which contain no traitors to the proletariat. You must show that you are devoted and disciplined militants of the Communist International, and it is in the name of the Communist International that we put the problem before you in the clearest and most explicit way. All of you, delegates of workers inscribed in the party, must make a choice when the moment of voting on the resolutions presented to you comes: either for the Communist International or for reformism; either for the road of the world revolution or for that of the counterrevolution.

"The Unity of the Party" is an ambiguous formula: it means unity between communists and enemies of communism. There is no place for this kind of unity in the ranks of the Third International. He who wishes to remain in the Communist International must align himself against the reformists and with the communists, and with those all over the world who stand firmly on the foundation of the inviolable decisions of their World Congress. Thus we repeat to you that the Communist International rejects every resolution which is not put before you by the Communist faction. We underline this, because we are convinced that only with the close union of communists all over the world will it be possible to overthrow the power of capitalism and establish the rule of communism on the whole earth.

Long live the Communist International!

Long live the Italian Communist party!

DOCUMENT 4: *"Order of the Day of the Unitary Communists"*

Il Partito Socialista Italiano e L'Internazionale Comunista.

The Italian Socialist party in its XVII National Congress, in discussing its political direction, considers that it is necessary to strengthen the unity of the party on the basis of a greater homogeneity of its organs as well as of its components. To obtain this it asks for greater centralization, in such a way that every single member and organ subordinates and disciplines its own activity to the law of common interest and common goals; and this should hold true also for control of didactic activity in the intellectual and propaganda fields.

For the same purpose, it wishes to make certain that, in opposition to economic organizations and those which have as their goal resistance, pre-eminence be given, on the level of both thought and action, to political considerations. These considerations should take precedence over contingent or trade union considerations, just as the central organs of the economic and trade union movement subordinate themselves to the organs of the political party.

The Italian Socialist party recognizes as a consequence the necessity that the unitary structure of the party be preserved so that we may more easily and more quickly arrive at the conquest of all political power. For this end every means—within the limits of absolute class intransigence—is acceptable, always, however, keeping in mind the goal of the communist revolution, which itself calls for the integration of political action with the economic action of the trade union forces.

The PSI makes legal and extra-legal preparation, not only for organizing the means of education and the instruments of revolutionary conquest, but also for creating organs to replace the existing ones.

In discussing, furthermore, the relations between the Italian Socialist party and the Third Communist International, it confirms its full and spontaneous adherence to that International and to the deliberations of the International Congress.

It therefore declares, after the Second Moscow Congress, that it accepts completely the Twenty-One Conditions derived from the motions which were voted upon, adding to these conditions the expulsion of the Masons. As for the execution of the conditions, it feels that the Twenty-One Points should be interpreted according to the circumstances and historical conditions of the country, in agreement with the Executive Committee of the Third International, which admits (Points 16 and 20) that this is the practice in other countries.

It takes as implicit the concept that whoever adheres to the principles of the Third Communist International does so with full agreement and with a firm desire to achieve them in practice.

Finally, with regard to the conditions demanded by the 17th Point, the Congress, considering that the Italian Socialist party did not stain her banner in the years of the World War, and to keep yesterday's and tomorrow's expellees from taking over the glorious name of Socialist party, under which banner the party is known to the proletarian masses, asks the Executive Committee of the Third International to consent that the name be provisionally retained. But it does not make of the exception an essential condition for adhesion to that same Third International, from whom the Italian Socialist party asks and hopes for closer, more continuous, and more fraternal support in the future.

DOCUMENT 5: *"Order of the Day of the Concentration Faction"*

Il Partito Socialista Italiano e L'Internazionale Comunista.

The Italian Socialist party, although fully aware of the new needs caused by the swift turn of events after the World War, appraises very highly the goals and educational spirit of its propaganda and the fine daily work of organization in political, administrative, cooperative, and trade union affairs. It plans to keep the name of Socialist party, the name under which it has earned until now, through its actions, the trust of the working classes. The Congress recognizes that there exist differences of judgment with regard to the nature of the present historical period, but holds that this is not sufficient motive for a division of forces. It reaffirms, therefore, that it wishes to maintain the unity of the socialist forces and declares itself against every division or exclusion which does not find its *raison d'être* in substantial disagreements on the fundamental principles of socialism. The unity of the party will be that much more spontaneous and secure when every comrade is allowed the liberty of expressing his own thoughts during the time in which the course of action which is to be imposed on members is discussed. To that liberty must correspond a rigid discipline in the action agreed upon by the majority of the party and its component organs.

The Socialist party confirms its adherence to the Third International, reaffirms the autonomy of interpretation in the application of the Twenty-One Points according to the conditions in each country, and asks for the complete exclusion from the sections of the International of anarchist and syndicalist groups and of Masonic elements.

The Italian Socialist party does not have prejudices with regard to historical socialist development and the means which should be employed for its definitive triumph. The dictatorship of the proletariat, understood in the maximalist sense as a transitory necessity imposed by special conditions and not as a programmatic obligation, is not denied by the Italian Socialist party. But that dictatorship must not, cannot, be the model for all countries on the basis of the experience of one country; and it would be a serious error to wish to prescribe to peoples—democratically evolved and who cannot bear authoritarianism—laws and systems held useful and necessary for other countries.

The Italian Socialist party does not ask for the use of violence and of illegal means in the class war and in the conquest of public power. The use of violence in the accomplishment of a passage of power from the middle class to the working class cannot be renounced, but it can only be the last measure to which the proletariat has recourse against the blind resistance and tyranny of the bourgeoisie and in order to break up a social organization incompatible with the new methods of production.

The Italian Socialist party holds that the war, by its inability to attain the ends for which it had been justified, has accelerated the crisis of the capitalist regime and has made the solution of the problems on which the revolutionary advent of the socialist regime depends a more urgent matter for the proletariat. This revolutionary period has become even more pronounced after the fall of the Czarist Empire and after the Peace of Versailles, which sanctioned the oppression by stronger capitalist states of weaker ones. But it would be childish to assert that this revolutionary period has come to a more acute phase everywhere and to assert the possibility of overthrows in the richest capitalist countries within a short time.

The Italian Socialist party believes that revolution in Italy in a violent and destructive form as desired by the communists, with the immediate formation of a regime of the Russian type, would be destined to fail within a short period of time if there were lacking the concurrent economic or political action of the proletariat of richer countries during the economic collapse which would inevitably follow the formation of such a regime.

The Italian Socialist party supports all possible attempts to arrive at an approximation of the socialist regime: when the conditions are right, the party does not renounce the conquest of political power in the form consistent with the times and the international situation. It will use the forces of all those political and trade union organizations which act in full accord with the party; and it will act in complete independence of any party or faction, however democratic, of the bourgeoisie.

DOCUMENT 6: Paul Levi, *The Beginning of the Crisis in the Communist Party and International*

Rede von Paul Levi auf der Sitzung des Zentralausschusses der V.K.P.D. am 24. Februar 1921 (Remscheid, 1921).

. . . Finished communists do not exist in this world. There is nobody who does not daily learn in the struggle and in the situation. There are no leaders who know everything better in advance, who know precisely how things go, and there are no masses who simply trot behind; instead it is a mutual political learning and experiencing in the course of which we shape our own tactic, our knowledge, and practice. In the Communist International the following tactic had been practiced at least since the Second Congress in Moscow: to try in the above sense to absorb masses with political experience into the communist parties and the Communist International. Comrades, if one splits parties, as we communists have done, which are organizationally not connected with us, then it is possible to draw the line either narrowly or widely. The Executive of the Communist International drew, for example, the line in Germany in accordance with our wishes in such a way that the Ledebour people were excluded and everybody left of Ledebour and Rosenfeld admitted to our side. One might quarrel over whether, for example, the line in France should have been drawn tighter or not. I want to tell you, comrade Frölich, that when Zinoviev arrived in Germany—and this was not my impression alone—he had totally changed; we who in Moscow had still been in his eyes semi-independents, as it were, had to hold him by his coattails in order to check him.

But, to continue, whether the line should have been drawn somewhat tighter in France is another question. In Italy we are concerned with something altogether different. In my article on the subject, I wrote the following with full consciousness:

> With the Italian party congress an event has occurred which is new in the history of the Third International. What has happened is not the split of a party of the Second International for the purpose of a union of its communist members with the Communist International, but a party already belonging to the Communist International has been split in order to be able to continue as a member of the Communist International. One may comfort oneself by saying: the split was necessary. . . .

I am saying that we are dealing here with a case where we do not split an alien party in order to create the basis for a mass party, but where we split a party which is organizationally connected with us. And this raises the large question of principle, a question, I think, of crucial importance to the Communist International. If we have connected these masses organizationally with us, these masses who are, as I said, as little finished communists as all of us and who experience the process of communism as their political life, what do we do to promote and realize their education? And here, comrades, one thing should be crystal clear: there exist two ways in which to achieve a higher degree of communist experience in these masses organizationally connected with the Third International. One way to carry out this education involves new splits; the other way implies that one trains politically the masses who have found their way to us, experiences with them the era, the revolution, and daily issues in order to arrive with and in the masses at a higher stage. That is the problem and with it a problem has been opened up which is not new in the history of socialism. It is the old problem regarding the formation of socialist parties. I do not want to conceal anything: the old difference between Rosa Luxemburg and Lenin emerges here again, the old difference which involved a question: how are social democratic parties—in the parlance of the day—formed? History has produced its judgment. Lenin was right: socialist and communist parties could also be created through the strictest screening proposed by him. In times of illegality he has produced a good party by means of the strictest screening and by the mechanical process of adding one communist to another; and perhaps, comrades, if we were confronted with a period of illegality of ten years we might also vote in favor of this way. . . . I am saying that if we had such a period ahead of us, maybe we would elect this way, although even then the one vast difference about which I just spoke would still remain: the organizational emphasis in addition to all the other considerable differences between the past Russian period and the present German and European period. But above all else, we do not expect such a period and for this reason we are of the opinion that we can only win over the masses, make communists out of them, create a big party, and engage in communist politics, if we are to maintain the closest relations with the masses, drawing them nearer to us ever more tightly instead of splitting them off. . . .

And thus I am saying, comrades, that in the case of Italy the road has been taken for the first time to achieve the education of the communist masses within the Communist International, not through an organic bringing-up but through a mechanical split. That I am not simply looking at the dark side, that I am perceiving in fact the underlying principle—as may be expected from the Russian comrades—and a well-thought-out principle at that, which will have its effect, that I infer again from the deliberations of comrade Marbosi.[4] Speaking of France he said: "There too we have many undesirable people, as for example Lafont, who had been expelled from Russia by Trotsky and who is now a member of the Communist party, and Cachin, who is a member of the Masons. . . ." He continued: ". . . Aside from the fact that *we wanted to create a precedent,* this question is not just an Italian question. This can be currently seen in the negotiations with the French party and with the Czechoslovakian party. . . ." The principle to create parties within the Communist International not through organic growth with the masses but through deliberate splits is thus now to be applied

---

[4] Levi is referring to two articles by Rákosi published in the *Rote Fahne,* No. 95 (Feb. 26, 1921) and No. 99 (March 1, 1921) in which Rákosi defended his and Kabekchiev's actions in Italy and the policy of splits in general.

to the French party; and I am telling you, comrades, with all the seriousness at my disposal—may the representative of the ECCI return to Moscow and report about it—that if the Communist International functions in western Europe in terms of admission and expulsion like a recoiling cannon; if the correction in France—where I admit the line was possibly drawn too loosely—is to be carried out not through the unification and direction of the masses who would then proceed with the correction *on their own*, but through a repeated split, then we will experience in western Europe the worst possible setback. And I add that the principle adopted in this instance is a principle which can be and will be applied to all parties. Among us in Germany too there are opportunists; Friesland may possibly say I am one of them, but I know others as well. There are opportunists in our midst; we will live through splits to the right and left in Germany too, in the same way as I had considered the Right split in Italy in the direction of Turati as absolutely necessary, because it could be carried out by keeping the masses, who are in favor of the Third International. To continue: it is possible that we too may have splits in Germany from the Right and from the Left; if, however, the process of the training and creation of still more stalwart cadres—and all of us are in need of more training—is to be achieved by means of repeated splits, then I say, comrades: communism will not survive the next split in Germany. It will suffer for many, many years from the remedy. I am telling you, comrades, the elections to the provincial diets and the picture they convey—I believe as many voters of the former USPD turned to the SPD as to us—speak volumes. I am not speaking about the number of seats which we might have gained through the elections, but I am speaking about the mood of these masses, who preferred to return to the party of Ebert and Noske rather than to come to us communists. . . .[5]

And now, comrades, I would like to return briefly to the Italian question. I maintain that it was possible in Italy to separate the right wing from the party without losing the masses. I appeal in this connection to no one else than Marbosi

[5] After the USPD was split at the Halle congress in October 1920, a little more than a third of its 800,000 members joined the KPD and roughly the same number joined the SPD.

himself, who says quite clearly in the section to which I have already referred: ". . . We would have swept the masses along with us—but we could have done so only by taking the leaders, that is, the Serrati people, into the bargain. For this reason we let go of the masses. . . ." and for this reason the case is clear to me. I had declared in a resolution submitted by me and in which I strictly avoided, as in all other statements, all identification and solidarity with the person of Serrati: "No price is too high for the unity of the Italian communists, short of the continued membership of the Turati people." I have always been of the opinion that if the masses can be retained within the Communist party of the International only by taking Serrati into the bargain, then the price is not too high. Comrades, I cannot help myself, but I think that on the whole question of the Italian split there has developed an all too mechanical view in the minds of our Russian friends and of the representatives present in Italy as well. I do not know whether our Russian friends are unanimous, for Zinoviev according to reports received by me, is said to have assumed a different position, but has been outvoted. But it seems to me that the comrades did not clearly realize that splits in a mass party with a different intellectual structure than, for example, that of the illegal Russian party—which performed brilliantly in its own way—*cannot be carried out on the basis of resolutions, but only on the basis of political experience.* If we had confronted the comrades of the USPD with a resolution from Moscow and declared: Now get out of the party, then we would not have mustered the 400,000 members we did on the basis of a political struggle lasting a year or more. In the course of this struggle the masses personally had experienced and understood the deep political differences, understanding at the same time that it had to draw the necessary conclusions. If we had come only with a resolution in Germany we would simply have flopped. It was a mistake on the part of the Italian comrades as well as of the ECCI, because the political differences had not been clearly enough worked out; they were not strong enough against the Turati people, though I continue to be of the opinion that they would have been sufficient. But in the understanding of the masses there existed no cause for a split with the Serrati people. . . . It may be the fault of the Italian communists that they did not stress this contrast strongly enough if the split with Serrati was indeed necessary, but it was also the fault of the ECCI. Things cannot be done this way. Until the middle of 1920, Serrati was, outwardly, in Italy, before the Italian masses and the party, the representative of the ideas of the Communist International, sitting at that in Moscow as a member of the Presidium of the Congress; and a quarter of a year later the masses are told Serrati is a traitor. The masses do not readjust their ideas that quickly; they have to recognize from the concrete questions of their daily struggle that a split is necessary. If they fail to do that and we split nonetheless, then, I say, we burden ourselves with the heavy opprobrium of splitters. We know that splits were and are necessary, but we must avoid splits in which the burden of guilt falls on us simply because the masses do not know that a matter of life and death is involved. . . .

DOCUMENT 7: Karl Radek, *"The Italian Question"*

Soll die Vereinigte Kommunistische Partei Deutschlands eine Massenpartei der revolutionären Aktion oder eine zentristische Partei des Wartens sein? (Hamburg, 1921).

To begin with, here are the *most important* particulars regarding the split in the Italian party. Prior to the Second Congress of the Communist International the Executive already received reports to the effect that the Italian Socialist party, the first large West European party to declare its adherence to the Communist International, did not actually engage in communist politics. Instead it pursued under the influence of avowed centrists such as Turati and Treves and under the influence of the trade union bureaucracy, as well as the parliamentarians and such vacillating, semi-centrists as Serrati, not only a confused agitation, but *abstained from doing anything which might sharpen the social crisis in Italy and lead to a conflict.* The *Turin party organization* adopted prior to the Second Congress of the Communist International resolutions confirming these reports and demanding a consistently revolutionary policy of the Italian party (cf. *Communist International* No. 12). As a result, a series of discussions were held with Serrati at the congress both in plenary and in committee sessions. Serrati and his followers conducted themselves extremely equivocally on almost all votes. The Italian delegation was split into fractions and voted differently. This situation convinced the Executive of the necessity of an appeal to the Italian workers. It decided for this reason to address a letter to the Italian party, applying criticism to the policies of the Italian Executive Committee, calling for the removal of the reformists from the party and its redirection toward the goal of revolution. (cf. *Communist International* No. 13). The representatives of the KPD participated in the composition of this letter. Lenin shortly thereafter expressed himself in clear and decisive terms about the Italian party question in a letter addressed to Serrati, in which he stated openly that Serrati belonged to those elements who avoided struggle and who were incapable of leading a revolutionary party. Although the Serrati group thrives best in semi-darkness, and because of its intellectual poverty avoids the expression of clear and unequivocal positions, Serrati could no longer withdraw and was obliged to make his view known. He did so in his answer to Lenin, which was amply exploited against the Communist International by the *Freiheit* as well as by the Longueists—and rightly so.[6] This letter denied the existence of reformism within the Italian party. *It refused to break with the reformist trade union bureaucracy,* portrayed the prospects of a world revolution in the blackest colors, and breathed the spirit of distrust in the power of the proletariat, which constitutes the basis of all centrist politics. . . .

The convention of the Italian Socialist party at Livorno thus confronted the Executive with the problem as to whether it should forgo the expulsion of the reformists from the Italian section or not. This and nothing else was the question. Serrati's declaration that he was in favor of a break with the reformists, provided they were expelled singly upon committing violations of discipline, stands not only in contradiction to the declaration of the same Serrati in his answer to Lenin, denying the existence of reformists within the Italian party, but stands in the sharpest contrast to the facts. Turati, leader of the Italian reformists and simultaneous member of the Italian party, had written just prior to the Congress an introduc-

[6] *Die Freiheit* was a newspaper of the USPD group, which had refused to join the Comintern at the Halle congress. The followers of Longuet comprised the right-center of the French Socialist party.

tion to a book by Nori and Pozzani, directed against Soviet Russia, in which he comes out quite clearly and openly against all the principles of the Third International. . . .

What was at stake? The question at stake was whether the *Communist International would permit the centrist elements who had infiltrated its organization because* in view of the mood of the workers *they* did not have the courage to oppose it openly, to *sabotage its policies from within by granting them the right to adapt, meaning in reality to invalidate, the resolutions of the congresses to the "conditions of a country."* This question could become a fateful issue for the Communist International. In view of the slow pace of development of the world revolution, there will exist within the rapidly growing communist parties everywhere elements who are revolutionary when driven by the impetuous mass, but who will seek to steer into quiet reformist waters as soon as it means to *prepare* the revolution intellectually and organizationally, in a situation which does not appear revolutionary to a superficial observer. And it is precisely the nature of centrism to see only the social surface and to remain observer in the struggle between the classes. It had thus become necessary to take up a position at the first sign of a test case. Every concession to Serrati constituted a concession to all semi-centrist elements operating within the International. It would mean the transition of the Communist International to the principles of the ifs and buts of the Two-and-a-Half International.[7] The attitude of the parties of the Communist International toward the Italian conflict was an *index of the extent to which they contained centrist or semi-centrist elements.* The discussion which raged for weeks in the German party over the Italian question was thus no quarrel about nothing, no quarrel concerning the past, *but rather one concerning the present and the future of the German Communist party itself.*

The chairman of the party, comrade Levi, published an ar-

---

[7] Many socialist centrist parties or groups formed the International Working Union of Socialist Parties, generally called the Two-and-a-Half International or Vienna International, founded on February 22, 1921. Its members included a French group under Longuet and Renaudel, the British Independent Labour party, the USPD group which had shunned Comintern affiliation, the Austrian and Swiss parties, and the Russian Mensheviks and Social Revolutionaries in exile.

ticle on January 23rd in the *Rote Fahne* on the Italian party convention, in which he sought to obscure this clear and unequivocal situation. He too declared himself in favor of the immediate expulsion of the reformists from the Italian party, but he expressed his conviction that the Serrati group would have separated itself from the reformists if the Executive and the Italian communists had not opened their sharp attack on Serrati. He sees the core of the Italian section of the Communist International within the Serrati group. He treats the communists who have separated themselves from Serrati as a confused crowd to whom he denies the appellation of a "firm and clear communist core." Lastly, he maintains that the quarrel in Italy concerns itself solely with the timing of the separation from the reformists, since both factions, including the Serratinists, wished to separate themselves from the reformists. *This article was a stab in the back of both the Executive and the newly founded Italian Communist party.* At the time of the first serious struggle within the Communist International the chairman of the KPD stood on the side of the right wing of the Communist International. Serrati declares that the reformists are no guardians of the bourgeoisie and that the quarrel between himself and the Communist International concerns itself solely with the point of time and form of the dictatorship of the proletariat. Serrati declares that he does not protect reformists because, firstly, they do not exist, and, secondly, he wants to expel them should they sin against the party statutes. All the while the chairman of the KPD declares that he does not at all defend Serrati, but that Serrati after all does want to exclude the reformists, the only question being the time of the expulsion; but should he not want to expel them the question would only revolve around the moment of the break with Serrati, with whom, after all, 90,000 revolutionary workers identify as their leader. *In this manner Turati supports the bourgeoisie and helps to sabotage the Italian revolution. In this manner Serrati supports Turati and helps him to sabotage the communist policies within the Italian party. The chairman of the KPD supports Serrati in the same manner and helps him to sabotage the very same resolutions of the Second Congress of the Communist International in the drafting of which he himself cooperated.*

II : The German March Action

Paul Levi, who had been an eyewitness to the split in the PSI, returned from Livorno with grave doubts about the Comintern's methods of forcing the adoption of the Twenty-One Conditions. In February 1921, he stood at the crossroads of his career: he had led the KPD to preeminence among communist parties, but his own position was made insecure by enemies within his own party and within the ECCI; he had followed the main line of the Comintern in building a mass party, but he had also begun to have reservations about the ECCI's authority in matters affecting the state and development of national parties. At the instigation of Rákosi, who was passing through Berlin on his return to Moscow, Levi's critique of Comintern activity at Livorno was put to a vote before the KPD's central committee and was condemned by a narrow majority.[1] Thereupon, in a surprise move, Levi, Clara Zetkin, and three others resigned from the *Zentrale*.

In the less than two years during which Levi led the KPD, his sights were continually on the creation of a mass party. To further this end he forced out the left extremists, initiated parliamentary participation, encouraged trade union activity, skillfully engineered a fusion with the left wing of the USPD, and sought other means of promoting class consciousness beyond the pale of communist cadres among the politically affiliated and unaffiliated proletariat. His most unique and daring maneuver was an Open Letter of January 8, 1921 in the *Rote Fahne*, addressed to the other working class parties and trade

[1] The central committee or *Zentralausschuss*, composed of delegates from each of the party's twenty-eight districts, was a new leadership instrument created by the KPD at the end of 1920. Thereafter, major policy decisions were made at joint meetings of the central committee and the *Zentrale*, which evolved into an executive organ. Not only did the central committee serve as a watchdog over the Zentrale, but, given its broader representation, it also became the breeding ground for dissenting factions.

unions, in which he called for cooperative action to attain certain limited goals. The failure of this appeal strengthened the hand of those who opposed Levi's cautious policy of building the party. Within the KPD Levi's critics included a left wing led by Ruth Fischer, Arkady Maslow, and Ernst Friesland [Reuter], which demanded revolutionary activity regardless of the foreign political needs of the Soviet Union, and an opposition faction sponsored by Radek and led by Ernst Meyer, Heinrich Brandler, August Thalheimer and Paul Frölich, which had a profound respect for Soviet and Comintern authority and became a ready convert to its mentor's theory of the offensive.[2]

This theory, developed by Bukharin and embraced by Zinoviev and his subordinate Radek, rested on the belief that in the light of a developing new revolutionary potential the European parties were too inactive, and that they had to assume the offensive at any cost. The offensive strategy of the Comintern ECCI directly contradicted Lenin's shift in Russian policy from war communism to the New Economic Policy (NEP) at home, and from revolutionary offensive to peaceful coexistence abroad. The anomalous position of Russian leaders in calling for both a revolutionary breathing spell and a revolutionary offensive was reflected in Germany in Levi's attempt to build party strength organizationally and in Levi's critics demand for revolutionary mass action.

The denouement of this ambiguity in Germany came two weeks after Levi's resignation from the *Zentrale*. The "offensive hawks" now in control of the party, together with Béla Kun, who as emissary of the ECCI contributed enthusiasm and conveyed the Comintern's endorsement, made plans for action. On March 16th Otto Hörsing, the social democratic governor of Saxony, announced a police occupation of Prussian Saxony on grounds that wildcat strikes, looting, robbery, terrorist acts, and other expressions of lawlessness had to be stopped. In making this unexpected move Hörsing anticipated

[2] The offensive strategy was not merely a foreign import. Many USPD members who had joined the KPD in 1920 had done so because they expected that a truly revolutionary party would as surely lead them into action. The offensive theory of Radek's disciples in the KPD corresponded to a similar tendency among the rank and file. Comintern endorsement of the strategy artificially strengthened is most subordinate faction in the KPD.

and undercut the *Zentrale*, which had planned to take the offensive after Easter week when the workers were back on the job. The government had taken the initiative, but the *Zentrale* refused to turn down the challenge, although the timing and momentum favored its opponents.

Even after the occupation had begun the KPD found it difficult to arouse the Saxon workers. An incendiary press campaign coupled with instigation by provocateurs from the party's secret apparatus finally succeeded in moving the workers in the mines of Mansfeld and the chemical works of Halle to declare a general strike and offer armed resistance. Once in motion the insurrection spread but slowly, and with the exception of Hamburg was generally restricted to central Germany. To accelerate the movement the KPD called a nationwide general strike on March 24th, but failed to arouse popular enthusiasm or to move the non-communist workers. The SPD and USPD had come out against the communists' action from the beginning and had prevented their followers from taking part in the strikes. This had led the KPD to use large numbers of unemployed in attempting to force the non-striking workers to shut down their plants. Within the ranks of the communists themselves there was great confusion. Not only were the local party officials working at cross-purposes with the members of the secret apparatus, but there was only intermittent contact with headquarters in Berlin which, instead of providing clear direction, contented itself with telling the masses to arm and denouncing those who refused to participate in the party's uprising. Although there was quite a bit of fighting between communists and government forces and between workers and *Lumpenproletarians*, the best organized combatants on the side of the insurrection were a troop of romantic anarchists under one Max Hoelz, who sympathized with the KPD. On March 31st, after thirteen days of "offensive action" punctuated by confusing and unrealistic directives, self-sacrifices on the part of local communist cadres, putschist adventures, and a growing hostility on the part of the masses, the *Zentrale* was finally forced to terminate the March Action. The KPD rank and file was beaten and bewildered; a large number were sent to jail and many others left the party.

The significance of the March Action and the responsibility for its failure immediately became a subject of controversy.

Levi, who had observed the uprising as a bystander, sent a letter to Lenin on March 29th absolving himself of responsibility for what he considered the catastrophic decisions and activities of the party leadership. When the *Zentrale*, which had led the party into battle, met on April 7–8 to assess recent events, it categorically turned down Zetkin's attempt to make it responsible for what she termed a major defeat. Instead, the *Zentrale* justified its offensive strategy and claimed that the KPD had taken an important step toward becoming a party of action. Levi refused to let this whitewash by the party leaders go unchallenged and, finding it impossible to reach the rank and file through normal party channels, decided to make his views public.

In his critique published on April 12th Levi held both the *Zentrale* and the ECCI responsible for the "greatest Bakuninist putsch in history" (Document 1). He accused the *Zentrale* of having misled the Saxon workers with its "offensive" slogans and of having attempted to create conditions for action by provocations instead of political means. The effect of this erroneous theory and putschist practice was to alienate the non-communist workers and to sacrifice loyal communist cadres in a wild adventure. If the KPD was to survive this debacle, he concluded, the full story would have to be told to the members, and those who bore the responsibility would have to leave the party. Shifting his tack, Levi insisted that the ECCI must bear a part of the blame for the abortive action, because its pressure for a forward strategy had encouraged the offensive theorists in Germany. Emissaries of the ECCI like Kun, he observed, had neither the stature nor the experience to make them useful to the parties to which they were dispatched, and in their eagerness to prove themselves sowed discord and supported undesirable tendencies in the parties.[3]

[3] It is still not clear whether Kun's encouragement of the KPD's offensive strategy was at the instruction of the Comintern. We do know that Kun had been made a member of the ECCI's powerful inner bureau earlier that year and that he was one of Zinoviev's trusted lieutenants. In all likelihood he was sent to promote a forward strategy but without clear directives about how far he might go in realizing it. This vagueness of mandate which allowed a mercurial personality like Kun considerable leeway of action is precisely what Levi complained about. On the one hand, he argued, it al-

Levi's breach of discipline in washing the KPD's dirty linen in public was considered treasonous by the *Zentrale*, which expelled him from the party. His appeal before the central committee was turned down, and the ECCI endorsed his expulsion. The party press broke into print with numerous attacks on Levi, and the "case of renegade Levi" became a convenient smoke screen for the party leaders, who were all too anxious to divert attention from the March Action itself. Outstanding among these vituperations was that of Radek, whose role as gray eminence to the offensive theorists was widely rumored (Document 2). Radek was not concerned with answering Levi's charges against the *Zentrale* or the ECCI, but devoted himself almost exclusively to a scurrilous attack on Levi's person. Radek called Levi a self-serving opportunist, salon Bolshevik, and intellectual dilettante and aesthete who, never having been trustworthy, had left his post like a coward. When epithets failed him Radek made up fictitious quotations from Levi's pamphlet to show how callous he was to the suffering caused by the uprising among the workers.

Whereas the party leaders and their mentor used character assassination as their main weapon, the Levi opposition responded with unpleasant documentary evidence. In August, Levi's periodical *Unser Weg* printed a series of letters written by Radek to the *Zentrale* members Brandler, Thalheimer, Frölich, and other disciples between March 14th and April 8th (Document 3). These letters revealed that Radek had been building a faction within the KPD and encouraging it to challenge Levi on the question of action.[4] Radek predicted an international crisis and exhorted his followers to take the offensive by getting arms and moving the masses in the event of war. The struggle against Levi remained his main concern even after he had been forced to accept the March Action as a setback.

---

lowed the emissary to raise havoc in the party to which he was dispatched, on the other it allowed the ECCI to disavow the nature or scope of his activities after the damage was done.

[4] This exposé had a more serious sequel in November when the social democratic *Vorwärts* published documents confiscated by German authorities from Zetkin while en route to the Third World Congress of the Comintern. This damning evidence consisted mainly of depositions by party functionaries about the *Zentrale*-inspired putschist activity of the party during the March Action.

Since the *Zentrale* and the Levi faction were at loggerheads in interpreting the March Action, a higher authority was needed to save the German party from collapse and to extrapolate the meaning of the German experience for the international movement. The Third World Congress meeting in Moscow between June 22nd and July 12th made this task its major concern. It was apparent from the 509 delegates representing 48 countries that the organization had grown since the last meeting. It was much less obvious that the power of the Russian party had increased even more markedly. Representatives of the German unreconstructed offensivist *Zentrale* who expected a hero's welcome, representatives of the Levi faction who hoped to exonerate their leader, as well as partisans of both sides from various delegations, had no idea that the issue already had been resolved in advance, and that the main theoretical and tactical lessons to be drawn had been determined.

Prior to the Congress the Russian leaders had been divided in their evaluation of the German situation. Zinoviev, Radek, and Bukharin, who were the architects of the offensive theory and whose agent Kun had been the instrument for activating the KPD, stuck to their guns and supported the *Zentrale*. Lenin, Trotsky, and Kamenev, who realized that the Soviet Union had entered a new phase of development, were anxious to interpret the German reversal as the beginning of a general temporary retreat from revolution. They argued that the resolution of Russia's internal crisis by the official proclamation of NEP on March 15th and the crushing of the Kronstadt uprising on March 17th, as well as the Anglo-Russian Trade Agreement of March 16th, made their new general line an absolute necessity. Their force of argument created a consensus within the Russian leadership which determined the decisions of the Congress.

Before the Congress opened Zetkin was able to present Levi's case to Lenin in a number of interviews (Document 4). Zetkin defended Levi as a dedicated communist who published his attack in the belief that only the whole truth would save his party. Lenin replied that he had no quarrel with Levi's fundamental position and that the Congress would uphold it, but that the *Zentrale* could not be humiliated too much. At any rate Levi had to be condemned and expelled for breach of discipline. Lenin brushed the subject of the offensive theory aside with the remark that it was an expression of German and Hungarian romanticism.

Thus the stage was set for a discussion of the German question, from which the Russian leaders had taken every care to exclude a consideration of the complicity of the ECCI as well as of Zinoviev, Radek, and Kun. In the course of the proceedings Levi's united front policy was adopted under the watchword "To the masses!" but as a sop to the *Zentrale* the March Action was characterized as a step forward; the ECCI was upheld in its right to intervene in the affairs of member parties. The tactics adopted by the Congress marked a retreat from aggressive revolutionary policy. In view of the likelihood that the downfall of capitalism would require a fairly long period of revolutionary struggle, extreme methods were condemned as an obstacle to genuine revolutionary activity. The Theses promulgated by the Congress on the preparation for battle directed communist parties to reach the broadest masses in the press through clarion calls for revolution, in parliament by wooing the "semi-proletarian petty bourgeois classes," and in trade unions through the organization of cells (Document 5). The lessons of the March Action, the Theses stipulated, were that: the KPD had not sufficiently stressed the defensive nature of the struggle; KPD members had exaggerated the importance of the offensive as a means of struggle; in the future the KPD must study and weigh the preconditions for action; and democratic centralism had to be observed and enforced.

The Third World Congress marked an important turning point in the history of the Comintern; its real lessons were apparent to only a few at the time. The Congress revealed the inability of mass parties created by enforcing the Twenty-One Conditions to take the revolutionary offensive, and accepted a gathering rather than a testing of strength as the order of the day. By acting as arbiter in resolving the conflict within the KPD the Comintern established the right to do so elsewhere in the future. The policies of the Comintern and of the member parties became more clearly and directly tied to the needs of the Soviet Union, where a breathing spell had been created which was to be used in consolidating the Bolsheviks' position at home and in strengthening their control over the international movement.

Perhaps most significant was the Congress' demonstration,

through the Levi case, that unarmed prophets, no matter how pure their lineage, penetrating their critique, or impassioned their plea, could not challenge or impede the bolshevization of the communist movement.

DOCUMENT 1: Paul Levi, *Our Course against Putschism*

(Berlin, 1921).

Preface

When I planned to write this pamphlet there existed in Germany a Communist party of 500,000 members. When I actually wrote it eight days later the same Communist party had been shaken to its very foundations and its continued existence was in doubt.

It may appear as a hazardous enterprise to come forward with such an unsparing criticism at the present time, when the Communist party finds itself in such a great crisis. However, even brief reflection will indicate not only the utility but the necessity of this criticism. The irresponsible play with the existence of the party, with the lives and fates of its members, must come to an end. It has to be terminated by the action of the members, particularly in view of the fact that those responsible refuse even today to recognize what they have wrought. The party cannot permit itself to be dragged blindly into an anarchism of Bakuninist complexion. Should it be possible to rebuild a *Communist* party in Germany, then the dead of central Germany, of Hamburg, the Rhineland, Baden, Silesia, and of Berlin, the many thousands of prisoners who became victims of this Bakuninist madness, they all demand in view of the events of last week:

"Never Again!"

It goes without saying that the fury of the white terror must not be the shield behind which those responsible may withdraw from their *political* responsibility. And it goes equally without saying that the fury and abuse which will be raised against me constitute no ground to abstain from this criticism. In this spirit I turn confidently to the members of the party with this description that must tear at the heart of everyone who helped to build what was here destroyed. These are bitter truths. But, "it is medicine, not poison, which I dispense." Written April 3–4, 1921.

. . . How Is the Power of the State Conquered?

The seizure of political power by the proletariat generally will be (exceptions such as the Hungarian do exist) the fruit of a successful uprising on the part of the proletariat alone, or with the aid of other classes drawn into the maelstrom of the revolution. What are the prerequisites for an uprising? Lenin has the following to say on this question (*Will the Bolsheviks Maintain State Power?*, p. 61):

If a revolutionary party lacks the allegiance of the majority of the vanguard of the revolutionary classes and of the rural population, an uprising is out of the question. In addition to this majority are necessary:

1. The swelling of the revolutionary wave throughout the country.
2. The complete moral and political bankruptcy of the old—for example the "coalition"—government.
3. Deep-seated insecurity in the camp of all vacillating elements, that is, those who are *not* wholeheartedly standing behind the government, though yesterday they were still its supporters.

We do want to take this opportunity here to reexamine these prerequisites for Germany and to criticize on that basis the events which recently occurred in Germany.

1. The chief prerequisite to which must be added all others, that is, "the majority of the revolutionary classes and of the rural population behind the revolutionary party," as we have seen, did not and does not exist in Germany. Even if we leave aside the rural population, which in Germany does not play the decisive role it did in Russia, the Communist party ("the revolutionary party") does not constitute the majority of the proletariat (the "vanguard of the revolutionary classes") either.

2. The revolutionary wave was not on the increase throughout the land. Admittedly, the exasperation of the more advanced part of the proletariat grew daily, the number of the unemployed swelled daily, and the poverty and misery of the masses increased. But the moment had not yet come when

manifest dissatisfaction becomes transformed into increased activity on the part of the masses, as happens frequently; for the time being it was translated into increased resignation.

3. To speak of complete moral and political bankruptcy of the old—that is, "coalition"—government was out of the question. In Prussia, where social democracy maintains a coalition with the bourgeois parties, it has just received twice as many votes as all the other proletarian parties combined, and has grown relative to the previous June.

4. Neither could there be any question as to the deep-seated insecurity in the camp of the vacillating elements; the Communist party had done nothing, given even excellent opportunities such as the London ultimatum, to make it feel insecure.

We think that there existed not the slightest doubt regarding these conditions in the mind of *anyone* in the German Communist party.

What then were the assumptions and how did the action come about?

As a preface we declare herewith: the situation in which the party finds itself is more difficult than ever before. The question as to whether there exists a German Communist party, whether communism exists in Germany as a party may be decided within weeks, possibly days. In this situation it is a duty toward the party to speak in all openness and honesty. Whoever assumed the responsibility for this action must bear it in the same manner as any ordinary party comrade. Accordingly, we will strive to prevent delivering new victims to the courts and to prevent the consequences of the present misfortune from extending beyond the German Communist party. However, within this framework the truth and nothing but the truth must reign.

How did the action come about? The first initiative toward this action did not come from within the German party. We do not know who bears the responsibility for it. It has often been the case in the past that emissaries of the ECCI exceeded their authority, that is, it became *subsequently* clear that they had lacked authority for this or that action. We are not in a position to put the blame on the Executive Committee of the Communist International, though it should not be concealed that there existed among members of the Executive a certain dissatisfaction with the "inactivity" of the KPD.

Aside from grave errors in connection with the Kapp Putsch, the German party could not, of course, be accused of concrete sins of omission.[5] There existed thus a measure of strong pressure on the *Zentrale* [of the German party] to enter into activity *now,* immediately, and *at any price.*

And this immediate action had then to be justified. A responsible speaker had the following to say at the meeting of the [German] central committee of March 17th:

As to the general situation, the same holds as outlined by Levi during the last sessions with the exception that since that time [four weeks earlier!!—the author] the antagonisms between the imperialist states have become intensified, that is, the conflicts between America and England have increased. Unless a revolution gives a different turn to the course of events, we will shortly [!!—the author] be faced with an Anglo-American war. . . .

. . . Domestic difficulties lie within the realm of the possible in view of the fact that [Allied reparations] sanctions will be imposed on March 20 [!—the author] and that the plebiscite will take place in Upper Silesia on the same day, leading in all likelihood to armed conflicts between the German and Polish imperialists. According to information received by us, the old French occupation force has been replaced by English troops; while the French troops had adopted a position friendly toward the Poles, it is assumed, according to reports [!!], that the present English troops are quite strongly in favor of the Germans. There exists a ninety percent likelihood that armed conflicts will occur. While the Polish counterrevolution arms itself, the German government, according to documentary evidence, prepares itself systematically since the beginning of October for mili-

[5] On March 13, 1920, Wolfgang Kapp and General Walther von Lüttwitz staged a right-wing putsch and drove the social democratic government out of Berlin. After four days a general strike led by the trade unions succeeded in restoring the legitimate government. Initially the KPD *Zentrale* in Berlin refused to participate in the general strike on grounds that communists had no business supporting one group of counterrevolutionaries against another. In the end the leaders reversed themselves and joined the strike. Levi, who was in jail, sent a scathing letter to the *Zentrale* accusing it of having let a promising revolutionary situation pass by.

tary conflicts. . . . [The speaker reads excerpts from these documents which, as he points out, cannot be published.]

Our influence will go beyond our organization of four to five hundred thousand members. I maintain that today we are able to influence through our communist organization two to three million non-communist workers, willing to fight under our banner even in offensive operations. If I am correct in my point of view, then we are obliged by this state of affairs to remain no longer passive in the face of domestic and foreign pressures and to confine ourselves to a merely agitational exploitation of the domestic and foreign situation, but we are instead obliged by the present situation to intervene with concrete actions in order to influence matters in our direction.

We, on the other hand, maintain that in every party which thinks highly of itself a responsible member of the leadership who asserts that the contradictions between the imperialist states have become intensified from the middle of February to the middle of March, that in fact the conflicts between England and America have increased to the point where we "will be faced shortly with an Anglo-American war," would be placed in the cellar of a hydropathic sanitarium rather than in the leadership of the party. It would speedily remove any member of the leadership from his post who would base himself in the making of such a weighty decision on "secret information," "unpublishable documents," on "ninety percent likelihood of war," who, in short, gives a report compared to which the report of a police agent assumes dimensions of historical merit. To this a responsible, leading comrade attaches the computation of an illiterate regarding the two to three million non-communists who would join us even in "offensive actions"—*and this was the political basis for the later action!*

In elucidation of what was actually meant by an "offensive action" another responsible member had the following to say:

What the executive committee now proposes constitutes a *complete break with the past.* Hitherto we were guided by the tactic, or rather were forced to accept this tactic, of biding our time until a situation conducive to action existed and to formulate our decisions on the basis of this situation. Now we say: we are so strong and the situation is so pregnant with possibilities that we have to begin *to force the fate of the party and of the revolution.* . . .

The party has now to assume the initiative, to indicate that we are no longer willing to bide our time, to wait until we are faced with accomplished facts; we intend to create these facts ourselves as far as those are dependent on us. . . . We could infinitely complicate the confusion in the Rhineland by leading the masses there in a strike which would be bound to intensify the differences between the Entente and the German government to an extraordinary degree. . . .

. . . The situation in Bavaria is the same as existed in Germany for a long time, that we had to wait until the other side opened the attack. What is our task in this situation? Through our activity we have to make sure that this eruption occurs, if necessary by provoking the state militia. . . .

And a third responsible party comrade added further: ". . . as a result, the *prevailing party line,* which aimed at avoiding partial actions and the issuance of slogans that appeared as if we might call for the final struggle, *has to be discarded.* . . ."

This is the theoretical system which decided the being or non-being of the German Communist party.

First of all. There are communists in whom words such as "intensification," "sharpening," "conflict," etc., awaken certain revolutionary hallucinations. No other interpretation is possible if this one speaker expects a sharpening of the conflict between the Entente and Germany as a result of mass strikes in the Rhineland. In the meantime this assertion has been tested. Workers in Düsseldorf went on strike; the Franco-German relations intensified to such a point that the French occupational authorities in Düsseldorf hastened to return the guns to the [German] police force to enable *it* to suppress the strike.

The press of April 4th reports another "intensification" in a report from Moers:

Obviously as a result of orders from higher quarters, Belgian military personnel intervened Sunday on behalf of the non-communist population and in the face of communist resistance resorted to the use of arms. The Belgian troops succeeded in restoring order. As a result of the exchange of fire with the communists, three insurgents were killed and twenty-seven wounded. Many were arrested by the Belgians. Since the communists attempted to set free their comrades, the Belgians, continually shot at and bombarded with bricks, returned the fire. Troop reinforcements are on the way to Moers. The mines have been occupied by Belgian soldiers.

This is a picture of the "intensification of the relations between Germany and the Entente"; if the speaker of the executive committee thought anything at all in the course of his speeches he must have expected that the German government would engage in a diatribe against the Entente because of the shooting of German communists.

For the rest, however, these conquerors of the fate of the German Communist party and of the German revolution recognize at least the necessity of the existence of an appropriate situation, that is, a situation in which the masses comprehend the need for struggle and are willing to engage in it. The "new tactic," "the break with the past," consists in the belief that such situations can be *created*. This is actually nothing new. We have always upheld the view that the conditions for struggle *can* be created by a political party and *must* be created by the *Communist party* through *clarity* and *decisiveness* of its attitude, through the *trenchancy* and *boldness* of its agitation and propaganda, through the intellectual and organizational *influence* which it gains over the masses; in short, it must create such conditions by *political means*. The novelty which truly signifies the break with the past of the KPD is the assumption that these conditions for battle can be created also by *unpolitical* means, by the *method of a police agent,* and by *provocation*. What is meant by provocation was revealed by another responsible party comrade in another meeting which took place during the action. He said:

> We are of the opinion that with the aid of an intensive propaganda campaign the prevailing calm of the police force will be lost, thus provoking that part of the working class which as yet stands outside the battle.

And the same speaker said later on March 30, when the action had long since been lost:

> We have to try to enter on a skillful retreat, to create conflicts, *to provoke the police, in fact to provoke all counter-revolutionary elements. Should we succeed in creating* [!!—the author] *the movement with the help of these means,* there will be clashes. . . .

This indeed is novel in the history of the party founded by Rosa Luxemburg: to expect communists to act like procurers, to provoke the murder of their brothers—this constitutes a complete break with the past. I hope I may be spared the proof that the last interpretation has not gone too far; but to repeat, this was the *new* theoretical foundation on which the game was based.

The action began. For the time being the *Zentrale* was spared to translate into practice the newly acquired theoretical foundation. Hörsing [the SPD district governor of Saxony] acted first. He advanced into the area of Mansfeld and thus already scored a victory for himself: the appropriate time. With the cunning of an old trade union bureaucrat he selected the week preceding the Easter holidays, knowing full well the significance of a four-day shutdown of the factories from Good Friday until Easter Monday. With this action the *Zentrale* had already in advance become the prisoner of its own "slogans." It was no longer in a position to exploit Hörsing's provocation within the limits of the situation. The workers of Mansfeld opened their attack. A member of the *Zentrale* said in a meeting taking place subsequently:

> Our comrades in Mansfeld interpreted the slogans of the *Zentrale* somewhat excessively and did not follow their true meaning. In Mansfeld we were faced not with the occupation of factories but with the entry of troops.

This description is nothing less than a defamation of the fighting comrades. If the slogan was issued opposing the occupation of the factories, then no reasonable man can assume, unless he happens to be a member of the *Zentrale* of the KPD, that it is invalid in the face of the evident preparation for

the occupation of the factories, that is, the entry of troops.
The comrades in Mansfeld also acted in accordance with the
instructions of the *Zentrale* when they resorted to arms. That
too seems to be disputed in the above-mentioned sentence.
In addition we are also faced with the case—not the first one,
mind you—in which the *Zentrale* does not know and notices
only later the nature of its slogans.

The *Rote Fahne* began with its call to arms of March 18th:
"*Every* worker disregards the law and *acquires* a weapon
wherever he may find it."

The *Rote Fahne* inaugurated the movement with this rather
curious wording in view of a mass action and retained this
tone throughout. On March 19th the *Rote Fahne* wrote: "The
Orgesch gang reigns with the sword.[6] It speaks the language
of open violence. The German workers would be cowards
were they not able to find the courage and strength to answer
the Orgesch gang in *their clear voice.*"

On March 20th the *Rote Fahne* wrote: "The example of
the workers in the district of Halle, who will answer Hörsing's
provocation with a strike, must be imitated. *The working class
must arm itself immediately in order to face the enemy armed.
Weapons into the Hands of the Workers!*"

On March 21st the *Rote Fahne* wrote: "Only the proletariat can destroy the infamous intentions of the Orgesch gangs.
It can accomplish this only through unity in action, by dis-
missing the chattering traitors of the social revolution and by
beating the counterrevolution in the only manner in which
it can be beaten—*With the Weapon in the Hand!*"

At the same time the "new theory" makes its way through
the organization, along with the call for action and the declaration to open the attack as soon as possible, if necessary by
provocation. Given the situation, the workers of Mansfeld in-

---

[6] Orgesch or Organisation Escherich was a national association
of home guards (*Einwohnerwheren*) organized in May 1920 by the
Bavarian Forestry Councilor, Dr. Georg Escherich. The home
guards had sprung up in the spring of 1919, ostensibly as auxiliary
forces to aid the regular police in maintaining order. In practice
they were right-wing paramilitary organizations concerned more
with crushing the Left (as in the case of the Bavarian Soviet Republic) than with protecting the Republic. Under continuous pressure
from the Entente, the German government finally disarmed and dis-
banded Orgesch in June 1921.

terpreted the slogan in the only possible manner in which it made sense to any reasonable person. To describe these very same Mansfeld workers now as "violators of discipline" constitutes a cowardly defamation of dead heroes who gave their lives in good faith. Nobody could imagine that a call to arms on the part of the *Rote Fahne* actually meant locking up the arms for the time being. Neither could every worker easily understand the babble about arms in the same manner as did obviously the chief of the advertising department of the *Rote Fahne* in the edition of March 24, 1921 (No. 139 supplement):

> ### The Arms of the Communists
> consist at the present time not least of all in their party press, which ruthlessly exposes the cancer of capitalism. It is the duty of every communist to participate in this
>
> ### Distribution of Arms
> and to gain ever new adherents. Make ceaseless propaganda for the party press at your place of work and in the circle of your friends so that
>
> ### The Red Army
> of the proletarian fighters may receive new recruits daily!

Thus the uprising in Mansfeld broke out during the most unfavorable week, in a politically completely untenable situation, on the defensive from the very start and without any organizational preparation—*all of this thanks to the toying with uprising by the Zentrale.*

Obviously, no member of the *Zentrale,* even "the best Marxist of West Europe," [as Radek called Thalheimer] read or took to heart the following words by Marx:

> Uprising happens to be an art like war, and like other arts it is subject to certain rules, the neglect of which leads to the ruin of the party indulging in it. These rules—logical inferences from the nature of the parties and the conditions to be reckoned with in such cases—are so clear and simple

that the Germans became quite familiar with them as a result of the short experience of 1848. *Firstly, one should never play with an uprising, unless one is prepared to weather the consequences of this play.* An uprising is a mathematical computation with highly indeterminate quantities whose value may change from day to day: the opposing military forces have all the advantages of organization, discipline, and traditional authority on their side; unless one can muster tremendous countervailing forces, one will be beaten and destroyed. Secondly, once the uprising has begun one must act with the greatest possible resolution and assume the offensive. *The defensive is the death of any armed uprising;* it has lost before it has even tested its strength against that of the enemy. [Marx, *Revolution and Counter Revolution in Germany,* 1919 edition, p. 117.]

Fate now took its course. The spark of Mansfeld kindled the fire in Hamburg. A rich harvest of dead was the immediate result there, and we cannot venture a guess whether the "new theory" fell on fertile soil. The Hamburg comrades were at any rate naïve enough to assume that a *Zentrale* of a party alluding to an uprising knows what it does and to believe that the *Zentrale* meant what it said. They therefore went "full steam ahead." A special messenger was then dispatched to them for the purpose of "slowing them down." After the messenger had carried out his task, it was discovered that he slowed them down too much. Another messenger was dispatched to remedy the work of the previous one, but when he arrived the movement in Hamburg had already been crushed. The whole "action" had essentially already run out of steam. The "action," conceived in *one head* [Kun] who on top of it did not have the faintest idea about German conditions, politically prepared and led by political numbskulls, had left the communists in the lurch.

Anticipating the story—it is actually the most natural thing in the world that the generals of this putsch should look elsewhere for the blame rather than to themselves. The talk about "saboteurs," "pessimists," and "defeatists" within the party has indeed begun already. The gentlemen engaged in this pursuit show a complete resemblance to Ludendorff in this respect, with whom they also share other characteristic features. They resemble Ludendorff not only in inventing a poor excuse designed to put the blame on *others*, but also in committing the same fundamental error. Ludendorff was a graduate of that school which taught that wars were made "on the basis of the principles of the general staff above and slavish obedience below." This may have been appropriate to a certain historical epoch. During the times of Old Frederick and the Potsdam Guards it was altogether sufficient if below the soldiers marched up in squares in blind obedience and if above the will of the king reigned. In the era of huge armies, of conscript armies, and mass armies this is no longer sufficient. The "moral factor" comes more and more into play. Large armies are not only a military, they are also a political instrument. They are tied by innumerable bonds to the non-uniformed masses; between them there takes place an invisible exchange of wills, feeling, and thought. A general who does not understand how to lead an army politically in this sense will destroy the best army—as was done by Ludendorff.

Political parties function similarly. It is entirely sufficient for an anarchist club if the will of the leader commands and the courage of the believers in the face of death obeys. It is, however, not sufficient for a mass party, which does not only want to set masses into motion but which is itself a mass. It is proper to expect of communists that they quickly detect and vigorously utilize every situation conducive to struggle and that they always point to the final aim beyond the aim of the immediate struggle. But no communist is obliged or qualified, for that matter, to detect—as a result of his admission into the Communist party and his carrying of a membership card—a fighting situation *where there is none,* and where nothing but the will of the *Zentrale* decides on the existence of such a situation in a secret meeting and for other reasons than those obvious to the proletariat. The *Zentrale* thus did not even display the simple skill of the Indian chieftain who in a demonstration of his omnipotence stepped outside his tent every morning and said: "Sun, follow the path which I show you." With that he pointed with his hand in the direction from east to west. The *Zentrale*, animated by the same feeling of omnipotence, pointed accidentally in the direction from west to east. It violated in this manner the basic principle which alone will activate a mass party; only the will, insight, and resolution of the masses themselves will put it into motion, and on the basis of these prerequisites a good leadership is enabled _to lead_. But the _Zentrale_ has also not recognized those conditions which alone can activate a mass party, a mass among masses which is everywhere connected to the proletarians in a personal or professional relationship in the factories and the trade unions, subjected to the strengthening and invigorating influence of sympathy or the paralyzing influence of antipathy or enmity. And this again raises the question: what should be the relationship of the communists to the masses during an action? An action which merely expresses the political needs of the Communist party and not the subjective needs of the proletarian mass is bound to fail. It is impossible for the communists, especially as long as they remain such a minority among the proletariat, to engage in an action _in place_ of the proletariat, or _without_ the proletariat, or in the end even _against_ the proletariat. They can do no more than create by dint of the above-mentioned _political_ means situations which will make plain to the proletariat the need to fight and will actually involve it in the fight. The communists are then in a position to lead the proletariat in this struggle by virtue of their slogans.

How did the _Zentrale_, however, imagine the relationship between the communists and the masses? As already mentioned before, it thought that the situation could also be created by _non-political_ means. The result was dead workers in both Hamburg and Mansfeld. But the situation from the beginning was lacking all the necessary prerequisites for action, so that even the dead were unable to get the masses to move. But the _Zentrale_ had recourse to yet another means. No. 133 of the _Rote Fahne_ of Sunday, March 20, contains an article entitled "He Who Is Not for Me Is against Me! An Address to the Social Democratic and Independent Workers." The article itself actually discusses only the "_for_ me" aspect and tells the workers only near the end under what conditions they may "participate." It says:

Independent [USPD] and Social Democratic Workers! To you we extend our fraternal hands. But beware, if you want to join us in our fight, you have to aim your blows not only at the capitalists, but equally at those who in your midst defend the interests of the capitalists and join the Orgesch gang in an attack upon your workers, as well as

against those fainthearted cowards who lull you to sleep
and discourage you while the dagger of the Orgesch band
is aimed at your heart.

Imagine: for the Independent and social democratic workers there existed no cause for action in this situation. The genius in whose head the action has been conceived was unknown
to them; a decision by the Communist party was no reason
to drag them into an action whose motivation they did not
know. We suspect that if they had known the motivation their
inclination to act would hardly have been increased. Imagine,
these workers who cannot make rhyme nor reason out of the
action are told as a precondition for their participation that
they should preferably string up their current leaders on street
lamps. And in case they are not willing to submit voluntarily
to this condition, they are given the alternative: "He who is
not for me is against me!" *A declaration of war is made on
four-fifths of the German workers at the beginning of the action!*

We do not know whether the author of the above article
is experienced enough to know that he has a predecessor. This
predecessor at least had the modesty to say: "He who is not
with us is against us." He was certainly neither a Marxist nor
a socialist; his name was Bakunin, the Russian anarchist who
in 1870 directed an appeal to the Russian officers under this
alternative. The author of the article in the *Rote Fahne* may
read up on Marx's verdict about it and other related matters
in the booklet by Marx and Engels entitled, "The Alliance
of the Socialist Democracy and the International Workers' Association." It should actually be noted that the whole attitude
to the revolutionary classes comprised in the statement. "He
who is not for is against" is characteristic of anarchism, and
that the sentence "He who is not for us is against us" was
virtually the favorite phrase of Bakunin and his disciple
Nechayev. Only this conception leads to the methods used
by anarchism, not for the purpose of defeating the counterrevolution, but, in the words of a member of the *Zentrale* of
the KPD, to "force the revolution." Communism is never opposed to the working class. The basically Bakuninist point of
view of action—making a mockery of everything Marxist—this
complete misunderstanding and denial of every Marxist
premise in the relation of the communists to the masses, re-

sulted almost automatically, as it were, in all the subsequent
conscious or unconscious, intended or unintended, forced or
voluntary, repented or unrepented, characteristically anarchist
features of the March insurrection. The fight of the unemployed against the employed, the fight of the communists
against the proletarians, the emergence of the *Lumpenprole-
tariat,* the acts of sabotage—all of these were the *logical* consequences. All of this characterizes the March movement as that
which it is:

the greatest Bakuninist putsch in history.

To continue, the declaration of war aimed at the working
class was made. The *Zentrale* seems not to have been aware
of this either, for an above-mentioned member of the *Zentrale*
placed the blame for this "incorrect prelude" to the movement
on the Mansfeld workers as well. And what happened subsequently defies definition. To apply the term Blanquism to this
action would amount to a desecration of the name of Blanqui.
For even Blanqui was after all merely of the opinion—condemned in all its aspects by Marx and Engels—"that revolutions on the whole do not make themselves but are made;
they are made by a relatively small minority" which sweeps
along the majority by virtue of its example. In the *Rote Fahne,*
on the other hand, a writer of articles speaking for the *Zentrale* declares war on the workers at the beginning of the action *in order to browbeat them into participation afterward.*
And the war began. The unemployed were sent ahead as
storm troops occupying the gates to the factories. They forced
their way into the factories, extinguished the furnaces here
and there, and attempted to force the workers out of the factories. Open war of the communists against the workers broke
out. From the district of Moerse the following report, for
example, was received:

> The Krupp forge Friedrich-Albert in Rheinhausen was the
> scene of fierce fights Thursday morning between commu-
> nists occupying the works and workers arriving for work.
> The workers finally charged the communists with clubs
> in hand and thus gained entrance to their place of work by
> force. In the end Belgian soldiers intervened in the brawl,
> separated the combatants and arrested 20 communists. The
> communists evicted from the works later returned with re-
> inforcements and reoccupied the forge.

Still more moving reports came from Berlin. It was a terrible sight, we are told, to see the unemployed crying because of the thrashing they received while being thrown out of the factories, and to hear them cursing those who had sent them there. The *Rote Fahne* appeared suddenly with pious instructions, after it was too late, to be sure, after the war of the communists against the workers had already begun and had already been lost by the communists. Obviously a different editor of the *Rote Fahne* than the one who had printed the article "He Who Is Not for Me Is against Me," published on March 26th admonitions saying no war of workers against workers! This Pontius Pilatus was washing his hands in innocence.

But that was not yet the end. As though there were not enough unemployed already, new ones were created. The communists in the factories were faced with the difficult problem of deciding whether they should leave those factories where they were in a minority and where consequently their strike would not lead to a shutdown nor even to a curtailment of operations. The executive committee claims to have given instruction to remain inside the factories in such cases. The secretary of the Berlin organization claims to have done the same, but there exists a circular letter from the Berlin organization dated March 29th which reads: "A communist, even when in the minority, should under no conditions proceed to work." The communists left the factories; in troops of 200 to 300 men, often more or less, they left the factories. Work continued, but they have joined the ranks of the unemployed. The managers have seized the opportunity to sweep the factories "clean of communists" in a situation in which they even had the support of a large part of the workers. In short, the "action," begun with a declaration of war of the communists against the proletariat and the unemployed against the workers, was lost from the very first moment; the communist will never be able to gain anything, not even moral support, from an action begun in that manner.

The *Zentrale* had to decide what to do next; it decided in favor of an "acceleration of the action." The insanely initiated action which left people in the dark as to its aims and in which the *Zentrale*—obviously due to lack of better ideas and because it considered the stratagem terribly smart—resurrected trade union demands from the time of the Kapp Putsch

(!), this madness was to be accelerated. It could be accelerated. The dead of Mansfeld and Hamburg were joined by the dead of Halle. They too failed to produce the "proper state of mind." The *Zentrale* grows nervous because of the absence of the expected state of mind. It is in this situation, on March 30th, that a member of the *Zentrale* expresses with a deep sigh the hope that the police of Berlin might possibly "lose its calm" so that the working class may be "provoked."

The working class which was to be "provoked" at the same time continued to be "manipulated" in the pages of the *Rote Fahne*. On the same day, March 30th, this paper wrote the following:

> We are telling the Independent and social democratic workers in all clearness: if you tolerate or just mildly protest against the white terror and lynch justice unleashed by Ebert, Severing, and Hörsing against the workers who are fighting in the vanguard of the whole proletariat, then this capital crime rests not only on the heads of your leaders but on the head of every one of you. . . .
>
> The *Freiheit* [newspaper of the Independent Socialist party] calls for an intervention on the part of the trade unions and the social democratic parties. We *scoff* at the intervention of the *knaves* who themselves let loose the white terror of the bourgeoisie, who in fact carry out the dirty work for the bourgeoisie. . . .
>
> *Shame and dishonor on the worker* who still stands apart: *shame and dishonor on the worker* who still does not know his place.

To "provoke" workers into entering the action in this manner constituted indeed a "complete break with the past" of the Communist party. Nothing was left; nothing was left of the spirit of Karl Liebknecht, to say nothing of that of Rosa Luxemburg. For this reason it should have been left unsaid what a scoundrel—may I be forgiven this one harsh word in the defense of the memory of dead ones who can no longer defend themselves—wrote in the issue of the *Rote Fahne* of March 26th, (the Call to Arms No. 1): "The spirit of Karl Liebknecht and Rosa Luxemburg marches at the head of the revolutionary proletariat of Germany."

Enough new corpses existed for the purpose of "provocation"; the old ones one could leave in peace.

What happened next resembled a deeply moving drama. The *Zentrale* "accelerated the action." Pennon after pennon arose. The distinction between "old communists" and "new communists," still looked down upon by the wholly anointed, disappeared. The comrades rose with unparalleled heroism and contempt for death. In the towns and villages of central Germany, in the Leuna works and in the small and large factories, pennon after pennon lined up for the attack as the *Zentrale* commanded. Pennon after pennon advanced into the battle as the *Zentrale* commanded. Pennon after pennon met their deaths as the *Zentrale* commanded. . . .

And the *Zentrale?* It met in Berlin and "accelerated the action." During a session of the *Zentrale,* convened days before the termination of the action, of the members present five voted against three for the termination of the action. But here as elsewhere they became victims as well of their own snares of "slackness," "opportunism," and "inactivity" laid for others. In the face of the three votes pressing for sticking it out, the other five did not dare to force through their own position for fear of being suspected of insufficient revolutionary drive. Three vague "reports" from three districts indicating "some action," that the farmhands of East Prussia were "on the move," were sufficient. Accordingly, new messengers were dispatched in order to "accelerate the action." And what were the reasons given by those three diehards? We do not know whether all three shared it, but one of them offered as a reason that the action had to be driven on, now that it had been lost, to forestall possible attacks from the "left," necessitating a defense only against the "right."

What could one possibly answer to that? Even the behavior of Ludendorff pales by comparison. He, at least, conscious of certain defeat, had enemies of his own class meet their deaths. The others, however, had their own flesh and blood perish in a cause which they themselves had already recognized as lost, simply to save the position of the comrades who did this and with whom we ourselves lived through many good and bad times. But may they burden themselves, for their own sake and for that of the party in whose interest they may have believed to have acted, with just one castigation: *To never again show their faces to the German workers. . . .*

In this connection the question of the relationship of the KPD to the Communist International remains to be discussed. Not only because a catastrophic defeat such as that suffered by the KPD affects the Communist International as well, but also—without going into details—because at *least* part of the blame must be borne by the Executive Committee of the Communist International.

First of all, the Executive Committee of the Communist International viewed and still views our rather strong antiputschist stand, and that of other comrades, with alarm. It is in fact so alarmed about it that it dispatched its most expert scouts and interpreters to look for indications of "opportunism." It is fitting to talk about this quite openly and to state that such a position is incorrect. As far as opportunism, that is, social reformism, is concerned, it should be borne in mind that in no other country has it revealed itself as clearly and as unequivocally, has indeed crystallized itself as unambiguously as in Germany. . . .

That the events which took place in Germany, that is, an uprising shot from a pistol against the bourgeoisie and four-fifths of the proletariat, represented a putsch hopefully needs no further verification. But we are not at all of the opinion that every action for limited demands represents a putsch. We were opposed to limited actions in 1919 when the revolution was on the decline, and when any armed action would only have given to the bourgeoisie and Noske the fervently hoped-for opportunity of smothering the movement in its own blood. Limited actions should be avoided in revolutionary situations on the decline. In ascending revolutionary situations limited actions are absolutely necessary. In spite of the great revolutionary consciousness of the German proletariat it should not be expected—unless the miracle of a Kapp Putsch, comprehended this time by the communists, were to recur— that the proletariat is made ready *from one day to the next*, as if programmed by a machine, as envisioned by the social democratic party secretary and by Hilferding. When the revolutionary wave in Germany is again on the ascendancy, then actions will again develop in parts, similarly as before 1918, with the exception that the greater maturity of the German proletariat, comparatively speaking, will express itself in more powerful and more united partial actions than formerly. But we understand only one thing by limited action, and that is the entry-into-the-battle on the part of the proletarians of a part of Germany, be it of a large city or an economic region. We do not understand by a limited action that communists engage in a strike or an action in a part of the Reich or throughout the Reich. Limited action always implies: partial in a vertical and not in a horizontal sense. . . .

To begin with. We think that the inadequacy of the leadership of the Executive [ECCI] is perceived not only here in Germany but everywhere else. The reason for this lies not in the fact that it is not headed by a Marx, like the First International, nor by a Lenin; the reason lies in great technical difficulties, the imperfection of postal communication, etc. As a consequence the Executive is isolated from West Europe, its most important field of activity. We think that the Executive itself is most acutely aware of this. As a remedy it chose the most unfortunate of all, a remedy about which as chairman of the party I could talk only with a certain reserve, about which, however, I may talk freely as a member of the party. It is the system of delegates. To begin with, Russia is not in a position to use its best people for this purpose. They occupy posts in Russia in which they are irreplaceable. As a consequence comrades arrive in Europe each one of whom is filled with good intentions and ideas of his own, zealous for the chance to demonstrate how he "brings a thing off successfully." Thus West Europe and Germany become the testing ground for all sorts of miniature statesmen who give the impression that they want to develop their skills here. I have nothing against the Turkestanians[7] and wish them no ill: but I often feel that these people with their clever tricks would wreak less damage there [in Turkestan].

The matter takes on fatal proportions, however, when representatives are dispatched who do not even have the necessary human sensibilities. Here too I have to come back to the Italian matter. Comrade Rákosi, who represented the Third International, came to Germany on his way back from Italy.

[7] Levi called delegates of the ECCI to the various national parties *Turkestaner*. He applied this term particularly to Béla Kun, Joseph Pogány, and August Guralsky, who were dispatched to Germany in March 1921 and whom he also sarcastically referred to as "the mullahs of Khiva and Bokhara."

He was introduced to the sessions of the *Zentrale* as well as of the central committee as a representative of the ECCI. He has literally stated there that Italy was to "serve as an example," and he has declared both privately and publicly that the German party would again have to be split. He defended the Italian split at *the* point at which it took place with this necessity of a renewed split. The speeches have been recorded, and a hundred witnesses are prepared to testify. Rákosi, however, reports to Moscow and what does the Communist International make of it? In the semi- or wholly official yet apocryphal article by comrade Radek it says:

> The attempt (of a further split) exists only in the imagination of Levi, who appeals to the alleged remark of the Hungarian comrade Rákosi, present in Italy as representative of the Executive, and who is to have said, according to Levi's assertion, that the KPD also needs purging. Comrade Rákosi, who participated in the session of the Berlin central committee as a visitor [private person] denies having said anything to that effect. But even if comrade Rákosi had said such a thing, he had not been authorized to do so.

This remark displays a candidly frivolous manner of playing with parties, things, and people. Comrade Radek knows that visitors have no access to the meetings of the central committee of the KPD. Comrade Radek declares that Rákosi had not been authorized to make such a remark. However, comrade Rákosi was the representative of the Executive Committee in Livorno and gave us the official explanation of the basic principles underlying the split carried out there. He supplied basic principles which tomorrow could lead to a split in the German party. He himself drew the consequences; we and twenty-three other members of the central committee explicitly disapproved of these basic principles, but the Executive declares afterward: Rákosi was not authorized to make such a statement. This leaves one with the impression that he was authorized to promote an unprincipled split. This is a frivolous game. The method of dispatching irresponsible people who may then be avowed or disavowed, as the occasion demands, is certainly very convenient; but even if this method is hallowed by long party tradition, it is disastrous in its consequences for the Third International.

For the rest we would like to comment that the game of new splits, at least on the part of foreign representatives of the Executive Committee, is very easily indulged in. I hope not to be placed in a position in which I would have to provide proof for the fact that circles close to the Executive in Germany—that is, circles for whom the Executive bears at least political responsibility—consoled themselves in the face of the terrible defeat of the party by saying: if the action leads to nothing more than to the purge of the right wing, then the sacrifice is not too high. The comrades killed in central Germany were not told this when they were brought face to face with death; they were not told that their corpses would be worked up as dynamite for the party. If the Executive does not learn to rid us and itself of unscrupulous fellows of this kind, it will ruin us and itself.

The officious commentary of comrade Radek reveals, however, yet another and even more pernicious effect of the system of delegates. That stems from the direct and secret communication of these delegates with the Moscow Executive. We believe that dissatisfaction with this method is equally widespread in most countries in which the envoys function. . . . They never work with, but always behind the back of, and frequently against the central committee of a given country. *They* are trusted in Moscow, *others are not.* This is a system which is bound to undermine all confidence in reciprocal work on *both* sides, on the side of the Executive as well as on the side of the member parties. These comrades are for the most part either unsuited or insufficiently trusted for *political* leadership. Thus the hopeless situation results in which political leadership from the center is missing. All that the Executive accomplishes in this direction are belated appeals or premature papal bulls. Such a political leadership of the Communist International leads either to nothing or to disaster. As a consequence, nothing remains of the organization but what has been described in the foregoing. The executive does not function differently than a Cheka projected beyond the Russian borders, obviously an impossible situation. The concrete demand for a change, making it impossible that the unauthorized hands of unauthorized delegates snatch up the leadership within the separate countries, the call for a political leadership and against a party police, is not the demand for autonomy. . . .

DOCUMENT 2: Karl Radek, *"The Levi Case"*

Die Kommunistische Internationale, II, No. 17 (Sept., 1921).

. . . A chapter began which all German workers, in fact the Communist International, should study as one of its saddest but at the same time most instructive chapters of its short history. The central committee of the party decided on March 17th after lengthy and careful deliberations, and in view of the threatening internal and external danger and the total world situation, to sharpen and to intensify the politics of the party, not to avoid conflicts but instead to intensify them. The party did not decide on a putsch but on an orientation toward a struggle. The soldier Levi heard the reveille. He assured himself, however, that the struggle would not begin tomorrow and left for Italy in order to gather strength for future struggles. The other plain soldiers of the party, the half a million proletarians, did not travel to Italy for a vacation; they were called upon to exert all their energy in order to put the party in fighting trim. But the soldier Levi, even as a soldier, demanded something out of the ordinary! He, the anti-putschist, knows that large actions of the party cannot be engaged in unprepared, that they have to be prepared by means of agitation and organization, but he had full confidence in the *Zentrale's* ability to handle the work by itself. The report on the outbreak of the fights, which took place earlier than the party had expected, reached him in Vienna. He then made a great sacrifice for the world revolution, for he did not travel to Italy, though he had the ticket in his pocket, but returned to Germany. Unfortunately, nobody saw him in central Germany. He was not seen in Hamburg or Berlin in an organizing and agitating activity. . . . The "plain soldier" did his revolutionary duty differently: he began his undermining work while the struggle was on. Not a single one of his friends participated in the struggle. The ordinary party members perceived their absence, a circumstance which naturally did not increase their pugnacity or fighting morale. On March 29th, when the fate of the movement had not yet been decided and when a concentration of all the forces on the fight was still necessary, Levi wrote a letter to Lenin in which he described the whole action as a calamitous putsch. And what did he say in view of this "calamitous putsch?" Did he accuse himself of having committed an error when he and all his friends resigned from the *Zentrale*, thus removing all obstacles before the calamity? To the contrary, he declares: "Everyone who is acquainted with my inclinations knows that I regarded my resignation from the leadership of the German Communist party as a *joyous* event rather than the opposite." The very same man who prophesied in this letter that "the present leadership of the party will bring about its complete ruin in six months" states that "he will not oppose its policy." "Even now I do not intend to go any further than possibly writing a pamphlet setting forth my views, *but I will not lodge complaints either with the proper authorities in Germany nor with the Executive. The comrades who bear the responsibility (for the party) should not feel themselves hindered by me.*" Levi handed in the pamphlet he intended possibly to write for publication on April 3rd. His views expressed in it are those of Stampfer and Hilferding.[8] In it he accuses the *Zentrale* of the party of crimes against the party; he demands the retirement from political life of men——just to mention Brandler and Thalheimer—whose shoes Levi is not worthy of pulling off their feet, which have grown sore in a life spent in self-sacrificing, relentless service in the ranks of the labor movement. The Executive of the Communist International, whose core is provided by the leaders of the Russian party, is described as a gang of unscrupulous adventurers. Comrades who were placed by the Russian Communist party, in spite of its own difficult situation, at the disposal of foreign communist parties and who, though hunted like animals, are doing their duty as internationalists, are dragged through the mud in this pamphlet by an individual whom they far surpass. But that is not all. At the moment in which thousands of faithful proletarians languish in prisons and hundreds of proletarian corpses await their graves, in which the bourgeois press screams for the heads of the Communist party, and the final betrayal of

---

[8] Rudolf Hilferding was leader of the right wing of the Independent Socialist party (USPD) who debated Zinoviev at the Halle congress of the USPD in 1920 when the party was split. Friedrich Stampfer was an editor of the SPD newspaper *Vorwärts*. Both were leading anti-communists and anti-Bolsheviks.

the Independents raises every bloodhound of Ebert's sham judiciary to the level of a legitimate representative of the nation acting against robbers and murderers instigated from abroad; at this moment the former Communist party leader and present "soldier" appears and says: "Those who died in the battle did not die while repulsing an attack by Hörsing on red central Germany; they died as victims of the criminal madness of the *Zentrale* of the German Communist party. . . . You orphans and widows of the proletarian casualties, do not hate capitalism; do not hate the social democratic lackeys and henchmen, do not hate the Independent scoundrels who attacked the fighting workers in the rear—hate the leaders of the Communist party! And you workers who, though mistreated in the prisons, still raise your bleeding heads high in the belief to have fallen into the hands of the enemy after a brave battle in the interests of the proletariat, you are mistaken; you have no right to be proud of your wounds, for you are victims of new Ludendorffs who have sent you to suffer death cynically and frivolously!" All of this is contained in the same pamphlet which describes on page 34 how one town and one village of central Germany after another marched like one pennon of the proletariat after another resolutely into battle. "As the *Zentrale* commanded," thus sneers the "Marxist," without even sensing that he is unmasking himself as a liar and a slanderer in the eyes of every thinking communist; for who will believe him that in a young party the *Zentrale* enjoys such a confidence of hundreds of thousands of proletarians that they will suffer death upon its appeal even when the battle is the result of a picked quarrel? Who will believe him, especially at a moment when, as everyone knows, the resignation of the comrades Zetkin, Däumig, and Levi further weakened the *Zentrale,* which even earlier did not command too large an authority? *Paul Levi does not besmirch a putsch but the revolutionary struggle of the German proletariat!* Denounce him to the public prosecutor and to the bourgeois press!

And Levi's case is not even the most depressing thing. I think that after what has been said about the natural history of Levi, the character of this collapse [March Action] has been fairly clearly revealed to the eyes of the proletariat. A gifted intellectual becomes a social democrat in the stuffy air of Wilhelmian Germany. Intelligent and clever, he is repelled by the philistine atmosphere of the party bosses. He comes from a wealthy family, but its petty bourgeois existence does not attract but repels him. Then comes the war with its wave of dirt and patriotic lies. The young intellectual with his knowledge of languages and of the world situation naturally does not believe in the patriotic fairy tales of invasion, etc. Naturally, without any connection with the trade unions and party organizations, he cannot cross the bridge which led many an honest social democrat to accept the position of social patriotism; what are proletarian organizations to him and what is he to them? Their preservation cannot serve as a means of his self-deception, which might cloak his compromise with the bourgeoisie. He is opposed to the war. His connections with Rosa Luxemburg, his aesthetic preference for classicism, for the magnificent, lead him to the Spartacus League. But even the Spartacus League is not his fatherland, sacrifice for which constitutes his sole craving. Freed from military service, he does not go into hiding to risk his life for the ideas of the Spartacus League, as was done by Johann Knief, Pieck, and Karl Becker. Paul Levi lives and travels abroad, engaging in Spartacist activities as a sideline. "What is compassion which does not consume itself?" asks Nietzsche. Levi was not possessed by the revolutionary idea as by a flame. The revolution elevated the gifted author and speaker into the leadership of the Spartacus League. The revolutionary wave declined; to work for the party involves hard work, work under constant peril, work involving extreme privation, not only of a physical nature. If one wants to serve the cause everything has to be renounced. This work becomes a heavy burden to the intellectual dilettante and aesthete. While youths become men in this work and men grow hard as steel, the aesthete, the dilettante and intellectual feels himself oppressed; he wants to escape in a thousand ways. He must be given injections of camphor, his egotism must be appealed to, and the warnings of Rosa Luxemburg must be repeated to him. But the ashes of our martyrs do not burn in his heart, and he always rebels again. Those accursed proletarians who do not understand his sacrifice when he contemplates his lovely vases only once a week! They dare shout in his face: Down with the bosses! and threaten him with a gun while he endeavors to convince them. Filled with a rage against the plebeian pack, he gets into a conflict with experienced comrades who sense the corruption in him and who are too far removed from the German movement to be induced, as I was, to cover up his shortcomings, because I recognized the poverty of literary talents in the German movement. He senses this distrust he provokes, but it does not drive him to reflect on his own weaknesses, on the inflexible duties of a revolutionary; instead it drives him to the right. Instinctively he seeks the support of those comrades who are still in a transitory stage toward communism. He is alarmed when he discovers that the International is prepared even to forego temporarily considerable numbers of workers in order not to vacillating leaders into its ranks. The centralization of the struggle and the support of younger Communist parties by older ones, which he himself had repeatedly called for, now appears to him as an unbearable compulsion. He rebels against the International, but does not dare to oppose it openly in the awareness that in the struggle against it he is bound to be the loser, because he has nothing else to oppose to its ideas than the ideas of the Hilferdings rejected by the workers; thus he becomes the creeping malady of the party. Following his unmasking he retires to private life. He had contemplated desertion a thousand times before: to retire to private life, to a cozy home, where he could devote himself after the completion of higher legal work to the enjoyment of his collection of vases and to horticulture; now, however, he leaves as an angry Achilles. Nobody shed a tear on his behalf, nobody asked him to return, and the salvation which he craved turned into torment. Then the moment arrived. The party marched into a battle the prospects of which were very poor. He raised his head to indicate that he would not interfere in the matter. He washed his hands in innocence; he announced himself as an admonisher at the International but declared at the same time that he did not think of opposing the party. The party suffered a terrible defeat, it bled from a thousand wounds. The intellectual imagined that the workers were a chip off the same block as himself, that they would be discouraged and demoralized. And the pamphlet begun as political hot air turns into a missile against the party. The passive weakling, the psychological enigma, the human being with all his contradictions stands, revealed in his totality, and the shout resounding from his lips says: Down with the Communist party, down with the International! The bourgeois

youth, driven to the side of the proletariat by the stench of
his decaying class, becomes a renegade! . . .

DOCUMENT 3: Waldemar, *"Behind the Scenes of the March Action"*

Unser Weg (Sowjet): Zeitschrift für Kommunistische Politik, III (Aug., 1921).

I

Open Letter to the *Zentrale* of the KPD

Berlin, August 20, 1921

Dear Comrades:

A number of documents have, for reasons known to you,
come into my possession, which I have returned to you in the
original in the meantime.

You have recently repeatedly emphasized that only the
open, complete elucidation of the past, without consideration
as to the criticism of our enemies, is capable of bringing
about a recovery of the situation within the party in the future. I may, therefore, assume to act in agreement with your
wish in handing the letters over for publication.

The letters are the documentary evidence of the pernicious,
not to say criminal, role which the representative of the Executive has played in our party. I trust that the whole German, indeed international working class has a right to know
where the abscess is located which poisons the party and the
International. . . .

II

The delegates to the party congress may note from the following documents *how* and *by what means* a party is ruined.
By way of supplement we might add the following. Since the
end of January 1921 an emissary of the Executive had begun
with its approval (at least from the Bureau) to sponsor an opposition, a "left" wing, within the party united only a month
and a half ago. The letters published below deliver up the
corona which adorned and led this left wing. In order to but-

tress the left wing a messiah [Béla Kun] was dispatched who brought the gospel of salvation called "offensive" to Germany, about which this much was known: the "opportunist" Paul Levi, the "Serrati of the German CP," does not like it. The anointed arrived. However, unexpected disturbance of the program: Paul Levi was no longer a member of the *Zentrale*, the leadership of which he had already earlier handed over to the left wing. And now fate took its course. That fool [Kun] arrived, but the obstacle which had been built into the calculation was no longer present; the left wing, not permitted to "apply the brakes," went along, and the result was the March Action.

The matter also has international significance; the writer of these letters is Karl Radek, secretary of the Communist International.

III

Letter from Radek, March 14, 1921
to: Brandler, Thalheimer, Frölich, Meyer,
Böttcher, Felix

. . . 2. Situation in your party is clear to me. Levi tries to form faction under watchword: Mass Party or Sect. Which is swindle since he breaks up the party by his policy, whereas we can attract new masses by activating our policy. Nobody here thinks of a mechanical or for that matter any split in Germany. It is necessary to clearly develop the above contrasts, *to prepare the left wing for intellectual leadership*. Levi will quickly ruin himself. However, everything has to be done to prevent Däumig and Zetkin from going down with him. . . .

3. Everything depends on the world political situation. If rift between Entente and Germany widens, possibly leading to war with Poland, we will talk. You must do everything to mobilize the party, if only because these possibilities exist. One cannot shoot an action out of a revolver. If you do not now do everything through incessant pressure for action to give the communist masses a sense of its necessity, you will again fail in the face of a great moment. In connection with the world political decisions, less emphasis on "radical" formulas, more on action, that is, on how to put the masses into motion. If war breaks out, do not think of peace, or only of

protest, but of how to obtain arms. All of this written in a hurry at the party congress. Everything else in the article.

Greetings.

IV

Letter from Radek to the *Zentrale*

April 1, 1921

Dear Friends:

At the moment of writing this letter I have only the news from Nauen about the situation. On the basis of this information it is difficult to determine whether the current movement is spontaneous or represents an action initiated by the party. The fact that the starting point of the movement lies in the central German district, where we are stronger than anywhere else, and that Hamburg is the second point of attack makes me believe that this is the *party's action*. I fear that you began the action *a couple of weeks too soon*. I fear that a tactical error is involved, since you did not wait until a conflict between Germany and Poland might have broken out. I can understand the general reasons within the context of German and European affairs which might have decisively influenced your decision, in case the action was initiated on your decision. Misgivings are for this reason superfluous, even if the action results in a defeat. This not only because you could not have been certain that it would come at all to a Polish-German conflict, but also because action had finally become necessary. I believe that regardless of the outcome of the action it will *advance* the party. A party of half a million members will not be smashed or declared illegal by that gang. What I am thinking of now is that should we be repulsed, the differences within the party will return to their proper dimensions. Levi, having dragged out the formula, Sect or Mass Party, will undoubtedly now raise the issue of putschism; all that noise will then reveal itself for what it really is: as the beginning of the clear crystallization of the right faction.

Be wide awake on this point and *catch him on the first word* with which he tries to transfer the struggle to this basis. Brass and Koenen are here. We will have an official meeting with them on Saturday. I have reviewed the material here and will propose the following:

1. A resolution on the resignation of the five which will declare the resignation evidence for their striving toward a bureaucratic party; the Executive will further suggest to the communist parties to expel in the future any party leader leaving a post entrusted to him by the party. At the same time it will be pointed out that the fact of their desertion proves that they have presently no business in the *Zentrale*. In the second resolution, Levi's whole formulation, Mass Party versus Sect, will be reduced to its proper proportion, which means that Levi and company do not desire a communist party but a party of the Two-and-a-Half International. I do not know whether these resolutions will be adopted in this pointed manner. But it is necessary that you pose the questions in this manner. I repeat what I have said in my last letter: it is a mistake for August [Thalheimer] to depict these matters as if they were phantoms. I understand why he did it. In view of Clara's [Zetkin] and Däumig's authority their resignation was a hard blow, the effects of which he wanted to check for the moment. But you must now fight out this affair in complete openness. The only question is how. Brass tried to prove to me that there exists a secret factional organization of the old Spartacists. The documents he showed me, such as the "cremation story," already indicate by their titles that we are dealing with trifles concocted by provincial comrades. I strongly advise against any secret factional dealings. You will undoubtedly have on your side the masses of former left Independents, aside from the old Spartacists. In view of the situation do not conduct the struggle in small closed caucuses but in full view of the membership and in the press. August and Frölich ought to write small concise pamphlets explaining the differences. I should be finished within the week with my pamphlet about the question of the third congress. . . .

v

Letter from Radek to the *Zentrale*

April 7, 1921

1. The result of the discussions with Brass, Koenen, and Geyer is as follows: all are convinced that it involves the formation of a right wing. Levi's declaration from Vienna indicates that he is just short of a break with us. The only question is whether he will retire to private life, as I assume, or

whether he will take up the fight. Däumig's declaration in the central committee, like many of Clara's statements in the *Zentrale,* invite doubt as to whether they will retreat from their position in time. It would have been appropriate under these circumstances for the ECCI not only to come out unequivocally against them, but to indicate that this was not merely an episode. The old man [Lenin] still hopes that these people will come to their senses. It also has to be taken into account that all of us are convinced that we are faced with a setback as a result of the miscarried *offensive.* This setback will induce the right wing to reveal its nature on German questions. For this reason it might possibly be appropriate for the ECCI to wait with its move against the Right until this movement of self-revelation. We have adopted two resolutions, *one for the party executive and the central committee, the other for the public.* Zinoviev asked me just prior to his departure to regard *even* the public resolution for the time being as *confidential.* Following his expected arrival in Petrograd today we are supposed to come to a final decision about it by phone. I am afraid this will not occur prior to the mailing of this letter. In that case, please communicate the resolution to the *Zentrale,* the central committee and the five, but do not publish it. Should we decide for the publication of resolution B, I will wire. This much concerning the ECCI.

As far as *I am concerned,* I will conduct the fight entirely in the *open.* Advise the same to: Thalheimer, Frölich, Brandler, and Stöcker. I am finally beginning with the writing of the pamphlet and beg you to forward all the material on the last action by special courier. I am in advance convinced that the weaknesses manifesting themselves in the existence of the right wing had to find their expressions in the shortcomings of the action. As long as these questions are not argued through *openly* before the workers' organizations, the party will remain without fixed course. . . .

DOCUMENT 4: Clara Zetkin, *Reminiscences of Lenin*

(Vienna/Berlin, 1929).

. . . "Since when have you joined the pessimists," he [Lenin] asked; "rest assured the 'theoreticians of the offensive' will not ride the crest of the wave during the Congress.

We have still to be reckoned with. Do you think we 'made' the revolution without learning from it? And we want you to learn from it as well. Can it actually be called a theory? Beware, it is an illusion, it is nothing but romanticism. It is for this reason that it was fabricated in the 'land of the poets and thinkers' with the aid of my dear Béla [Kun], who also belongs to a poetically gifted nation and who considers himself obliged to be constantly more left than the left. We cannot afford to write poetry and to dream. We have to view the world economic and political situation soberly, entirely soberly, if we want to take up and win the battle against the bourgeoisie. And we want to win and have to win. The decision of the Congress on the tactic of the Communist International and all the controversial questions connected with it has to be related to and viewed in conjunction with our theses on the international economic situation. All of this must have unity. For the time being we will listen more to Marx than to Thalheimer and Béla, although Thalheimer is a good, well-trained theoretician and Béla is an excellent and faithful revolutionary. The Russian Revolution continues, after all, to teach more than the German 'March Action.' As I said, I am not uneasy about the position of the Congress."

"The Congress will also have to give its verdict on the 'March Action,' which, after all, constitutes the fruit, the application of the 'theory of the offensive,' its historical example, as it were," I interrupted Lenin. "Can one separate theory from practice? And yet I have noticed that there are many comrades here who, while rejecting the 'theory of the offensive,' passionately defend the 'March Action.' I find that illogical. All of us will certainly bow our heads in sincere sympathy before the proletarians who fought because they believed themselves provoked by Hörsing's henchmen and wanted to protect their rights. We will all declare ourselves in solidarity with them, regardless of whether hundreds of thousands were involved, as some story tellers would have us believe, or just a few thousands. But a different matter was and is the fundamental and tactical position of our party's *Zentrale* toward the 'March Action.' It was and remains a putschist offense, and the perpetrator of this state of affairs cannot be whitewashed with any political or literary soap."

"Naturally, the defensive action of proletarians ready for action and the offensive thrust of the poorly advised party, or

rather its leadership, would have to be judged differently."
Lenin said this rapidly, with determination. "You 'opponents
of the March Action' share responsibility for the fact that this
has not taken place. You have seen only the mistaken policy
of the *Zentrale* and its serious consequences, but not the
struggling proletarians in central Germany. In addition, Paul
Levi's wholly negative criticism, which indicated no sense of
solidarity with the party and which perhaps exasperated the
comrades more by its tone than by its content, diverted attention from the most important aspects of the problem. As
far as the probable position of the Congress is concerned, you
have to realize that we have to have room for a compromise.
Yes, just go on looking at me surprisedly and reproachfully,
but you and your friends have to swallow a compromise. You
have to be satisfied with carrying home the lion's share of the
proceeds of the Congress. Your basic political line will win,
will in fact win brilliantly. That will also prevent a repetition
of the 'March Action.' The decisions of the Congress must be
carried out strictly; the Executive will take care of that without a doubt.

"The Congress will throttle this splendid 'theory of the
offensive' and decide on a tactic corresponding to your view.
In return the Congress has to give to the supporters of the
'theory of the offensive' some crumbs of solace. If in the
analysis of the 'March Action' we stress that proletarians provoked by the lackeys of the bourgeoisie were involved, and
if for the rest we exercise somewhat paternal 'historical' mild-
ness, this approach will be possible. You, Clara, will object to
it as an attempt to cover up and the like, but to no avail. If
it is assumed that the tactic to be decided by the Congress
should succeed in the fastest possible way and without too
much friction, should in fact become law for the activity of
the communist parties, then it is imperative that our dear
'leftists' do not return home too humiliated and embittered.
Above all, we have to think about the mood of the genuinely
revolutionary workers within and outside the party. . . ."

"What about Paul Levi! What is your attitude toward him
and that of your friends, and what position will the Congress
take?" This question had been on my lips for a long time.
"Paul Levi has unfortunately become a case all of its own,"
replied Lenin. "The fault lies mainly with Paul himself. He
has removed himself from us and has obstinately run his head

against a brick wall. You must have observed this yourself in the course of your intensive agitation among the delegations. Such agitation is not necessary with me. You know how greatly I appreciate Paul Levi and his capabilities. I met him in Switzerland and had hopes for him. He has proved himself in times of the worst persecution; he was courageous, intelligent, and devoted. I believed him to be closely linked to the proletariat, although I noticed a certain coolness in his relation to the workers, a certain 'desire to remain distant' as it were. Since the appearance of his pamphlet I have developed doubts about him. I am afraid he has a strong tendency toward eccentricity and individualism and is not free from literary vanity. A ruthless criticism of the 'March Action' was necessary. What, however, did Paul Levi accomplish?—a cruel mangling of the party. He does not only criticize in a highly one-sided, exaggerated, in fact malicious manner, but he provides nothing with the help of which the party could orient itself. He lacks the spirit of solidarity with the party. And it is this which has outraged the rank and file so much, has made them deaf and blind to much of what is correct in Levi's criticism and particularly to his fundamentally correct political position. In this manner a mood arose, affecting also the non-German comrades, in which the quarrel about the pamphlet and particularly about Levi personally became the exclusive object of the altercation, rather than the incorrect theory and poor practice of the theory of the offensive and the 'leftists.' They may thank Paul Levi for having gotten off unscathed up to now, much too unscathed. Paul Levi is his own worst enemy."

The last sentences I had to let pass, but I objected vigorously to other remarks of Lenin. "Paul Levi is no conceited, complacent man of letters," I said. "He is no ambitious political careerist. It was his fate and not his wish that he assumed the leadership of the party at a young age and without great political experience or profound theoretical education. Following the murder of Rosa [Luxemburg], Karl [Liebknecht] and Leo [Jogiches] he had to take over, though he often enough resisted it. This is a fact. Even if our comrades never feel terribly warm in their relations with him and he is a solitary person, I am convinced that he lives for the workers with every fiber of his being. He was deeply shaken by the calamitous 'March Action.' He firmly believed that it had frivolously endangered the existence of the party and destroyed that for which Karl, Rosa, Leo, and many others had given their lives. He cried, literally cried in pain at the thought that the party was lost. He believed that its salvation was possible only by the application of the strongest remedies. He wrote his pamphlet in the same mood in which the legendary Roman threw himself voluntarily into the gaping abyss in the hope of saving his fatherland by sacrificing his life. Paul Levi's intentions were the purest, the most disinterested."

"I have no argument with you about it," replied Lenin. "You are a better attorney for Levi than he himself. Alas, you know yourself that in politics it is not the intent that counts but the consequence. Don't you Germans have a proverb which says something like 'The road to hell is paved with good intentions'? The Congress will condemn Paul Levi, will be hard on him. That is unavoidable. However, Paul's condemnation will be based on his violation of discipline, not on his fundamental political points of view. How would that be possible at any rate at the moment, when this point of view is in reality recognized as the correct one? With this act the road is wide open for Paul Levi to make his way back to us. I hope he will not himself barricade this road. He holds the key to his political fate in his own hand. He has to submit to the decision of the Congress as a disciplined communist and to disappear from political life for a while. He will certainly find it very hard. I sympathize with him and I feel genuinely sorry for him. Please do believe me. I cannot save him from this difficult trial period. . . ."

DOCUMENT 5: *"Preparation for the Struggle" and "Lessons of the March Action"*

Thesen und Resolutionen des III. Weltkongresses der Kommunistischen Internationale (Hamburg, 1921).

6. Preparation for the Struggle

The character of the transitional epoch makes it the duty of all communist parties to heighten to the utmost their preparedness for struggle. Every single battle can develop into a struggle for power. The party's preparedness for action can, however, only be developed if the party gives its whole agitation the character of a passionate attack on capitalist society, if it is capable of linking itself in this agitation with the broadest masses by talking to them in a manner which will convince them that they are led by a vanguard genuinely struggling for power. The publications and proclamations of the Communist party should not be house organs concerned with proving the validity of communism theoretically, but clarion calls for the proletarian revolution. The activity of communists within parliaments should not consist of discussions with the enemy, should not serve to persuade him, but should rather serve in the ruthless and relentless exposure of the agents of the bourgeoisie, in the arousal of the will to action of the working masses, and in the drawing nearer to the proletariat of the semi-proletarian petty bourgeois classes. Our organizational work in the trade unions as well as in the party organizations should not consist of a mechanical build-up or a purely numerical enlargement of our ranks, but must be pervaded by the consciousness of the coming struggle. Only if the party grows to embody the will to action in all its vital expressions and in all its organizational forms will it be in a position to execute its tasks in those moments when the conditions for larger actions will be present.

Wherever the Communist party represents a mass force, extending its influence beyond the framework of its party organization to broader masses of workers, it has the duty to rouse the working masses to struggle by action. Huge mass parties cannot confine themselves to criticizing the failures of other parties and to opposing their demands with communist ones. As mass parties the responsibility for the development of the revolution rests naturally with them. Where the condition of the working masses becomes progressively more intolerable, the communist parties must do everything to involve them in the struggle for their interests. In western Europe and America, where the workers are organized in trade unions and political parties, spontaneous movements cannot be reckoned with except in the rarest cases. In view of this it is the duty of the communist parties to strive for concerted action in the struggle for the immediate interests of the proletariat by using its influence in the trade unions and by increasing the pressure on other working class parties. Should the non-communist parties be pressured into this struggle, the task of the communists then consists in preparing the working masses in advance for the possibility of a betrayal on the part of the non-communist parties at some future stage, in intensifying and driving forward the situation as much as possible, in order to be prepared to lead the struggle independently if necessary (see the Open Letter of the KPD which may be used as a model for the opening phase of actions). Should the pressure of the communist parties on the trade unions and in the press not suffice to lead the proletariat into united action, it becomes the duty of the Communist party to try to lead large masses of workers independently into action.

This independent policy by the most active and class-conscious part of the proletariat for the defense of the vital interests of the proletariat will be crowned by success and lead to the arousal of the backward masses if its goals derive from concrete situations, if they are comprehensible to the masses, and if the broad masses are able to identify these goals with their own even though they are not yet capable of fighting for them.

But the Communist party should not limit itself to defense against the dangers threatening the proletariat, to the warding off of blows striking down the working masses. In accordance with its nature the Communist party constitutes, in the period of world revolution, the attacking party on the offensive against capitalist society; it is obliged to extend every defensive action, wherever it develops in breadth and depth, into an attack on *capitalist society*. Wherever these conditions exist it also has the duty to do everything possible to lead the working masses directly into an attack. Whoever opposes in principle the policy of the offensive against capitalist society violates the principles of communism.

These conditions are, first of all, the *intensification of the struggle in the bourgeois camp itself, both nationally and internationally*. When the struggles in the bourgeois camp have reached the point of opening up the prospect that the proletariat will be faced with a divided and separate enemy, the party has *to assume the initiative* in leading the masses into action after careful political and, wherever possible, organizational preparation. The second condition for offensive advances, that it attack on broad fronts, consists of *great discontent existing in decisive segments of the working class*,

opening up the prospect of a willingness by the working class
to enter into a general offensive against the capitalist government. While it is necessary to progressively intensify the
fighting slogans during the ascending phase of the movement,
it is also the duty of the communist leadership to lead the
fighting masses out of the battle in as orderly and united a
fashion as possible, should the movement assume a retrograde
direction. . . .

7. The Lessons of the March Action

The March Action represents a struggle forced on the KPD
by the government's attack on the proletariat of central Germany.

In the course of this first great struggle since its foundation,
the KPD committed a series of errors; the most important of
these consisted in not clearly emphasizing the defensive character of the action. By emphasizing the offensive aspect the
KPD offered the unscrupulous enemies of the proletariat, such
as the bourgeoisie, the SPD, and the USPD, the opportunity
to denounce it before the proletariat as the plotter of
putsches. This error was compounded by a number of party
comrades who represented the offensive as the primary
method of struggle by the KPD in the present situation.
Official spokesmen of the party, such as its chairman, comrade Brandler, have railed against this error. The Third Congress of the Communist International views the March Action
as a step forward. The March Action was a heroic struggle
of hundreds of thousands of proletarians against the bourgeoisie. By placing itself courageously in the vanguard of
the defense of the workers of central Germany, the KPD has
proven itself to be the party of the revolutionary proletariat of
Germany. The congress is of the opinion that the KPD will
be more assured of success in carrying out mass actions in
the future if it adapts its fighting slogans more successfully to
the real situations, analyzes these situations most carefully,
and carries out the actions in the most unified fashion.

In evaluating the prospects for action, the KPD must carefully consider all the facts and facets bearing on the difficulty
of the action, and it must carefully weigh the reasons advanced against the action. However, as soon as the party authorities have resolved on an action, all comrades have to sub-

mit to the decisions of the party and to carry out these actions. The criticism of actions may begin only after their conclusion; it may be practiced only within the organizations and the press of the party, and must take account of the situation in which the party confronts the class enemy. Since Levi has disregarded these obvious requirements of party discipline and the conditions of party criticism, the congress confirms his expulsion from the party and prohibits any political cooperation of a member of the Communist International with him.

III: Voices of Orthodoxy——Critics and Jeremiahs

Between the First and Third World Congress the policy of the Comintern, expressed in theoretical formulations and tactical pronouncements, underwent an almost revolutionary turnabout in its appraisal of the world situation. During the First Congress communism was in its heroic phase and the onset of world revolution appeared to be imminent. During the Second Congress revolutionary fires had been dampened, reversals had to be assimilated and explained, and a new course had to be charted by which national parties and the International would be strengthened through discipline and purified by the exclusion of centrists and reformists. During the Third Congress it became apparent that the times were not ripe for revolutionary action, that the communist parties were too isolated and represented too small a force within the working class to serve even as a catalyst for action. In short range at least a program of practical reforms was substituted for revolutionary goals and the member parties were directed to build bridges to the other working class parties and associations in the hope of winning members.

The Bolshevik leaders, with many years' experience in maneuvering, and the ECCI members, operating very much above the immediate battle for world revolution, were able to realize the need for a radical change in policy and to adjust to it much more readily than the leaders of national parties and their rank and file. On the theoretical front the latter found it difficult enough to forswear revolution for concrete transitional demands and to accept the premise that the decisive battles of the proletariat were not yet on the agenda. A number of parties (especially the Italian, French, and Spanish) found it impossible to accept the veiled united front policy of the Third World Congress. They could not understand how the social democrats were suddenly transformed from class enemies into misguided class brothers to be converted to the cause. Few could follow the ECCI's argument (and some considered it pure casuistry) that whereas yesterday the parties had to be split for the sake of purity, today they were to pursue a policy of united front; that the "pure parties" created by the expulsion of centrists and reformists could now undertake the hazardous task of wooing the non-communist masses precisely because they were steadfast and united in their belief and purpose.

The opposition to the united front was more than a natural resistance by sluggish party organizations to a reversal of policy in two years' time. It stemmed in large measure from resistance to Comintern authority by the Left in various communist parties which (ironically much like Levi had done) challenged the applicability of the Comintern's new general line to their own countries and political conditions. Although sensitive to this residue of resistance, the ECCI was not prepared to compromise with it. A truce between the Right and Left of the German party had been forced at the Third World Congress over Levi's political corpse, and the ECCI expected that other parties would draw the proper conclusions and accept it as a model.

At the end of 1921, the ECCI issued a set of directives to be followed by communist parties in implementing the united front (Document 1). The movement, it began, had entered a new transitional stage in which capitalism had taken the offensive and thereby engendered a desire for unity in the whole working class. Communist parties, it instructed, must undertake joint actions with non-communist parties and trade unions against the capitalist offensive, but were free to work out specific tactics in relation to prevailing national conditions. Above all, communist parties must retain the right to criticize their temporary partners and thus drive a wedge between complacent leaders and restive members. The united front experience of the Bolsheviks between 1903 and 1917 was offered as a model for all parties which had not yet captured power. The directives included a glowing report of conditions in Germany, France, England, and Italy, where each party was found to be pursuing the united front in a unique and disciplined way.

In 1922, when most parties were forced to consider these directives, hardly anyone was prepared to accept the Comintern's new orthodoxy. In Germany the KPD leadership constantly was assailed by the left wing which wanted to return

316 of Bolshevik Hegemony

to the revolutionary offensive; in France, where the communists controlled the largest political party of the Left, the
united front was rejected outright; in Britain the party was
too insignificant and weak to exercise any serious political
influence; and in Italy the PCI rejected the united front in
political activity but accepted it in trade union work. The
Comintern refused to alter its new course in the face of this
resistance and the February and June meetings of the ECCI
affirmed the united front theses over Italian and French objections. During the Fourth World Congress in November–
December 1922 the Italian and French parties were taken to
task for their intransigence, but the real differences over the
united front policy were plastered over and no disciplinary
measures were taken against its most uncompromising opponents.

One of the most outspoken of these was Amadeo Bordiga,
whose strong syndicalist leanings had already found expression in the Rome Theses of 1922, in which the PCI rejected
the political united front. Even after he was imprisoned in the
first important *razzia* against the Left after Mussolini's coup,
he tried to liberate his party from what he considered the
Comintern's erroneous policy in Italy by issuing a challenging
manifesto (Document 2).[1] The Comintern's overall united
front strategy, he charged, threatened to undermine the principles of communist militancy of the PCI and called into question the reasons for the split at Livorno which brought the
PCI into being. In sponsoring an actual fusion between the
PCI and the Maximalists (socialists of the PSI under the leadership of Serrati), he complained, the Comintern was not only
forcing the communists to become the bedfellows of opportunists and anti-revolutionaries, but was also undermining the

[1] The Manifesto was written in April 1923. The first indication
of its existence is found in a letter of May 1, 1923 from Palmiro
Togliatti to Antonio Gramsci. The text of the Manifesto has survived because it was confiscated by the police from Togliatti when
he was arrested on September 23, 1923. Archival work done by
the editors of the *Rivista storica del socialismo* has only recently
brought it to light. It is not known how Bordiga managed to forward
the document from his prison. For the details on the history of
this document and its reception, see Palmiro Togliatti, *La forma-
zione del gruppo dirigente del Partito comunista italiano nel 1923–
1924* (Milan, 1962).

united front attempts by the PCI to win the Maximalist rank and file from their leaders.[2] Far from achieving any success, the policies of the Comintern had demoralized the PCI and encouraged the formation of a right-wing minority within it. Bordiga demanded a full discussion of the Italian situation by the PCI and the Comintern, with the challenge that if such a debate did not sustain the present policies of the leadership, those with different principles be given an opportunity to take command.[3]

The united front, which was to remain in force for seven years, proved to be difficult to enforce. The policy based on open temporary alliances with social democracy to further the aims of communism could not be applied in the growing number of countries where communist parties were outlawed. When it was put to the test in relatively favorable conditions in 1923 it failed abysmally. The united front was above all a policy of retreat from revolution, whose acceptance naturally diminished the importance of the Comintern as a revolutionary organization. In view of the failure of the world revolution to materialize, the Comintern had to bide its time and devote itself to the defense of Soviet Russia, the only mainstay of proletarian revolution.

[2] At its Rome congress in October 1922 the PSI expelled Turati and his reformist followers. In the following month, at the Fourth World Congress of Comintern, the PCI was directed to fuse with the purified PSI.

[3] Gramsci's refusal to sign the Manifesto marked the first step in the eventual creation, with the help of the Comintern, of a new party leadership composed of Gramsci, Togliatti, and Umberto Terracini. They acquiesced in the fusion with the PSI and ended the Syndicalist orientation of the Italian party which had for so long plagued the Comintern. Not only in Italy but elsewhere differences over the united front were resolved by the promotion of national leaders willing to abide by the Comintern's general line. A more tractable leadership naturally accelerated the course of bolshevization.

DOCUMENT 1: *"Directives on the United Front of the Workers and on the Attitudes to Workers Belonging to the Second, Two-and-a-Half, and Amsterdam Internationals, and to Those Who Support Anarcho-Syndicalist Organizations"*

Jane Degras, *The Communist International 1919–1943,* Vol. I. By permission. First appeared in *Bulletin des Exekutivkomitees der Kommunistischen Internationale,* No. 5 (Jan. 21, 1922).

1. The international labor movement is passing at present through a peculiar transition stage, which presents both the Communist International as a whole and its individual sections with new and important tactical problems.

The chief characteristics of this stage are: The world economic crisis is growing more acute. Unemployment is increasing. In practically every country international capital has gone over to a systematic offensive against the workers, as shown primarily in the fairly open efforts of the capitalists to reduce wages and to lower the workers' entire standard of life. The bankruptcy of the Versailles peace has become ever more apparent to the broadest strata of the workers. The inevitability of a new imperialist war, or even of several such wars, is clear, unless the international proletariat overthrows bourgeois rule. . . .

The "democratic" reformist illusions which, after the end of the imperialist slaughter, were reborn among the workers (the better-off workers on the one hand, and the most backward and politically inexperienced on the other) are fading before they reach full bloom. The "labors" of the Washington conference will shake these illusions even more.[4] If, six months ago, it was possible to speak with some justification

---

[4] A conference of the great powers on disarmament and the Pacific area was convened in Washington in November 1921. The agreement by the powers to limit their naval strength and bases in the Far East proved embarrassing for Soviet foreign policy, because it contradicted the accepted thesis of growing contradictions and antagonisms in the capitalist world.

of a general swing to the right among the working masses in Europe and America, there is no doubt that today, on the contrary, the beginning of a swing to the left can be observed.

2. On the other hand, under the influence of the mounting capitalist attack, there has awakened among the workers a spontaneous *striving toward unity* which literally cannot be restrained, and which goes hand in hand with a gradual growth in the confidence placed by the broad working masses in the communists. . . .

3. Communist parties can and should now gather the fruits of the struggle which they waged earlier on when conditions were most unfavorable because of the indifference of the masses. But while the workers are coming to feel greater and greater confidence in the uncompromising and militant elements of the working class, in the communists, they are as a whole moved by an unprecedented urge toward unity. Those strata of the workers now awakening to active life but with little political experience are dreaming of the unification of all workers' parties and even of all workers' organizations in general, hoping by this means to increase their power of resisting the capitalists. . . . Considerable sections belonging to the old social democratic parties are no longer content with the campaign of the social democrats and centrists against the communist vanguard, and are beginning to demand an understanding with the communists. But at the same time they have *not yet* lost their belief in the reformists, and considerable masses still support the parties of the Second and the Amsterdam Internationals.[5] These working masses do not formulate

[5] The so-called Amsterdam International was the postwar revival of the International Federation of Trade Unions (IFTU), which before 1914 was a loose organization sharing the general outlook of the Second International. In April 1920, the IFTU helped organize the Washington conference at which the International Labor Organization (ILO) of the League of Nations was founded. At the Second World Congress of Comintern an International Trade Union Council (Mezhosvprof) was created and given the task of organizing an international congress of red trade unions to compete with the IFTU. The congress took place in July 1921, and the Red International of Trade Unions or Profintern became a subsidiary of the Comintern. The majority of organized labor continued its allegiance to the Amsterdam International, which was dubbed with the pejorative "yellow" in communist literature.

their plans and aspirations clearly enough, but by and large the new mood can be attributed to the desire to establish the united front and to attempt to bring about joint action by the parties and unions of the Second and Amsterdam Internationals with the communists against the capitalist attack. To that extent this mood is progressive. In essentials the belief in reformism has been undermined. In the general situation in which the labor movement now finds itself any serious mass action, even if it proceeds only from partial demands, inevitably brings to the forefront more general and fundamental questions of the revolution. The communist vanguard can only gain if new sections of workers are convinced by their own experience of the illusory character of reformism and compromise.

4. In the early stage of germination of a conscious and organized protest against the treachery of the leaders of the Second International, these latter had the entire apparatus of the workers' organizations in their hands. They ruthlessly used the principle of unity and proletarian discipline to stifle the revolutionary proletarian protest and to eliminate any resistance to their placing the entire power of the workers' organizations at the service of national imperialism. In these circumstances the revolutionary wing was forced to win at any cost freedom of agitation and propaganda, i.e., freedom to explain to the working masses the unexampled historical treachery committed and still being committed by the parties created by the working masses themselves.

5. Having secured organizational freedom to influence the working masses by their propaganda, the communist parties of all countries are now trying to achieve the broadest and most complete unity possible on practical action. The Amsterdamers and the heroes of the Second International preach this unity in words, but in their actions work against it. Having failed to suppress organizationally the voice of the proletariat and of revolutionary agitation, the reformist compromisers of Amsterdam are now seeking a way out of the deadlock for which they themselves are responsible by initiating splits, by disorganizing and sabotaging the struggle of the working masses. It is at present one of the most important tasks of the Communist party to expose publicly these new forms of an old treachery.

6. Profound internal processes are, however, forcing the

diplomats and leaders of the Second, Two-and-a-Half, and Amsterdam Internationals to push the question of unity into the foreground. But while, for those sections of the working class with little experience who are only beginning to awaken to class-conscious life, the slogan of the united front expresses a most genuine and sincere desire to mobilize the forces of the oppressed classes against the capitalist onslaught, the leaders and diplomats of these Internationals advance that slogan only in a new attempt to deceive the workers and entice them by new means onto the old road of class collaboration. The approaching danger of a new imperialist war (Washington), the growth of armaments, the new imperialist secret treaties concluded behind closed doors—all this will not induce the leaders of the three Internationals to beat the alarm in order to bring about the international unification of the working class not only in words, but also in fact; on the contrary, it will provoke inevitable friction and division within the Second and Amsterdam Internationals, roughly of the same kind as that apparent in the camp of the international bourgeoisie. This phenomenon is inevitable, because the solidarity of the reformist "socialists" with the bourgeoisie of their "own" countries is the cornerstone of reformism. . . .

7. Confronted by this situation, the ECCI is of the opinion that the slogan of the Third World Congress of the Communist International, "To the Masses," and the interests of the communist movement generally, require the communist parties and the Communist International as a whole to *support the slogan of the united front of the workers* and to take the initiative in this matter. The tactics of each communist party must of course be worked out concretely in relation to the conditions in each country.

8. In *Germany* the communist party at its last national conference supported the slogan of a workers' united front and declared its readiness to support a workers' government that was willing to take up with some seriousness the struggle against the power of the capitalists. The ECCI considers this decision completely right and is convinced that the KPD, while maintaining in full its independent political attitude, is in a position to permeate broad sections of the workers and strengthen the influence of communism on the masses. In Germany more than anywhere else the broad masses will be daily more convinced how right the communist vanguard were

when at the most difficult time they did not want to lay down their arms and steadily emphasized the worthlessness of the reformist actions proposed, since the crisis could be resolved only by the proletarian revolution. By pursuing those tactics the party will in time also rally around itself the revolutionary elements among the anarchists and syndicalists who now stand aside from the mass struggle.

9. In *France* the communist party has a majority among the politically organized workers. Hence the united front question has a different bearing there from what it has in other countries. But even there it is necessary that the entire responsibility for the split in the united workers' camp should fall on our opponents. The revolutionary section of the French syndicalists are rightly fighting against a split in the French unions, that is, fighting for the unity of the working class in the economic struggle against the bourgeoisie. But the workers' struggle does not stop in the factories. Unity is necessary also in the face of growing reaction, of imperialist policies, etc. The policy of the reformists and centrists, on the other hand, led to the split in the party and now also threatens the unity of the trade union movement, which shows that Jouhaux just like Longuet objectively serves the cause of the bourgeoisie. The slogan of the united front of the proletariat in the economic and political struggle against the bourgeoisie remains the best means of counteracting these splitting plans.

Even though the reformist CGT [Confédération Générale du Travail], led by Jouhaux, Merrheim, and Co., betrays the interests of the French working class, French communists, and the revolutionary elements among the French working class in general, must, before every mass strike, every revolutionary demonstration, or any other revolutionary mass action, propose to the reformists support for such mass action, and if they refuse to support the revolutionary struggle of the workers they must be exposed. This will be the easiest way of winning the non-party working masses. In no circumstances, of course, must the Communist party of France allow its independence to be restricted, e.g., by supporting the "left bloc" during election campaigns, or behave tolerantly toward those vacillating communists who still bemoan the break with the social patriots.

10. In *England* the reformist Labour party has rejected Communist party affiliation, although other workers' organiza-

tions are accepted. Under the influence of the growing desire among the workers for the united front, the London workers' organizations recently passed a resolution in favor of the affiliation of the CPGB to the Labour party.

England is, of course, in this respect an exception, because as a result of peculiar circumstances the English Labour party is a kind of general workers' organization for the entire country. It is the task of the English communists to begin a vigorous campaign for their acceptance by the Labour party. The recent treachery of the union leaders during the miners' strike, the systematic capitalist pressure on wages, etc. have stirred up a deep ferment among the English proletariat, who are becoming more revolutionary. English communists should make every effort, using the slogan of the revolutionary united front against the capitalists, to penetrate at all costs deep into the working masses.

11. In *Italy* the young Communist party is beginning to conduct its agitation according to the slogan of the proletarian united front against the capitalist offensive, although it is most irreconcilably opposed to the reformist Italian Socialist party and the social-traitor labor confederation, which recently put the finishing touch to their open treachery to the proletarian revolution. The ECCI considers this agitation by the Italian communists completely correct and insists only that it shall be intensified. The ECCI is convinced that with sufficient foresight the CP of Italy can give an example to the entire International of militant Marxism which mercilessly exposes at every step the half-heartedness and the treachery of the reformists and the centrists, who clothe themselves in the mantle of communism, and at the *same time* conduct an untiring and ever mounting campaign among ever broader masses *for the united front of the workers against the bourgeoisie.*

The party must of course do its utmost to draw all the revolutionary elements among the anarchists and syndicalists into the common struggle. . . .

16. In a number of other countries the position differs according to different local circumstances. Having made the general line clear, the ECCI is sure that the individual communist parties will know how to apply that line in accordance with the conditions prevailing in each country.

17. The principal conditions which are equally categorical for communist parties in all countries are, in the view of the

ECCI . . . the absolute independence of every communist party which enters into an agreement with the parties of the Second and Two-and-a-Half Internationals, its complete freedom to put forward its own views and to criticize the opponents of communism. While accepting a basis for action, communists must retain the unconditional right and the possibility of expressing their opinion of the policy of all working class organizations without exception, not only before and after action has been taken but also, if necessary, *during its course.* In no circumstances can these rights be surrendered. While supporting the slogan of the greatest possible unity of all workers' organizations in every *practical action against the capitalist front,* communists may in no circumstances desist from putting forward their views, which are the only consistent expressions of the defense of the working class interests as a whole.

18. The ECCI considers it useful to remind all brother parties of the experiences of the Russian Bolsheviks, that party which up to now is the only one that has succeeded in winning victory over the bourgeoisie and taking power into its hands. During the fifteen years (1903–1917) which elapsed between the birth of bolshevism and its triumph over the bourgeoisie, it did not cease to wage a tireless struggle against reformism or—what is the same thing—menshevism. But at the same time, the Bolsheviks often came to an understanding with the Mensheviks during those fifteen years. The formal break with the Mensheviks took place in the spring of 1905. Influenced by the stormy developments in the workers' movement, the Bolsheviks formed a common front with the Mensheviks . . . and these unifications and semi-unifications happened not only in accordance with changes in the fractional struggle, but also under the direct pressure of the working masses, who were awakening to active political life and demanded the opportunity of testing by their own experience whether the Menshevik path really deviated in fundamentals from the road of revolution. . . . The Russian Bolsheviks did not reply to the desire of the workers for unity with a renunciation of the united front. On the contrary. As a counterweight to the diplomatic game of the Menshevik leaders the Russian Bolsheviks put forward the slogan of "unity from below," that is, unity of the working masses in the practical struggle for the revolutionary demands of the workers against

the capitalists. Events showed that this was the only correct answer. As a result of those tactics, which changed according to time, place, and circumstance, a large number of the best Menshevik workers were won for communism.

19. While the Communist International puts forward the slogan of the workers' united front and permits agreements between the various sections of the International and the parties and unions of the Second and Two-and-a-Half Internationals, it can itself not reject similar understandings at the international level. The ECCI made a proposal to the Amsterdam International in connection with relief action for the Russian famine. It repeated this proposal in connection with the white terror and the persecution of workers in Spain and Yugoslavia. The ECCI is now making a further proposal to the Amsterdam, Second, and Two-and-a-Half Internationals, in connection with the opening of the Washington conference, which has shown that the international working class is threatened by a new imperialist slaughter. Up to now the leaders of these Internationals have shown by their conduct that *in fact* they ignore their unity slogan when it comes to *practical action.* In such cases it will be the task of the Communist International as a whole and all of its sections separately to explain to the broad working masses the hypocrisy of these leaders who prefer unity with the bourgeoisie to unity with the revolutionary workers, and who, for example, by remaining in the International Labor Office of the League of Nations, form part of the Washington imperialist conference instead of organizing the struggle against imperialist Washington. But though the leaders of the Second, Two-and-a-Half, and Amsterdam Internationals reject one or another practical proposal put forward by the Communist International, that will not persuade us to give up the united front tactic, which has deep roots in the masses and which we must systematically and steadily develop. Whenever the offer of a joint struggle is rejected by our opponents the masses must be informed of this and thus learn who are the real destroyers of the workers' united front. Whenever an offer is accepted by our opponents every effort must be made gradually to intensify the struggle and to develop it to its highest power. In either case it is essential to capture the attention of the broad working masses, to interest them in all stages of the struggle for the revolutionary united front.

20. In putting forward the present plan, the ECCI directs the attention of all brother parties to the dangers which it may in certain circumstances entail. Not all communist parties are sufficiently strong and firm, not all have broken completely with the centrist and semi-centrist ideology. Some may overstep the mark, there may be tendencies which would amount in fact to the dissolution of communist parties and groups into the united but formless bloc. To carry out the new tactics successfully for the communist cause, it is necessary for the communist parties who put them into operation to be strong and firmly welded together, and for their leaders to possess great theoretical clarity.

21. Within the Communist International itself, there are two tendencies among the groups, which may with more or less reason be classed as right and semi-centrist. One has not really broken with the ideology and methods of the Second International, has not emancipated itself completely from reverence for its former numerical strength, and half-consciously or unconsciously, is looking for a path of intellectual understanding with the Second International and consequently with bourgeois society. Other elements, who are opposed to formal radicalism, to the mistakes of the so-called "left," are anxious to give the tactics of the young Communist party greater flexibility and maneuverability, in order to ensure for it the possibility of more rapid penetration among the masses.

The rapid development of the communist parties has occasionally thrust both apparently into the same camp, to some extent into the same group. The use of the methods noted above, which are designed to provide a prop for communist agitation in the united mass actions of the proletariat, is the best way of exposing the really reformist tendencies within the communist parties, and if rightly used will contribute in a high degree to their internal revolutionary consolidation, both by educating the impatient and sectarian elements through experience, and by ridding the parties of reformist ballast.

22. The united front of the workers means the united front of all workers who want to fight against capitalism, which includes those who still follow the anarchists, syndicalists, etc. In many countries such workers can help in the revolutionary struggle. From the first days of its existence the Communist International has taken a friendly line to these workers, who

are gradually overcoming their prejudices and drawing nearer to communism. Communists must pay even greater attention to them now, when the united front of the workers against the capitalists is becoming a reality.

23. In order to give definite form to future work on the lines laid down, the ECCI resolves to convene a meeting of the Executive in the near future at which the parties will be represented by double the usual number of members.

24. The ECCI will follow carefully every practical step taken in the field under discussion, and ask every party to inform the Executive of every attempt and every success, giving full factual details.

DOCUMENT 2: Amadeo Bordiga, *"Manifesto"*

"Nuova documentazione sulla 'svolta nella direzione del Partito Comunista d'Italia nel 1923–1924," *Rivista storica del socialismo*, VII, No. 23 (Sept.–Dec., 1964).

To All the Comrades of the Communist Party of Italy:

With good conscience and after mature deliberation, we believe we are carrying out our duty as communists by directing the present appeal to the comrades. The party is going through a crisis of such a nature that it can be resolved only by the participation of the whole mass of its members.

We are not alluding to the crisis in efficiency and organization which is the inevitable consequence of the victory of the antiproletarian forces in Italy. This crisis also deserves full attention, but it could be faced—if there were no others—by opportune measures taken by the directive organs and faithfully carried out.

Here it is a question of another crisis which unfortunately aggravates the consequences of the first: an internal crisis of general policies, which from individual tactical questions has now broadened to include the whole framework of principles and the tradition of the political line of the party.

This crisis did not originate from internal disagreements, but from divergencies between the Italian party and the Communist International in its present majority and in its central organs. Precisely because the crisis has taken on such a character—of absolute abnormality—it could lead to the paralysis of the life of the party and to the sterility of its action if the question is not placed before the whole party, with the comrades being completely informed through a basic discussion and a final and definitive evaluation of what must be the platform of thought and action of our party.

This document proposes the initiation of such a task, in spite of the difficulties caused by the inability to have open meetings of the party and a free press.

The platform on which our party was built at the congress of Livorno is known to the comrades. They know the results of [our] criticism carried out within the Socialist party as a reaction to its essential shortcomings, especially in the years after the war.

What was the situation of the party and its task immediately after Livorno for the men entrusted with its leadership? The theory of the party was clearly established on the revolutionary and Marxist bases brought to light by the Russian Revolution and the founding of the Third International. The new organization of struggle of the Italian proletariat, distinguished by the strength of its international connection, must develop more and more in such a way as to avoid the pernicious and traditional defects of superficiality, disorder, and personal cliques fatal to the old party; and with new criteria of seriousness and cool reflection, together with the unlimited dedication of all the individual militants to the common cause.

And there is also the vast problem of the action and tactics to be applied in the special Italian situation in order to arrive at communist goals.

The condition of the proletarian struggle at the beginning of 1921 had been compromised by the inadequacies of the Socialist party, so much so that a revolutionary offensive did not seem possible on the part of a minority party like ours. But the party action could and should have been calculated to obtain the greatest efficiency of resistance of the proletariat to the unleashed bourgeois offensive, and through resistance obtain the concentration of the workers' forces in the best possible condition around the banner of the party, the only one possessing a method capable of guaranteeing the preparation of a recovery.

The communists saw the problem in this way: assuring the maximum of proletarian defensive unity before the pressure of the industrialists' offensive, but at the same time avoiding that the masses in the illusion of that apparent unity, a sorry mixture of contradictory directions which already had been denounced as impotent by the sad experience acquired by the Italian masses [incomplete sentence].

At this time we shall not repeat the history of the communist attempt to build a united front of the workers' organizations against reaction and fascism. The attempts failed because of the behavior of the other parties . . . but from this very failure our criticism, based on facts, gained the advantage of an increased tendency of the militant proletariat to gather around the communist party.

Our propaganda never hesitated to assert that the proletariat could win only with a clearly communist direction, even if—precisely to win that goal—the communists offered to struggle together with workers of any political party. The results of this experiment, in a period of extraordinary political importance, must be discussed by the party and the International with an exact evaluation and complete account.

But today there is this danger: such a question may be liquidated by saying, The tactics of the party were wrong and caused the proletarian defeat!

Here the point is not to defend the work of individuals, to whom nobody in the other parties denies goodwill and even other qualities, but something quite different: a judgment on a totality of experiences of the first order, a thing of vital importance for a Marxist party, and augmented by the international significance of the present phase of Italian history. And it is a question of asking whether the party, after the outcome of such an experiment, should review and modify its fundamental bases. Such a question demands the interest of the whole party, as well as a much more mature examination by the whole International. And, after having said that which is obvious to any witness of Italian politics of this last year—that the Communist party could not have prevented in any way the course that events have taken because of causes too profound and remote to reverse—it is to be immediately emphasized that the line which we established at Livorno could be followed only for a brief moment. Here we are only presenting the outline of the question in the hope of persuading the comrades of the need for a profound discussion.

Three facts must be considered:

1. The Italian party has had different opinions than those

of the International regarding the communist "international" tactic.

2. The divergence regarding Italian things is even more serious, since it departs from the limits of "tactics" to touch upon the very bases of the constitution of the party.

3. Up to now the International has modified and is still in the process of modifying its policies with regard to tactics, but now also with regard to its program and its fundamental organizational norms.

Here we shall not deal with the first point. It is well known through the discussion at the Congress of Rome of our party (March, 1922), and is spelled out in the theses on tactics which were there approved.

The second point, on which the mass of the party is little informed, deserves greater attention.

On the question of the tactics to be applied in Italy within the proletarian movement, the divergence came to a head very slowly. Even though the Italian delegation to the Third Congress was already in the opposition regarding the tactics of the International, the concrete work of the party up to that time and beyond was still approved and praised.

Later, with regard to the slogans of the "united front" and a "workers' government," we never precisely knew what the International wanted us to do. But in the meantime our party spelled out its line with the aim of preventing tactical means from conflicting with the needs of propaganda, not only in theory but in fact. This was done from two fundamental points of reference: "Only with the political line upheld by the Communist party and with its leadership can the proletariat defeat the bourgeoisie," and "Only in a revolutionary dictatorship can proletarian power be built." Consequently, [the party] did work in the "united trade union front," but with an open campaign against any trace of opportunism.

From time to time, the International did make specific criticisms, but even in June 1922 it merely asked the party to launch the slogan of a "workers' government," but so defining it as to render it a "pseudonym of the proletarian dictatorship," whereas it was afterward said that it was really ministerial and parliamentary participation.[6] On the trade

[6] With its weather eye cocked to Germany, where the possibility of a communist-socialist coalition government existed in Saxony and Thuringia, the ECCI put forward the slogan "workers' government"

union question and on fascism it was never made clear what the International wished to modify in the method we had followed.

But the divergence broadened and deepened to a field of substantial importance with the question of fusion with the Maximalist party [Serrati faction].

Whereas we viewed the "pedigree" of the party [PCI] as having been historically established in its foundations at Livorno, and always maintained that the influx of other proletarian elements, the chief goal of the party, was to be attained by wrenching them from the cadres of other movements and inserting them in ours, and we were against any idea of a mass fusion with other parties and against any creation of factions of sympathizers within the latter rather than having them come [directly] into our ranks (that is, we were against "noyautage" or cell building), it is clear today that the International considers the Livorno solution as transitory and aspires to a mass adherence of another "slice" of the Socialist party. According to it, the Maximalists were divided from us solely by the fact that they hesitated to separate themselves from the reformists. According to us, Maximalism is a form of opportunism as dangerous as reformism. In its tradition and leadership it will never be revolutionary, but will continue its task of leading the masses astray with its charlatanic language, which hides the most pernicious cultivation of a state of impotence and inertia.

The International, in seeing the Italian proletariat lose ground and the consequent reduction in the ranks of our party, thought it could displace the development of the situation and at the same time achieve an international success

---

in its Directive of December 1921. Opponents of the united front were quick to point out that if the slogan meant nothing more than proletarian dictatorship, they would support it, but that if it implied parliamentary horse trading, they would have nothing to do with it. The Fourth World Congress stipulated the types of government in which communists might participate: governments of workers and poor peasants and workers' governments. But both of these were to be considered only as a possible transitional stage toward proletarian dictatorship. Communist parties were to participate in such governments on the condition that they had the consent of the Comintern and retained their own identity and unrestricted independence of agitation.

with the adherence of the Maximalists. We wished to denounce this openly as defeatism and to reinforce, even in
the inevitable retreat of the militant proletariat, the pre-
dominance of the Communist party with the liquidation of
the other parties.

Facts have demonstrated the resistance of the Maximalists
as a political organization to put themselves on the revolutionary terrain and loyally to accept adherence to the International. There was the opinion that Serrati [incorrect phrase
—probably to the effect that Serrati was the most representative Maximalist leader] and we have seen that same
Serrati liquidated by his party, or rather by a few dozen
leaders who do everything in the name of the Maximalist
workers, whereas the latter can be won only by breaking the
net in which they are caught. And they say . . . that the
communists have prevented the fusion!

What have been the consequences of this attitude of the
International in Italy? The tactical work of the party in the
united front was impeded, thus providing the other parties
with a diversion from the situation in which our tactics had
bound them. They proposed a "political" coalition to hide
their repugnance for action along the lines of communist proposals. The Maximalists could play to the hilt the game of the
reformists in the General Confederation of Labor and in the
Alliance of Labor, thus deceiving the workers—thanks also
to the fact that Moscow invited them to adhere, thus perpetuating the old and fatal mistake. Let us recall only that the
last chance to eliminate the trade union leaders and reestablish the movement of August 1922 on very different bases
occurred at the conference of the Confederation [of Labor]
in July [1922] at Genoa. There the reformists were a minority, yet the Maximalists bade them remain at their posts after
their declaration against parliamentary collaboration, which
was in fact not less pernicious than their do-nothing formula
urging neither proletarian action nor collaboration [with the
bourgeoisie].

Evidently, besides the old distaste for struggle, there was
the game of Serrati and others to barter little by little their
position and influence for a readmission to the International.

The formation of the Third Internationalist faction, in
which those elements which might have come to us were invited to stay [in the PSI] basically served to perpetuate the

mistake. And in conclusion the Maximalist party—which should have disappeared after its division from the reformists—while it trifled with the International, undertook no commitments, and exploited the situation in a facile opportunism. Unfortunately [Maximalism] exploits the tendencies of the workers toward inertia in this difficult moment by continuing to win them over to a certain degree to its banner of passive and simulated fidelity to a few revolutionary phrases. Even if the situation changes, it is a force destined to exhaust itself in a worse impotence.

And the politics pursued by the International, though not obtaining the fusion, did prevent the Communist party from utilizing some situations in which the workers tended to recur to it—even though in numbers "relative" to the decline of effective [members] caused by other reasons.

So it was after the August strike. However, the International regarded the socialist schism as the most important event—in a certain sense even after the advent of fascism and the unleashing of reaction against our party. Within the latter, subjected to a permanently abnormal condition of delay and profound structural modification, a state of uneasiness developed and grew which is in contradiction with any eventual probability of a turn for the better.

Moreover, the differences with the International had produced the formation of a current, the so-called "minority," which while posing as orthodox communism, in reality unites those who after Livorno remained somewhat attached to the old socialist methods [even though] disapproving of its clumsy systems of work and responsibility. This group upheld the theses of the International not by elevated and solid arguments but by recalcitrance and undercover gossip.

The party suffers from all this. A remedy is necessary.

The outcome of this "fusionist" direction threatens the "liquidation" of the party as it was at Livorno and it was in its struggles of more than two years, which were not without honor. That would mean once again to cast the Italian proletariat into the stagnation of vile and chattering Maximalist "centralism." Thereby the Italian working class would not even draw a useful lesson for tomorrow from its Calvary.

It may appear that a warning should have been sounded earlier. But, as we have said with regard to the tactical question, for some time the dissension was in practice elusive. The method of the International was to present its particular slogans one at a time, whereas we wanted them outlined and defined in broader relief. Something similar occurred with regard to the fusion itself, according to the various alternatives presented by the successive socialist congresses. For example, after the one in '21, it seemed that fusion was no longer considered, and even relations with the Third Internationalist faction were, as far as we knew, at least not considered to be official. It was at the end of '22 that the divergence appeared in all its gravity, and only later events showed that it developed in a way scarcely known to the party. And it is in the most recent times that hope has been lost for a solution through a real and vast discussion within the International and not with palliatives contrived in long and painful dealings and with expedients of hardly more than a personal character.

Let us at least refer to a typical point which we have proposed to examine. The new tactical slogans of the International, not yet well clarified in their meaning, which appeared after the Third Congress—and the Fourth did not have time to discuss tactical theses—also brought a danger of modifications of program and principles, a danger now evident in the repeated postponements of the question of the program and the statutes to 1924. At the same time, the grave problem of organizational discipline has become a desultory and often discontinuous expedient resulting in unpleasant internal crises in many parties and in their relations with the center.

The danger to which we refer can become very serious. We are perhaps on the eve of a crisis in the international camp; as the Italian party we are in the depths of a crisis.

Driven by all these grave considerations, which we promise to further illuminate when it will be possible for us, we propose attaining an agreement of the comrades on these concluding points:

a. To provoke within the party, despite the obstacles of the present situation, a broad discussion and consultation on the value of the experiences and struggles acquired by the party and on its programmatic and tactical direction.

b. To provoke in the competent organs of the International an analogous discussion of broad import on the conditions of the proletarian struggle in Italy during the last years and up to today, avoiding the contingent and transitory accomodations which [illegible word] suffocate examination of the most important problems.

c. To participate in a discussion of the program, organization, and tactical action of the International, struggling against any revision toward the right, and above all obtaining maximum clarity in the establishing of policy.

d. After achieving a unanimous evaluation of the fundamental problems through such debates, to ensure that a clear and complete plan be outlined for the direction and action of the party. On this basis, active work will begin for intensifying the activity and efficiency of the party on a line clear in the minds of all the militants and with the most rational participation of all their energies, since the reasons and causes of the present grave state will have been overcome.

e. If such a debate does not bring about a substantial consensus in a series of decisions based on common principles— though remaining at our posts in the ranks of the communist militia guided according to the will of the majority of the International—not to take part in the organs of leadership of the party, since these should be composed in accordance with the policies which they are called to apply.

Important.

Would the comrade who receives this document make copies of it and distribute them to the party members, also copying this postscript.

Each comrade is asked to send his agreement, or even his opinion, however dissenting, and any communication concerning this document by means of the same comrade who gave him this copy. The reply will travel the same road in a reverse direction.

This document has been sent to the central committee of the party and to the International.

It would also be of great interest to diffuse it abroad. We would be very grateful to anyone doing this in the form of a translation.

The Initiators

Further Reading

The most authoritative, indeed the only comprehensive account of developments in the communist movement from the Second to the Fourth World Congress of the Comintern can be found in E. H. Carr's *The Bolshevik Revolution 1917–1923* ("A History of Soviet Russia," New York, 1953), Vol. III. This magisterial work, which broke new ground and became the point of departure for virtually every subsequent study of the subject, remains the definitive work in spite of emendations by other scholars.

Although no monograph has yet been written on the communist parties' reaction to the Twenty-One Conditions, two special studies deal with their reception in France and Germany. Robert Wohl's recent examination of the origins and early years of the French Communist party, *French Communism in the Making 1914–1924* (Stanford, 1966), traces the attitude of the French party toward directives from Moscow from the Twenty-One Conditions to the united front. Eugen Prager's *Geschichte der USPD: Entstehung und Entwicklung der Unabhängigen Sozialdemokratischen Partei Deutschlands* (Berlin, 1921), written in the heat of controversy, remains the only detailed history of the Independent Socialists. Particularly useful is the account of the party immediately preceding and during the split at the Halle congress in 1920, during which time the Twenty-One Conditions were a central issue.

A comprehensive history of the Italian Communist party is still to be written. Until that time John M. Cammett's *Antonio Gramsci and the Origins of the Italian Communism* (Stanford, 1967) will remain the most scholarly source of the split in Italian social democracy which brought the PCI into being. Although Gramsci and the later history of the party are Cammett's main subject, the array of forces in 1921, and the role of leading personalities and importance of ideological differences at that time, have been described with painstaking care. Neither biographies nor full-length political studies of either Amadeo Bordiga or G. M. Serrati appear to exist. For a sketch of the career of the former, see Enzo Santarelli, *La Revisione del marxismo in Italia* (Milan, 1964). For a contemporary Italian communist evaluation of the role of the latter, see Pietro Secchia, "Giacinto Menotti Serrati," *Movimento operaio*, IV (1956).

An excellent review of the KPD's activities up to the ill-starred March Action can be found in Werner T. Angress' *Stillborn Revolution: The Communist Bid for Power in Germany, 1921–1923* (Princeton, 1963). Particularly valuable is his treatment of the March Action itself, with its careful chronology, revelations about the activities of Max Hoelz, Hugo Eberlein, and Béla Kun, and exposition of the controversy between Paul Levi and the KPD *Zentrale*. A challenging interpretation, although less thoroughly researched than Angress' work, of the growth of Bolshevik influence in the German party can be found in Richard Lowenthal's "Bolshevisation of the Spartacus League," David Footman (ed.) *International Communism* ("St. Antony's Papers," No. 9, London, 1960). For the activities of the KAPD, German communism's extreme Left, see the partisan account of Bernhard Reichenbach, a former member of that party, "Zur Geschichte der KAPD," *Archiv für die Geschichte des Sozialismus und der Arbeiterbewegung* (Leipzig, 1928), Vol. XIII. A highly colored but fascinating memoir of the activities of the romantic and anarchistic extreme Left in central Germany during the March Action can be found in Max Hoelz, *From White Cross to Red Flag: The Autobiography of Max Hoelz, Waiter, Soldier, Revolutionary Leader* (London-Toronto, 1930). Karl Radek's remarkable career and activities as Comintern expert on Germany have been sketched in H. Schurer's "Radek and the German Revolution," *Survey*, Nos. 53 and 55 (Oct., 1964, Apr., 1965). Bernard Reichenbach has also recorded an interesting personal account of the climate of opinion in Moscow at the time of the Third World Congress in "Moscow 1921: Meetings in the Kremlin," *Survey*, No. 53 (Oct., 1964).

PART FOUR

1923—END OF
WORLD REVOLUTION:
BULGARIAN JUNE
AND GERMAN OCTOBER

Nineteen twenty-three was a pivotal year, in which the Comintern turned from a revolutionary international of communist parties into a centralized and bureaucratic organization firmly tied to the developments in and policies of the Soviet Union. In that year revolutionary reversals in Bulgaria and Germany not only accelerated the process of bolshevization within national parties, but also gave impetus to the russification of the Comintern, which henceforth adapted itself to the framework of Soviet foreign policy.

Russification did not stem from some conscious plan or conspiracy, but was the natural outcome of the growing prestige and authority of Soviet Russia and the relative decline of the other communist parties in the absence of world revolution. Its subtle origins can, no doubt, be found in various revolutionary experiences of the movement during its formative years; its first clear manifestation came in the attempt to place the stamp of Russian state and party organization on the structure of the Communist International. Russian influence in the Comintern was growing continually from the First World Congress, but it was not until the Fourth World Congress that this concentration of power took a new form which gave the Russians control over the international organization.

The Comintern was originally organized as a federation of communist parties to be governed by broad lines of policy and specific tactics necessary for their realization. Both of these were developed by delegates from national parties at world congresses and, in the interim between them, by the ECCI, whose members were appointed at the congresses. Thus, although the authority of the directing center of the movement was derived indirectly from the diverse interests of members, the weaknesses of previous internationals were to be avoided by making this authority binding on all members through various disciplinary means. Yet, every change in the formal structure of the organization, beginning with the Twenty-One Conditions, contributed to the transformation of the Comintern into a world party of which national communist parties were in effect subordinate organs in a descending hierarchy.

The shift from a federal to a centralized structure became really marked during the Fourth World Congress at the end of 1922. There the constitution of the ECCI was altered so that its members, who had formerly been appointed by national parties to act as their representatives on the Executive, would henceforth be elected by the congresses. Biennial sessions of an "enlarged executive" consisting of the ECCI and one or two members of each party, depending on its size, were to be held between congresses, a practice which corresponded to the "party conferences" held by the Russian party. The inner bureau of the ECCI, which had been renamed the presidium, was to act as a political bureau and was also to appoint an organizational bureau of seven members, two of whom could be members of the presidium.[1] To complete the duplication of the Russian party organization, the office of secretary-general responsible to the presidium was created. The striking change taking place in the nature of the organization was underlined by the recommendation that national parties should hold their congresses after, and not before, the world congresses of the Comintern. This instruction made it clear that the Comintern was to act as a self-sufficient directorate whose decisions would be handed down to be interpreted and applied by national congresses, and not as a forum whose collective decisions could be reached through debate and compromise by delegates representing the views of national party congresses.

Russification was not only implicit in the conversion of the

[1] The "organizational bureau" was charged with supervising the methods by which important offices in the national parties were filled and with controlling illegal work of member organizations.

Comintern's structure to a Russian model, but had become explicit in the power struggles of Russian leaders which, after the middle of 1923, were fought out increasingly in the arena of the Comintern. During the first three years of the Comintern differences among the Bolshevik leaders about Russian affairs and developments in the International seldom reached the limelight, and the Russian leaders themselves made an effort to keep their involvement in state and Comintern matters separate. Indeed, it was not until the summer of 1923, when the interregnum in Russian leadership following Lenin's second stroke in December 1922 became critical, that the official separation (in reality already somewhat fictitious) of Russian and Comintern affairs broke down. The struggle for the mantle of Lenin was centered on the resolution of the "scissors crisis" but, with the ascending of the triumvirate, Stalin-Zinoviev-Kamenev, it more and more assumed the properties of a naked contest for power.[2] At this juncture the contestants extended their conflict to the Comintern where, particularly in the analysis of the defeats of 1923, they sought allies among national delegations and attempted to forestall or neutralize support by national parties for their opponents. Centralization together with the direct interjection of Russian questions and problems into the activities of the International virtually completed the Russification of the Comintern and made it subordinate to the Soviet Union.

[2] The term "scissors crisis" was coined by Trotsky to describe the anarchy of prices which was at the heart of the economic chaos of 1923. It was characterized by: the rapid rise in prices of consumers' goods, which were raised artificially by industrial managers who withheld commodities from the market; the rapid decline of agricultural prices; the stagnation of the capital goods sector; the instability of currencies and credits; growing unemployment and working-class discontent; and profiteering by the NEP-men more experienced than state employees in manipulating a market economy. This crisis threatened to prevent that solidarity between urban and rural workers on which NEP was predicated. The controversy was over the means by which heavy industry, the backbone of a developing socialist economy, could be lifted from its doldrums. Trotsky proposed a tightening of control over the peasants to provide primitive socialist accumulation for rationalized industry. The triumvirate was prepared to make further concessions to the peasants in order to stimulate a grain surplus which, when sold abroad, would serve to capitalize industry.

Nineteen twenty-three was also a crucial year in the history of the ill-starred united front policy. By a decision to act too late in Bulgaria and Germany the ambiguities of the policy and the resistance to it clearly were brought to light. Consequently, the notion of "workers' government" and "workers' and peasants' government" had to be abandoned, and the whole general line had to be shifted to a tangent from which the bastion of social democracy, now considered the first line of capitalist defense, would be besieged by unrestricted warfare from above and united fronts from below. Both in a symbolic and real sense the abortive "German October" of 1923 was the swan song of world revolution and of the revolutionary international.

I: Bulgarians Spurn the United Front

By the spring of 1923 the united front policy had found only hesitant support and received limited application by various communist parties. It was yet to be tested in action growing out of a political situation rather than through pacts and maneuvers. The occupation of the Ruhr by French troops in January in retaliation for Germany's failure to keep pace with its reparation commitments, and the German's organized passive resistance against the foreign occupation were viewed by the Russian leaders as a sign of the waxing of the revolutionary potential in Europe. But they were cautious in their response, partly because of domestic difficulties occasioned by the growing pains of NEP and Lenin's illness and partly because of the precariousness of Russia's international position, which the Curzon Ultimatum recently had illustrated.[1] While the maturation of the new revolutionary potential was awaited in the West and particularly in Germany, which traditionally was considered the revolutionary weathercock by the Comintern, developments in Bulgaria unexpectedly made East Europe a potential theater of revolutionary operations. Suddenly, the opportunity presented itself for the realization of a united front through a workers' and peasants' government—a method which the Fourth World Congress of the Comintern had recommended.

On June 9th a block of Bulgarian parties of the Right, supported by the army and police and by Macedonian refugees

[1] On May 8, 1923 the British Foreign Office sent a memorandum (later called the Curzon Ultimatum) to the Soviet government listing a number of grievances about Soviet policy toward Britain. The memorandum threatened that if these grievances were not redressed in ten days' time, the Anglo-Soviet trade agreement would be nullified and diplomatic relations severed. In Moscow this ultimatum conjured up the specter of a new foreign intervention, and the Soviet government made every effort to placate the British. A series of notes were exchanged, as a result of which harmonious relations were reestablished by June 16th.

organized in the International Macedonian Revolutionary Organization (IMRO), carried out a coup d'etat against the peasant government of Alexander Stambulisky.[2] The rising was immediately successful in Sofia and, after a few days of sporadic fighting in the countryside, during which Stambulisky was killed, a new regime under Tsankov representing the middle class and the army was established. While all of this transpired the Bulgarian Communist party (KPB), with nearly 40,000 members, control of most trade unions, domination of many municipalities, and support of one-fourth of the electorate, stood by and declared its neutrality in the struggle.

The KPB's passivity at this crucial moment can be explained in part by its historic development. The party had its origins in the Bulgarian Socialist party, from which the Left split in 1903, assuming the name of Tesnyaki or narrow-minded ones to signify their support of Lenin's organizational principles. During the war the anti-war position of the Tesnyaki brought them mass support, and their association with the Zimmerwald Left made them sympathizers of the Bolsheviks. In September 1918 the Tesnyaki cooperated with the Peasant Union of Stambulisky in promoting desertions from the army, which led to the collapse of the Bulgarian front and hastened Germany's suit for peace. A further offer by Stambulisky for collaboration in overthrowing the Bulgarian government that September was rejected by the Tesnyaki on the grounds that such a struggle was nothing but a fight within the bourgeoisie, and Stambulisky was defeated by troops of Macedonian refugees loyal to the government. The failure of the Tesnyaki in this instance to mobilize the urban workers for an alliance of the poor against the rich can be explained by a tendency of Marxists at the time to equate

[2] Macedonian nationals played the role of a particularly unstable leaven in Bulgaria's complicated political affairs. After Bulgaria's defeat in the Second Balkan War of 1913 a large part of Macedonian territory was ceded to Serbia and many Macedonians fled to Sofia. As members of the notorious extremist IMRO they fought in the Bulgarian army during the World War in the hope of wresting Macedonia from the Serbs and establishing its autonomy. In the postwar period the Macedonians gave their support to anyone (from the extreme right to the extreme left) who might advance their nationalist aspirations.

alliances with opportunism and also by their unwillingness
to accept half a loaf in the form of a bourgeois democratic
republic when the proletarian world revolution loomed so
large. In 1919 the Tesnyaki became a charter member of
the Comintern as the KPB, and as the significant labor party
in its country organized along bolshevik lines it was considered a model for the movement.

Although the KPB's inaction in June 1923 no doubt had
roots in the Tesnyaki's unwillingness to support Stambulisky's
Radomir uprising of September 1919, the later history of the
party and particularly of its theoretical position provides a
more substantial explanation of its puzzling behavior. The
membership and electoral strength of the party, although considerable, was restricted to the working class and the population of the cities; the peasants, who accounted for more than
eighty per cent of the total population, increasingly looked
upon urban dwellers as aliens, enemies, and exploiters.
Against this background the party proceeded to discuss the
Comintern's recommendation for a workers' and peasants'
government as a practical application of the united front. The
party gave the Comintern's general and specific line its formal
endorsement but in such equivocal terms as to make it meaningless. A coalition with the Peasant Union was ruled out on
the grounds that it represented the interests of the Bulgarian
rural bourgeoisie and served as a blind tool of Entente imperialism. A workers' and peasants' government, the resolution
of the KPB suggested, was desirable only if the party could
win the disaffected small and landless peasants from Stambulisky's ranks. The party's stand in supporting the united front
but only "from below" set the stage for its "plague on both
your houses" neutrality of June 9th.

A meeting of the KPB's central committee convened on
June 11th to take stock of Tsankov's coup merely seconded
the party's decision taken several days earlier (Document 1).
The central committee declared that what had transpired in
Bulgaria was a struggle for power between two branches of
the capitalist class from which the KPB proudly had stood
aloof.[3] It called upon the small-holding and landless peas-

[3] The KPB's response to this crisis is reminiscent of the Kapp
Putsch in 1920, during which the German party leaders explained
their initial inactivity as an unwillingness to support the social
democratic-bourgeois side against the reactionary-bourgeois side.

ants to shed their illusions about their bourgeois leaders and rally to the standard of the sole champion of the people. Stambulisky's government, it insisted, which had dug its own grave by its tyrannous policies, differed only slightly from the Tsankov forces which had come to power. Nevertheless, it sounded the alarm and called for self-defense by the masses against the severe repressions which had already begun under the new government. A session of the enlarged ECCI, meeting from June 12th to 23rd, came to the conclusion that the Bulgarian communists had missed a golden opportunity for actuating the united front (Document 2). The ECCI's Manifesto on the subject found Stambulisky guilty of having failed to ally himself with the urban working class and exhorted the peasants to correct this error before it was too late. The greater error, the ECCI implied, had been committed by the KPB, in viewing the coup d'etat as a struggle within the bourgeoisie about which the working class could remain neutral. The workers, the ECCI directed, must now join hands not only with the peasant masses but also with their surviving leaders in a united struggle for a workers' and peasants' government against Tsankov's tyranny.

Although the ECCI's criticism of the KPB was guarded, its prescription for the future course of the party was clear and to the point. But the Bulgarian party, long considered a model of discipline, balked and refused to heed the directive of the Comintern. In a resolution of its central committee passed in early July the KPB entered a plea with which right and left deviationists in other parties had justified their cases in the past: that a national party was better informed about conditions in its own country than the ECCI and therefore better able to evaluate them (Document 3). The difference of opinion, the resolution asserted, with respect to tactics on June 9th between the ECCI and the KPB, stemmed from the fact that the ECCI was informed insufficiently about the events in question. Conditions for a workers' and peasants' government simply did not exist at the time, and once the ECCI was aware of the facts it would undoubtedly support the KPB. It would be an error, the resolution concluded, to follow the ECCI's demand for a united front from above with peasant leaders, since they had already lost their influence among the agrarian masses, which were turning to the party for guidance.

Such an open breach of discipline would most likely have been met with censure by the Comintern, but the growing repression of the KPB by the Tsankov dictatorship, for which persecution of communists was an important aspect of policy, saved the Bulgarian party from this formal step. Instead, the ECCI mobilized opinion in the communist movement against the recalcitrant Bulgarians. The fiercest and most telling attack on the KPB came from the pen of Mátyás Rákosi, one of the Comintern's most ruthless polemicists and trouble-shooters (Document 4). The party's claim, he charged, that the ECCI lacked sufficient information in making its judgment was nothing but cheap subterfuge for its opportunism. The outcome of the coup d'etat would have been very different, he insisted, if the KPB had not declared its neutrality at the outset but had evaluated the news of armed struggles from many places and called for active resistance, the general strike, and a united front with the peasants. If the latter course had been followed, striking workers would have prevented the dispatching of troop trains to the centers of insurrection and the peasants would have won time to mobilize their forces which, in union with the communists, could have defeated the weak Bulgarian bourgeoisie. Such a positive stand by the KPB would have demonstrated to hundreds of thousands of peasants what communist propaganda had failed to teach them: that the KPB was the only defender of peasant interests. The party, Rákosi warned, had let the propitious moment, when united action with the Peasant Union would have led to victory, slip by, and today faced a life-and-death struggle against an aggressive and strengthened bourgeoisie. So far the KPB had not learned from its errors; it had to alter its course lest it repeat them.

For all intents and purposes the discussion was now closed, but its repercussions in the party led to a leadership crisis in which Kabakchiev and Tudor Lukanov, held mainly responsible for the false tactics of June 9th, was superseded by Kolarov and Dimitrov, who were prepared to follow the Comintern's directive. Tsankov had destroyed the Peasant Union, and now turned the full force of repression on the KPB. The better part of valor might have been for the Bulgarian party to go underground. But under the prodding of the ECCI, which expected that Tsankov could be resisted even though the masses were demoralized and divided, and partly to atone for the mistakes of June, the KPB sought to establish a united front from above with peasant and Macedonian leaders. These negotiations, which were carried on in August preparatory to an armed uprising planned for late fall, came to naught. The party was forced to go it alone by a government which had declared open season on it and by resistance to its new policy within its own ranks. Tsankov, fully aware of the plans afoot, made the first move by arresting a large number of party functionaries on September 12th, and thereby forced the KPB to push up the date for its revolt. During the uprising, which was staggered from September 19th to 28th, the peasants were the mainstay of the communist forces and the workers generally remained quiescent. The revolt was crushed systematically and followed by a ruthless terror. Neither the new bolshevized Bulgarian leadership nor the Comintern had been able to turn the historical clock back to June 9th.

When Zinoviev turned to evaluate the Bulgarian defeat he praised the KPB for the courage with which it had fought to make good its former doctrinal errors. In what was slowly becoming a Comintern tradition of retrospectively snatching parties from the jaws of defeat by interpretation, the September uprising was viewed as the KPB's storm of steel in which it had become a stronger and more disciplined party. No mention was made of the fact that the united front had failed its first significant practical test. The eyes of the movement at any rate were on Germany, where the united front was the counter in a game for much higher stakes.

DOCUMENT 1: *"The Situation in Bulgaria and the Communist Party"*

International Press Correspondence (INPRECORR), III, No. 48 [28] (July 5, 1923). First appeared in *Rabotnicheski Vestnik,* June 11, 1923.

The parties of the bloc [Tsankov], including the national party and the social patriots [epithet for socialists], have issued a common appeal, in which they call upon the Bulgarian people to support the new government. The fact that representatives—if not the chief leaders—of all bourgeois parties are participating in the new government is a fresh proof that this government is a great bourgeois coalition, comprising all of the bourgeois parties, from the people's party and the national liberals to the social patriots.

The bourgeois press is endeavoring to screen this fact behind the veil of a "general national cabinet." But in vain! Why do the bourgeois parties not openly state the truth to the people? Why are they afraid to admit that they—the old bourgeois parties—have seized power? Because they are convinced that the toiling masses in town and country neither regard the old bourgeois parties with any enthusiasm, nor will they support these parties. This is why these parties chose a military coup for forcing their seizure of power.

The new government is headed by a few individuals who do not openly belong to the bourgeois parties. But this does not alter the real character of this government, which, by the way, is but a temporary one, preparatory to a definite bourgeois coalition.

The armed struggle between the followers of the fallen government and those of the new government is not yet at an end. The Communist party, and the hundreds of thousands of workers and peasants united beneath its flag, are not taking part in this conflict. We do not know how this struggle may develop; but up to the present moment the broad masses of the people have not been drawn into it. It is a struggle for power between the bourgeoisies of the city and of the village, that is, between two wings of the capitalist class.

In whose name is this armed struggle being carried on? The fallen agrarian government [Stambulisky] disclosed its real program by its policy of plunder and suppression applied to the toiling masses in town and village. The last months of its rule were marked by the wildest acts of violence against the Communist party, and against the hundreds of thousands of workers and peasants fighting under its banner. The general policy pursued by the agrarian government is summed up in the 2 1/2 milliard levy of indirect taxation which it imposed under the new state budget.

The program of the new government—its written program —is still unknown to us. But we know the actual program of the parties backing up this government; the parties which ruled for forty years, which plunged the nation into disastrous wars, which supported for four years the reactionary policy pursued by the agrarian government against the Communist party, against the working class, and against the working peasantry.

The new government says that it will respect the rights and liberties established by the Constitution—this is its present declaration.

The new government, in its declaration, declares that a "civil police will be organized." And in actual fact a "civil police" of the bourgeoisie is being formed of people belonging to old bourgeois parties, and the new government is distributing weapons among them. This fact throws a bright light on the situation. It proves that the workers, the toilers in town and country, must be on their guard, that they must unite and be prepared, in order to protect their vital interests and their political liberties against every attack.

The Communist party, while exposing the actual aims of the city and rural bourgeoisie, and in pointing out that these aims have nothing in common with those of the toiling masses in town and country, at the same time calls upon the workers and toilers in city and village to unite, and to fight independently for the preservation of their interests and for the realization of the slogans issued by the Communist party. The Communist party calls upon the small-holding and non-propertied peasants of the Peasants' League to break with the village bourgeoisie, to cease to support the large landowners and village mayors, and to give no support to the capitalists, bankers, and usurers of the cities, or to their parties. The agrarian government, by its policy and by its deeds, has shown itself to be the defender of the interests of the exploiters and oppressors, and the enemy of the toiling population of the villages. The toiling peasantry that have followed this government must now oppose the policy and actions of their leaders, and grasp the brotherly hand of the Communist party, which unites the working people in town and country for the common struggle against the bourgeoisies of city and village.

In the midst of this fight between two wings of the bourgeoisie, each striving to draw the masses of the people into the struggle for its own purposes, we call upon the working people in town and country to form the united front of the workers, and to fight for the slogans of the Communist party:

Annulment of the peace treaty of Neuilly, of the repara-

tions and national debts. People's tribunal for those guilty of
the war. Abolition of the taxation pressing upon the workers
and small-holding masses. Abolition of obligatory work. Payment of the whole taxation by the city and village bourgeoisies. Taxation of income, of capital, and of property, by
progressive taxes; progressive taxation of large bequests. Confiscation by the state of a part of the capital invested in industry, in commerce, and in the banks; this capital to be placed
under the control of the labor organizations. Limitation of the
exploitation by commercial, speculative, and usurious capital,
this to be done by placing cheap credits at the disposal of
small-holding farmers and craftsmen by the state, by the development and support of the workers' and peasants' cooperatives, consumer credit, and productive cooperatives, and
cooperatives for the export of agricultural products, and the
introduction of a state monopoly of foreign trade. Letting of
land to landless and small-holding peasants. Compulsory seizure of the first necessities of life in the possession of the big
capitalists, landowners, trades-people, and banks, by the state,
and their distribution by municipalities at reasonable fixed
prices, under the control of the organizations of the workers
and small holders. Solution by the compulsory seizure of the
superfluous dwelling rooms possessed by the big house owners; reduction and fixing of house rent; provision of healthy
conditions in working districts; erection of cheap and healthy
dwelling houses. Increase of workers' wages, and of the civil
servants employed by the state, municipalities, and rural districts, in correspondence with the rise in prices. Labor legislation, labor inspection, control of production by the shop
stewards and trade unions. Extermination of monarchism,
expansion and security of the political rights of the working
people; women's suffrage; full right of combination; freedom
of speech, press, and meeting. Disarmament of the bourgeoisie,
and of its fascist and other bands; arming of the workers and
small farmers for the defense of the people against internal
coups d'etat and external invasions. Peace with Turkey, peace
and alliance with Soviet Russia. National independence for
the suppressed people in Macedonia, Thrace, Dobrudscha,
and all other Balkan states; creation of a Federal Republic
of the Balkans.

The Communist party raises these demands, and fights for
their realization. These demands can be partly realized today,

but solely by means of pressure by the united fighting workers and working peasantry; these demands will be completely fulfilled solely through the establishment of the workers' and peasants' government.

APPEAL TO THE WORKERS AND TOILERS
IN TOWN AND COUNTRY

The armed struggle between the new power and the followers of the agrarian republic overthrown by the military putsch of June 9 is now approaching its end.

The toiling masses fighting under the flag of the Bulgarian Communist party side with neither one party nor the other in this armed struggle. They have preserved their complete independence, and continue to follow the path that they have pursued before the change of government.

The government of the Peasants' League, which maintained its power by means of the bayonets of the police and gendarmerie, and which exerted a cruel and boundless tyranny against the masses, could deserve nothing at the hands of the working people but profoundest contempt during this duel with those overthrowing the government.

The agrarian government dug the pit it fell into by its policy of violence and hostility to the people, and smoothed the way for the military coup of the city bourgeoisie.

The bourgeoisie and the old bourgeoisie parties, as well as their tools, the social patriots, are not, however, content to merely put an end to the regime of the agrarian government and to establish a new power. They demand more:

They are filled with the most cruel class hate against the working people. They regard the present moment of armed action as the most favorable for the gratification of their hate.

At the same time they are trying to utilize the change which has taken place for the purpose of strangling the emancipation movement of the toiling masses and its political leader—the Communist party—to crush this movement, in order that they may thus secure themselves the unhindered exploitation, plundering, and subjection of these masses for a long time to come.

Workers in town and country!

The extremely reactionary "law against robbers," passed by the agrarian government, will be used for having hundreds and thousands of peasants and workers arrested—on the pretext that they have offered armed opposition to the new power, though their sole crime consists in the fact that during the days when the situation was quite unclear, in the moment of the collision, their endeavor has been to save themselves and their relations from the flames of a conflict between two opposing powers. Armed representatives of the bourgeoisie parties utilize the weapons in their hands for terrorizing and attacking their political opponents, the hated communist champions, for arresting and even murdering them. Besides the official armed forces of the government, "volunteer troops" are also being organized, which conduct open programs and political murders against the Communist party. The labor clubs are closed, the labor meetings prohibited; the rights and liberties vitally necessary to the working people are being attacked. The whole bourgeois press—from the national liberal and the people's party to the social patriots—teems with raging incitements to a bloody settlement with the Communist party, with the party which united more than two hundred thousand working voters from town and country around its program, during the most frightful period of terror under the agrarian government, at the last elections to parliament, and which has proved that it is the most powerful party of the people in our country.

Why these cruelties, persecutions, and attacks?

Is it not perfectly plain that all this is being done, not because the toiling masses have opposed the new power with weapons in their hands, but because the bourgeoisie (from the national liberals to the social patriots)—utilizing the wretched situation—is anxious to create pretexts for bleeding the working people and for justifying the attacks being prepared on the Communist party? Is it not perfectly plain that the bourgeoisie and its parties are striving to substitute the dictatorship hitherto exercised by the village bourgeoisie of the Peasants' League by an even sharper bourgeois dictatorship and that the bourgeois parties—despite the loud and solemn declarations made by the new government—is striving for the renewed suppression of the rights and liberties of the people, and for the establishment of a regime of force and reaction for this purpose?

Workers, in the cities and the villages! The bourgeoisie is mobilizing! It is making use of the state apparatus, and of its armed power, for robbing you of your political rights and liberties, for perpetuating the exploitation and enslavement of the masses of the people.

The bourgeoisie and its parties, which are *talking*, as they always do, of lawlessness, but continue to trample the rights and liberties of the people underfoot, and who are endeavoring at this moment to fasten chains upon the toiling masses, and to crush the Communist party, by illegal means, fascist organizations, armed attacks, and pogroms—this bourgeoisie and its parties is opposed by one party only; today the Communist party is the sole party representing the political rights and liberties of the people.

Be vigilant at your posts! Gather more closely together beneath the ensign of the Communist party, for your self-defense against the diabolical intentions of the bourgeoisie, of their white guard and fascist organizations!

The whole country reechoes with the mighty protests uttered by the people against the deeds of violence, against the arrests and murder of the faithful sons of the working people, against the tyranny of the military power, and of the bourgeois dictatorship raising its head in the country!

The armed troops of the bourgeoisie must be disarmed! The arrested innocent workers and peasants must be liberated; the "law against robbers" must not be applied! The safety of the lives of the toiling masses must be secured! The right of combination, the freedom of speech, of meetings, must be completely restored! The provocation of the working people and their political party must cease, the insolent provokers must be curbed!

And if the new power, despite its solemn declarations, should not be able or willing to fulfill all this, then be ready boldly and determinedly to defend your lawful rights and liberties by means of the political struggle! Never forget that there is no right so supreme as the right to a free life, worthy of the human race, for the working people!

Long live the Bulgarian working people!

Long live the Communist party of Bulgaria!

Sofia, June 15, 1923.

THE CENTRAL COMMITTEE OF THE
COMMUNIST PARTY OF BULGARIA

DOCUMENT 2: *"Manifesto of the Enlarged Executive of the Communist International on the Events in Bulgaria"*

INPRECORR (English Edition), III, No. 48 [28] (July 5, 1923).

The following Manifesto was unanimously adopted at the concluding session of the Enlarged Executive of the Communist International on June 23rd last.

Forward to the battle against the government of the white coup d'etat in Bulgaria. Up with the government of workers and peasants.

To the Bulgarian workers and peasants. To the international working class!

Comrades! Brothers and sisters! In Bulgaria a small clique of bankrupt bureaucrats, unemployed officers and profiteers have seized the government by means of a military coup d'etat. The very same people who drove the Bulgarian people into the World War, who have 200,000 lives upon their consciences, who have been thrice kicked out of office by the Bulgarian people in democratic elections, this very clique has dared to seize power. It introduces a reign of the most atrocious terrorism against the great majority of the population, against the workers and peasants. The prisons of Bulgaria are being filled with workers and peasants, the villages are abandoned to the mercy of reactionary adventurers under the guise of so-called punitive expeditions. They shoot the leaders of the peasantry, but they have not the courage to confess their responsibility for the deeds. Tomorrow they will begin the assassination of the leaders of the working class.

The white coup d'etat of the Bulgarian bureaucrats, generals, and profiteers was perpetrated with the aid of the Social Democratic party, which is part of the Second International. This party, which shares the guilt for the crime of the Bulgarian war government, is a party upon which all workers have turned their backs, so that it has shrunk to nothing, and serves only as a fig leaf to the counterrevolutionary coup d'etat. By this it has proved itself worthy of Noske, Turati, and their like, who paved the way for the white coup d'etat in Germany and Italy respectively.

The coup d'etat was consummated with the aid of the scum of the European counterrevolution, with the aid of Wrangel officers and with the support of Horthy's hangmen and the Rumanian boyars. Capitalist Europe, which has so hypocritically attempted to arouse the so-called civilized world against the Red Terror, makes haste to recognize these murderers and incendiary adventurers. The British government, the government of the English Junkers and manufacturers, supports them, in the hope that Bulgaria will become a bulwark against Soviet Russia. The Italian government supports them because it considers the military adventurers of Sofia as a possible aid in a campaign against Yugoslavia. The capitalist world has approved of the white coup d'etat in Bulgaria. The fascist bands of all countries see in it the proof that the desire alone is sufficient to enable one to put his foot upon the neck of the people of the working class. We, the Communist International, the union of all the militant workers of East and West, call the Bulgarian workers and peasants and the international working class to the battle against the Bulgarian usurpers of power.

Peasants of Bulgaria! To you the victory of the white clique is a lesson which you ought to assimilate, if you wish to throw off the yoke which is being imposed on you. The peasant government of Stambulisky was overthrown because it failed to form an alliance with the workers of the cities. The interest of the great majority of the Bulgarian peasants, who are poor, go hand in hand with the interests of the workers and artisans of the cities. Stambulisky persecuted the working class. He lost the only support which he might have gained in the cities, against the clique of bureaucrats and officers who had been exploiting and enslaving the Bulgarian people during four decades, and will now continue to do so, since Stambulisky has paid for his policy with his life. But the Bulgarian peasants continue to live. They will be compelled to fight, if they do not wish to be further treated like cattle. We call upon them to unite with the workers of the cities and to start the fight under the slogan of the establishment of a government of the workers of the cities and villages.

Workers of Bulgaria! The Stambulisky government, in the

interest of the bourgeoisie and usurers of the villages, persecuted the labor movement and sacrificed the interests of the
workers of the towns as well as those of the poorer peasants.
But whereas the Stambulisky government persecuted the
workers, the Tsankov government will go further than that,
for it seeks to destroy them. Those who held the mistaken belief that the struggle of the now victorious white clique
against Stambulisky was a struggle between two bourgeois
cliques, to which the working class could afford to be neutral,
can now see the best proof of their error by the bloody persecution of the labor organizations. The usurpers of the state
are now the enemy, who must be defeated. Join hands for the
fight against the white coup d'etat, not only with the wide
masses of the peasantry, but also with the leaders of the Peasant party who have survived. Point out to them the consequences of the cleavage between the workers and the peasants, and call them to the united fight for a workers' and
peasants' government.

Peasants of Macedonia! Revolutionaries of Macedonia! You
have allowed the Bulgarian counterrevolution to use you for
their coup d'etat, although your interests, as shown by your
past, are most closely interwoven with the interests of the
working people, with the interests of the revolution in the
Balkans and throughout the world. The Stambulisky government delivered Macedonia to the Serbian bourgeoisie in order
to gain their support. It persecuted you in a bloody fashion.
But do not believe for a moment that the counterrevolutionary movement will be able to liberate the Macedonian people. It will fight against the Bulgarian peasants and workers,
against your own brothers, but not for the liberation of the
Macedonian peasants. In order to entrench itself in power it
will a thousand times betray Macedonia and oppress you, because it cannot tolerate any revolutionary peasant movement
in Macedonia. Only a workers' and peasants' government in
Bulgaria will arouse the sympathies of peasants and workers
in Rumania, Yugoslavia, and Greece.

Only such a government will blaze the path for the establishment of a Balkan Federation of Workers' and Peasants'
Governments, which alone can bring about your deliverance,
so that Macedonia should not become again the arena of san-
guinary battles, in which your huts are burned to the ground,
your fields devastated and trampled underfoot. Peasants and

revolutionists of Macedonia! None of you, however great your anger against the Bulgarian Peasant party and its leaders, must lend the slightest support to the government of White Terror in Bulgaria. Moreover, for the sake of your own national freedom, you must join hands with the Bulgarian workers and peasants in the common struggle.

Workers and peasants of Yugoslavia, Rumania, and Greece! Show your utmost resentment to those in the Balkans who are supporting the Tsankov government, show your hatred to the envoys of that government, surround the Bulgarian white guards with the wall of your resistance, hasten to the aid of the Bulgarian workers and peasants at every opportunity, to the aid of the valiant industrious people of Bulgaria now starting the fight against the white government. Workers of Austria and Germany! The victory of the fascist bands in Bulgaria will give encouragement and hope to the fascist adventurers in your own country. Be on your guard, be watchful, do not allow yourselves to be misled or lulled to sleep. Fight with your utmost determination against any aid being rendered to the Bulgarian white guards, and draw the necessary conclusions from the conduct of the Bulgarian reaction and from the errors committed by the Bulgarian peasants and workers. Exert all your efforts to bring about an alliance of the poor peasants and the workers against the hirelings of capital and of the military cliques. Dare to venture upon even a difficult fight when danger is nigh, if you do not wish to pay with your lives for your hesitation.

Worker of all countries! We call on you to watch with utmost attention the development of events in Bulgaria. We call on you to bring to the notice of the wide masses all the misdeeds perpetrated by the fascist clique in Bulgaria against the working people of Bulgaria, with the aid of the capitalist governments of all countries, and to mobilize the masses against the murderous government of Sofia. The message from Sofia speaks to you just as eloquently as did the message from Rome [regarding Mussolini]. The working class of all countries is in danger! Know this, and prepare for the defense!

Down with the fascist bands, the hirelings of capital!

Down with the militarist usurpers and usurers of Sofia!

Long live the Bulgarian Workers' and Peasants' Government!

Long live the Balkan Federation of Workers' and Peasants' Governments!

Long live the solidarity of the international working class in the struggle against the fascist menace!

THE ENLARGED EXECUTIVE
OF THE COMMUNIST INTERNATIONAL

DOCUMENT 3: *"The Communist Party of Bulgaria and the Recent Coup D'Etat"*

INPRECORR (English Edition), III, No. 53 [31] (July 26, 1923). First appeared in *Rabotnicheski Vestnik*, July 10, 1923.

The attitude of the Communist party of Bulgaria to the events of June 9.

The committee of the party, after hearing the report of the party central [committee] on the attitude of the party to the events of June 9, unanimously passed the following resolution:

1. The committee of the party completely approves of the attitude adopted by the party central [committee] to the events of June 9, and declares that the attitude and instructions of the party central [committee] are in complete accord with the resolution passed by the party committee in January and April 1923. The attitude which was taken by the Bulgarian Communist party to the events of June 9 was the only possible one under the circumstances. The Communist party of Bulgaria could not, on June 9, intervene arms in hand between the fallen government and the new government on behalf of the agrarian policy, a fact amply proved by the failure of the masses to rise in defense of the agrarian government. The Communist party could not take any action for the immediate establishment of a workers' and peasants' government, because the overthrow of the agrarian government did not bring about any revolutionary movement among the working and peasant masses, and because the conditions for the formation of a workers' and peasants' government did not yet exist. The attitude of the Communist party to the events of

June 9 was not an attitude of passivity and neutrality, but rather an attitude of independent political struggle in defense of the interests and rights of the working masses, for the realization of the slogans of the Communist party and for the establishment of a workers' and peasants' government. The party committee further points out that the attitude of the central [committee] to the events of June 9 was unanimously approved by the party. Exceptions in two or three places do not signify the existence of differences of opinion, but are to be explained by the special conditions existing for our comrades in these places.

2. The party committee is of the opinion that the differences of opinion which have arisen with respect to the tactics of the party on the occasion of the coup d'etat between the Executive of the Communist International, on the one hand, as shown by comrade Zinoviev's explanation at the session of the Enlarged Executive, as well as by the appeal to the Bulgarian workers and peasants, and the Communist party of Bulgaria, on the other hand, are to be attributed to the insufficient information of the Executive on the events of June 9. The central [committee] of the Bulgarian party had not yet had the possibility of informing the International and brother parties on the events of June 9. The party central [committee] has been commissioned to do this now. The party committee is convinced that the Executive of the Communist International, once in receipt of accurate information, will recognize the correctness of the attitude of the Communist party of Bulgaria.

3. With respect to the appeal made by the Executive of the Communist International to the working masses, in which these are summoned to join forces with the leaders of the Peasant Union, the party committee is of the opinion that at the present moment—when the rural working masses themselves recognize the bankruptcy of their leaders, when they are deserting the village bourgeoisie and the men of the agrarian government previously in power, and when the rural masses are already seeking to unite with the workers and peasants who are fighting under the flag of the Communist party—it would be an error for the Communist party to restore to the agrarian leaders, who have betrayed the interests of the rural working people, their lost influence. But the Communist party will not refuse to cooperate with the Peasant Union and its leaders, if the Union and its leaders should prove ready to form

a united front for the common struggle for the demands of the Communist party and for the workers' and peasants' government.

DOCUMENT 4: Mátyás Rákosi, *"The Latest Attitude of the CP of Bulgaria"*

INPRECORR (English Edition), III, No. 53 [31] (July 26, 1923).

The party committee of our Bulgarian brother party, which met from July 1 till July 6 for the purpose of defining its attitude to the coup d'etat, has now published in the central organ of the KPB, the *Rabotnicheski Vestnik* of July 9, two of its resolutions on the "attitude of the Communist party of Bulgaria to the events of June 9," and on the "situation after June 9th, and the tasks of the KPB."

In the first resolution "the party committee fully approves of the attitude adopted by the party central," as "the attitude adopted by the KPB to the events of June 9 was the only possible one under the circumstances." It was no "passivity and neutrality, but rather the attitude of independent political struggle in the defense of the interests and rights of the working masses." The contrary opinion of the Enlarged Executive is "to be attributed to the insufficient information of the Executive on the events of June 9."

We shall not enter into discussion of the cheap subterfuge which it is always our fate to hear when opportunists are short of other arguments—that of insufficient information on the part of the EC. The Bulgarian comrades must be very hard up for arguments in support of their point of view, if they resort to this means. Let us rather once more consider the situation as it was in Bulgaria at the time of the upheaval. On June 9, that is, on the day of the outbreak of the putsch, the situation was still quite unclear, and in 12 districts the peasants took up arms—in some places together with the communists. At this juncture the party central issued, among others, the slogan of neutrality for the communists, as in the opinion of the central it was solely a question of a fight of the village bourgeoisie against that of the city.

The resolution on the situation, passed on July 6, substantiates the attitude adopted by means of a lengthy analysis, demonstrating that the fallen agrarian government fought more against the workers than against the bourgeoisie, just as any other government trying to pursue a "middle line" is obliged to do. This is doubtless perfectly true. But, on the other hand, this government still had many adherents among the poor of the villages, indeed the majority of the poorer villagers were its followers. The bourgeoisie could not offer the poor peasants anything to induce them to desert Stambulisky. The communists carried on agitation to this end, but this has its limits, and it is only in conjunction with well-thought-out action and tactical maneuvers—particularly in combination with the united front—that this can be widened to a conquest of power. Our Bulgarian comrades have regarded the united front as highly important for other countries, but at home they have *not* employed it. A certain stagnation has been the inevitable result. The elections, which took place seven weeks before the coup d'etat, showed a falling off in our votes; but they also showed our strength, for we received more votes than all the bourgeois parties put together.

When the city bourgeoisie, which did not receive even a fifth of the votes at the election, prepared to launch the coup d'etat, our party issued the following slogans (approved and enumerated in the resolution of July 6): "Combating of high prices, decrease of taxation, alleviation of the housing problem, rises in wages, shortening of working hours, guarantees for the rights, liberties, peace of the Bulgarian people, etc." The slogan of neutrality is now being bashfully concealed behind this "etc."

In reply to all this, the Executive, after having received the most important documents, appeals, and articles, declared it to have been a tremendous error not to have gone to the help of the peasants in the struggle against the white guard bourgeoisie. The excuse that the peasants themselves had no wish to fight does not hold. Days have to pass before such tidings penetrate into the villages, and before peasants just preparing to bring in their crops resolve on armed resistance. But our party took immediate steps in favor of neutrality, on the first day, before there was any possibility of obtaining a clear view of the situation, and whilst news of armed struggles was reaching Sofia from many places. The party thus proved that it did not want to fight. If it had not merely issued general slogans —such as our Argentine or Norwegian comrades may well issue, but which are totally inadequate in a situation where bloody fights are taking place in a dozen districts—but had raised the slogan of active resistance, of the general strike, of the united front with the peasantry against the capitalists, then the situation would have been very different. Then the bourgeoisie would not have had the opportunity of sending their officers and gendarmes to the seats of immediate insurrections by means of railway trains run by Bulgarian workmen; then the peasants would have found a few days' time to mobilize their powers, and to deal a powerful blow at the weak Bulgarian bourgeoisie, with the aid of the communists. And hundreds of thousands of poor peasants would have been able to learn from this *one* deed that which thousands of communist meetings and leaflets have not yet taught them: that the communists, and the communists only, are the real defenders of the toiling villagers.

Our party has missed this opportunity; it looked on, neutral, while the peasants so dangerous to the bourgeoisie were murdered—and many good communists with them. And the resolution passed by the party committee goes into long-winded explanations as to how the new government is striving for the bloody dictatorship of the bourgeoisie, an "open war" against the Communist party. Six weeks ago our party could have taken up this war in conjunction with the Peasants' League, and could have emerged victorious. Today the most energetic leaders of the peasantry have been defeated, the peasants' organizations are scattered, disarmed, and confused. The party has now to take up arms without the aid of the organized peasantry, and against a bourgeoisie strengthened in self-confidence by its easy victory, and has now to face a life-and-death struggle. And when the party committee "fully approves" of the attitude of the central, and opines that the condemnation of the Executive is "to be attributed to insufficient information," then the committee proves that it has not yet comprehended the error, that it either cannot or will not see this error, and that it will repeat it in some form or another. And this would mean that the fate of our Bulgarian brother party would be sealed for long to come!

Despite the unanimous criticism of the Enlarged Executive, the party committee remains equally unanimous in its approval of the neutrality of the central. It goes even further. At the very moment when it admits that the knife is at the throat of the party, it still refuses to form a united front with the elements utilizable in the struggle against the bourgeoisie! In the resolution on the situation we read literally: "The socialists (who are still in the government, but are aware of the danger) are already beginning to call for a bloc of the Left, but the prerequisites for such a bloc do not yet exist." The proposition made by the Executive, that the party combine with the leaders of the peasantry, is replied to in the resolution on the events of June 9 as follows: "It would be a mistake on the part of the KPB to restore to the agrarian leaders, those betrayers of the interests of the rural working population, their lost influence. But the Communist party will not refuse . . ." to join with these, "should they be prepared to form a united front for a joint struggle for the demands of the Communist party, and for the workers' and peasants' government."

And these same comrades, who decline a united front with the socialists, and "do not refuse" to join forces with the peasantry under certain circumstances, write an article in their central organ, two days after the publication of the above resolution, and appear literally as follows to the officers of the white government: "The active and reserve officers are bound to the working people by an indissoluble blood brotherhood."

These are no communist tactics. If the Communist party of Bulgaria cannot realize its errors by means of immediate and relentless self-criticism, if it cannot come into line with the Communist International, it is certain of defeat in the coming battles. It is still possible to save much, but only if the party leaders possess sufficient courage to admit and retrieve their errors.

II : A Second Red October?

At the beginning of 1923 the eyes of Russian and Comintern leaders once again were focused on Germany, where a quickening of internal conflicts and an increase of pressures on the Republic appeared to augur the second coming of the October Revolution. As perhaps never before the times seemed propitious for a German revolution, which in turn might rekindle revolutionary fires elsewhere that had grown cold in the past two years. The occupation of the Ruhr and passive resistance of the Cuno government, the runaway inflation which threatened the existence of the lower middle class, increasing working class discontent characterized by mass resignations from trade unions and wildcat strikes, the growth of right-wing organizations and paramilitary units struggling against the Franco-Belgian occupying forces but inherently hostile to the November Republic, and the threatened separatism of Bavaria which had become a veritable rightist witches' cauldron—all seemed to provide a rich humus for the late blooming of revolution. And yet this revolution was stillborn, and brought to an end the fervent hopes of communists dating back to 1918 that Soviet Russia would soon be surrounded by a fraternity of communist states. The German October was more than a local failure and did more than shatter illusions. It demonstrated conclusively the impracticality of the united front under fire and thereby occasioned another shift in Comintern policy. It also marked an important crossroad in the communist movement, because for the first time not only the Comintern but also the Russian party participated on a large scale in preparing and directing a revolutionary operation.

This last chapter in the Comintern's serious bid for world revolution had its origins in the occupation of the Ruhr on January 11, 1923 by French and Belgian troops in reprisal for Germany's default in reparations payments. This act created a state of national emergency to which the right-of-center government of Wilhelm Cuno responded with a call for passive

resistance in the occupied zone. The KPD reacted by denouncing French actions as the most recent and flagrant example of the imperialist policies of the Western powers which
had been ushered in by the Versailles Treaty. For the next
four months the party contented itself with the formula
"Smite Poincaré and Cuno on the Ruhr and on the Spree,"
indicating communist opposition to both French and German
capitalism. Whereas the overall design of KPD policy was
clear-cut, there was no agreement on the tactics to be employed in its execution. Seething below the surface of official
pronouncements were the bitter conflicts between the right-
wing *Zentrale* and a left-wing opposition that dated back to
the March Action. The most recent sutures applied to this rift
by the Fourth World Congress gave way during this crisis.

Brandler, who had become leader of the party at its Leipzig
congress in January 1923, was intent on winning the masses
through a broad application of the united front. In this approach he received the theoretical assistance of Thalheimer
and the blessing of Radek, who was once more entrusted by
the Comintern with shepherding the German party. The *Zentrale* representing the majority of the rank and file concentrated its efforts on moving the German Socialist party (SPD)
from its position on the left wing of the bourgeoisie to the
right wing of the working class. To further this end the
Zentrale negotiated with SPD leaders, employed the factory
councils as a communist stalking horse for the trade unions,
and laid the groundwork for the creation of workers' governments, particularly in Saxony and Thuringia, where the KPD
held the parliamentary balance of power. The party's Left opposition, under the leadership of Fischer, Maslow, and Ernst
Thälmann and with predominant strength in the districts of
Berlin, Hamburg, and the Ruhr, considered the KPD's official
position opportunistic and, because it allegedly neglected the
ultimate goal of revolution, even akin to reformism. The Left
demanded a united front from below through which the non-
communist masses but not their leaders would be won for
the cause, and denigrated the party's attempts to build workers' governments as a futile effort to combine democracy with
dictatorship of the proletariat. The Leipzig party congress
demonstrated that a reconciliation between the *Zentrale* and
the Left was impossible, and even though the official resolu-

tions upheld a prudent united front policy, the party remained divided.[1]

The emerging crisis of 1929 had its basis in the occupation of the Ruhr, but was exacerbated and accelerated by a galloping inflation which erased savings, paupered those on fixed incomes, drastically reduced the real wages of workers, and ultimately brought the economy to a virtual standstill. The progressive deterioration of the economy both in the occupied and unoccupied parts of the nation was accompanied by attempts on the part of Germany's leading industrialists to badger and bribe the government into removing economic controls, leading to an abolition of the eight-hour-day and the right to strike. Consequently, large numbers of workers, brought to despair by the inflation and feeling themselves unprotected against the threats of big industry, left the impotent trade unions and turned to the KPD. Another source of domestic instability was the sudden appearance of Free Corps and other illegal rightist paramilitary organizations in the Ruhr. The government's policy of passive resistance answered by French reprisals had brought chaos to the occupied territory. The rightists turned passive resistance into a guerilla war, which increased the misery of the population and set in motion a wave of intense nationalism that aroused the suspicion of labor. Throughout the first four months of this gathering storm the KPD *Zentrale* and the Left remained divided and often worked at cross-purposes. Moscow, itself in the throes of an interregnum, offered little guidance to the party slowly groping its way along the united front path.

In May, after the worsening condition of the Ruhr workers gave rise to a series of spontaneous and endemic strikes over which the KPD neither exercised control nor from which it benefited demonstrably, the party began to search for a more productive course. The first step in a new direction was the startling move to extend the party's united front efforts beyond the ranks of the proletariat, which was undertaken on a note of blatant nationalism. It was Radek who legitimized previously sporadic attempts by the KPD to win sympathizers

---

[1] A significant event at the Leipzig congress was the election of August Guralski, alias Kleine, to the *Zentrale*. During the March Action he (like Kun and Pogány) had been an emissary of the ECCI. In 1923 he was Zinoviev's man in Germany, where the party took him into its inner circle.

from the nationalist and rightist petty bourgeoisie. At a meeting of the enlarged ECCI on June 20th he made a sensational speech in which he openly wooed the German nationalists. Taking as a point of departure the recent execution by the French of the Free Corps officer Schlageter, whom he dubbed "the brave soldier of the counterrevolution" who died in vain because his nationalism had been in the service of the bourgeoisie, Radek declared that the majority of the misguided nationalist masses belonged in the camp of the workers, which alone was able to protect Germany against the evil effects of the Versailles Treaty.[2] In presenting the KPD as the party of the whole German people Radek appealed to nationalists of the lower middle class suffering from the effects of inflation and wounded in their patriotism by the humiliation in the Ruhr, and to the Schlageter-like goalless soldiers of fortune who fought mainly against the pedestrian Republic. Even though the "Schlageter line" strikes the contemporary reader as a radical departure, it was not considered so at that time by the ECCI, which also passed a strong resolution calling for an all-out struggle against international fascism. It was viewed by Radek and the ECCI as a tactical maneuver for splitting the ranks of the nationalists by demonstrating that in the long run only the communists could effectively oppose the Versailles Treaty; it could therefore be made logically consistent with a vigorous struggle against fascism. The Schlageter campaign undertaken by the KPD between June and August, and frequently carried to embarrassing extremes by the party's Left, was a patent failure, for neither the Right nor the Left was affected by their intellectual exchanges in print and on lecture platforms.[3] Furthermore, the wooing of the nationalists alienated the SPD, which was after all the primary target of the overriding united front policy.

The KPD's search for a new course was accompanied by several tests of communist strength. The first of these came on July 29th, which the party had proclaimed as an antifascist day. Throughout July the party waged a vigorous propaganda campaign to warn the public against the growing dan-

[2] Radek received Zinoviev's approval for this speech before delivering it.

[3] Communist speakers before nationalist audiences on more than one occasion made embarrassing remarks about "Jewish capital" and the possibility of an alliance with National Socialism.

ger of fascism and to demonstrate the necessity for a united front of workers, peasants, and employees. The strident tone of these appeals and several premature demonstrations, which ended in clashes with the police, prompted the state governments to ban all open air assemblies on the 29th. On the appointed day the KPD held its demonstrations indoors, except in Saxony and Thuringia, where the sympathetic left-wing SPD government permitted outdoor processions. Even taking this handicap to the party's test of mass appeal into account, the turnout throughout the nation was not impressive. Almost immediately another opportunity arose for the party to prove its mettle. On August 10th, when the economic crisis was at its zenith and inflation had assumed tragi-comic proportions, the Berlin printers union struck, and under the influence of the communists shut down the government printing presses which produced the paper money. As the strike spread spontaneously to other industries, the KPD attempted unsuccessfully to create a united front with the SPD and trade unions for the purpose of calling a general strike. Before the KPD, thrown back on its own resources, had the opportunity to transform the spontaneous movement into a general strike, Chancellor Cuno resigned on August 12th. With Cuno gone the popular movement collapsed. A new government was formed under Gustav Stresemann, sympathetic to the Ruhr industrialists, who demanded an end to passive resistance, and created a "great coalition" cabinet from his own German People's party on the right to the SPD on the left.

It frequently has been asked why, when conditions had become so chaotic in July and August, the KPD was indecisive and restrained instead of taking the plunge for revolution. It seems that Radek, Brandler, and a majority in the *Zentrale* were unprepared to risk a bid for power without substantial mass support which, as proved by recent experience, the party still lacked. Although aware of the fact that communist strength and influence had grown during the past half-year, they were not prepared to chance another March fiasco. Consequently, they opted for a policy of attrition whereby through a deft use of the united front and in capitalizing on each new crisis symptom the party would attain decisive strength. Radek and his fellow architects of this strategy undoubtedly received approval for it from Russian leaders at various stages of its development.

Although it certainly was not realized at the time, the revolutionary wave in Germany was moving toward ebb tide by the middle of August. It was precisely at this time that the Russian leaders, who for months had watched German developments as bystanders, agreed that the moment for decisive action had come. This conclusion rested on the belief that the German crisis had deepened with the resignation of Cuno and that Stresemann would be unable to cope with it. The Russians no doubt also feared that Stresemann, known for his Western foreign political inclination, would have little use for the Eastern orientation that had prevailed since Rapallo.[4] More important than these considerations was the Russians' almost naïve belief that Germany was about to experience a "second October," revealed in their tendency to draw analogies between Russian conditions in 1917 and German events in 1923.[5]

At a secret session on August 23rd the Russian Politburo decided to gird itself, the Comintern, and the KPD for action. A high command of five for Germany was appointed, consisting of Radek, the ECCI representative, to supervise the *Zentrale;* Pyatakov, Vice President of the Council of National Economy, to take charge of agitation; Unshlikht, Vice President of the secret police, to supervise the formation of "Red Army" units; Schmidt, commissar of labor, to organize revolutionary cells in the trade unions; and Krestinsky, Soviet Ambassador to Germany, to disburse the secret funds needed in preparing the revolution. Toward the end of the month Brandler was called to Moscow for consultation and was soon followed by Fischer, Maslow, and Thälmann representing the

[4] The Rapallo Treaty signed between Germany and Russia on April 16, 1922 came as an unpleasant surprise to the Western powers. At Rapallo the two outcasts of European society concluded a diplomatic *rapprochement* which had been carefully prepared on both sides for several years. Economic and military collaboration was the essence of this consolidation in Soviet-German relations. The subsequent friendly association of the two states was based, above all, on their mistrust of the West.

[5] A typical example of this tendency was Zinoviev's belief that General Müller, the newly appointed commander of the army in Saxony, could be ignored in the same way the Bolsheviks had successfully disregarded the appointment of the Cadet Pepelyaev as commissar of Kronstadt by the Provisional Government in 1917.

KPD Left opposition. What followed, in a series of high caucuses between Russian and German leaders which lasted until the first week in October, is not entirely clear. Brandler, cautious and painfully realistic as ever, certainly had not changed his view that his party lacked the necessary popular support for a revolution in the near future. It appears that the unrestrained optimism of the Russians, who were after all successful revolutionary practitioners, and the wishful thinking of his own colleagues of the Left allayed Brandler's fear that a collision course would be a foolish gamble with the fate of his party, and ultimately converted him. Indeed Russian enthusiasm went very far with Zinoviev, predicting that twenty-two million German workers would constitute the cornerstone of the forthcoming revolution and with Trotsky demanding that the date for the onset of revolution be fixed at November 7th.

A master plan was devised whereby the KPD was to prepare the ground for an armed uprising by entering the left-wing SPD government of Erich Zeigner in Saxony, which for months had owed its existence to communist votes. Once a "workers' government" had been created in Saxony, and also in Thuringia where the same favorable conditions prevailed, stocks of arms could be collected to equip "proletarian hundreds" which were being organized throughout the country, and the revolutionary tocsin could be sounded.[6] The substance of the plan was a matter of great controversy; only at the last moment were Brandler's nagging doubts erased that entry into the Saxon government would tip the party's hand before the masses had been politically prepared for revolution, and finally even he was able to share in the enthusiasm and great expectancy which surrounded him in such profusion. The plan which Zinoviev activated with a telegram to the *Zentrale* on October 1st rested on a number of dangerous illusions. The proletarian hundreds were not intended as a match for the army or police but as a counterweight against rightist paramilitary units. The army and police, it was believed, could

[6] The "red" or "proletarian hundreds" were created by the KPD in the spring of 1923. The purpose of this workers' militia was to defend the proletariat against the increasing threat of rightist paramilitary organizations, to stimulate a united front of all workers based on self-preservation, and to build a military apparatus which could be used in carrying out a revolution.

be neutralized from within by working-class elements which would refuse to defend the bourgeoisie, and nationalist elements which would refuse to defend the Republic. At least the KPD leaders should have known better than to make such assumptions, for both the army and police carefully excluded workers and leftists, and although the former previously had demonstrated no great desire to save the Republic, it was not going to surrender it to the communists. This misconception was crucial, since a force of 250,000 well-trained and heavily armed men was a match for an uprising even with a broad popular base. In this case, as in others, the Russians obscured the danger by discovering homologues to their October Revolution.

Brandler and his fellow *Zentrale* members returned to Germany on October 8th. In their absence the KPD press had launched a campaign of unrestrained agitation, which called for economic measures to relieve the misery of the workers but also openly insulted and threatened the government. The government had responded to these provocations with repressive measures against the party. An ominous situation developed during this interim, when National Socialist newspaper attacks on President Ebert, Chancellor Stresemann, and General von Seeckt, seconded by General Otto von Lossow, commandant of the army in Bavaria and Gustav von Kahr, general state commissioner, nearly brought Bavaria to the point of secession.

With the target date for the uprising set for sometime in the first half of November, the KPD's preparation began in earnest with the return of Brandler. One of the principal aspects of the master plan was the creation of a revolutionary striking force, and the secret apparatus feverishly undertook to recruit, train, and arm the proletarian hundreds and to create the subsidiary organizations necessary to direct and sustain their operation. In spite of numerous Russian experts and advisors these preparations, considering the formidable opponent, were amateurish. They were hampered by conflicting chains of command divided between Germans and Russians, as well as between those acting for the Comintern and for the Russian Politburo. Consequently, at most eight hundred proletarian hundreds were organized, many of which existed only on paper, and the stock of weapons collected was pitifully inadequate. If the secret operation left much to be desired, the

legal one initially went according to plan. The KPD negotiated with Zeigner about entry into the Saxon government
and he, fearing a rightist threat from Bavaria, agreed to form
a coalition and appointed three communist ministers on October 12th.[7]

The communists had hardly begun to prepare Saxony as a
springboard for revolution when Stresemann moved against
them. On October 13th General Müller, the military commander of the army in Saxony, banned the proletarian hundreds and all similar organizations. Müller answered the Zeigner government's resistance to this measure with a further
directive on the 16th placing the Saxon police force under the
immediate authority of the army. Pressure was increased to
the point of forcing the KPD's hand when Müller informed
Zeigner on the 20th that the army was moving in to restore
and maintain constitutional and orderly conditions. Brandler
called a hurried meeting of Saxon workers' representatives for
the next day to determine whether they would approve calling a general strike and thus give the signal for the uprising.
The meeting refused to make such an important decision on
the spur of the moment and without probing the mood of the
masses. The KPD *Zentrale* was therefore forced to conclude
that nothing further could be done. The revolution was defeated before the first blow was struck.[8]

On October 29th this conclusion was made inescapable by
Ebert, who deposed the Saxon coalition government by federal executive action as authorized by Article 48 of the Weimar Constitution. Having neutralized the communists, Stresemann moved quickly to deal with other aspects of the political
and economic crisis. On November 8th full emergency powers
were granted to General von Seeckt, who used them to crush

[7] In Thuringia an agreement on similar terms was concluded
on October 13th.

[8] Although the German October was abortive, it had one brief
and bloody sequel in Hamburg. There the communists rose on October 23rd, partly because they had not been informed clearly about
the cancellation of the revolution and partly because the local party
organization refused to accept the rumored general retreat and decided to take the initiative. Although the Hamburg rising went according to plan and met with some initial success, it lasted only
a few days. The masses refused to support the communists, and
they alone were no match for the government forces.

the Hitler putsch in Munich on the following day. On the 16th a new *Rentenmark* was introduced, which stabilized the currency. Finally, on the 24th, the KPD was banned along with parties of the extreme Right.

Without a doubt the KPD had suffered its third major defeat in five years but, because so many of the preparations and plans had remained secret and the masses had never been activated, only the leaders could have known how decisive the latest reversal was. Yet, the Brandler *Zentrale* which met on November 3rd to evaluate the October experience remained undaunted in its belief that revolution was still on the agenda. The resolution adopted at the meeting accused the social democrats and their leaders of having betrayed the communists at the crucial moment by refusing to fight against the military dictatorship. Henceforth the party planned to pursue the united front only from below. The resolution's central conclusion was that fascism had won a victory over the November Republic.[9]

This pleasant postmortem, which made no reference to the defeat of the party or the working class, was totally unacceptable to the Left opposition in the *Zentrale*. Ruth Fischer lost no time in presenting her own evaluation, which gave her the long-awaited opportunity to take the party leadership to task (Document 1). The united front as practiced by the party, she charged, was carried out too much from above and too little from below. Every effort should have been made to discredit the leaders of the SPD Left. Instead, the *Zentrale* staked everything on parliamentary horse-trading and neglected the masses. The cardinal error, she maintained, was the party's entry into the Saxon government, because it entangled the communist leaders in the machinery of the bourgeois state and thereby discredited the party among the workers. That the strength of the party in Saxony had turned out to be nothing but a legend, she concluded, stemmed from the policy of compromise which the *Zentrale* had followed for the past two years. Fischer's pointed attack forced Brandler and Thalheimer to come to terms with the fact that the October experience had been a defeat (Document 2). The fundamental

[9] This line, that the military was promoting fascism and working against the Republican government, became indefensible after November 9th when General von Seeckt, on government orders, put down the National Socialist coup in Munich.

cause of the October defeat, they insisted, did not lie in tactical errors by the party but in the unwillingness of the majority of the working class to either defend the November Republic or to fight for a soviet dictatorship. Both the ECCI and the KPD, they argued, were responsible for the incorrect estimate of communist strength in relation to the SPD. The *Zentrale* leaders had warned the ECCI about this condition but had not been heeded because they were not forceful enough. They concluded that both the premature onset of the final struggle and the insufficient connection between the political and technical preparation were the result of this incorrect estimate.

The Left refused to accept the explanation of the party leaders, and by its renewed attacks succeeded in turning a substantial group within the *Zentrale* against Brandler and his circle. This new central group within the party sided with the Left in demanding a drawing of accounts for October. The final reckoning was delayed because the authorities in Moscow, only a short time before so active in German affairs, were not inclined to intervene. The Russian leaders' failure to become involved was not a matter of reticence; it stemmed from the leadership crisis in the Kremlin, which had reached its height and come out into the open in October and November. The two sides—Radek, Trotsky, Pyatakov representing the party opposition, and the triumvirate Stalin, Zinoviev, and Kamenev, representing the party majority—confronted each other, grappled for advantage, and sought allies. Given the relationship between national communist parties and the Comintern and the Comintern's ties with the Russian party, it was only a matter of time before foreign communists took an active interest in the disputes in Moscow and the Russian contenders became involved in the affairs of other communist parties. When this entanglement of Russian and foreign communist affairs came to pass in the middle of December, the German question could no longer be judged on its merits; the KPD itself became a battleground in the struggle within the Russian Politburo. In the tug-of-war which ensued over the German party and its October defeat Zinoviev championed the left wing and Trotsky defended the right wing of the *Zentrale*. Zinoviev made the first significant gain when, at the end of the month, the Politburo officially censured Radek for his present and past activities in the KPD.

The real test of strength took place in the presidium of the ECCI, where Zinoviev's authority was paramount. Representatives of the three German factions were invited to a meeting which began on January 11, 1924. The German spokesmen for the Right, Center, and Left had nothing new to add to their well-worn arguments. Radek, who gave the opening report, attempted to defend the *Zentrale* leaders by insisting that a revolutionary situation simply did not exist in Germany at the time of the planned uprising. The final word, the judgment so to speak, was left to Zinoviev, who masterfully skirted the complicity of the Russians in the debacle, save by innuendo that of Trotsky and Radek, and skillfully maneuvered his own followers to power in the KPD (Document 3). The responsibility for the KPD's entry into the Zeigner government, he began, was his, but this policy had led to defeat only because of its faulty execution. The communist ministers in the Saxon government had been more concerned with being responsible members of a bourgeois government than with attacking the left-wing SPD, and had thereby debased the idea of a workers' government into an opportunist entanglement with social democrats. He, for one, had always considered workers' government synonymous with dictatorship of the proletariat. Brandler, he accused, had fathered the kind of united front which stood for evolutionary processes and under the guidance of Radek had pursued Menshevik tendencies. The collapse in Saxony, therefore, was simply due to these rightist deviations in the party. Adroitly Zinoviev shifted to the heart of his subject, the reallocation of power in the KPD. The old *Zentrale* had not made sufficient use of people like Thälmann, he chided, who were "the gold of the working class." A new leadership was absolutely necessary, he insisted, and proposed that it consist of the new Center and the Left. Zinoviev's demand was duly ratified by the ECCI and KPD.

The German October brought to a close an era of international communism that had been inspired by the short-term prospects for world revolution. Thereafter the Comintern's form remained, but its substance became a mere shadow of what it had been in its dynamic years as the national communist parties became domesticated and as Russian internal and external affairs increasingly became the *raison d'être* of the movement.

DOCUMENT 1: Ruth Fischer, *"On the Situation in Germany and on the Tactics of the Party"*

DIE INTERNATIONALE, VI, Ergänzungsheft No. 1 (January, 1924).

I. On the Situation in Germany

1. The fascist initiative has forced the proletariat into the defensive. The enemies of the working class have thereby gained a great advantage, which can only be balanced by two factors: through the objective impossibility of ending quickly the general crisis with capitalist methods (reparations, financing, starvation, unemployment), and through the numerical superiority and organization of the proletariat.

2. The internal contradictions within fascism together with the struggles between individual fascist groups, as well as the contradictions within the leading circles of the bourgeoisie (separatists, great-German, *völkisch* Germans, nationalists, heavy industry, manufacturing industry, etc.) give the working class a time, albeit short, to prepare for the offensive.

3. Even a mere "external" solution of the present crisis is only possible through the dictatorship of the vanguard of one or the other class, and the entire population of Germany has understood this for some time already.

4. The farsighted among the German bourgeoisie do not balk at the prospect of a complete fragmentation of Germany in the case of a revolutionary movement. The workers must realize that they will at first take power in what will be only a nucleus of Germany.

5. The symptoms of crisis will increase during the winter months. The hunger riots breaking out everywhere are still the explosions of masses ready for action. There is a danger, if the crisis lasts much longer, that they will become a passive, hungry, and apathetic mass, rising up only in acts of desperation.

II. On the Tactics of the KPD in Saxony

1. The line of the party in Saxony has proven itself, through brutal facts rather than through discussion, to be disastrously wrong in every respect. The mistakes were:

a) the frivolously optimistic, vain, and self-deceiving analysis of the relationship of forces.

b) the disastrously incorrect application of the "united front tactic" not only for the past two years, but also particularly during our participation in the government.

c) the dangerously reformist view of the questions concerning the government, participation in the government, the state, state power, and the "utilization of the state apparatus."

2. It was a legend, cultivated and diffused officially, that the KPD was strong in Saxony and that the SPD was weak and "disintegrating." This was untenable even after only mechanical study of the bare statistics. But the relationship of forces cannot be determined alone by numbers of members. Our influence in Saxony could not have been strong because already for almost two years we were an example of a dependent, wavering, weak policy of compromise, based primarily on parliamentary intrigues which were in the end only of use to the SPD (this is shown particularly drastically in the elections at the Metal Workers' congress, in the Anti-Fascist Conference, in the strike of August, and during our participation in the government, particularly at the end). Added to this were the entirely unproven stories about the red hundreds in Saxony, about the "sawing off of the right-wing leadership in the SPD," etc.

3. Our "united front tactic" in Saxony was determined by those frequently used words regarding our "goodwill in working together with the Left SPD to wage working class politics within the context of democracy." Every word of this main theme in our Saxony policy is a mistake in principle as well as in tactics.

The tactic of the united front applied by the communists *assumes the conviction and the awareness that the SPD is incapable of "waging working class politics"* (that is, if words still have some meaning, *revolutionary* politics). Our "goodwill" therefore also should have been concentrated on destroying the social democrats through our united front with them. That as a first point. Second, the fetishism with which we dealt with the "leftness" of the oppositional-sounding (never acting) spokesmen of the really oppositional-minded SPD workers served as credit for this society of opportunist politicians and wavering petty bourgeois. Instead of discrediting them practically as well as theoretically in every way, instead of exposing them, we made them into "heroes," and even managed it so that our own comrades started believing in their virtues. This was possible because of the basically false, revisionist, liquidationist (probably unconscious) perspectives of the leading party circles who allowed the thesis to exist that "social democracy (as a party) could also lead revolutionary struggles" (from the discussion at the Leipzig party congress). That is the third point.

But apart from that, our "united front tactic" in Saxony consisted in eternal parliamentary combinations and negotiations among the top leaders who consciously refused to have factory-council congresses because of fear that such "demands" would "break up" the united front (with whom?).

And finally, even in those cases where a break was unavoidable and compromise direct treachery, we upheld this "united front" of exclusively party leaders while at the same time refusing to take absolutely necessary steps. This was the case after the murder of workers by the Zeigner government in Dresden, Bautzen, Leipzig (in the spring of 1923) and after the insolent sabotage of the general strike during our participation in the government. But precisely the breakup of this "united front" of top party leaders (a united front of inaction, of reformist compromise, and of discredit to the KPD) could have laid the basis of a united front *from below* because the masses would have seen revolutionary will, revolutionary goal, and a certain minimum of action from us.

4. Through our tactic in Saxony, we have held up the development of the KPD, arrested the disintegration of the SPD and consolidated its "left wing," the most dangerous barrier to the revolution, and have made the best elements of our own party and the proletariat suspicious of the KPD. Our assessment of the Zeigner government as a "bulwark of the proletariat" (or even as the only bulwark of the proletariat) does not differentiate itself in any way from the SPD's reformist assessment of a government "per se." A bourgeois government (with an intact apparatus of police, bureaucracy, courts, education) and with a leadership made up of people with social democratic (or communist) membership cards, is still a bourgeois government and will act like one.

5. Our entry into this government could only have had one aim—to break up its apparatus, to set up a proletarian one in its place, and to begin the attack on the bourgeoisie. The pre-

condition for this was mass mobilization, a congress of soviets, beginning the armament.

6. Already the name of this "government for proletarian defense" was not accidentally (and not only demagogically) chosen. The KPD, on the basis of a revisionist attitude, made the disastrous mistake of assuming that one could, without a new apparatus, "carry on working class politics" (as it was called in this point of the theoretically untenable Leipzig party congress theses) in "the context of democracy" and "of a bourgeois democratic constitution." Leading party members really believed that Brandler, Böttcher or other communists could really perform this miracle without changing the type of state apparatus from a bourgeois into a proletarian state machine (for if this belief had not existed, neither the theoretical discussion of the last year and a half nor the constantly stressed opinion that the workers' government is essentially completely different from the dictatorship of the proletariat would be comprehensible). The refusal of this "workers' government" to take responsibility before a congress of councils is practical revisionism.

7. Besides this, unusually grave mistakes of another sort were also made, the most important of which are listed here.

The unconditional entry into the Saxony government (for secretly made conditions are worth less than nothing in a time of civil war); the disgraceful speeches of the communist cabinet ministers, in which they declared themselves to be responsible only to parliament, the national government and the constitution; each minister's omission of even one revolutionary word in the *Landtag;* the coresponsibility for a government project to give the former royal family enormous valuables at a time of great starvation; the renunciation of independent actions for the defense of the very government we entered for revolutionary purposes, so as not to "break up" the united front (with Graupe and Zeigner!). All these are unforgivable mistakes which have done great damage to the party.

8. After this Saxon experiment the task is now to destroy all its roots. The benefit from this experiment is minimal: the shabbiness of the "Left" SPD could have been very well proven in practical action, without our participation in the government, without our being discredited. The damage is great. Through our activity in the government, we have de-

layed the decomposition of the SPD ("if even the communists are with us, we cannot be as bad as we thought") and brought it into our own ranks; undoubtedly we have repelled the best revolutionary workers, thereby narrowing the already sparse trust in communist leadership.

9. We will best transcend this episode by clear-cut, unambiguous, ruthless revolutionary politics. Time passes so quickly nowadays that we will take up the slack if we publicly acknowledge and finally abandon the way which has proven to be an impasse. . . .

DOCUMENT 2: A. Thalheimer and H. Brandler, *"Theses on the October Defeat and on the Present Situation"*

DIE INTERNATIONALE, VI, Ergänzungsheft No. 1 (January, 1924).

I. The October Defeat

1. The October retreat was inevitable and correct.

2. The basic causes of the October defeat are of an objective nature and are not the fault of basic tactical mistakes of the KPD. The decisive cause is the still too strongly hindering influence of social democracy. The majority of the working class was no longer willing to fight for the democratic regime of November [1918] from which they no longer had any material benefit, and not as yet ready to fight for the soviet dictatorship and socialism.

In other words, the majority of the working class was not yet won for communism.

3. The mistake common to the ECCI and the *Zentrale* of the KPD was the incorrect estimation of the relationship of forces between SPD and KPD within the working class.

The KPD was in this respect critical of the position of the ECCI but was not energetic enough. The ECCI did not grant enough importance to this criticism.

4. The consequences of this incorrect analysis of the relationship of forces were:

   a) a premature date for the final struggles;
   b) neglect of partial struggles;
   c) because of the faulty connection between political

and technical preparation, the military technical preparations also suffered.

5. Secondary and tertiary deficiencies were:

a) in Saxony and Thuringia there was not enough use made of given positions in respect to the break-up of the SPD and the winning over of the SPD workers to the KPD, as well as in respect to the organizations of military defense.

b) the cumbersome nature of the party's reorganization for civil war.

6. All these mistakes and inadequacies do not essentially change the fundamental relationship of forces between the bourgeoisie and the working class.

II. The Present Situation

1. The military dictatorship of Seeckt has its social base in heavy industry and among large landholders. It seeks to subordinate the independent movement of the middle class (petty bourgeois fascism) partially through concessions and partially through reprisals. It seeks to preserve and deepen the split in the working class on the one hand by keeping up the pretense of bourgeois democracy, thereby winning over social democracy as a force of protection, and on the other, by reprisals against the KPD.

2. The duration of the dictatorship depends on:

a) the possibility of restoring a temporary economic stabilization through increased exploitation of the working class and the middle classes, through decreasing expenditures and adequate taxation of the propertied. The first two are possible by virtue of the existing power relations, the last is questionable and will be decisive;

b) the pace at which the majority of the workers will be won for communism and at which the disintegration and neutralization of the middle classes will occur.

3. It is not yet possible to guess the tempo at which the situation will again come to a head. However, a sharpening of class contradictions and struggles must be generally expected.

4. The tempo at which the majority of workers will be won for communism depends on the KPD. All efforts must be concentrated on the political and organizational liquidation of the SPD.

5. The political platform for this liquidation must be:

negative: the destruction of democratic and social reformist illusions;

positive: the winning over of the workers to the struggle for proletarian dictatorship and socialism.

6. Partial struggles in political, economic, and military matters must be connected with this fundamental and critical propaganda. The decisive struggle is the culmination and result of these partial struggles.

7. The next link in the chain is conquering freedom of mobility (in the streets, etc.) through revolutionary mass actions (at first peaceful, armed demonstrations; strikes; armed and defended meetings, etc.).

8. Placing organizational emphasis on factory cells.

9. Increasing the activity and discipline of the party. Elimination of passive elements in the party, at the same time broader contact with the masses.

DOCUMENT 3: *"Speech of Comrade Zinoviev on the Situation in the KPD"*

DIE INTERNATIONALE, VII, No. 2/3 (March 28, 1923).

Zinoviev: Comrades, first of all, we must realize in which situation we have begun this discussion.

We are in agreement that we have suffered a serious defeat. I think it would be exaggerated to say a collapse; however, a serious defeat in any case. And a defeat is, according to our experience, the most important test of strength for a revolutionary party. It is precisely after a defeat that we must prove whether or not we are capable of passing the test. It can ruin the party to sink into a mood of pessimism. Now, after the defeat, there is all the more reason for the German comrades to show what they can do. After a victory, this is no great feat. Above all, it is a question of maintaining loyalty now that the party is in such a bad situation.

I would like to make a few observations before I go into matters more concretely.

It was said here that a split in the German Communist party would mean the decline of the German revolution, or

at least its postponement for five years. This is absolutely correct. I think we must enter concrete discussion with the
awareness that whoever threatens unity with factionalism, at
this stage, out of factional conviction, naturally, is a criminal
for the German working class. We all know that there are
situations in which splits have to occur. In such cases we split.
But there are also situations when everything should be
swallowed down in order to prevent a split. I maintain that
in Germany at present we have the latter situation. He who
presses for a split today, even if he has only the best of motives, is objectively nothing else but a lackey of the social
democrats and the bourgeoisie, and does not serve the interests of the German working class.

Now, on to the concrete side of the discussion.

First of all, a few words about certain documents. It was
an attempt to cover things up when it was said here that
the first mistake was not made in October, that it was not in
October that we underestimated the situation for the first
time, but already earlier, during the Ruhr crisis; and because
of this, we have the situation today.

But that is really self-evident! Had we begun to make preparations during the Ruhr crisis, then, certainly, we would
have been better prepared. Had we begun even earlier, then
even more so. This is a chain which can be followed backward forever, and this is pure sophism being used to obscure
real mistakes and sins of omission made at a specific time. We
must, above all, be honest with ourselves. Then we can also
find the real mistakes.

The Ruhr crisis was indeed the beginning for the whole
development of things. I have in front of me the instructions
for the Ruhr crisis, dated March 12, 1923.

"Directives for the delegation of the Executive of the CI
at the International Conference in Cologne on March 17,
1923."

Read these instructions. What is in them?

"The Conference at Essen was primarily a demonstration.
The Conference of March 17 had to become a workers' conference.

"In the conditions under which the Essen Conference was
held, a simple demonstration was already quite a great political event. The more or less successful coordination of the
activity of the French and German Communist parties in re-

gard to the occupation of the Ruhr should not be underestimated. But to simply repeat Essen now would be a great step backward."

And our directive had the following text:

"The Conference of March 17 and the pre-Conference (particularly the pre-Conference) have two tasks:

a) to work out a genuine, joint, clear, firm, concise, and agitational program for the most important sections concerned;

b) to work out a number of organizational and in part conspiratorial measures and to actually carry these out." [*Radek:* And we carried them out.] Wait a minute, comrade Radek—So the Executive saw the task quite clearly and showed it to the Conference. We admit that its execution was inadequate even though the youth of France worked very well. We have already done that sufficiently. But this should not be used as an excuse for sophistry by saying that because we did not put forward the issue of an armed uprising we were incorrect at that time.

No, the mistake in October lay with the German party and partially also with the Executive.

Further, here is another document, a document about Saxony dated October 1, 1923:[10]

"Since we estimate the situation to be such that the decisive moment will not come later than four-five-six weeks from now, we consider it necessary to occupy any position which can be of immediate use. On the basis of the [present] situation we believe that the question of our entry into the Saxony government must be approached practically. On the condition that Zeigner's people are really ready to defend Saxony against Bavaria and the fascists, we must enter [the Saxon government] and immediately carry out the arming of fifty thousand to sixty thousand people; ignore General Müller. The same goes for Thuringia."

This directive was decided upon after intensive discussion. Was it right or wrong? Absolutely correct, if it was assumed that the Zeigner people really wanted to fight the fascists and arm fifty to sixty thousand workers.

[10] The document is the telegram sent by Zinoviev, in the name of the ECCI, to the *Zentrale*, outlining mobilization steps for the planned uprising.

How did we envisage the matter? As an episode in the development of the civil war, which is contained in the text. Further, I would like to cite that passage which deals with our relations with Left social democracy and with social democracy in general. In the presence of Brandler and everyone else, we resolved at that time that:

"The main enemy is Left social democracy. It must be clear that we will have to lead a struggle not only without the Left social democrats, but against them as well." That is the text of the Moscow resolution.

Comrades! I admit that I and the other comrades bear the main responsibility for entry into the Saxony government; Brandler wavered on this point. He said, "I do not know whether it has been planned sufficiently in advance." But he gave in. I do not want to dodge any of the responsibility. I accept it completely. This was the general opinion emerging from talks with the French, Polish, and Czechoslovak parties. The Polish comrades now write in a letter that there were big mistakes in the German affair. But the Polish comrades were there! Comrade Warski was here. We drew them in for counsel, although they were not members of the Executive. We were of the opinion that if it were only a matter of weeks, Saxony had to be used for the preparation of the civil war.

That was our general position.

And its execution, comrades? That is, of course, the decisive point in the whole matter.

First of all, in Saxony. Comrade Remmele asked yesterday whether it was really so important to investigate now what the ministers failed to do and to hold it against them now. Is that not a sort of opportunism? What can be expected from ministers anyway?

What is correct in this? The main thing, certainly, is the behavior of the masses. The behavior of the ministers, however, is a symptom for us of the whole bad attitude of the party. The main issue is self-evident: why did the civil war not happen, why could the masses not be mobilized? If, apart from that, we attribute much significance to the actions of the ministers, it is because they were symptomatic of the incorrect attitude of the German party. Who were the ministers anyway? Our best comrades. Leading comrades like Brandler and Böttcher. Their performance is to us proof of the existence of something rotten in the party. Compare the train of thought contained in the telegram I mentioned with the way in which our ministers behaved. Two completely different attitudes. Why no one strode forward, why the masses did not start moving remains a main issue but does not alter the fact that at the same time the actions of the ministers bespoke an incorrect attitude of the party. Comrade Fischer certainly exaggerated yesterday when she said Brandler is aware of the game he is playing. These are exaggerations. Here lies precisely one of the drawbacks of the otherwise good talk given by comrade Fischer. Through such exaggeration, a caricature can be made of something which is correct. That is, indeed, the biggest mistake of the [German] Leftists, as we have repeatedly said here. Brandler could not possibly have done consciously what he did. [*Walcher:* That was her only argument.] No, that was merely her worst argument. Incidentally, her talk contained a whole series of good arguments with which one must agree. We turned our attention to the behavior of the communist ministers because, coming from an incorrect line, it made of the Saxony workers' government a banal entanglement with the social democrats.

Let us assume that the situation was incorrectly analyzed, a mistake was made, and the possibility of arming sixty thousand workers was over-estimated. But why did you have to come forward as social democrats? What compelled you to say that you "stood by the Constitution"? Why did you say that we were "only responsible to the *Landtag*?" This is an old-fashioned attitude, at best, a Bebel standpoint, right out of the 1890's. That is what Bebel said in his best days. At that time it was correct, but today the revolutionary strength of the masses of workers should have been appealed to directly. Now it was your duty to tell the masses that the main enemy was Left social democracy—which goes with the Right while the Right goes with Seeckt and the latter goes with Ludendorff—but not to say that we stand by the Constitution.

The carrying out of the directives was therefore shockingly bad, and signaled to us the existence of greater dangers in our party than any of us had imagined. That is why our letter to the German central committee criticizing its position was unanimously decided upon. We ask that that not be forgotten. I do not like to pass the responsibility from myself to other comrades. I wrote the letter. But it was in no way a purely personal letter, as it is tended to be called in Germany. A commission was formed in which sat comrades Kolarov and Zetkin and in which various changes were suggested which I in turn accepted completely. [*Zetkin:* I would like to point out that the letter was written before we received any detailed reports, before we received anything at all.] It is true that we were not as well-informed as we are now. I admit that I now see many details differently. In the main, though, we were right. Trotsky approved our letter. He demanded only small changes. If we want to defend the actions in Saxony we had better join the Second International. All this has to be spoken about. Incidentally, very much has already been spoken about in the theses by the present majority of the *Zentrale*.

A few words about our relationship to social democracy in general. It was resolved here to recognize Left social democracy as the main enemy and to fight in spite of it, even against it. I wrote that in an article in the middle of October, at a time when some of our comrades were meeting with those scoundrels for a whole week and working out a program, only to declare shortly thereafter that they wanted to postpone the whole matter by two days and then come up with a new program. [*Walcher:* The Berliners were involved in this.] Fine, the Berliners are also accountable for it. However, this is not the way to treat social democracy in such a situation.

And now, comrades, the question of the united front.

First of all, a general question: Did we in the Communist International have up until now differing opinions on this issue? Yes, there were shades and nuances of differences. We did not fight them out. But now they must be fought out until there is complete clarity.

What was my mistake when, in the meeting of the Enlarged Executive, I defined the workers' government as a pseudonym for the dictatorship of the proletariat and was attacked for this by a representative of the [German] majority? It was argued that it hurt agitation and that such a designation was inopportune. I yielded at that time because, as I told myself, not everything should be disclosed in practical agitation. Now it is clear, however, that the objections at that time did not come out of consideration for the needs of prac tical agitation but from a principally mistaken view. The workers' government is either really nothing but a pseudonym for the dictatorship [of the proletariat] or it is simply a social democratic opposition.

Radek can confirm what I and Stalin said immediately after Leipzig: there is here either a big stylistic deviation or the existence of an opportunistic danger.[11] Soon thereafter—if I am not mistaken, one week later—the Czechoslovak party congress took place. They had the same democratic formulations. It was quite natural that Brandler should agree with them. My mistake was not having fought the issue out then. I thought it was better to wait. The affair was still new. Perhaps we could clear it up in a peaceful manner. Now it is clear that the hubbub about the "pseudonym" was the beginning of opportunist deviations, as was proven in the Leipzig resolutions and immediately thereafter in the resolutions in Czechoslovakia. We must recognize this openly and correct it or we will ruin the party.

What does the united front mean? In the theses which we presented, it is stated:

"The united front is a tactic of revolution, not evolution; a method for agitation among the masses and for their mobilization against social democracy in a given period of the class struggle." No more. He who believes it is more than just this is already a lost soul. It is no more and should be no more than this. Whoever has another opinion makes concessions to the counterrevolutionary social democrats.

The question, comrades, must be clarified now not only nationally but internationally. I stand completely on the resolution of the Fourth [World] Congress. And what does it say? It says, "Not every workers' government is a proletarian government." In a few days we will have a MacDonald govern-

---

[11] The eighth congress of the KPD was held at Leipzig from January 28th to February 1, 1923. On that occasion the long-standing and fundamental differences between the *Zentrale* and its left-wing opposition led to another bitter confrontation. In the main discussion of tactics and short-range objectives the Left branded the party's policy as passive, opportunist, and revisionist, ridiculed attempts to form a workers' government from above, and demanded an aggressive, uncompromising forward strategy. The *Zentrale's* resolution, which was passed, disregarded the Left's critique and endorsed the party's cautious united front policy already in practice.

ment in England. Will it be a workers' government? [*voice:* No.]

If you deny it then you are against the resolutions of the Fourth Congress. We mentioned the case of Australia at the Fourth Congress and we said in the resolution that such a liberal workers' government would also be possible in England in the near future. Compare Saxony and England. The Saxony government seems trivial in comparison with the Mac-Donald government. However, on the eve of the proletarian revolution in Germany it represents a significant step. A comparison of these two governments will also show that there are essential differences. The MacDonald government will be the English version of a Scheidemann government. It will nevertheless represent a great historical event, for it means that English workers will feel themselves in power. It will still be a Scheidemann government. In Saxony we had communists attempting to carry on a revolution when objectively matters already had turned into cheap intrigue.

Comrade Fischer reminded us quite correctly yesterday of the effect the announcement of the communists' intention of entering the Saxony government had on the Fourth Congress. [*voice:* It was disapproved.] That is of no consequence, comrades. The authoritative representatives of the KPD were in Moscow at the time. There were about twenty comrades, among them Thalheimer and Meyer. But they were *for* entry into the government. This is a fact. We had to fight with them one whole evening. Afterward we decided unanimously in the Russian delegation, and this included Lenin and Trotsky, to take a position against this, as it would be pure opportunism.

I was and am still of the opinion that we would lose the practical possibility of making agitational use of our contrast with social democracy the minute we entered such a government.

The same thing happened with the united front. You will remember that when we decided on the tactic of the united front the idea of a conference of the three Internationals came up. I believed that we must postpone such an attempt as long as possible, because it could easily become a blow to the united front. Nothing more would have come out of it but concessions to social democracy or inconclusive talking. The slogan of the united front would have thereby lost its attraction. The united front is thus only a method of agitation which one must understand how to apply differently, according to the different stages of development. Whoever expects more of this tactic is with the social democrats. Comrade Brandler said something very interesting to me yesterday. He said that one must admit that one of the consequences of the application of the united front tactic has been the development of a sort of psychological expectation among the masses of an evolutionary process, according to which there would first be a bourgeois coalition, followed by a social democratic government with the support of the communists, then a half-and-half government, etc. If it is true that such a notion has been formed among the masses, then there is a strong argument against the sort of united front tactic managed by you. Particular attention should be paid to Brandler's remarks, because he is the father of the united front tactic in Germany, by which I do not mean to cast any aspersions on him. We all pushed for it. If he now states that things have objectively reached such a point that the masses understand the united front tactic to mean that one government gradually transforms itself into another, if that is a fact, then we must with all thoroughness find out the fundamental mistake in tactics. I believe that it does not lie with the united front tactic in itself but, again, in the execution of it. This must not be overlooked. The matter must not be taken too lightly.

That is the way things stand, comrades, on the issue of the united front. It seems to me that we have no reason to basically revise it. It was principally correct and remains so. The matter is similar to that of revolutionary parliamentarism, which we also maintained with determination. And was not this also fought? One need only recall Bombacci or the weakness of the parliamentary faction in Germany and France. But that is no principled position on the question. How to carry through a good idea has to be learned. This tactic is imperative because we are still a minority in the working class; the social democrats, on the other hand, are in the majority, and we are largely still on the defensive while capitalism wages an offensive against us. It [the united front] will, accordingly, be supported for some years still throughout the communist movement. But in order to defend this idea, a merciless struggle must be waged against its bad implementation. For the simple worker will ask himself, what sort of a policy is this if things are going badly in France, Czechoslovakia, and even in Germany, which has the best party? And he will ask further, what sort of a great idea is the united front if, in practice, it turns out to be such a monster? That is why we must emphasize that the united front not become a fleshless, bloodless idea.

In regard to the various formulations of the united front now confronting one another, it is above all necessary to honestly think the matter through to all its consequences. I propose for acceptance in the name of the Russian delegation the following definition:

"The united front tactic is nothing more than a method of mobilizing proletarian forces in the present period."

Any other view would be social democratic. It would be easy to find a rubber stamp formula. But we will not do that. If we should remain a minority in the Executive, then we will make all efforts to become a majority. We hope, however, not to remain a minority. A period of democratic cooperation with the social democrats is henceforth impossible. Whoever believes a political alliance is still possible between communists and social democrats shares the standpoint of social democracy, and is actually a centrist. The good in these bad experiences in Germany will be that we have finally attained clarity in these matters.

I will now come to the question of German social democracy in general, and in relation to the question of fascism; in other words, to the question, who won over whom in Germany?

Yesterday Radek stated correctly that the first question that a politician asks himself is, who rules in a country, who rules in Germany? Radek, however, answers this question much too simply. He says, the fascists. But I ask further, do the fascists rule alone or are there in Germany co-rulers? And who are they? My answer to that is that the social democracy rules with them. [*Brandler*: very true.] Well, so you find this true. Then let us draw the conclusions from this.

Since 1918 a bloc has been ruling Germany. Things are not that simple that we may speak merely of a rule of fascism. As is well-known, the bourgeois revolution broke out against the will of social democracy. It was for the preservation of the monarchy until the last, and the bourgeois revolution broke out in Germany in spite of social democracy, even against its expressed will. I refer you to Scheidemann's book, for example, in which he tells how he began to sweat when he heard about the outbreak of the revolution, so much so that his collar went soft. Incidentally, I thought Scheidemann would be too smart to say something like that. It is therefore a fact that social democracy was against the bourgeois revolution. The bourgeois revolution came anyway. Germany was called a socialist republic. Now they want to popularize the name of "November Republic." This designation is meaningless. We are Marxists and as such should use the old terminology of Marxism, particularly when it is a question of scientific definitions.

What have we had the whole time in Germany since the collapse? A bourgeois democracy. It differs from the French as well as from the American and Swiss; the content is the same. During five years of bourgeois democratic rule, social democracy has done everything to give all power or at least the greater part of it step by step to the bourgeoisie. Since the revolution, there is a bloc in the government. Recently, the relationship of forces within it has changed somewhat. I say somewhat on purpose, comrades. You reply that now the situation is totally different; the Communist party is being prohibited. You have a short memory, comrades. Didn't Noske also prohibit the party? And is not Severing a minister? But Severing is a social democrat. Social democracy therefore rules as well.

And we have still today a bloc at the helm of state. Ebert is president, although that may be unimportant. We know that thousands, even tens of thousands of social democrats, even social democratic workers hold state positions and carry out state functions. They are in the apparatus and have something at stake to defend. More exactly, there rules in Germany now not only fascism, but fascism plus social democracy. And the nice formula about the victory of fascism over the "November Republic" is therefore useless and nothing is correct in that statement. If it is examined carefully, very little remains of it. First of all, the designation of "November Republic" is incorrect, because it emphasizes an external feature of this republic, instead of characterizing its nature. As a Marxist, one can only speak of a bourgeois democracy. A principally different ruling system does not obtain. It is analogous to the French system. Or do you believe that generals do not rule in France as well?

Further, it is said that the republic was defeated, but not the working class. That is either a literary flourish or opportunism à la Leipzig. If it were but a literary flourish, it would not be so bad. Why is such a thesis politically dangerous? Because an incorrect analysis of social democracy is the result, which can lead to new deviations. If it were correct that social democracy is now defeated, then precisely because of that it would be necessary to cooperate with it. [Exclamation.]

Comrade Piatakov asks, very naïvely, why we use this formulation. Because this formulation motivates our present abandonment of partial slogans and struggles. But, comrades, everything has been turned upside down here. For the sake of a comfortable reason for abandoning partial demands, a thoroughly incorrect formulation was created. If it is true that social democracy has been defeated, then it follows that it is necessary to come closer to the social democrats. Marx teaches that already in the *Communist Manifesto,* where it says that when reactionary forces and a wavering petty bourgeoisie confront each other, we have to go with the latter. In Germany the situation is completely different. In Germany reaction rules together with social democracy. Both must therefore be fought. From your incorrect terminology a totally different position results. I have before me a letter from the delegates of the Comintern from November 18, in which we read,

"We propose in place of the demands of the Leftists for an immediate general struggle, that is, for a general defeat, a line for general mobilization of the party and the proletariat in the form of a series of battles from which the final victory must emerge. For such a revolutionary line we need the recognition of the victory of fascism, for alone this fact provides the basis for a change in our tactics."

Now comrades, this is entirely false. [*Maslow:* Very comfortable!] Not comfortable, but false. It is again either a deviation or opportunism, for here, once again, everything is expected from the famous victory of fascism. No one is asking himself, as a Marxist should, who is in power? What bloc of forces do we see before us? What is the role of social democracy?

The matter is suddenly presented as if a complete turnabout had occurred in social democracy, the very social democracy which since 1920 has been performing the same dance step. These people are very elastic. I do not mean that in the sense of their individual qualities, but in the sense of their class ideology. They represent precisely that petty bourgeoisie whose nature it is to waver back and forth. Such a turn in social democracy can occur a dozen times, but objectively the bloc with the fascists remains.

That is the situation. We must demand a more pronounced tactic for Germany because social democracy has become—and this is crystal clear to us today—a fascist wing of the workers' movement. German social democracy is a fascist social democracy. From this understanding comes the necessity of modifying our tactics. [*Walcher:* That is exactly what we said.] No, you did not say that. You scold the social democrats, but to enlighten the workers about the nature of social democracy, that you do not comprehend. Scolding is easy. "Handymen of the bourgeoisie" is easily said. But the main thing is to recognize that social democracy is not defeated, but has become a part of fascism, just as international social democracy is developing in this direction. What are Pilsudski[12] and his cohorts but fascist social democrats? But were they that ten years ago? No! Potentially, *in nuce,* they were that of course already at that time. But they disclose their character so unmistakably now because we live in a revolutionary epoch which makes fascists of them. What is the Italian social democracy? Another example: the Broad Socialists of Bulgaria and Janko Sakazov.

They have always been opportunists. Could they have been called fascist social democrats ten years ago? No, it would have been stupid to do so then. Now, on the contrary, it is a reality. The proof? Sakazov is a member of the Tsankov government. Sakazov maintains that he belongs to the Second International, that he is a social democrat. The essence of these things must be understood if one does not want to merely

---

[12] Joseph Pilsudski began as a socialist who struggled against Russian czarism and for Polish independence before the World War. During the war he became leader of the Polish Legions organized to fight against Russia. In the immediate postwar years, after having fought briefly against Soviet Russia in 1920, he became the figurehead of socialist forces in the country. In 1926 he was assisted by the Left in staging a coup d'etat but turned against it once he had established himself in power.

scold social democrats. MacDonald, the chairman of the Second International, comes to power. The English bourgeoisie asks him to take over the government. Therein lies proof of the weakness of the bourgeoisie, at the same time proof that the significance of the working class has grown, that the proletariat has become a powerful factor. Nonetheless, it proves that social democracy appears proper and fit for the bourgeoisie. That is why the English bourgeoisie can place the wheel of the ship of state into the hands of the president of the Second International.

One can rant at MacDonald for being a traitor and a helper of the bourgeoisie, but we must keep in mind at all times the epoch in which we are living. International social democracy is today a wing of fascism. That must be made clear to the German workers.

That is a view, diametrically opposed to yours, which throws a completely different light on the political line and agitation. The thesis that the victory of fascism over the "November Republic" is not a victory over the working class is, I repeat, either nonsense or opportunism. Scolding the social democrats does not help you get by this. That is why the majority theses of the *Zentrale* are absolutely false. They are a first attempt at self-orientation. We would, however, be pure formalists if we declared that the *Zentrale* be strangled for having made such an incorrect resolution. It was simply an unsuccessful attempt at self-orientation in a new situation.

We must oppose this formulation with another. The majority theses sound more like an article by Radek than a party resolution. I wrote an article against the majority theses about Koltschak, which seems to me to explain the circumstances far better than Radek's article, which you have raised to a resolution. [*Scholem:* We distributed your article.] Thank you. Walcher observes that exactly this characterizes my article. I in no way fear that. The Left comrades are a part of our International. [*Maslow:* And not bad ones.] And not the worst. They make mistakes, they exaggerate, but are essentially correct. I am therefore not in the least ashamed that my article was distributed by the Berlin workers.

What did the Right do, on the other hand? It attached the remark to my article that a new one by Radek would follow. They were afraid that certain elements could understand my article.

It is of course your right to oppose our standpoint, but then you have no right to deny that a right wing exists. The Right is that tendency in the party which published and distributed that remark. The Right is a minority and will probably shrink to a little nest once the International has spoken. And even this little nest will acquiesce. We are completely convinced that we belong together. We should, however, not shut our eyes to the existence of such a tendency. If you bear in mind the Leipzig resolutions, the hue and cry about the pseudonym, the majority resolutions of the *Zentrale*, the application of our resolutions in Saxony, finally the editorial remark about the appearance of an article by Radek, all this is enough for any political person to conclude that there is here a system, a tendency. [*Radek:* A system, yes. But is it incorrect?] This system is Menshevist.

What is Menshevism? One often hears that Radek is a Menshevik. Of course he is not. He is, of course, a communist. But he sometimes makes Menshevist mistakes. If he were a Menshevik and I a Bolshevik, we would have fought very differently.

Radek says I would be right if things were as they were in Russia then. Now, comrades, you as foreigners are not obligated to know all our political leaders. But Radek should know them. We also once had a Purishkevich, a Russian Hitler. There was in our country once a strong, utterly reactionary movement which we called the Black Hundred. It was really Russian fascism which used social demagogy very cleverly. The "Black Hundred" movement arose from among the monarchists and supported the monarchy. It had a chapter in almost every village, every city. All the little people, the watchmen, servants, etc., went with them. This movement also used religious conflicts for its purposes. In a way, it was a popular movement, for it knew how to secure allegiance of broad social strata, which it gathered under its cloak of demagogic pursuit of Jews. It was a big movement which attracted not only the large landholders, not only the aristocracy, but also thousands of petty bourgeois, and was much more a mass party than the Milyukov party.[13] So if you

13 Pavel N. Milyukov was leader of the Constitutional Democrats popularly known as Cadets. Before the Russian October Revolution it was the most important liberal party, with substantial representation in the Duma.

want to make comparisons with Germany, you must not overlook this tendency. And you have overlooked it. [*Radek:* In regard to the petty bourgeoisie, I am in complete accord with what Zinoviev said.] Radek is completely right when he underscored the significance of the petty bourgeoisie. We must hasten to the aid of the petty bourgeoisie. That is why we followed Radek. This remains one of our most important tasks. Your meetings for the agitational cultivation of these petty bourgeois strata were tactically good and prove that you really sought contact with the masses. This task remains. We must win the petty bourgeois elements. I never heard that the Left was against this. If, on the other hand, differences between the Wittelsbach and the Hohenzollern are construed, as in the resolutions of the *Zentrale*, then we call this opportunism. To build the politics of the working class up on such things, to raise such differences as essential factors for the revolution is to fall into crude error.

What did Lenin and Martov fight about? Certainly not over whether to make use of nuances in the opponent's camp. The fight was rather over the fact that Martov, in looking for nuances, had forgotten the main issue; namely, that the people were divided into three: into bourgeoisie, petty bourgeoisie, and proletariat. He was a Menshevik. One example should be sufficient warning.

Another point of Radek's. Radek says that we are either one communist agitational party or a mass combat party; either an agitational sect or a mass party. That is a wrong attitude. I am not saying that Radek is on the same footing with Levi, but it is the same mistake in a general way, the same assumption that Levi had. The dispute is precisely over that—how can we become a combat party with good agitation—hence it is precisely over the need for a communist or centrist agitation. Please do not keep coming around with that old sect bogey! We are more than familiar with it. In Russia we became not a sect, but a mass party. What our parties lack, on the other hand, is a communist agitation. That is true of the English party as well as of the French, Czech, and German parties. They all do not as yet understand how to wage popular, communist agitation to rouse the masses. They do not feel themselves to be people's tribunes as yet. Why were we so bothered by the behavior of our comrades such as Heckert, who did not feel himself to be a tribune of the people in Saxony?[14] Because we know him to be an earnest communist who we know stands solidly with the Communist International and would die with it. [*Walcher: Did you ever read one of his speeches?*] I read everything that there was to read, no less than Walcher. We did not reach our opinions frivolously. We read dozens of reports. [*Walcher: Everyone said it was a good communist speech.*] For the average listener it may have been a good speech. But Heckert did not feel himself a leader whom the revolutionary tide had swept on to the shoulders of the laboring masses. He did not feel this. But something like that cannot be felt if one believes one's responsibility is to the *Landtag* and to stand with the Constitution. [*voice: There was no tide.*] No, it was there. If not at the given moment in Leipzig, then it was there visibly in October throughout the nation. Remmele told us how the masses stayed out on the street overnight, how aroused was the mood of the women. Comrades, such phenomena are the most essential for us and much more important than tomes of fabricated theses. It is this feeling for the movement of the masses which one ought to have above all. The picture that Remmele painted, the mood of the masses as reflected in comrades König and Thälmann, are of the greatest significance in estimating what was happening in Germany. If this mood was not seen in Leipzig on October 25, it was nonetheless seen in the rest of Germany. Were you an expression of this mood? [*voice: It was spontaneous.*] Fine, the masses act spontaneously, but Heckert, a member of the *Zentrale*, does not act spontaneously. If he is a leader then he must feel what is going on among the masses. What is reflected in Thälmann, Remmele, and König is just what is missing in his speeches, and that is exactly what is frightening in the matter, because it is a bad symptom. We are not appearing before you as Shylocks, incessantly demanding why you did not get hold of any weapons for ten days. That we understand. This was not possible and had to be understood quickly. Our accusations are not at all on that score. What stopped you from becoming the passionate spokesmen of the people? That is what we do not understand and exactly that is symptomatic.

[14] Fritz Heckert was one of the three communists who became ministers in Zeigner's coalition government on October 12th. The others were Heinrich Brandler and Paul Böttcher.

We are of the opinion that a retreat at the time of the Chemnitz conference [October 21st] was inevitable. It is not worth fighting over this point now. It was probably inevitable in the given situation. That things reached such a point in the Saxony affair is proof that certain rightist tendencies exist which have not been confronted by an adequately organized opposition in the party. We have not resisted these tendencies in a sufficiently decisive manner and will now oppose them more strongly.

Now, as for the internal situation in the party. Frankly, comrades, ten comrades such as Remmele and Thälmann in the *Zentrale* is what is needed. That would be a *Zentrale!* Such a *Zentrale* would have to attract other political and organizational forces in the party to assure itself of the appropriate composition. These comrades are the best and most valuable that the German party has. I am not giving you the theory about the calloused hand. I only maintain that this is the most valuable material which we have. Our greatest reproach to the *Zentrale* is that it does not know how to value this—if we may be allowed to put it this way—gold of the working class. Instead of fighting over theses or raising every article of Radek's to a resolution, it should rather learn to give careful thought to such representatives of the workers. They do not understand that as yet. I do not mean to say that we will get along without the intelligentsia. Such a statement would be pure demagogy. We also need intellectuals. But we need a firm basis first.

What should happen now? A change in leadership? But to what sort of leadership? One in which the present majority of the *Zentrale* will govern together with the Left, based on the support of the Communist International. This is the advice which we give you.

Relations with the Left, different from the ones created by Radek and Brandler, must now be set up. [*voice:* Radek was for taking Ruth (Fischer) and Thälmann into the leadership.] I grant that during the October talks, Radek was with me and Bukharin against Trotsky, who asked that Ruth Fischer and others be removed. Nevertheless, in the end his general attitude toward the Left was wrong. He let himself be carried away by his temperament more than by an incorrect position. There was civil war in the party. The people in Berlin —the functionaries there—are bad, you [the right wing of the

Zentrale] say. Comrades, I am the head of the Petersburg organization and know well what it means to lead twenty-five
to thirty thousand workers. Such masses cannot be mechanically led; one cannot simply impose oneself on them. Maslow
could be Satan and Ruth Fischer a sorceress, but there would
still only remain two thousand workers who are functionaries.
I have been with the Petersburg workers for twenty years
and I still cannot force them to do anything. Do you think
the workers will do everything because of the color of your
eyes? The behavior of the Berlin workers is no accident. One
has to understand how to accept that. You have the central
apparatus and the newspapers, and have enjoyed up until
now much more of the support of the CI than the Left. Why
didn't you win Berlin and Hamburg over? The reply is because Zinoviev favored the Left. That is all that is said about
it. Incidentally, you overestimate the role of the individual in
history. [*Radek:* Very true! *Piece:* You always stake on individuals in Germany.] Not at all. You are referring to our
line in October. Well, we did believe that Brandler best em-
bodied our politics. Even now, we believe that Brandler will
do much good. We know all too well that one has to go
through a good dozen defeats before victory is won. That is
the way the world is. We say candidly that you made big
mistakes. [*Brandler:* I made mistakes, but different ones from
those you mean.] I remind you that you said yesterday the
masses comprehend the united front tactic as an evolutionary
tactic. [*Brandler:* Is there a tactic without mistakes and deviations?] Comrade Brandler! The leader is responsible for his
acts. If after two years one is compelled to acknowledge that
the masses are in such a mood, then this is proof that there
was something bad in the way the tactic was carried out.

The only conclusion is that we must have a change in the
leadership. This does not in any way mean a crusade against
the Right. . . .

Comrades, my talk has gone on too long. I do not need to
go into our perspectives anymore. We are quite in agreement on these. We do not know, of course, how things will
turn out. We made a mistake on the issue of tempo, but we
can comfort ourselves with the thought that even Marx and
Lenin erred at times about that. The general estimate of the
perspectives remains essentially correct. When some comrades say that everything will start rolling in three months,

I must say I am a bit skeptical and I say, let us wait and see. In the final analysis everything will depend on the impetus of our party. As far as we are concerned, we can assure that the Russian party and the Communist International will give its lifeblood to make any clash of forces come out to our advantage as quickly and surely as possible. The illegal organization must be strengthened and the material preparations for combat must be continued, and the same goes for the closest fraternal sections, such as the French party, which must be attuned to support your final struggle. We have already sent a letter accordingly to the French party. Comrade Zetkin can testify that the perspectives in the German question remain what they were, namely the expectation of a new revolutionary wave. We will say the same thing to the other sections. We must be prepared for quick decisions. But as sober leaders we dare not overlook the danger of a deceleration in the tempo of revolutionary development. This we know from recent experience. At the time of the 1905 revolution, we Bolsheviks were able only after a year and a half to see where things were going. In 1906, Lenin warned of the outbreak of an uprising three times: once in the spring, once for late summer at the time of the harvest, and finally for a later date. The Mensheviks laughed at him. There was nothing funny about it. Mistakes could be made in tempo. Only after a year and a half did one see that it would take longer. We also are obliged to take short aim at present, according to the limits of the present situation, and think in terms of spring or summer, in any case in terms of a short time.

If we agree on these main points, then our vehement struggling was not in vain. We have lost some illusions, but gained understanding of the realities of life.

Further Reading

Unfortunately there is only a small amount of literature on the events of 1923 of interest to the general reader. Most conspicuously lacking are suitable political or biographical monographs on the main actors in Bulgaria and Germany. At present there exists no better overview of the Comintern's fateful year, 1923, than E. H. Carr's *The Interregnum 1923–1924* ("A History of Soviet Russia"; New York, 1954). Against the background of Russia's economic and leadership crisis Carr portrays the communist movement's tests of strength in Bulgaria and Germany with his usual command of sweep and detail. The description of the blurring of lines between Comintern and Soviet Russia interests is particularly skillful.

Anyone interested in the Bulgarian crisis of 1923 will have to consult Joseph Rothschild's *The Communist Party of Bulgaria: Origins and Developments, 1883–1936* (New York, 1959). This is a judicious and comprehensive history of Bulgarian social democracy and the Bulgarian Communist party, in which there is a good balance between domestic Bulgarian affairs, Soviet-Bulgarian relations, and Comintern-KPB relations. The events of June 1923 and its September aftermath are related dramatically without sacrificing the important nuances. A brief and balanced survey of the Macedonian problem and communist policies relating to it can be found in Elizabeth Barker's *Macedonia: Its Place in Balkan Power Politics* (London, 1950).

Considering the wealth of documentation in Werner T. Angress' *Stillborn Revolution: The Communist Bid for Power in Germany, 1921–1923* (Princeton, 1963) and the pace and skillfulness of his account, it will remain the authoritative work on the German October for some time. Angress traces the KPD's attempts to establish a united front, which he believes failed because it acted from a desire to reconcile two essentially irreconcilable aims: acquisition of greater influence over the labor movement and unremitting pursuit of the party's revolutionary ideals. The result was the misfired uprising of 1923. The account of the negotiations and plans in Moscow preparatory to the German action is particularly vivid. For local aspects and effects of the German October, see Richard A. Comfort's *Revolutionary Hamburg: Labor Politics in the Early Weimar Republic* (Stanford, 1966). A succinct and compelling sketch of the isolated Hamburg rising is part of this fascinating and detailed study of labor and the Left in Germany's second largest city.

SELECTED GENERAL BIBLIOGRAPHY

Among general works dealing with socialism, communism, and the Internationals the best is Carl Landauer's *European Socialism: A History of Ideas and Movements from the Industrial Revolution to Hitler's Seizure of Power* (Berkeley and Los Angeles, 1959), 2 vols. In addition to a review of socialist theory emphasizing Marx there is a clear exposition of the major events in the history of socialism and communism. Special attention is given to communism in Germany, Russia, Italy, and France and to the Comintern. Landauer has structured a vast amount of detail into a coherent and balanced narrative; his ability to create order out of chaos is matched by his concern for scholarly procedures. Less successful is George D. H. Cole's *A History of Socialist Thought* (London and New York, 1953–1960), 5 vols. This sprawling narrative by the doyen of British socialism stretches from the utopians to the condition of labor and the Left at the outbreak of the Second World War. The work is encyclopedic in detail but verges on the pedantic and, in the absence of selectivity or analysis, frustrates rather than informs the reader.

Franz Borkenau's *The Communist International* (London, 1938) also in paperback as *World Communism* (Ann Arbor, 1962) remains the standard history of the Comintern from its origins to the popular-front days in the thirties. In spite of important lacunas, the scantiness of the sources upon which the book is based, and the partisanship of the author, who was a former member of the German Communist party and agent of the Comintern, it abounds in keen insights about the development of the communist movement. More limited in scope and objectivity is Alfred Rosmer's *Moscou sous Lénine: les origines du communisme* (Paris, 1953). This memoir, by a founder of the French Communist party and member of the ECCI who broke with the Comintern in 1924 and became a leading Trotskyist, covers the period from 1920 to Lenin's death with particular emphasis on the Second, Third, and Fourth World Congress of the Comintern. The work is most valuable for a picture of the movement's inner life at the higher echelons. An interesting supplement to an overview of communism in Lenin's era is Leon D. Trotsky's *The First Five Years of the Communists International* (New York, 1945), 2 vols., which contains a representative collection of his writings on the subject during that period.

Unfortunately, few scholarly works exist on the subsidiary organizations of the Comintern. The best of these is George D. Jackson's *Comintern and the Peasant in East Europe 1919–1930* (New York, 1966). Through a careful sifting of material Jackson presents the Comintern's complicated line on the peasant question and traces the clearly embarrassing history of the Krestintern (Peasant International). The most useful study of the Red International of Trade Unions or Profintern and its relations with the IFTU is Lewis L. Lorwin [Louis Levitzki], *Labor and Internationalism* (New York, 1929).

Much work still needs to be done on the leading personalities of the Comintern executive. Two recent doctoral dissertations are an important first step in that direction. The first, William Korey's "Zinoviev on the Problem of World Revolution, 1919–1927" (Columbia University, 1960), is a revealing study of the ideas of the first head of the Comintern. It is particularly successful in tracing the genesis of Zinoviev's views on world revolution and his retreat from apocalyptic doctrines. The second, Warren Lerner's "Karl Radek on World Revolution" (Columbia University, 1960) presents highlights from Radek's colorful career as Comintern gray eminence and troubleshooter. In the absence of a monograph on Trotsky's activities on behalf of the Third International one must turn to the second volume of Isaac Deutscher's definitive biography, *The Prophet Unarmed; Trotsky: 1921–1929* (London and New York, 1959). Although the emphasis of the work is on Trotsky's involvement in Russian domestic affairs, his appearances in the international arena receive due attention. A truly satisfactory scholarly biography of Lenin is still to be written. Adam B. Ulam's *The Bolsheviks: The Intellectual and Political History of the Triumph of Bolshevism in Russia* (New York, 1965), in reality a biography of Lenin, comes closest to the mark. Although Ulam has mastered a huge body of sources, his tone is flippant throughout. Lenin is viewed from the perspective of his alleged hatred for the intelligentsia—considered a typical Russian leftist flaw—upon which his political personality is made to turn.

One important obstacle to the study of international communism is the lack of serious and scholarly books on the national communist parties. In large measure this can be explained by the absence of regional and specialized monographs upon which comprehensive histories of whole parties must depend. Of the national histories now available Joseph Rothschild's *The Communist Party of Bulgaria: Origins and Development, 1883–1936* (New York, 1959) is the most satisfactory. Based on what appear to be ample sources and judicious in its judgments, it approximates a high standard unique among the national histories. George Lichtheim's *Marxism in Modern France* (New York, 1966) is less a history of the French Communist party than a brilliant analysis and interpretation of French communism based on the existing spotty research into that subject. Each of the other more traditional histories suffers from serious flaws. Ossip K. Flechtheim's *Die Kommunistische Partei Deutschlands in der Weimarer Republik* (Offenbach/M, 1948) contains a valuable chapter on the sociology and ideology of the KPD, but on the whole is based on a very limited selection of sources. Henry Pelling's *The British Communist Party: A Historical Profile* (New York, 1959) is fragmentary and based on only a limited number of printed sources. Ivan Avakumovic's *History of the Communist Party of Yugoslavia* (Aberdeen, 1964), Vol. I, is a long and frequently confused account which contains masses of undigested facts. M. K. Dziewanowski's *The Communist Party of Poland: An Outline of History* (Cambridge, 1959) is full of undocumented assertions and judgments.

Anyone interested in the changing theoretical and tactical positions of the Comintern and the light that political differences within it shed on the relationship between the ECCI and the member parties must turn to the major publications of the Comintern. Most important among these are the proceedings of the first five world congresses. These Protocols appeared in German, Russian, French, and English versions, of which the first two are the most complete and reliable. A study of the debates at the congresses should be combined with a reading of the Theses and Resolutions adopted, which were published separately. Further information about the changing policies in the movement can be found in the Comintern's periodicals. One of the two most important of these was _Die Kommunistischen Internationale,_ first published in May 1919, which appeared in German, Russian, French, and English editions, of which the first two are the most complete. Articles were contributed by the leaders of the movement on a wide variety of theoretical subjects. The other significant periodical was _Internationale Presse-Korrespondenz_ (_Inprekorr_), first published in October 1921, which appeared in several language editions, of which the German and Russian are most reliable. It contains verbatim reports of world congresses and plenums of the ECCI and detailed accounts of the congresses of member parties.

Fortunately for the layman, an excellent collection of documents drawn from Comintern publications has been selected and edited by Jane Degras, a leading authority on the subject. _The Communist International 1919–1943: Documents_ (London and New York, 1956, 1960), Vol. I (1919–1922), Vol. II (1923–1928) contains a wide range of material from official sources arranged chronologically and accompanied by brief informative notes.

Probably the most valuable part of any reading list is the additional bibliographic guides it contains. These make it possible for the interested reader to pursue the subject in question along lines other than those the author has suggested. As yet no bibliography exists that comes close to introducing the reader to the huge volume of sources and monographs and to the archives and libraries in which they are to be found. It is highly unlikely that such a task could be accomplished by conventional means; most probably data processing and information retrieval will be the techniques employed in the future. Although all the existing bibliographies are a mere sampling of the sources and literature, they do point the serious student in the direction which he should follow to satisfy his interests. The best of these is that edited by Thomas T. Hammond, _Soviet Foreign Relations and World Communism: A Selected, Annotated Bibliography of 7,000 Books in 30 Languages_ (Princeton, 1965). Although the quality of the selections and annotations varies radically (probably in direct relation to the quality of the contributing editor) this volume is a valuable guide to the most important literature. The bibliography edited by Giuliano Procacci, "L'Internazionale dal I al VII Congresso 1919–1935," Istituto Giangiacomo Feltrinelli, *Annali*, I (Milan, 1958), lists the most pertinent (but by no means all) of the publications containing the proceedings and official acts of the Comintern. Much more ambitious but disappointingly unsuccessful is Witold S. Sworakowski's, *The Communist International and its Front Organizations* (Stanford, 1965). An entirely mechanical and uncritical selection of titles, leading to frequent duplication and omission of standard works, greatly reduces the usefulness of this volume. The attempt to indicate the location of each item in various American libraries and European archives is commendable but marred by the general, haphazard approach, which makes this volume a blot on the Hoover Institute's publishing record.

CHRONOLOGY

1889

July 14–20   First Congress of the Second International in Paris.

1900

Sept. 23–27   Fifth Congress of Second International in Paris; ISB organized; ministerialism condemned.

December   *Iskra* founded.

1902

February   Lenin's *What Is To Be Done?* published.

1903

July 30– Aug. 23   Second Congress of RSDLP in Brussels and London: split into Bolsheviks and Mensheviks.

1904

Feb. 9   Beginning of Russo-Japanese war.

June   Luxemburg's "Organizational Questions of Russian Social Democracy" published.

1905

Jan. 22   Bloody Sunday in St. Petersburg.

March   First Moroccan crisis.

Oct. 30   "October Manifesto" announced.

1907

Aug. 18–24   Seventh Congress of the Second International at Stuttgart: resolution on war.

1911

July 1   Third Moroccan crisis.

1912

Oct. 8   Outbreak of First Balkan War.

Nov. 24–25   Extraordinary Congress of the Second International at Basel.

1914

June 28   Assassination of Archduke Francis Ferdinand at Sarajevo.

July 28   Austria declares war on Serbia.

July 29–30   Meeting of the ISB in Brussels; anti-war meetings and demonstrations.

Aug. 1   Germany declares war on Russia; Serbian Social Democrats refuse to vote for war credits.

Aug. 4   War credits unanimously approved in Germany and France.

Sept. 6–7   Lenin's theses on the war adopted by Bolsheviks in Bern.

Sept. 27   Italian and Swiss socialists confer at Lugano.

1915

Sept. 5–8   Zimmerwald Conference; ISC elected.

1916

Jan. 1   Rosa Luxemburg's Theses adopted by the German *Internationale* group.

Feb. 5–8   Meeting of the enlarged ISC at Bern preparatory to calling of Second Zimmerwald Conference.

Apr. 24–30   Second Zimmerwald Conference at Kienthal.

1917

March 14   Russian Provisional Government formed.

March 15	Nicholas II abdicates.
April 6	The United States declares war on Germany.
April 6–9	German Independent Socialist party (USPD) founded.
April 16	Lenin and other political émigrés arrive in Petrograd.
Sept. 5–12	Third Zimmerwald Conference at Stockholm.
Nov. 7	Bolsheviks seize power in Petrograd.

1918

Jan. 8	Wilson's "Fourteen Points" made public.
March 3	Germany and Russia sign Brest-Litovsk treaty.
Sept. 29	Bulgarians sue for peace; Stambulisky's Radomir uprising defeated.
Oct. 16	Emperor Karl issues manifesto turning the Dual Monarchy into a federated state.
Nov. 8	Republic proclaimed in Bavaria with Kurt Eisner as head.
Nov. 9	William II abdicates; Ebert head of provisional socialist government.
Nov. 11	Armistice signed between Germany and Allies.
Nov. 12	Austrian Republic is proclaimed.
Nov. 16	Károlyi proclaims the Hungarian Republic.
Dec. 19	First National Congress of German Councils surrenders its powers to the future National Assembly.
Dec. 30	German Communist party (KPD) founded.

1919

Jan. 5–15	Spartacist uprising in Berlin.
March 18	Formation of Bavarian parliamentary govern-

ment under Majority Socialist Johannes Hoffmann.

March 20	Vyx note of the Allies demanding further Hungarian withdrawal from its eastern territories.
March 21	Hungarian Soviet Republic established.
April 7	First Bavarian Soviet Republic (Socialist) proclaimed.
April 13	Second Bavarian Soviet Republic (Communist) proclaimed.
May 1	Second Bavarian Soviet Republic crushed by Berlin government with use of Free Corps.
June 15	Abortive communist uprising in Vienna.
June 28	Germany signs Versailles Treaty with Allies.
Aug. 1	Fall of Béla Kun regime.
Sept. 10	Austria signs St. Germain Treaty with Allies.

1920

Jan. 10	League of Nations is created.
March 13–16	Kapp Putsch in Germany defeated by general strike.
April	Lenin's *"Left-Wing" Communism: An Infantile Disorder* circulated.
June 4	Hungary signs Trianon Treaty with Allies.
July 15	Profintern founded.
July 19–Aug. 7	Second World Congress of the Comintern.

1921

Jan. 15–21	Italian Socialist party is split at congress of Livorno; Italian Communist party is founded.
Feb. 28–March 8	Sailors revolt in Kronstadt.

March 15	NEP announced.
March 16	Anglo-Russian Trade Agreement concluded.
March 19–31	German March Action.
June 22– *July 12*	Third World Congress of the Comintern.
July 3–19	First congress of the Profintern.

1922

Feb. 6	Treaty of Washington signed on limitation of naval armaments.
Apr. 10– *May 19*	The Genoa Conference on the economic and financial reconstruction of Europe.
Apr. 16	Russia and Germany sign Rapallo treaty.
Nov. 5– *Dec. 5*	Fourth Congress of the Comintern.

1923

Jan. 11	Ruhr occupied by French and Belgian troops.
May 8	Curzon Ultimatum to Soviet Russia.
June 9	Stambulisky's peasant government in Bulgaria overthrown by Tsankov.
Aug. 12	Chancellor Wilhelm Cuno resigns; Gustav Stresemann forms "Great Coalition" government.
Sept. 19–28	Communist uprising in Bulgaria crushed by Tsankov regime.
Oct. 10–16	First World Conference of Peasants held in Moscow; Krestintern founded.
Oct. 12–13	Communists enter the left-wing socialist governments of Saxony and Thuringia.
Oct. 21	The German October is stillborn.
Oct. 23–28	Communist rising in Hamburg is isolated and fails.

Nov. 9	Hitler's attempted putsch in Munich is crushed by German army.
Dec. 8	Trotsky publishes *The New Course*.

1924

Jan. 21	Lenin dies; triumvirate Stalin-Zinoviev-Kamenev emerges as leading force in party and government.
Feb. 1–March 24	Soviet Russia receives *de jure* recognition from Britain, Italy, Norway, Austria, Greece, Sweden, and Canada.
Apr. 16	Germany accepts the Dawes Plan.
June 17–July 8	Fifth Congress of the Comintern.

INDEX

A

Adler, Friedrich, 44, 176, 177, 179, 182, 187ff, 200
Adler, Max, 176
Adler, Victor, 11, 46, 187
Albert, Max (Eberlein, Hugo), 78–81
American Communist Party, 203
anarcho-syndicalism, 6
Arbeiter Zeitung, 181
Arco-Valley, Count Anton von, 154
Auer, Erhard, 154
Austria (see also Vienna)
  German-Austria Republic, 175
  organizations:
    Christian Social Party, 176, 179
    German-Austria Communist Party (KPO), 186, 187, 191, 194, 197ff
    Peoples' Militia (*Volkswehr*), 177, 178, 179
    Revolutionary Soldiers' Committee (RSK), 195, 201
    Social Democratic Party (SPO), 44, 175ff, 188, 195, 198, 199
    Workers' Council, 182, 183
Archduke Ferdinand, assassination of, 13
Axelrod, P. B., 17, 57

B

Babeuf, François, 92
Baden, Max von, 100
Bakunin, Mikhail A., 9, 287–88
Balabanoff, Angelica, 46
Balkan states, 197
Bauer, Otto, 176, 177, 179, 187, 188
Bavaria, 365, 372, 385
Bavarian Assembly, 154–55, 158
Bavarian Soviet Republic, 153–59, 176
  Communist Party declaration, 159–62
  Munich experience (Frolich), 162–68
    opposing view (Levi), 168–74
Bebel, August, 11, 387
Becker, Karl, 299
Belgian Social Democratic Party, 50
Benisch, Joseph, 182
Berlin (see Germany)
  Spartacus experience (1918), 100–14, 175, 203
  March action (1921), 289, 296, 401
Berne Socialist conferences
  (1915), 44, 46
  (1919), 77, 80
Bernstein, Eduard, 10, 47, 94
Bettelheim, Ernst, 7, 178, 180, 189ff
Black Hundreds, 52, 397
Blagoev, Dmitrii, 2

Blanqui, Jérôme A., 32–33, 288
Bobrov, M., 57
Bogar, Ignaz, 139
Bolsheviks, 3, 46, 58, 76–78,
        97, 98, 119, 175, 176,
        190, 196, 203, 209, 213,
        221, 231*ff*, 314, 324,
        344, 370
Bolshevism, 98, 154, 211
Bolshevizing Comintern
    Second   World   Congress,
        231*ff*
        voting system, 234, 248
        21 admission conditions,
            235–37, 241–46, 248,
            255
        Italian Socialist Party, split
            in, 238–41, 258*ff*
Borchardt, Julian, 74
Bordíga, Amadeo, 240, 316
Böttcher, Paul, 302, 380, 386,
        399
Bourderon, A., 57
Brandler, Heinrich, 7, 268, 302,
        366, 369*ff*, 380, 381–82,
        386, 392, 399, 401
Braunthal, Julíus, 181, 184,
        185–94
Brest-Litovsk, treaty of, 100,
        222
Britain, 196, 221, 223
    organizations
        Communist   Party,   203,
            218
        Independent Labour Party,
            61, 92, 219, 265, 323
        Shop Stewards, 235
        Socialist Party, 61, 74, 98
Budapest   Soviet   experience,
        117–52, 176, 187, 203
        (see Hungary)
    and Austria, 196
Bukharin, Nikolai, 3, 268, 272,
        400
Bulgaria, 6, 196, 339–64
    organizations

Broad Socialists, 395
    Communist   Party   (KPB),
        344–48, 349–54, 355–
        58, 361, 363–64
    Manifesto of, 355
    slogans,   1923   uprising,
        350–51
    International   Macedonian
        Revolutionary   Organiza-
        tion (IMRO), 343–44
    Peasants' League, 350, 363
    Peasant Union, 345, 347,
        360
    Radical Party, 227
    Social Democrats, 45, 355
    Socialist Party, 61, 74, 98,
        344
    Tesnyaki Narrow Socialist
        Party, 344, 345
    Tsankov coup d'etat, 343–44

                C

Cachin, Marcel, 2, 236, 260
Carr, E. H., 4
Central Powers Socialist confer-
        ence (Vienna), 45
Clemenceau, Georges, 88, 109
Cole, G. D. H., 94
Comintern, 2–7, 78–81, 123,
        155, 157, 177, 179, 180,
        203*ff*, 223, 227, 231*ff*,
        267, 314, 315–17, 339,
        341*ff*, 365, 366, 370, 375,
        394
    Communist "leftism," 203–26
        Lenin, Vladimir I., 203–16
        Gorter, Hermann (reply),
            216–26
    Communist Manifesto (Marx-
            Engels), 30, 51, 82–92
    Congress of Stuttgart (1907),
            13
    Copenhagen   Socialist confer-
            ence, 45
    cordon sanitaire, 77

Cuno, Wilhelm, 365, 369
Curzon ultimatum, 343
czarism, 51, 52, 53
Czechoslovakia, 196, 197

D

Däumig, Ernst, 298, 302, 304
Degras, Jane, 82–93, 318
DeLeon, Daniel, 207
Deutsch, Julius, 177, 178, 183
Die Freiheit, 264, 290
Die Internationale, 137, 162, 168
Die Rote Fahne, 144, 260, 266, 282–83, 286–90
Dutch Communist Party, 203, 208, 223
Dutch Tribunists, 45

E

Eberlein, Hugo (see Albert, Max)
Ebert, Friedrich, 101–3, 114–16, 145, 158, 159, 290, 298, 372, 373, 393
Economism, 18, 20, 38, 40
Eichhorn, Emil, 103, 115
Eisner, Kurt, 153–55
Emperor Karl, 117, 175
Engels, Friedrich, 17, 82, 208
Entente Powers, 83, 84, 178, 179, 181, 190, 197, 198, 302, 345
Entente Socialist Conference (London), 45

F

Fabian Socialists, 11
Fischer, H. H., 61–65, 65–69, 69–72
Fischer, Ruth (Friedländer, Elfriede), 200, 268, 366,

370, 374, 377–80, 387, 390, 400–1
France, 196, 258
organizations
Centrists, 236
Communist Party, 314, 316, 322
Social Democratic Party, 50
Socialist Party, 61, 92, 98, 234
Syndicalists, 235
socialist movement, 235
Friedländer, Elfriede (Ruth Fischer), 176
Friesland (Reuter) Ernst, 268
Frölich, Paul, 74, 157, 258, 268, 302, 304
Frossard, L. O., 2, 236

G

Gankin, O. H., 61–65, 65–69, 69–72
George, Lloyd, 88, 109
Germany, 221, 223; and Congress of Councils, 102
organizations
Bremen Left Radicals, 103
Communist Party (KPD), 48, 103–4, 114–15, 122, 156, 161ff, 177, 186, 203, 207, 235, 237, 240, 263–64, 266, 267–73, 274–95, 296–301, 301–13, 315, 322, 365ff, 377, 380, 381–83, 383–402
Communist Workers Party (KAPD), 207, 220, 221, 235, 269–305
Free Corps, 155, 156, 366
Independent Social Democratic Party (USPD), 74, 92, 101, 116, 153, 154, 166, 208, 235, 237, 261, 262, 265

Germany (*cont'd*)
  Internationale Group, 48, 61–65
  Majority Socialists, 100–2, 153, 154, 164, 175
  National Socialist Party, 374
  People's Party, 369
  Republican Guards, 167
  Revisionists, 11, 51
  Revolutionary Shop Stewards, 101, 103, 116, 160, 166
  Social Democratic Party (SPD), 11–12, 26–27, 44, 50, 153, 261, 366, 369, 374, 378ff, 381–82
  Spartacists and Spartacus League, 48, 74, 101, 103, 138, 144, 145, 299, 304
    aims of, 104–14, 123
Socialist movement, 39
uprisings
  Bavarian Soviet Republic (1918), 153–74, 175, 187, 203
  Berlin Spartacus experience (1918), 100–14, 175, 203
  March Action (1921), 7, 268–95, 306ff, 366
  Saxony, 268–69 (see Saxony)
  Rhineland, 276–77
  Mansfeld, 281–84
  Hamburg, 284–86, 296, 303, 401
  Rheinhause, 288
  Berlin, 288, 296, 401
  Central Germany, 291, 298, 303
  Communist setback (1923), 6, 365
  basis for Red hope, 365–67

  Party action, 366–69
  Stresemann regime, 369, 372–73 (see Stresemann)
  Russian action (see Saxony), 369–73, 377ff
  reasons for failure, 366, 374
  Ruhr, 365–67, 384–85
Gorter, Hermann, 2, 204–5, 223
Gramsci, Antonio, 316, 317
Grimm, Robert, 46, 57
Gruber (Steinhardt), 78, 200
Guesde, Jules, 46, 59
  followers of, 11
Guralsky, August, 293, 367

H

Haenisch, Konrad, 51
Hamburg uprisings, 284–86, 296, 303, 373
Hanecki, Cz., 57
Heckert, Fritz, 399
Heine, Wolfgang, 51
Henderson, Arthur, 59
Hilferding, Rudolph, 220, 297
Hillquit, Morris, 11, 243
Hindenburg, Gen. Paul von, 100
Hitler, Adolf, 176, 374
Hoelz, Max, 269
Hoffmann, Adolf, 57
Hoffmann, Johannes, 155, 156, 163, 165
Höglund, Z., 57, 74
  followers of, 45
Holland Social Democratic Party, 58
Hörsing, Otto, 268, 281, 290, 298, 306
Horthy, Miklós, 143
Hungary (see also Budapest)
  aristocracy, 117
  organizations

Hungary (*cont'd*)
    Communist Party, 118–19,
      132, 138, 139, 141, 142,
      196
    Radical Party, 118
    Revolutionary Shop Stew-
      ards, 118
    Revolutionary Socialists,
      118
    Social Democratic Party,
      118, 119, 133, 138, 139,
      197
    Socialist Party, 119, 133
    Soviet Republic of
      proclaimed, 119–20
      collapse of, 121
        reasons for, 132–37
        lessons from, 137–42
Hyndman, Henry M., 11

I

International Socialist Bureau
    (ISB), 13, 45*ff*, 55, 73,
    75
International Socialist Commit-
    tee (ISC), 47, 48, 49,
    75
    German Internationale thesis,
      61–65
International Socialist Con-
    gresses
    Stuttgart (1907), 13, 55, 71
    Copenhagen (1910), 55, 71
    Basel (1912), 55, 71, 83
Internationale Flugblätter, 74
Internationales
    First, 9, 91, 92
    Second, 91, 92, 141, 220,
      232
      collapse of, 44, 45, 50, 63,
      73, 75, 92
      organization of, 9*ff*
    Third (Communist), 92,
      189, 208 (ECCI

formed), 219, 220, 224,
    225, 294, 306, 312,
    313, 328–35, 400, 402
    background, 9
    Comintern, 78, 233, 236,
      241*ff*
Congresses:
1st World, 314, 339
2nd World (1920), 231*ff*,
    250–66, 267, 327, 330,
    333–34 (see bolsheviz-
    ing Comintern), 306–9,
    314
3rd World (1921 Moscow),
    232, 271, 273, 314, 321,
    334
4th World (1922), 316,
    334, 339, 340, 342, 366,
    390
5th World
    founding of, 73–78, 79–81
    delegates and voting, 77
    New Communist Mani-
      festo, 78, 82–92
    United Front, 318–27
    Amsterdam, 319–20, 323,
      325
Iskra (*The Spark*), 29, 31
Italy, 195, 197, 258; and
    Livorno Congress of So-
    cialist Party, 252–66,
    267, 327, 330, 332–33
    organizations
    Communist Party, 314,
      316, 323–24, 327–35
    Manifesto of Bordiga,
      327–35
    Socialist Party, 61, 74, 98,
      233*ff*, 254–66, 327
    Socialist Concentration,
      238–39
    Unitary Communists, 238–
      39, 254
    Socialist Movement, 39, 45

J

James, C. L. R., 5
Jaures, Jean Leon, 11, 66
Jogiches, Leo, 2, 308
Joll, James, 2
Jouhaux, Léon, 322

K

Kabakchiev, Khristo, 3, 7, 238, 250, 260
Kahr, Gustav von, 372
Kamenev, Lev B., 272, 341, 375
Kapp Putsch, 277–78, 345
Kapp, Wolfgang, 277–78
Károlyi, Count Michael, 117–19, 138, 141, 144
Kautsky, Karl, 10, 46, 81, 220, 243
Kiel, revolt of sailors, 100, 153
Kienthal Conference, 44–49, 176
    manifesto of, 65–69
    proletariat, peace attitude of, 69–72
Knief, Johann, 299
Kolarov, Vasil, 3, 57, 388
Kolchak, Aleksandr V., 140, 195
Kommunismus, 194
Kommunistische Internationale, 296
Koritschoner, Franz, 176, 187, 193, 194, 199–200, 201
Kornilov, Gen. Lavr G., 218
Kremlin leadership crisis, 375–76
Kronstadt, uprising at, 272, 370
Krupskaya, N. K., 50
Kun, Béla, 3, 118–21, 132ff, 136, 139, 141, 146, 152, 176, 178, 180, 199, 268, 270, 272, 291, 302, 306

Kuusinen, Otto, 3

L

Landauer, Gustav, 155, 164
Lapinski, Stanislaw, 57
Laufenberg, Heinrich, 207
Lazzari, Constantino, 57
League of Nations, 86, 243, 325
Ledebour, Georg, 57, 258
Lenin, V. I.
    Comintern, 1, 2, 231, 235, 259
    era of, 1–29
    German Communist Party, 268, 271, 272, 297, 306–9, 390, 398, 402
    illness, 341–42, 343
    Kienthal Conference, 74
    "leftism" in communism, 203–16, 223
    1914–18 War, 45, 50–53, 58–60
    revolution, stages of, 14ff, 31, 32, 34ff
    What Is to Be Done?, 15–29
    world revolution, 119
    Zimmerwald conference, 48, 58–59
Leninism, 29–43, 344
Lensch, Paul, 51
Levi, Paul, 12, 122, 143–52, 157, 168–74, 235, 237, 240–41, 258–63, 265–66, 267–96, 296–301, 302, 307–9, 313, 315, 398
Levien, Max, 156
Leviné, Eugen, 155, 156, 164
Liebknecht, Karl, 11, 44, 45, 48, 59, 74, 92, 104, 291
Longuet, Jean, 46, 243, 265, 322
Loriot, Fernand, 98
Lossow, Gen. Otto von, 372

Ludendorff, Gen. Erich von, 100, 285, 291, 387

Lugano Socialist Conference, 44, 45

Lüttwitz, Gen. Walther von, 277

Luxemburg, Rosa, 2, 11, 12, 14–15, 29–43, 48, 61, 74, 94, 102, 103–4ff, 107, 123, 138, 139, 147ff, 200, 259, 281, 291, 299

M

MacDonald, J. Ramsay, 46, 243, 390, 396

MacLean, John, 74

Maehl, William, 94

Mannheim agreement, 11

Marchlewski, Juljan, 2

Marx, Karl, 9, 17, 82, 93, 140, 207, 306, 394, 402

Marxism, 9, 11, 12, 29–43, 93, 140, 186, 212, 216, 217, 219, 288, 328, 393, 394

Maslow, Arkadr, 268, 366, 371, 394

Masses, rise of, 18

Mehring, Franz, 11, 74

Mehring, Walter, 48

Mensheviks, 14, 46, 59, 92, 206, 207, 213, 265, 324, 397, 398, 402

Merrheim, A., 57, 322

Meyer, Alfred G., 2

Meyer, Ernst, 268, 302, 390

Milyukov, Pavel N., 397

Modigliani, G. E., 57, 243

Molnar, Miklos, 93

Monatte, Pierre, 74

Mühsam, Erich, 155

Münchener Rote Fahne, 159

Munich, Soviet experience, 153–74, 175, 187, 203 (see also Germany)

Mussolini, Benito, 358

N

Naine, Charles, 57

Narodniki, 40

Narodniks, 17, 52

Nashe Slovo, 47, 74

New Economic Policy (NEP), 268, 272, 341, 342

Nerman, Ture, 57

Neue Zeit, 29

Nollau, Günther, 2

Noske, Gustav, 144, 154, 158, 159, 261, 393

Norwegian Labor Party, 98

O

One Step Forward, Two Steps Backward (Lenin), 31

Oven, Gen. von, 156

P

Pankhurst, Sylvia, 2

Pannekoek, Anton, 2, 223

Peidl, Julius, 136

Petrograd Soviet, 75

Pilsudski, Joseph, 395

Plekhanov, Georgii V., 11, 17, 46

Pogány, Joseph, 135, 291

Poland, 302, 303

Polish Social Democrats, 45

Portuguese Socialist Party, 59

Possibilists, 11

Postgate, R. W., 93

Pyatakov, Grigorio, 370, 375, 394

R

Rabochaia Myst, 18, 38

Rabotnitscheski Vestnik, 348, 359

Radek, Karl, 48; and
  Austrian revolt, 180, 186–94
  Comintern, 3, 240, 263–66
  German Communist Party,
    103, 268, 271–72, 294–
    95, 296–301, 302–5,
    384, 389, 392, 396–97,
    398, 400, 401
  Germany, 366, 367–68, 375–
    76
  Kienthal Conference, 74
Rákosi, Mátyás, 3, 238, 250,
    260, 267, 294, 347,
    361–62
Rakovsky, Christian, 3, 57, 74,
    81
Rapallo, Treaty of, 370
Red Army, 91, 119, 122
Renaudel, Pierre, 46, 265
Renner, Karl, 187, 188, 193
Roland-Holst, Henrietta, 46,
    57, 223
Rosenfeld (see Kamenev, Lev)
Rosmer, Alfred, 5, 74
Rühle, Otto, 59
Ruhr, 365–67, 384–85
Russian Constituent Assembly
    (1917), 209
Russian Politburo, 370, 372,
    375
Russian Revolutions (1905),
    11–12, 75
  (1917), 75, 76
Russian Social Democratic La-
    bor Party (RSDLP),
    13, 18, 31
Russian Socialist Party, leaders'
    position on 1914–18
    War, 61
Russification, 5, 339–42
Rutgers, S. J., 223

S

St. Petersburg industrial war
    (1896), 16

Sakalov, Janko, 395, 396
Saxony, 268–69, 373, 377ff.,
    386–87, 390, 399
Scandinavian Social Democrats,
    59
Scheidemann, Philipp, 81, 115–
    16, 138, 139, 145, 158,
    393
Schneppenhorst, Ernst, 156,
    159, 163
Serbia, 52
  Social Democrats, 59, 98
  Socialist Party, 61
Serrati, G. M., 2, 235, 238–40,
    247–49, 262–66, 302,
    316
  followers of (Maximalists),
    262, 331–33
Socialist parties, *see* under
    countries
Sombart, Marcel, 59
Soziatistiche Monatshefte, 51
Spanish Communist Party, 314
Stalin, Joseph, 4, 341, 375,
    389
  era of, 4–6
Stambuliski, Alexander, 344,
    349, 356, 357
Stampfer, Friedrich, 297
Stockholm Conference, 75
Strasser, Joseph, 186, 192
Stresemann, Gustav, 369, 370,
    372, 373
Stürgkh, Karl von, 176, 187
Swedish Left Social Democratic
    Party, 98
Swedish Social Democratic
    Party, 81
Swiss Social Democratic Party,
    58
Szántó, Béla, 122, 132–37, 141,
    143

T

Tanner, Jack, 2, 235

Thalheimer, August, 268, 302, 304, 306, 366, 374, 381–82, 390
Thälmann, Ernst, 366, 370, 399, 400
Togliatti, Palmiro, 316
Toller, Ernst, 155, 164
Tolstoi, Leo N., 40
Tomann, Karl, 3, 176, 193
Trotsky, Leon D.
  Bolsheviks, 3
  Comintern, 78
  Germany, 272, 371, 375, 390, 401
  1914–18 War, 74
  "scissors crisis," 341
  Zimmerwald Conference, 46
Tsankov, Aleksandr, 344, 345, 347, 348, 357
Turati, Filippo, 238, 243, 263, 266, 316

U

Ulam, Adam B., 2
United Front, 317–27, 343, 365, 374, 391–92
U.S. Socialist Party, 45, 59, 74
universal political struggle, 21–23
  organization for (Lenin), 24ff
  organization for (Marxist), 30ff
Unser Weg, 271, 301

V

Vandervelde, Emile, 46, 59
Versailles, Treaty of, 175, 257, 318, 365, 368
Vienna
  organizations
    Red Guard, 177, 190

Workers' Council, 179, 185–216
Soviet experience, 175–202, 203
  putsch, 191–94
  lessons of (Radek), 186–94
  warning of, 185–86
  criticism of (Radek), 189–94
  reply by Bettelheim, 194–202
  and Budapest, 196
Soviet Republic, 188
Volkswehr (see Austria, Peoples' Militia)
Vollmar, Georg von, 153
Von Laue, Theodore H., 2
Vorbote; Internationale Marxistiche Rundschau, 74
Vorwärts, 297

W

Waldman, Eric, 114
Walling, William E., 94
Warski, A., 57
Werner, Paul (Frölich, Paul), 157–58, 159–62, 162–68
West Europe, 216ff
West European Bureau (Comintern), 223
White Russians, 98
Wilson, Woodrow, 84, 109, 120
  program of, 86, 87
Wolfe, Bertram D., 2
Wolffheim, Fritz, 207
World Revolution, 97ff, 119
  Austria, 175–202, 203
  Bulgaria, 5, 339–54
  Germany, 100–14, 153–74, 175, 187, 203, 268–95, 296, 298, 303, 306ff, 365–74, 377, 383–85, 401

Hungary, 117–52, 176, 178, 179, 181–82, 187, 195, 196, 203

Y

Young Guards of Belgian Labor Party, 98
Yugoslavia, 196

Z

Zasulich, Vera, 17
Zeigner, Erich, 371ff, 379, 380, 385, 399
Zetkin, Clara, 2, 11, 74, 267, 272, 298, 302, 304, 305, 306–9, 388, 402
Zimmerwald Conference, 44–49, 236, 237

Manifesto of, 53–57
Manifesto (Lenin draft), 58–60
Zimmerwald, left, 97, 344
Zimmerwald movement, 1, 73, 81
Zinoviev, Grigorii, 190, 341, 370
    Bolsheviks, 3
    Bulgaria, 348, 360
    Comintern, 235, 237, 258, 262
    German Communist Party, 268, 272, 297, 305, 383–402, 398, 401
    Germany, 366, 371, 375–76
    World revolution, 119
    Zimmerwald Conference, 48, 74